EDUCATION IN AMERICA

ISSN 2332-3809

EDUCATION IN AMERICA

Stephen Meyer

INFORMATION PLUS® REFERENCE SERIES
Formerly Published by Information Plus, Wylie, Texas

GALE
CENGAGE Learning·

Farmington Hills, Mich • San Francisco • New York • Waterville, Maine
Meriden, Conn • Mason, Ohio • Chicago

Education in America

Stephen Meyer

Kepos Media, Inc.: Steven Long and Janice Jorgensen, Series Editors

Project Editors: Laura Avery, Tracie Moy

Rights Acquisition and Management: Ashley Maynard, Carissa Poweleit

Composition: Evi Abou-El-Seoud, Mary Beth Trimper

Manufacturing: Rita Wimberley

For product information and technology assistance, contact us at
Gale Customer Support, 1-800-877-4253.
For permission to use material from this text or product,
submit all requests online at **www.cengage.com/permissions.**
Further permissions questions can be e-mailed to
permissionrequest@cengage.com

Cover photograph: © Goodluz/Shutterstock.com.

Gale
27500 Drake Rd.
Farmington Hills, MI 48331-3535

ISBN-13: 978-0-7876-5103-9 (set)
ISBN-13: 978-1-5730-2667-3

ISSN 2332-3809

This title is also available as an e-book.
ISBN-13: 978-1-5730-2709-0 (set)
Contact your Gale sales representative for ordering information.

Printed in the United States of America
1 2 3 4 5   20 19 18 17 16

TABLE OF CONTENTS

merit pay and teacher unions. The chapter concludes with statistics regarding crimes against teachers.

CHAPTER 9

College and university enrollment is analyzed in this chapter by various demographic factors. Other topics addressed include studying abroad; postsecondary institutions serving specifically women, African Americans, Hispanics, and Native Americans; degree-granting trends; faculty; student costs and financial assistance; student debt and the rising costs of higher education; and substance abuse on campus. Nonprofit and for-profit postsecondary institutions are compared, and the rise of for-profit colleges (career schools) is tracked.

Chapter 10 examines public opinion on education, as reflected by public opinion polls that posed questions about satisfaction with and expectations of public school education, problems facing local public schools, grading schools, and employment prospects for high school and college graduates.

PREFACE

Education in America is part of the *Information Plus Reference Series*. The purpose of each volume of the series is to present the latest facts on a topic of pressing concern in modern American life. These topics include the most controversial and studied social issues of the 21st century: abortion, capital punishment, care for senior citizens, the environment, health care, immigration, national security, social welfare, sports, women, youth, and many more. Although this series is written especially for high school and undergraduate students, it is an excellent resource for anyone in need of factual information on current affairs.

By presenting the facts, it is the intention of Gale, Cengage Learning, to provide its readers with everything they need to reach an informed opinion on current issues. To that end, there is a particular emphasis in this series on the presentation of scientific studies, surveys, and statistics. These data are generally presented in the form of tables, charts, and other graphics placed within the text of each book. Every graphic is directly referred to and carefully explained in the text. The source of each graphic is presented within the graphic itself. The data used in these graphics are drawn from the most reputable and reliable sources, such as from the various branches of the U.S. government and from private organizations and associations. Every effort has been made to secure the most recent information available. Readers should bear in mind that many major studies take years to conduct and that additional years often pass before the data from these studies are made available to the public. Therefore, in many cases the most recent information available in 2016 is dated from 2013 or 2014. Older statistics are sometimes presented as well if they are landmark studies or of particular interest and no more-recent information exists.

Although statistics are a major focus of the *Information Plus Reference Series*, they are by no means its only content. Each book also presents the widely held positions and important ideas that shape how the book's subject is discussed in the United States. These positions are explained in detail and, where possible, in the words of their proponents. Some of the other material to be found in these books includes historical background, descriptions of major events related to the subject, relevant laws and court cases, and examples of how these issues play out in American life. Some books also feature primary documents or have pro and con debate sections that provide the words and opinions of prominent Americans on both sides of a controversial topic. All material is presented in an evenhanded and unbiased manner; readers will never be encouraged to accept one view of an issue over another.

HOW TO USE THIS BOOK

From violence in the classroom to the production of high school graduates capable of competing in the global marketplace of the 21st century, education is a hotly debated topic in the United States. This book presents a snapshot of education in the United States. Areas covered include an overview of the U.S. educational system; primary, elementary, and secondary schools; public versus private schooling; special education; education of gifted children; testing and achievement of students at the primary, secondary, and college levels; national education goals; and trends in dropout rates, drug use, and violence in schools. Also discussed are colleges and universities; online learning, universities, and institutes; issues such as homeschooling, school choice, and vouchers; trends in teacher supply and demand; public opinions about education; and the Obama administration's educational initiatives.

Education in America consists of 10 chapters and three appendixes. Each chapter is devoted to a particular aspect of education in the United States. For a summary of the information that is covered in each chapter, please see the synopses that are provided in the Table of Contents. Chapters generally begin with an overview of the basic facts and background information on the chapter's topic, then proceed to examine subtopics of particular interest. For example, Chapter 3: Education for Special Needs Students, opens with an overview of legislation aimed at addressing the educational needs of disabled students, beginning with the pioneering Individuals with Disabilities Education Act of 1975. The chapter proceeds to examine the dramatic growth in special needs enrollment between the 1976–77 and 2012–13 school years, while offering a breakdown of students served, by disability type, race/ethnicity, and geographic location. The chapter continues with an analysis of various approaches to special needs education, including individualized education programs and inclusive education. Data concerning how special needs students ultimately exit the education system, including graduation statistics, are considered. The chapter continues with an inquiry into efforts to address the educational needs of gifted and talented students, while considering scholarly investigations into diverse types of intelligence. The chapter proceeds to evaluate government efforts to provide educational opportunities to disadvantaged students, notably the landmark Title I program, a federal initiative designed to provide school funding for low-income student populations. The chapter describes different categories of disadvantaged students, including students with limited English proficiency and homeless children, before concluding with a discussion of the Head Start program. Readers can find their way through a chapter by looking for the section and subsection headings, which are clearly set off from the text. They can also refer to the book's extensive Index if they already know what they are looking for.

Statistical Information

The tables and figures featured throughout *Education in America* will be of particular use to readers in learning about this issue. These tables and figures represent an extensive collection of the most recent and important statistics on education and related issues—for example, graphics cover school enrollment, expenditures per student, high school graduation rates, trends in average reading and math scores, public opinion on school choice, and the percentage of dropouts by race and ethnicity. Gale, Cengage Learning,

believes that making this information available to readers is the most important way to fulfill the goal of this book: to help readers understand the issues and controversies surrounding education in the United States and reach their own conclusions about them.

Each table or figure has a unique identifier appearing above it for ease of identification and reference. Titles for the tables and figures explain their purpose. At the end of each table or figure, the original source of the data is provided.

To help readers understand these often complicated statistics, all tables and figures are explained in the text. References in the text direct readers to the relevant statistics. Furthermore, the contents of all tables and figures are fully indexed. Please see the opening section of the Index at the back of this volume for a description of how to find tables and figures within it.

Appendixes

Besides the main body text and images, *Education in America* has three appendixes. The first is the Important Names and Addresses directory. Here, readers will find contact information for a number of government and private organizations that can provide further information on aspects of education. The second appendix is the Resources section, which can also assist readers in conducting their own research. In this section, the author and editors of *Education in America* describe some of the sources that were most useful during the compilation of this book. The final appendix is the detailed Index. It has been greatly expanded from previous editions and should make it even easier to find specific topics in this book.

COMMENTS AND SUGGESTIONS

The editors of the *Information Plus Reference Series* welcome your feedback on *Education in America*. Please direct all correspondence to:

Editors
Information Plus Reference Series
27500 Drake Rd.
Farmington Hills, MI 48331-3535

CHAPTER 1
AN OVERVIEW OF AMERICAN EDUCATION

The history of education in the United States has been replete with controversy, debate, and innovation. Educators, parents, politicians, and social scientists debate the purposes of schools, the benefits of education, the best approaches to teaching and learning, and how to afford the necessary costs. Since the 1980s the nation has been working to resolve critical issues such as low academic performance, high dropout rates, and drug use and violence in schools. Political and community leaders stress the importance of preparing high school graduates to compete in a technical, global environment. Educational leaders raise concerns about the impact of poverty on education and about the adequacy of school resources. Voters and legislators debate the merits of alternative schools, including whether parents who enroll their children in private schools should receive federal or state subsidies. Calls for school accountability are heard from both taxpayers and elected officials.

Despite such controversies, the United States remains one of the most highly educated nations in the world, and the educational system is central to American society. As indicated in Table 1.1, the U.S. Department of Education estimates that approximately 85.2 million Americans were involved either directly or indirectly in providing or receiving formal education during the fall of 2013. With a total population of approximately 316.6 million at that time, the United States had more than a quarter (27%) of its people involved in its educational system. Of the total, about 75.4 million were students enrolled in elementary, secondary, and postsecondary degree-granting institutions, and 4.5 million were teachers. Another 5.3 million were professional, administrative, and support personnel.

THE QUALITY OF EDUCATION IN THE UNITED STATES

The United States has many of the best universities in the world, a fact showcased in "World University Rankings, 2014–15" (2015, https://www.timeshigher education.co.uk/world-university-rankings/2015/world-ranking#). These rankings were developed by Times Higher Education, a leading higher education news publication located in the United Kingdom. The 2014–15 rankings showed that 29 U.S. universities were listed among the top 50 in the world. (See Table 1.2.) In addition, the United States held three of the top-five spots (California Institute of Technology was ranked first, Harvard University was ranked second, and Stanford University was ranked fourth) and 11 of the top-15 universities.

Many universities in the United States are among the world's best, but what about U.S. primary and secondary schools? Results of research conducted by the Organisation for Economic Co-operation and Development (OECD) provide a snapshot of the level of proficiency of U.S. school students. The OECD is an international group of 34 countries that are committed to democracy. As part of its work, the OECD collects international economic and social statistics to help governments solve common problems, identify good practices, and coordinate domestic and international policies. In 2000 the OECD began the Program for International Student Assessment (PISA), which measures the literacy levels of 15-year-olds in reading, mathematics, and science every three years. The results from PISA provide one perspective on the quality of the U.S. primary and secondary educational system by comparing the proficiency of U.S. students with that of students from other countries.

Table 1.3 and Table 1.4 show the results of the mathematics and science literacy assessments of 15-year-old students. Dana Kelly et al. of the National Center for Education Statistics (NCES) explain in *Performance of U.S. 15-Year-Old Students in Mathematics, Science, and Reading Literacy in an International Context: First Look at PISA 2012* (December 2013, https://nces.ed.gov/

TABLE 1.1

Projected number of participants in educational institutions, by level and control of institution, fall 2013

[In millions]

Participants	All levels (elementary, secondary, and degree-granting postsecondary)	Elementary and secondary schools			Degree-granting postsecondary institutions		
		Total	Public	Private	Total	Public	Private
Total	**85.2**	**61.7**	**55.9**	**5.8**	**23.5**	**16.7**	**6.8**
Enrollment	75.4	54.8	49.8	5.1	20.6	14.9	5.7
Teachers and faculty	4.5	3.5	3.1	0.4	1.0	0.6	0.4
Other professional, administrative, and support staff	5.3	3.4	3.1	0.3	1.9	1.2	0.7

Note: Includes enrollments in local public school systems and in most private schools (religiously affiliated and nonsectarian). Excludes federal Bureau of Indian Education schools and Department of Defense schools. Excludes private preprimary enrollment in schools that do not offer kindergarten or above. Degree-granting institutions grant associate's or higher degrees and participate in Title IV federal financial aid programs. Data for teachers and other staff in public and private elementary and secondary schools and colleges and universities are reported in terms of full-time equivalents. Detail may not sum to totals because of rounding.

SOURCE: "Table 105.10. Projected Number of Participants in Educational Institutions, by Level and Control of Institution: Fall 2013," in "Most Current Digest Tables," *Digest of Education Statistics*, U.S. Department of Education, Institute of Education Sciences, National Center for Education Statistics, March 2014, https://nces.ed.gov/programs/digest/d13/tables/xls/tabn105.10.xls (accessed July 16, 2015)

pubs2014/2014024rev.pdf) that the term *literacy* denotes a "broad focus on the application of knowledge and skills" and the "application of knowledge in mathematics, science, and reading literacy to problems within a real-life context."

The mean (average) of the mathematics literacy scores for OECD countries in 2012 was 494. (See Table 1.3.) The mean score for the United States was somewhat lower, at 481, although the public school systems in the states of Massachusetts (514) and Connecticut (506) both ranked higher than the OECD average. The Republic of Korea (South Korea; 554) topped the list of OECD countries that had the highest mathematics literacy scores, followed by Japan (536), Switzerland (531), the Netherlands (523), and Estonia (521). The non-OECD list included cities and special administrative regions of China at the top, with scores that were higher than the OECD average.

The mean of the science literacy scores for OECD countries in 2012 was 501. (See Table 1.4.) The mean score for the United States was 497. Japan (547) topped the list of OECD countries that had the highest science literacy scores, followed by Finland (545), Estonia (541), South Korea (538), and Poland (526). As with mathematics, the non-OECD science list included cities and special administrative regions of China at the top, with scores that were higher than the OECD average.

Returning to the question about the quality of U.S. primary and secondary schools, the answer is that based on student performance in these two assessments, they appear to be average to slightly below average. Chapter 4 discusses the results of other international tests and measurements of U.S. school student performance.

LEVEL OF EDUCATIONAL ATTAINMENT

Based on U.S. Census Bureau data estimates for the years before 1940 and on data collected from 1940 onward, the number of school years completed among Americans aged 25 years and older increased dramatically during the 20th century and into the 21st century. (See Table 1.5.) In 1940 only 38.1% of Americans completed high school. That meant that more than three out of five of the U.S. adult population did not have a high school education in 1940. Furthermore, only 5.9% of Americans earned a college degree.

Since 1940 the percentage of the U.S. adult population completing high school has increased consistently over the decades. (See Table 1.5.) By 2014, 90.8% of Americans had completed high school. Furthermore, slightly more than one-third (34%) of Americans had earned a bachelor's degree or higher.

Table 1.5 reveals differences in educational attainment between males and females. In 2014 a slightly higher percentage of females aged 25 years and older (91.5%) had graduated from high school than did males (90.1%). Among Americans with college degrees, the discrepancy became even more dramatic. In 2014, 37.2% of women had earned a bachelor's degree; by comparison, 30.9% of men had completed college that year.

The differences in educational attainment among whites, African Americans, and Hispanics are more notable than the differences between the sexes. Table 1.5 shows that in 2014, 95.6% of whites aged 25 years and older had graduated from high school, whereas 91.9% of African Americans and 74.7% of Hispanics had done so. In addition, 40.8% of the white population had graduated from

TABLE 1.2

The world's top universities, by rank and country, 2014–15

World rank	Institution	Country/region
1	California Institute of Technology	United States
2	Harvard University	United States
3	University of Oxford	United Kingdom
4	Stanford University	United States
5	University of Cambridge	United Kingdom
6	Massachusetts Institute of Technology (MIT)	United States
7	Princeton University	United States
8	University of California, Berkeley	United States
9	Imperial College London	United Kingdom
10	Yale University	United States
11	University of Chicago	United States
12	University of California, Los Angeles	United States
13	ETH Zürich—Swiss Federal Institute of Technology Zurich	Switzerland
14	Columbia University	United States
15	Johns Hopkins University	United States
16	University of Pennsylvania	United States
17	University of Michigan	United States
18	Duke University	United States
19	Cornell University	United States
20	University of Toronto	Canada
21	Northwestern University	United States
22	University College London	United Kingdom
23	University of Tokyo	Japan
24	Carnegie Mellon University	United States
25	National University of Singapore	Singapore
26	University of Washington	United States
27	Georgia Institute of Technology (Georgia Tech)	United States
28	University of Texas at Austin	United States
29	University of Illinois at Urbana-Champaign	United States
30	Ludwig Maximilian University of Munich	Germany
31	University of Wisconsin-Madison	United States
32	University of British Columbia	Canada
33	University of Melbourne	Australia
34	École Polytechnique Fédérale de Lausanne	Switzerland
35	London School of Economics and Political Science	United Kingdom
36	University of Edinburgh	United Kingdom
37	University of California, Santa Barbara	United States
38	New York University	United States
39	McGill University	Canada
40	King's College London	United Kingdom
41	University of California, San Diego	United States
42	Washington University in St. Louis	United States
43	University of Hong Kong	Hong Kong
44	Karolinska Institute	Sweden
45	Australian National University	Australia
46	University of Minnesota	United States
47	University of North Carolina at Chapel Hill	United States
48	Peking University	China
49	Tsinghua University	China
50	Seoul National University	South Korea

SOURCE: Adapted from "World University Rankings 2014–15," in *THE World University Rankings*, Times Higher Education, 2015, https://www.timeshighereducation.co.uk/world-university-rankings/2015/world-ranking#/ (accessed July 16, 2015)

TABLE 1.3

Average scores of 15-year-old students on mathematics literacy scale, by country, 2012

Education system	Average score		Education system	Average score	
OECD average	494	⌃	Lithuania[a]	479	
Shanghai-China[a]	613	⌃	Sweden	478	
Singapore[a]	573	⌃	Hungary	477	
Hong Kong-China*	561	⌃	Croatia[a]	471	⌄
Chinese Taipei[a]	560	⌃	Israel	466	⌄
Korea, Republic of	554	⌃	Greece	453	⌄
Macao-China[a]	538	⌃	Serbia, Republic of[a]	449	⌄
Japan	536	⌃	Turkey	448	⌄
Liechtenstein[a]	535	⌃	Romania[a]	445	⌄
Switzerland	531	⌃	Cyprus[a]	440	⌄
Netherlands	523	⌃	Bulgaria[a]	439	⌄
Estonia	521	⌃	United Arab Emirates[a]	434	⌄
Finland	519	⌃	Kazakhstan[a]	432	⌄
Canada	518	⌃	Thailand[a]	427	⌄
Poland	518	⌃	Chile	423	⌄
Belgium	515	⌃	Malaysia[a]	421	⌄
Germany	514	⌃	Mexico	413	⌄
Vietnam[a]	511	⌃	Montenegro, Republic of[a]	410	⌄
Austria	506	⌃	Uruguay[a]	409	⌄
Australia	504	⌃	Costa Rica[a]	407	⌄
Ireland	501	⌃	Albania[a]	394	⌄
Slovenia	501	⌃	Brazil[a]	391	⌄
Denmark	500	⌃	Argentina[a]	388	⌄
New Zealand	500	⌃	Tunisia[a]	388	⌄
Czech Republic	499	⌃	Jordan[a]	386	⌄
France	495	⌃	Colombia[a]	376	⌄
United Kingdom	494	⌃	Qatar[a]	376	⌄
Iceland	493	⌃	Indonesia[a]	375	⌄
Latvia[a]	491	⌃	Peru[a]	368	⌄
Luxembourg	490	⌃			
Norway	489				
Portugal	487				
Italy	485		**U.S. state education systems**		
Spain	484		Massachusetts[b]	514	⌃
Russian Federation[a]	482		Connecticut[b]	506	⌃
Slovak Republic	482		Florida[b]	467	⌄
United States	481				

⌃ Average score is higher than U.S. average score.
  OECD = Organization for Economic Cooperation and Development.
⌄ Average score is lower than U.S. average score.
[a]Non-OECD countries and education systems.
[b]Results for Connecticut, Florida, and Massachusetts are for public school students only.
Note: Education systems are ordered by 2012 average score. The OECD average is the average of the national averages of the OECD member countries, with each country weighted equally. Scores are reported on a scale from 0 to 1,000. All average scores reported as higher or lower than the U.S. average score are different at the .05 level of statistical significance.

SOURCE: Dana Kelly et al., "Table 1. Average Scores of 15-Year-Old Students on PISA Mathematics Literacy Scale, by Education System: 2012," in *Performance of U.S. 15-Year-Old Students in Mathematics, Science, and Reading Literacy in an International Context: First Look at PISA 2012*, U.S. Department of Education, Institute of Education Sciences, National Center for Education Statistics, December 2013, https://nces.ed.gov/pubs2014/2014024rev.pdf (accessed July 16, 2015)

college, compared with only 22.4% of the African American population and 15.1% of the Hispanic population.

SCHOOL ENROLLMENT

Primary and secondary education is compulsory in the United States. Depending on the state, students may be required to begin school at age five and to remain in school until age 18. Some states have later starting ages and earlier ages for withdrawal, but no state allows students to enter later than age seven or to drop out before the age of 16 without a special exemption. The terminal grade in the U.S. public school system is grade 12. Parents may send their children to private schools or homeschool them if they prefer.

Virtually all U.S. children aged seven to 15 years old were being schooled in 2013. Schooling for children of these ages is compulsory in all states, but some states may provide exemptions for some students beginning at the age of 14 years. Many states allow young people to leave school legally when they reach the age of 16 or 17.

TABLE 1.4

Average scores of 15-year-old students on science literary scale, by country, 2012

Education system	Average score	Education system	Average score
OECD average	501		
Shanghai-China[a]	580 ◭	Russian Federation[a]	486 ◮
Hong Kong-China[a]	555 ◭	Sweden	485 ◮
Singapore[a]	551 ◭	Iceland	478 ◮
Japan	547 ◭	Slovak Republic	471 ◮
Finland	545 ◭	Israel	470 ◮
Estonia	541 ◭	Greece	467 ◮
Korea, Republic of	538 ◭	Turkey	463 ◮
Vietnam[a]	528 ◭	United Arab Emirates[a]	448 ◮
Poland	526 ◭	Bulgaria[a]	446 ◮
Canada	525 ◭	Chile	445 ◮
Liechtenstein[a]	525 ◭	Serbia, Republic of [a]	445 ◮
Germany	524 ◭	Thailand[a]	444 ◮
Chinese Taipei[a]	523 ◭	Romania[a]	439 ◮
Netherlands	522 ◭	Cyprus[a]	438 ◮
Ireland	522 ◭	Costa Rica[a]	429 ◮
Australia	521 ◭	Kazakhstan[a]	425 ◮
Macao-China[a]	521 ◭	Malaysia[a]	420 ◮
New Zealand	516 ◭	Uruguay[a]	416 ◮
Switzerland	515 ◭	Mexico	415 ◮
Slovenia	514 ◭	Montenegro, Republic of[a]	410 ◮
United Kingdom	514 ◭	Jordan[a]	409 ◮
Czech Republic	508 ◭	Argentina[a]	406 ◮
Austria	506	Brazil[a]	405 ◮
Belgium	505	Colombia[a]	399 ◮
Latvia[a]	502	Tunisia[a]	398 ◮
France	499	Albania[a]	397 ◮
Denmark	498	Qatar[a]	384 ◮
United States	497	Indonesia[a]	382 ◮
Spain	496	Peru[a]	373 ◮
Lithuania[a]	496		
Norway	495		
Hungary	494	**U.S. state education systems**	
Italy	494	Massachusetts[b]	527 ◭
Croatia[a]	491	Connecticut[b]	521 ◭
Luxembourg	491	Florida[b]	485
Portugal	489		

◭ Average score is higher than U.S. average score.
OECD = Organization for Economic Cooperation and Development.
◮ Average score is lower than U.S. average score.
[a]Non-OECD countries and education systems.
[b]Results for Connecticut, Florida, and Massachusetts are for public school students only.
Note: Education systems are ordered by 2012 average score. The OECD average is the average of the national averages of the OECD member countries, with each country weighted equally. Scores are reported on a scale from 0 to 1,000. All average scores reported as higher or lower than the U.S. average score are different at the .05 level of statistical significance.

SOURCE: Dana Kelly et al., "Table 2. Average Scores of 15-Year -Old Students on PISA Science Literacy Scale, by Education System: 2012," in *Performance of U.S. 15-Year Old Students in Mathematics, Science, and Reading Literacy in an International Context: First Look at PISA 2012*, U.S. Department of Education, Institute of Education Sciences, National Center for Education Statistics, December 2013, https://nces.ed.gov/pubs 2014/2014024rev.pdf (accessed July 16, 2015)

As Table 1.6 shows, school enrollment among students aged 16 to 17 years rose from 89% in 1980 to 96.1% in 2010, before dipping to 95.8% in 2012 and 93.7% in 2013. In 1980, 90.7% of African American students aged 16 to 17 years were enrolled in school; 89.2% of white students aged 16 to 17 years were enrolled in school that year, whereas only 81.8% of Hispanic students in that age group were enrolled in school. By contrast, in 2013 Hispanics aged 16 to 17 years (93.9%) were the most likely to be enrolled in school, followed by whites (93.6%) and African Americans (92.7%).

As shown in Table 1.6, a higher percentage of African American girls from ages 10 to 13 to ages 16 and 17 dropped out in 2013 (5.9 percentage points) than did African American boys (3.9 percentage points). This gender difference shifted among white and Hispanic students. In 2013 school enrollment among white boys dropped 5.6 percentage points between ages 10 to 13 and 16 to 17, whereas enrollment among white girls in these age groups fell only four percentage points. Among Hispanic boys enrollment fell 4.2 percentage points between the ages of 10 to 13 and 16 to 17 in 2013, compared with a decrease of 3.4 percentage points among Hispanic girls.

The percentage of people enrolled in school drops sharply after the age of 18. By this age young people either graduate from or drop out of high school and may not immediately (or ever) go on to any form of higher education. Nonetheless, the proportion of older teens attending school has increased since 1980. In 2013 the percentage of 18- and 19-year-olds enrolled in school was 67.1%, up from 46.4% in 1980. (See Table 1.6.) In 2013 a greater percentage of females (69.2%) attended school than males (65.1%) at age 18 to 19. In addition, a greater percentage of whites (69.6%) than African Americans (64.2%) or Hispanics (59.3%) attended school at this age in 2013.

Changes in School Enrollment over Time

Overall, school enrollment at all levels has risen steadily since 1990. Total enrollment rose from to 60.7 million in 1990 to 68.7 million in 2000, an increase of 13.2 percent. (See Table 1.7.) The next decade saw continued growth, and by 2010 overall enrollment reached 75.9 million. Enrollment dipped somewhat over the next four years, dropping to 75.2 million in 2014, before rising slightly to 75.23 million in 2015. Overall school enrollment was projected to climb steadily over the next decade, surpassing 81 million by the year 2024.

Elementary school enrollment, which includes both public and private prekindergarten to grade eight, reached 34.4 million students in 1990. (See Table 1.7.) Total elementary school enrollment rose steadily over the next decade, reaching 38.6 million in 2000. Elementary school enrollment saw little change over the next decade and a half, however, reaching 38.7 million in 2010 and 38.9 million in 2015. It was projected to grow slowly through 2024, reaching 41.6 million public and private elementary school students.

Public and private high school enrollment experienced notable growth between 1990 and 2010. In 1990 total high school enrollment stood at 12.5 million; this figure rose to 14.8 million in 2000, and 16.2 million in 2010, an overall increase of nearly 30 percent over a

TABLE 1.5

Percentage of persons aged 25–29, by years of school completed, race/ethnicity, and sex, selected years 1920–2014

Sex, selected level of educational attainment, and year	Total	White[a]	Black[a]	Hispanic	Asian/Pacific Islander			American Indian/ Alaska Native	Two or more races
					Total	Asian	Pacific Islander		
Total									
High school completion or higher[b]									
1920[c]	—	22.0	6.3	—	—	—	—	—	—
1940	38.1	41.2	12.3	—	—	—	—	—	—
1950	52.8	56.3	23.6	—	—	—	—	—	—
1960	60.7	63.7	38.6	—	—	—	—	—	—
1970	75.4	77.8	58.4	—	—	—	—	—	—
1980	85.4	89.2	76.7	58.0	—	—	—	—	—
1990	85.7	90.1	81.7	58.2	91.5	—	—	—	—
2000	88.1	94.0	86.8	62.8	93.7	—	—	—	—
2010	88.8	94.5	89.6	69.4	93.7	94.0	89.7	89.9	88.5
2013	89.9	94.1	90.3	75.8	95.4	95.4	95.5	84.7	97.4
2014	90.8	95.6	91.9	74.7	96.6	96.6	‡	83.9	96.0
Bachelor's or higher degree[d]									
1920[c]	—	4.5	1.2	—	—	—	—	—	—
1940	5.9	6.4	1.6	—	—	—	—	—	—
1950	7.7	8.2	2.8	—	—	—	—	—	—
1960	11.0	11.8	5.4	—	—	—	—	—	—
1970	16.4	17.3	10.0	—	—	—	—	—	—
1980	22.5	25.0	11.6	7.7	—	—	—	—	—
1990	23.2	26.4	13.4	8.1	43.0	—	—	—	—
2000	29.1	34.0	17.8	9.7	54.3	—	—	—	—
2010	31.7	38.6	19.4	13.5	52.5	55.8	10.0	18.6	29.8
2013	33.6	40.4	20.5	15.7	58.0	60.1	24.7	16.6	29.6
2014	34.0	40.8	22.4	15.1	60.8	63.2	‡	5.6	32.4
Master's or higher degree									
2000	5.4	5.8	3.7	2.1	15.5	—	‡	—	—
2010	6.8	7.7	4.7	2.5	17.9	19.2	‡	‡	5.3
2013	7.4	8.6	3.3	3.0	20.6	21.8	#	‡	4.8
2014	7.6	9.0	3.9	2.9	17.9	18.8	‡	#	7.1
Males									
High school completion or higher[b]									
1980	85.4	89.1	74.7	57.0	—	—	—	—	—
1990	84.4	88.6	81.4	56.6	95.3	—	—	—	—
2000	86.7	92.9	87.6	59.2	92.1	—	—	—	—
2010	87.4	94.6	87.9	65.7	93.8	93.5	‡	93.2	87.9
2013	88.3	93.3	87.8	73.1	94.4	94.3	‡	‡	96.8
2014	90.1	95.4	93.5	72.4	96.1	96.1	‡	‡	96.9
Bachelor's or higher degree[d]									
1980	24.0	26.8	10.5	8.4	—	—	—	—	—
1990	23.7	26.6	15.1	7.3	47.6	—	—	—	—
2000	27.9	32.3	18.4	8.3	55.5	—	—	—	—
2010	27.8	34.8	15.0	10.8	49.0	52.3	‡	18.9	24.9
2013	30.2	37.1	17.4	13.1	53.0	55.1	‡	‡	29.3
2014	30.9	37.7	20.8	12.4	56.9	59.0	‡	‡	26.4
Master's or higher degree									
2000	4.7	4.9	2.1	1.5	17.2	—	—	—	—
2010	5.2	6.3	2.9	1.5	15.0	16.2	‡	‡	#
2013	5.7	6.3	1.5	2.1	20.8	22.1	‡	‡	5.9
2014	5.9	7.0	2.6	2.2	15.9	16.6	‡	‡	‡
Females									
High school completion or higher[b]									
1980	85.5	89.2	78.3	58.9	—	—	—	—	—
1990	87.0	91.7	82.0	59.9	85.1	—	—	—	—
2000	89.4	95.2	86.2	66.4	95.2	—	—	—	—
2010	90.2	94.4	91.1	74.1	93.6	94.5	‡	86.8	89.1
2013	91.5	94.9	92.5	78.8	96.2	96.3	‡	82.0	98.2
2014	91.5	95.9	90.5	77.4	97.1	97.1	‡	84.1	95.2

20-year span. (See Table 1.7.) Over the next five years total high school enrollment remained roughly the same, dipping to just under 16 million in 2013 before reaching 16.1 million in 2015. Growth over the next 10 years was projected to be more modest, with total high school enrollment expected to reach 16.3 million in 2024.

TABLE 1.5

Percentage of persons aged 25–29, by years of school completed, race/ethnicity, and sex, selected years 1920–2014 [CONTINUED]

Sex, selected level of educational attainment, and year	Total	White[a]	Black[a]	Hispanic	Asian/Pacific Islander Total	Asian	Pacific Islander	American Indian/ Alaska Native	Two or more races
Bachelor's or higher degree[d]									
1980	21.0	23.2	12.4	6.9	—	—	—	—	—
1990	22.8	26.2	11.9	9.1	37.4	—	—	—	—
2000	30.1	35.8	17.4	11.0	53.1	—	—	—	—
2010	35.7	42.4	23.3	16.8	55.8	58.9	‡	18.4	34.0
2013	37.0	43.8	23.2	18.6	62.4	64.3	‡	16.4	30.0
2014	37.2	43.9	23.8	18.3	64.3	66.9	‡	‡	38.4
Master's or higher degree									
2000	6.2	6.7	4.9	2.7	13.9	—	—	—	—
2010	8.5	9.2	6.2	3.8	20.6	21.8	‡	‡	10.0
2013	9.2	10.8	4.8	4.0	20.4	21.6	‡	‡	3.3
2014	9.3	11.1	5.0	3.6	19.7	20.8	‡	#	7.5

—Not available.

#Rounds to zero.

‡Reporting standards not met.

[a]Includes persons of Hispanic ethnicity for years prior to 1980.

[b]Data for years prior to 1993 are for persons with 4 or more years of high school. Data for later years are for high school completers—i.e., those persons who graduated from high school with a diploma as well as those who completed high school through equivalency programs, such as a GED (General Educational Development) program.

[c]Estimates based on Census Bureau reverse projection of 1940 census data on education by age.

[d]Data for years prior to 1993 are for persons with 4 or more years of college.

Note: For 1960 and prior years, data were collected in April. For all other years, data were collected in March. Race categories exclude persons of Hispanic ethnicity except where otherwise noted.

SOURCE: Adapted from "Table 104.20. Percentage of Persons 25 to 29 Years Old with Selected Levels of Educational Attainment, by Race/Ethnicity and Sex: Selected Years, 1920 through 2014," in "Most Current Digest Tables," *Digest of Education Statistics*, U.S. Department of Education, Institute of Education Sciences, National Center for Education Statistics, October 2014, https://nces.ed.gov/programs/digest/d14/tables/xls/tabn104.20.xls (accessed July 16, 2015)

As the NCES reports in "Back to School Statistics" (2015, http://nces.ed.gov/fastfacts/display.asp?id=372), total enrollment in public elementary and secondary schools was projected to reach 50.1 million in the fall of 2015. Of all public school students in 2015, 35.2 million were enrolled in prekindergarten through eighth grade, and 14.9 million were enrolled in high school. Overall, approximately 3 million students were expected to graduate from public high schools at the end of the 2015–16 school year.

In addition, the NCES estimates that roughly 20.1 million students were enrolled in postsecondary educational institutions in the fall of 2015. Of these, approximately 12.6 million were enrolled as full-time students, and 7.6 million were attending a college or university on a part-time basis. Enrollment in postsecondary institutions typically declines between the fall and spring semester in a given year. As the National Student Clearinghouse Research Center reports in "Current Term Enrollment Report—Fall 2014" (December 10, 2014, https://nscresearchcenter.org/currenttermenrollmentestimate-fall2014), total enrollment in all postsecondary institutions topped 19.6 million in the fall of 2014. According to the National Student Clearinghouse Research Center, in "Current Term Enrollment Report—Spring 2015" (May 13, 2015, http://nscresearchcenter.org/currenttermenrollmentestimate-spring2015), overall enrollment in postsecondary institutions fell to 18.6 million the following spring, a decline of 5%. As the National Student Clearinghouse Research Center notes, postsecondary enrollment in the spring of 2015 also represented a decrease from the spring of 2014, when 18.9 million students were enrolled in postsecondary institutions.

EDUCATION SPENDING

According to the Department of Education, expenditures for public and private education from preprimary to graduate school approached $1.2 trillion for the 2012–13 school year. (See Table 1.8.) Expenditures for elementary and secondary schools were estimated to reach $669 billion (57% of total education spending), and outlays for colleges and universities were estimated at $496 billion (43% of total education spending). The United States spent an estimated 7.2% of its gross domestic product (GDP; the total value of goods and services produced within the United States) on education during the 2012–13 school year. Nearly 60 years earlier, during the 1949–50 school year, the United States spent much less—$8.5 billion, or 3.1% of its GDP, on education.

The New America Foundation, a nonpartisan organization that publishes data on education funding, offers a breakdown of current education spending in "Federal, State, and Local K–12 School Finance Overview"

TABLE 1.6

Percentage of the population 3–34 years old enrolled in school, by sex, race/ethnicity, and age, selected years 1980–2013

Year and age group	Total				Male				Female			
	Total	White	Black	Hispanic	Total	White	Black	Hispanic	Total	White	Black	Hispanic
1980												
Total, 3 to 34 years old	49.7	48.8	54.0	49.8	50.9	50.0	56.2	49.9	48.5	47.7	52.1	49.8
3 and 4 years old	36.7	37.4	38.2	28.5	37.8	39.2	36.4	30.1	35.5	35.5	40.0	26.6
5 and 6 years old	95.7	95.9	95.5	94.5	95.0	95.4	94.1	94.0	96.4	96.5	97.0	94.9
7 to 9 years old	99.1	99.1	99.4	98.4	99.0	99.0	99.5	97.7	99.2	99.2	99.3	99.0
10 to 13 years old	99.4	99.4	99.4	99.7	99.4	99.4	99.4	99.4	99.4	99.3	99.3	99.9
14 and 15 years old	98.2	98.7	97.9	94.3	98.7	98.9	98.4	96.7	97.7	98.5	97.3	92.1
16 and 17 years old	89.0	89.2	90.7	81.8	89.1	89.4	90.7	81.5	88.8	89.0	90.6	82.2
18 and 19 years old	46.4	47.0	45.8	37.8	47.0	48.5	42.9	36.9	45.8	45.7	48.3	38.8
20 and 21 years old	31.0	33.0	23.3	19.5	32.6	34.8	22.8	21.4	29.5	31.3	23.7	17.6
22 to 24 years old	16.3	16.8	13.6	11.7	17.8	18.7	13.4	10.7	14.9	15.0	13.7	12.6
25 to 29 years old	9.3	9.4	8.8	6.9	9.8	9.8	10.6	6.8	8.8	9.1	7.5	6.9
30 to 34 years old	6.4	6.4	6.9	5.1	5.9	5.6	7.2	6.2	7.0	7.2	6.6	‡
1990												
Total, 3 to 34 years old	50.2	49.8	52.2	47.2	50.9	50.4	54.3	46.8	49.5	49.2	50.3	47.7
3 and 4 years old	44.4	47.2	41.8	30.7	43.9	47.9	38.1	28.0	44.9	46.6	45.5	33.6
5 and 6 years old	96.5	96.7	96.5	94.9	96.5	96.8	96.2	95.8	96.4	96.7	96.9	93.9
7 to 9 years old	99.7	99.7	99.8	99.5	99.7	99.7	99.9	99.5	99.6	99.7	99.8	99.4
10 to 13 years old	99.6	99.7	99.9	99.1	99.6	99.6	99.9	99.0	99.7	99.7	99.8	99.1
14 and 15 years old	99.0	99.0	99.4	99.0	99.1	99.2	99.7	99.1	98.9	98.9	99.1	98.8
16 and 17 years old	92.5	93.5	91.7	85.4	92.6	93.4	93.0	85.5	92.4	93.7	90.5	85.3
18 and 19 years old	57.2	59.1	55.0	44.0	58.2	59.7	60.4	40.7	56.3	58.5	49.8	47.2
20 and 21 years old	39.7	43.1	28.3	27.2	40.3	44.2	31.0	21.7	39.2	42.0	25.8	33.1
22 to 24 years old	21.0	21.9	19.7	9.9	22.3	23.7	19.3	11.2	19.9	20.3	20.0	8.4
25 to 29 years old	9.7	10.4	6.1	6.3	9.2	10.0	4.7	4.6	10.2	10.7	7.3	8.1
30 to 34 years old	5.8	6.2	4.5	3.6	4.8	5.0	2.3	4.0	6.9	7.4	6.3	3.1
2000												
Total, 3 to 34 years old	55.9	56.0	59.3	51.3	55.8	55.8	59.7	50.5	56.0	56.1	59.0	52.2
3 and 4 years old*	52.1	54.6	59.8	35.9	50.8	54.1	58.0	31.9	53.4	55.2	61.8	40.0
5 and 6 years old	95.6	95.5	96.7	94.3	95.1	94.5	96.0	95.4	96.1	96.4	97.5	93.1
7 to 9 years old	98.1	98.4	97.5	97.5	98.0	98.1	98.2	96.6	98.2	98.6	96.7	98.4
10 to 13 years old	98.3	98.5	98.5	97.4	98.3	98.2	98.8	98.4	98.3	98.8	98.1	96.4
14 and 15 years old	98.7	98.9	99.6	96.2	98.7	98.8	99.6	96.9	98.6	99.0	99.6	95.4
16 and 17 years old	92.8	94.0	91.7	87.0	92.7	94.7	88.9	85.7	92.9	93.3	94.6	88.3
18 and 19 years old	61.2	63.9	57.2	49.5	58.3	61.2	51.5	48.0	64.2	66.7	62.2	51.1
20 and 21 years old	44.1	49.2	37.4	26.1	41.0	45.8	31.3	24.2	47.3	52.7	42.3	28.1
22 to 24 years old	24.6	24.9	24.0	18.2	23.9	25.0	22.0	15.2	25.3	24.8	25.8	21.6
25 to 29 years old	11.4	11.1	14.5	7.4	10.0	10.5	11.6	5.1	12.7	11.8	16.7	9.5
30 to 34 years old	6.7	6.1	9.9	5.6	5.6	4.7	8.5	5.7	7.7	7.4	11.2	5.5
2010												
Total, 3 to 34 years old	56.6	56.1	58.7	55.1	55.9	55.5	58.4	52.9	57.4	56.7	58.9	57.4
3 and 4 years old*	53.2	56.1	57.2	44.2	53.0	55.9	57.0	43.3	53.4	56.3	57.4	45.0
5 and 6 years old	94.5	94.2	94.1	94.3	93.7	93.3	93.5	93.4	95.3	95.2	94.7	95.2
7 to 9 years old	97.7	97.4	96.9	98.5	97.6	97.1	97.3	98.1	98.0	97.7	96.5	98.9
10 to 13 years old	98.2	98.3	99.2	97.3	97.9	97.7	99.6	96.9	98.6	98.9	98.8	97.7
14 and 15 years old	98.1	98.0	98.8	97.9	98.0	98.0	98.4	97.5	98.3	98.1	99.3	98.3
16 and 17 years old	96.1	96.2	95.7	96.0	94.9	94.7	93.7	96.0	97.3	97.8	97.6	96.0
18 and 19 years old	69.2	71.0	62.9	66.2	66.9	67.8	62.3	64.9	71.5	74.3	63.4	67.6
20 and 21 years old	52.4	55.5	51.1	37.0	49.2	52.1	45.7	34.0	56.0	59.2	56.0	40.5
22 to 24 years old.	28.9	29.1	29.8	23.8	27.0	27.8	29.5	18.6	30.8	30.4	30.0	29.2
25 to 29 years old	14.6	14.6	16.5	11.4	13.5	13.8	13.9	9.6	15.8	15.4	18.8	13.6
30 to 34 years old	8.3	8.5	11.0	5.7	6.7	7.2	6.6	4.9	9.9	9.8	14.8	6.6
2012												
Total, 3 to 34 years old	56.6	55.6	58.9	56.4	55.9	55.0	58.8	54.7	57.4	56.2	59.1	58.2
3 and 4 years old*	53.5	56.5	54.8	46.3	52.7	55.6	51.7	45.4	54.4	57.4	57.8	47.1
5 and 6 years old	93.2	93.8	91.9	92.1	93.2	93.6	92.4	92.2	93.3	94.0	91.4	92.1
7 to 9 years old	98.0	98.1	96.8	98.1	97.7	97.7	96.7	98.2	98.4	98.5	97.0	98.1
10 to 13 years old	98.0	97.5	99.1	98.3	98.2	97.7	99.3	98.6	97.8	97.3	98.8	98.0
14 and 15 years old	98.2	98.2	97.4	98.5	98.3	97.9	98.4	98.9	98.2	98.4	96.4	98.1
16 and 17 years old	95.8	96.4	94.5	94.8	95.7	96.0	96.5	95.1	95.9	96.8	92.4	94.5
18 and 19 years old	69.0	68.8	68.9	68.1	65.8	65.4	62.0	65.7	72.3	72.3	75.7	70.7
20 and 21 years old	54.0	55.9	50.7	49.5	49.5	49.7	51.3	44.4	58.3	61.7	50.2	55.0
22 to 24 years old	30.7	30.2	28.4	27.1	29.4	29.6	26.2	24.7	32.1	30.8	30.3	29.7
25 to 29 years old	14.0	14.6	16.6	9.4	11.9	13.0	11.4	7.4	16.0	16.2	20.9	11.5
30 to 34 years old	7.5	6.6	12.4	6.2	5.8	6.1	7.9	3.3	9.2	7.1	16.0	9.3

TABLE 1.6

Percentage of the population 3–34 years old enrolled in school, by sex, race/ethnicity, and age, selected years 1980–2013 [CONTINUED]

Year and age group	Total				Male				Female			
	Total	White	Black	Hispanic	Total	White	Black	Hispanic	Total	White	Black	Hispanic
2013												
Total, 3 to 34 years old	**55.8**	**54.7**	**57.8**	**55.5**	**55.2**	**54.1**	**57.3**	**54.0**	**56.4**	**55.4**	**58.3**	**57.0**
3 and 4 years old*	54.9	57.4	61.1	45.4	53.2	55.2	58.2	44.2	56.7	59.7	63.8	46.7
5 and 6 years old	93.8	93.6	94.7	93.9	93.8	93.7	95.2	93.6	93.7	93.5	94.1	94.1
7 to 9 years old	97.9	97.9	96.4	98.4	97.9	97.8	96.2	98.6	97.9	98.0	96.6	98.2
10 to 13 years old	98.2	98.5	97.6	97.7	98.1	98.4	97.6	97.7	98.2	98.5	97.6	97.7
14 and 15 years old	98.4	98.4	98.6	98.3	98.2	98.4	98.7	97.9	98.6	98.4	98.5	98.8
16 and 17 years old	93.7	93.6	92.7	93.9	93.3	92.8	93.7	93.5	94.1	94.5	91.7	94.3
18 and 19 years old	67.1	69.6	64.2	59.3	65.1	68.6	60.8	55.4	69.2	70.8	67.5	63.2
20 and 21 years old	52.8	55.2	48.7	43.9	48.5	51.0	43.5	38.0	57.3	59.6	53.5	50.6
22 to 24 years old	29.7	29.1	28.0	26.7	27.6	26.2	25.7	24.4	31.7	31.9	30.2	29.1
25 to 29 years old	13.3	12.9	17.1	10.4	12.2	11.4	13.2	10.8	14.4	14.3	20.5	10.0
30 to 34 years old	6.7	6.5	9.1	5.7	5.3	5.6	5.7	3.9	8.1	7.4	11.8	7.6

*Beginning in 1994, preprimary enrollment data were collected using new procedures. Data may not be comparable to figures for earlier years.

Note: Includes enrollment in any type of graded public, parochial, or other private schools. Includes nursery schools, preschools, kindergartens, elementary schools, high schools, colleges, universities, and professional schools. Attendance may be on either a full-time or part-time basis and during the day or night. Total includes persons from other racial/ethnic groups not shown separately. Race categories exclude persons of Hispanic ethnicity.

SOURCE: Adapted from "103.10. Percentage of the Population 3 to 34 Years Old Enrolled in School, by Sex, Race/Ethnicity, and Age Group: Selected Years, 1980 through 2013," in "Most Current Digest Tables," *Digest of Education Statistics*, U.S. Department of Education, Institute of Education Sciences, National Center for Education Statistics, July 2014, https://nces.ed.gov/programs/digest/d14/tables/xls/tabn103.10.xls (accessed July 16, 2015)

(*PreK–12 Financing Overview*, June 29, 2015, http://atlas.newamerica.org/school-finance). In fiscal year 2014 state and local funding accounted for approximately 88% of all elementary and secondary school spending, while the federal government accounted for the remaining 12%. According to the NCES, in *Digest of Education Statistics: 2013* (October 2014, http://nces.ed.gov/programs/digest/d14/tables/dt14_401.30.asp?current=yes), of the $80.1 billion the federal government devoted to primary and secondary education in fiscal year 2014,

nearly half ($37.8 billion, or 47.2%) was administered through the Department of Education. Other government agencies involved in allocating education funds included the U.S. Department of Agriculture ($21.9 billion, or 27.3%), which oversees nutrition programs for students; the U.S. Department of Health and Human Services ($10.9 billion, or 13.6%), which funds the Head Start program; and the U.S. Department of Labor ($5.6 billion, or 7%), which funds a range of youth training and employment programs.

TABLE 1.7

Enrollment in education institutions, by level and control of institution, selected years 1990–2024

[In thousands]

Level and control of institution, enrollment level, and attendance status and sex of student	Actual				Projected											
	1990	2000	2010	2012	2013	2014	2015	2016	2017	2018	2019	2020	2021	2022	2023	2024
All levels	**60,683**	**68,685**	**75,886**	**75,595**	**75,412**	**75,219**	**75,227**	**75,563**	**76,372**	**77,049**	**77,661**	**78,263**	**78,948**	**79,662**	**80,405**	**81,007**
Elementary and secondary schools[a]	**46,864**	**53,373**	**54,867**	**54,952**	**55,036**	**54,965**	**54,994**	**55,077**	**55,447**	**55,719**	**56,031**	**56,404**	**56,779**	**57,151**	**57,524**	**57,872**
Public	41,217	47,204	49,484	49,771	49,942	49,986	50,094	50,229	50,584	50,871	51,183	51,547	51,910	52,260	52,601	52,920
Private	5,648[b]	6,169[b]	5,382[b]	5,181[c]	5,094	4,979	4,899	4,848	4,863	4,848	4,848	4,856	4,869	4,891	4,922	4,952
Prekindergarten to grade 8	34,388	38,592	38,708	38,924	39,045	38,938	38,926	39,010	39,363	39,642	39,937	40,204	40,450	40,728	41,147	41,574
Public[d]	29,876	33,686	34,625	35,018	35,188	35,159	35,182	35,282	35,595	35,856	36,125	36,366	36,587	36,839	37,223	37,615
Private	4,512[b]	4,906[b]	4,084[b]	3,906[c]	3,858	3,779	3,744	3,728	3,768	3,786	3,813	3,839	3,863	3,889	3,924	3,959
Grades 9 to 12	12,476	14,781	16,159	16,028	15,990	16,026	16,067	16,067	16,084	16,078	16,094	16,199	16,330	16,424	16,377	16,298
Public[d]	11,341	13,517	14,860	14,753	14,754	14,826	14,912	14,947	14,989	15,015	15,058	15,182	15,324	15,421	15,378	15,304
Private	1,136[b]	1,264[b]	1,299[b]	1,275[c]	1,236	1,200	1,155	1,120	1,095	1,063	1,035	1,017	1,006	1,003	998	994
Degree-granting postsecondary institutions	**13,819**	**15,312**	**21,019**	**20,643**	**20,376**[e]	**20,255**	**20,234**	**20,486**	**20,925**	**21,330**	**21,630**	**21,859**	**22,168**	**22,511**	**22,881**	**23,135**
Undergraduate	11,959	13,155	18,082	17,732	17,475[e]	17,322	17,280	17,472	17,823	18,156	18,404	18,591	18,843	19,119	19,423	19,640
Full-time	6,976	7,923	11,457	11,098	10,938[e]	10,966	10,904	11,033	11,261	11,463	11,601	11,708	11,857	12,019	12,211	12,345
Part-time	4,983	5,232	6,625	6,635	6,536[e]	6,356	6,376	6,439	6,562	6,693	6,804	6,883	6,986	7,100	7,211	7,295
Male	5,380	5,778	7,836	7,714	7,660[e]	7,466	7,446	7,490	7,612	7,745	7,836	7,898	7,998	8,113	8,236	8,330
Female	6,579	7,377	10,246	10,019	9,815[e]	9,855	9,834	9,982	10,210	10,412	10,569	10,692	10,845	11,006	11,187	11,310
2-year	5,240	5,948	7,684	7,164	6,969[e]	7,009	7,011	7,090	7,235	7,378	7,487	7,562	7,664	7,782	7,907	7,996
4-year	6,719	7,207	10,399	10,568	10,506[e]	10,313	10,269	10,381	10,587	10,778	10,917	11,029	11,179	11,337	11,516	11,645
Public	9,710	10,539	13,703	13,474	13,347[e]	13,245	13,221	13,366	13,633	13,890	14,083	14,225	14,418	14,631	14,863	15,029
Private	2,250	2,616	4,379	4,259	4,128[e]	4,077	4,059	4,106	4,189	4,266	4,321	4,365	4,425	4,488	4,560	4,611
Postbaccalaureate	1,860	2,157	2,937	2,910	2,901[e]	2,933	2,953	3,013	3,102	3,173	3,225	3,268	3,325	3,391	3,458	3,495
Full-time	845	1,087	1,630	1,639	1,659[e]	1,698	1,710	1,749	1,804	1,842	1,866	1,888	1,917	1,953	1,991	2,007
Part-time	1,015	1,070	1,307	1,271	1,242[e]	1,234	1,243	1,264	1,298	1,331	1,359	1,381	1,408	1,438	1,467	1,488
Male	904	944	1,209	1,205	1,201[e]	1,260	1,271	1,293	1,329	1,360	1,382	1,399	1,424	1,454	1,483	1,500
Female	955	1,213	1,728	1,705	1,700[e]	1,673	1,682	1,720	1,773	1,813	1,843	1,869	1,901	1,937	1,975	1,994

[a]Includes enrollments in local public school systems and in most private schools (religiously affiliated and nonsectarian). Excludes homeschooled children who were not also enrolled in public and private schools. Private elementary enrollment includes preprimary students in schools offering kindergarten or higher grades.
[b]Estimated.
[c]Projected.
[d]Includes prorated proportion of students classified as ungraded.
[e]Data are actual.

Note: Postsecondary data for 1990 are for institutions of higher education, while later data are for degree-granting institutions. Degree-granting institutions grant associate's or higher degrees and participate in Title IV federal financial aid programs. The degree-granting classification is very similar to the earlier higher education classification, but it includes more 2-year colleges and excludes a few higher education institutions that did not grant degrees. Detail may not sum to totals because of rounding. Some data have been revised from previously published figures.

SOURCE: "Table 105.20. Enrollment in Elementary, Secondary, and Degree-Granting Postsecondary Institutions, by Level and Control of Institution, Enrollment Level, and Attendance Status and Sex of Student: Selected Years, Fall 1990 through Fall 2024," in "Most Current Digest Tables," *Digest of Education Statistics*, U.S. Department of Education, Institute of Education Sciences, National Center for Education Statistics, March 2015, https://nces.ed.gov/programs/digest/d14/tables/xls/tabn105.20.xls (accessed July 16, 2015)

TABLE 1.8

Total expenditures of educational institutions related to the gross domestic product, selected years 1929–30 to 2011–12

			Expenditures for education in current dollars					
	Gross domestic product (GDP) (in billions of current dollars)	School year	All educational institutions		All elementary and secondary schools		All degree-granting postsecondary institutions	
Year			Amount (in millions)	As a percent of GDP	Amount (in millions)	As a percent of GDP	Amount (in millions)	As a percent of GDP
1929	$104.6	1929–30	—	—	—	—	$632	0.6
1939	93.5	1939–40	—	—	—	—	758	0.8
1949	272.8	1949–50	$8,494	3.1	$6,249	2.3	2,246	0.8
1959	522.5	1959–60	22,314	4.3	16,713	3.2	5,601	1.1
1969	1,019.9	1969–70	64,227	6.3	43,183	4.2	21,043	2.1
1975	1,688.9	1975–76	114,004	6.8	75,101	4.4	38,903	2.3
1980	2,862.5	1980–81	176,378	6.2	112,325	3.9	64,053	2.2
1985	4,346.7	1985–86	259,336	6.0	161,800	3.7	97,536	2.2
1990	5,979.6	1990–91	395,318	6.6	249,230	4.2	146,088	2.4
1995	7,664.0	1995–96	508,523	6.6	318,046	4.1	190,476	2.5
2000	10,289.7	2000–01	705,017	6.9	444,811	4.3	260,206	2.5
2005	13,095.4	2005–06	925,246	7.1	571,669	4.4	353,577	2.7
2010	14,958.3	2010–11	1,123,424	7.5	652,215	4.4	471,209	3.2
2011	15,533.8	2011–12[a]	1,140,000	7.3	652,000	4.2	488,444	3.1
2012	16,244.6	2012–13[b]	1,165,000	7.2	669,000	4.1	496,000	3.1

—Not available.

[a]Data for elementary and secondary education are estimated; data for degree-granting institutions are actual.

[b]Estimated by the National Center for Education Statistics based on teacher and enrollment data, and actual expenditures for prior years.

Note: Total expenditures for public elementary and secondary schools include current expenditures, interest on school debt, and capital outlay. Data for private elementary and secondary schools are estimated. Expenditures for colleges and universities in 1929–30 and 1939–40 include current-fund expenditures and additions to plant value. Public and private degree-granting institutions data for 1949–50 through 1995–96 are for current-fund expenditures. Data for private degree-granting institutions for 1996–97 and later years are for total expenditures. Data for public degree-granting institutions for 1996–97 through 2000–01 are for current expenditures; data for later years are for total expenditures. Postsecondary data through 1995–96 are for institutions of higher education, while later data are for degree-granting institutions. Degree-granting institutions grant associate's or higher degrees and participate in Title IV federal financial aid programs. The degree-granting classification is very similar to the earlier higher education classification, but it includes more 2-year colleges and excludes a few higher education institutions that did not grant degrees. Some data have been revised from previously published figures. Detail may not sum to totals because of rounding.

SOURCE: Adapted from "Table 106.10. Expenditures of Educational Institutions Related to the Gross Domestic Product, by Level of Institution: Selected Years, 1929–30 through 2012–13," in "Most Current Digest Tables," *Digest of Education Statistics*, U.S. Department of Education, Institute of Education Sciences, National Center for Education Statistics, February 2014, https://nces.ed.gov/programs/digest/d13/tables/xls/tabn106.10.xls (accessed July 16, 2015)

CHAPTER 2

PREPRIMARY, ELEMENTARY, AND SECONDARY SCHOOLS

SCHOOL ENROLLMENTS

Total School Enrollment

School enrollments grew rapidly during the 1950s and 1960s as a result of the post–World War II baby boom (1946–1964). This growth continued into the 1970s, before declining steadily during the late 1970s and early 1980s. It did not begin to increase again until 1985, when a significant number of children born to baby boomers began entering school. The increase in total school enrollment continued at a slow and steady pace, and by 2012 total school enrollment was 75.6 million. (See Table 1.7 in Chapter 1.) Total school enrollment was expected to steadily increase through 2024, with a projected total school enrollment of 81 million students.

Public School Enrollment: Preschool to High School

In the United States, depending on the state, students must begin school between the ages of five and seven years and remain in school until at least the age of 16 years. Some states, however, require enrollment to age 18, and others allow some students to leave before age 16 under special circumstances. Regardless of age, students are considered to have finished school in the U.S. public school system when they complete grade 12. The public school systems in most states offer kindergarten programs for children aged five and six years; some states also offer prekindergarten (pre-K) programs (also called nursery school or preschool) for children aged three and four years. Certain states offer these programs only for students with disabilities, whereas others offer other programs or multiple programs, such as Head Start (for at-risk children) and state pre-K for all three- and four-year-olds. Figure 2.1, which shows public school enrollment from 2000–01 to 2012–13 with projections to 2024–25, includes enrollments in grades pre-K to 12.

Public school enrollment in grades pre-K to 12 has grown slowly but steadily since 2000, reaching 49.8 million students in 2012–13. (See Figure 2.1.) Projections show the increase continuing through 2024–25. This pattern of growth is mirrored by the growth in enrollment in grades pre-K to eight, but the growth in enrollment in grades nine to 12 has proceeded at a slightly slower pace and is expected to stabilize.

The Growth in Preprimary Enrollment

As Table 2.1 shows, preprimary school enrollment in the United States nearly doubled between 1970 and 1995, rising from 4.1 million to 7.7 million over that span. After dropping to 7.6 million in 2000, total preprimary enrollment rose to 7.9 million in 2003, before dipping to 7.8 million in 2005. Overall preprimary enrollment experienced steady growth over the next six years, topping 8.3 million in 2011, before falling again to 7.9 million by 2013.

Pre-K enrollment experienced the biggest increase during these years. In 1970 nearly 1.1 million children were enrolled in pre-K programs nationwide, while more than 3 million students were attending kindergarten; by 1995 pre-K enrollment had more than quadrupled, to 4.3 million. (See Table 2.1.) Kindergarten enrollment experienced more modest growth during this period, reaching 3.4 million in 1995. Pre-K enrollment rose to nearly 4.9 million in 2003, before dropping to 4.5 million in 2005. Enrollment in pre-K programs experienced a steady increase over the next six years, exceeding 4.9 million in 2011, before falling to a little more than 4.6 million in 2013. Kindergarten enrollment fell to 3.1 million in 2003, the lowest figure since 1980. The number of children enrolled in kindergarten subsequently rose to 3.4 million in 2010, before slipping to a little over 3.3 million a year later. In 2013 kindergarten enrollment stood at just under 3.3 million.

In 2013, 7.8 million three-, four-, and five-year-old children out of 12.2 million (64.8%) in the United States were enrolled in preprimary programs. (See Table 2.1.)

FIGURE 2.1

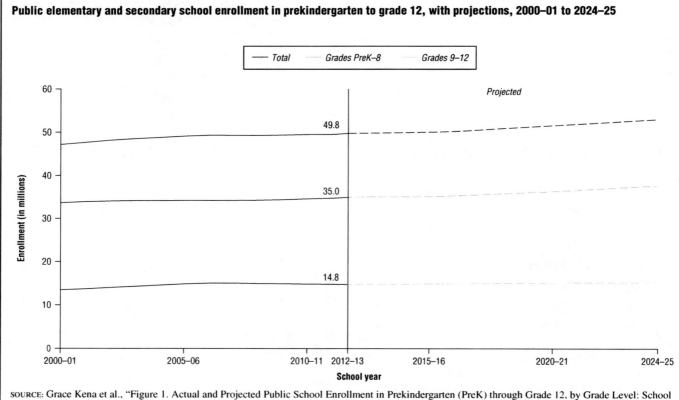

Public elementary and secondary school enrollment in prekindergarten to grade 12, with projections, 2000–01 to 2024–25

SOURCE: Grace Kena et al., "Figure 1. Actual and Projected Public School Enrollment in Prekindergarten (PreK) through Grade 12, by Grade Level: School Years 2000–01 through 2024–25," in *The Condition of Education 2015*, U.S. Department of Education, Institute of Education Sciences, National Center for Education Statistics, May 2015, http://nces.ed.gov/pubs2015/2015144.pdf (accessed July 16, 2015)

TABLE 2.1

Enrollment of three–five-year-olds in preprimary programs, selected years 1970–2013

Age of child, level and control of program, and attendance status	1970	1980	1990	1995[a]	2000[a]	2003[a]	2005[a]	2010[a]	2011[a]	2012[a]	2013[a]
3 to 5 years old[b]											
Total population (in thousands)	10,949	9,284	11,207	12,518	11,858	12,204	12,134	12,949	12,965	12,259	12,166
Enrollment of 3- to 5-year-olds (in thousands)											
Total	4,104	4,878	6,659	7,739	7,592	7,921	7,801	8,246	8,260	7,883	7,878
Level											
Preschool	1,094	1,981	3,379	4,331	4,326	4,859	4,529	4,797	4,911	4,602	4,625
Kindergarten	3,010	2,897	3,280	3,408	3,266	3,062	3,272	3,449	3,349	3,281	3,254
Control											
Public	2,830	3,066	3,971	4,750	4,847	5,051	5,213	5,829	5,823	5,638	5,448
Private	1,274	1,812	2,688	2,989	2,745	2,870	2,588	2,417	2,438	2,245	2,430
Attendance status											
Full-day	698	1,551	2,577	3,689	4,008	4,429	4,548	4,813	4,884	4,760	4,753
Part-day	3,406	3,327	4,082	4,051	3,584	3,492	3,253	3,432	3,376	3,123	3,125

[a]Beginning in 1994, preprimary enrollment data were collected using new procedures. Data may not be comparable to figures for earlier years.
[b]Enrollment data for 5-year-olds include only those students in preprimary programs and do not include those enrolled in primary programs.
Note: Preprimary programs include kindergarten and preschool (or nursery school) programs. "Preschool," which was referred to as "nursery school" in previous versions of this table, is defined as a group or class that is organized to provide educational experiences for children during the year or years preceding kindergarten. Data are based on sample surveys of the civilian noninstitutional population. Detail may not sum to totals because of rounding. Some data have been revised from previously published figures.

SOURCE: Adapted from "Table 202.10. Enrollment of 3-, 4-, and 5-Year-Old Children in Preprimary Programs, by Age of Child, Level of Program, Control of Program, and Attendance Status: Selected Years, 1970 through 2013," in "Most Current Digest Tables," *Digest of Education Statistics*, U.S. Department of Education, Institute of Education Sciences, National Center for Education Statistics, August 2014, https://nces.ed.gov/programs/digest/d14/tables/xls/tabn202.10.xls (accessed July 16, 2015)

Nearly 4.8 million of these children (60.3%) were enrolled in full-day programs.

Geographic Differences in School Enrollment

Although the trend in recent years in total school enrollment has been a slow and steady increase, this trend does not bear out equally in all parts of the country. Figure 2.2 shows the percentage changes in public elementary and secondary enrollments in all 50 states and the District of Columbia between the fall of 2006 and the fall of 2011. During this period, Utah was the only state that experienced an increase of more than 10% in elementary and secondary enrollments. Five states (Colorado, Delaware, South Dakota, Texas, and Wyoming) experienced enrollment increases of between 5% and 10%. Twenty-two states had enrollment increases of less than 5%, and 22 states had decreases.

Likewise, the number of public schools and the sizes of their enrollments differ throughout the country depending on locale. As of the 2011–12 school year, less than a quarter (22.6%) of all public elementary and secondary schools were located in large suburbs; that is, within an urbanized area and outside a principal city with a population of 250,000 or more. (See Table 2.2.) Schools in this type of locale had nearly one-third (28.8%) of all school enrollment. Another 13.5% of public schools were located in urbanized areas in large cities with a population of 250,000 or more. These schools had 15.3% of all public school enrollments. Thus, 36.2% of all public schools were located in either large suburban or large urban cities, and together schools in these locales had 44.2% of the total public school enrollment. By contrast, schools located in rural areas of the country totaled 32.9% of the nation's public schools, but accounted for only 25.2% of all public school enrollment.

FIGURE 2.2

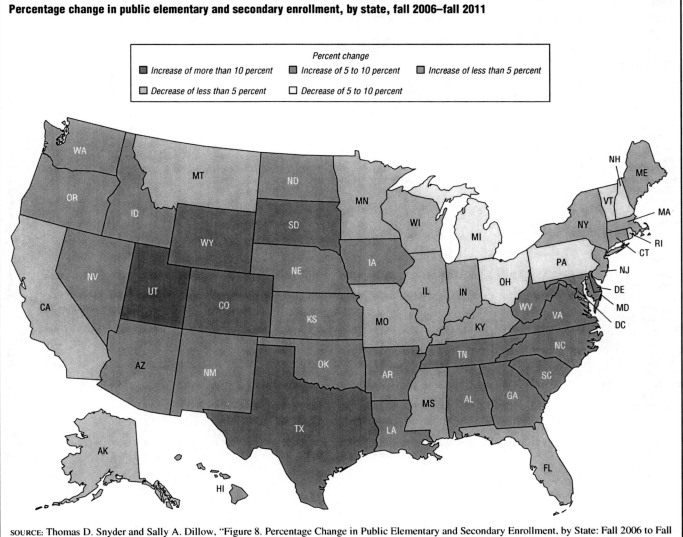

Percentage change in public elementary and secondary enrollment, by state, fall 2006–fall 2011

Percent change
- Increase of more than 10 percent
- Increase of 5 to 10 percent
- Increase of less than 5 percent
- Decrease of less than 5 percent
- Decrease of 5 to 10 percent

SOURCE: Thomas D. Snyder and Sally A. Dillow, "Figure 8. Percentage Change in Public Elementary and Secondary Enrollment, by State: Fall 2006 to Fall 2011," in *Digest of Education Statistics 2013*, U.S. Department of Education, Institute of Education Sciences, National Center for Education Statistics, May 2015, http://nces.ed.gov/pubs2015/2015011.pdf (accessed July 20, 2015)

TABLE 2.2

Public elementary and secondary school enrollment, number of schools, racial/ethnic distribution, and other characteristics, by type of locale, 2008–09 to 2011–12

Enrollment, number of schools, and other characteristics	Total	City				Suburban				Town				Rural				Locale unknown
		Total	Large[a]	Midsize[b]	Small[c]	Total	Large[d]	Midsize[e]	Small[f]	Total	Fringe[g]	Distant[h]	Remote[i]	Total	Fringe[j]	Distant[k]	Remote[l]	
Fall 2008																		
Enrollment (in thousands)	49,054	14,323	7,425	3,146	3,752	17,048	14,438	1,590	1,019	5,999	2,087	2,325	1,586	11,684	6,933	543,5	1,197	†
Percentage distribution of enrollment, by race/ethnicity	100.0	100.0	100.0	100.0	100.0	100.0	100.0	100.0	100.0	100.0	100.0	100.0	100.0	100.0	100.0	100.0	0.010	†
White	54.9	31.8	21.2	35.0	50.3	56.5	54.7	65.6	67.6	69.0	72.8	68.4	64.8	73.5	68.8	81.7	76.1	†
Black	16.9	27.0	30.0	29.3	19.0	14.8	15.6	10.8	10.7	11.2	8.6	13.7	10.9	10.6	12.3	8.4	7.6	†
Hispanic	21.5	32.7	39.6	28.2	22.9	21.2	22.0	17.7	16.4	15.6	15.5	14.6	17.3	11.1	13.9	6.9	7.7	†
Asian/Pacific Islander	5.0	7.1	7.9	6.1	6.2	6.2	6.6	4.2	3.6	1.9	1.7	1.2	3.1	2.3	3.3	0.8	0.7	†
American Indian/ Alaska Native	1.2	0.8	0.8	0.7	0.9	0.5	0.5	0.7	0.9	2.1	1.1	1.9	3.7	2.2	1.2	2.1	7.8	†
Other	0.5	0.5	0.4	0.8	0.6	0.7	0.7	1.0	0.8	0.3	0.4	0.2	0.2	0.3	0.4	0.1	0.1	†
Schools	98,706	25,675	12,927	5,780	6,968	27,168	22,482	2,786	1,900	14,228	4,258	5,639	4,331	31,635	12,625	11,792	7,218	†
Average school size[m]	517	579	588	575	566	647	662	591	558	450	512	443	396	384	579	311	171	†
Pupil/teacher ratio[n]	15.7	16.0	16.2	15.9	15.8	15.9	15.9	16.0	16.4	15.4	15.9	15.2	15.0	15.0	15.9	14.4	12.4	†
Schools (percentage distribution)	100.0	26.0	13.1	5.9	7.1	27.5	22.8	2.8	1.9	14.4	4.3	5.7	4.4	32.0	12.8	11.9	7.3	†
Fall 2009																		
Enrollment (in thousands)	49,082	14,377	7,511	3,174	3,692	16,873	14,296	1,574	1,003	5,899	956	3,089	1,854	11,932	7,267	3,495	1,171	#
Percentage distribution of enrollment, by race/ethnicity	100.0	100.0	100.0	100.0	100.0	100.0	100.0	100.0	100.0	100.0	100.0	100.0	100.0	100.0	100.0	100.0	0.010	100.0
White	54.1	31.4	21.2	34.9	49.3	55.5	53.7	64.5	66.7	68.0	71.7	69.2	64.0	72.6	67.8	81.5	76.0	44.4
Black	16.8	26.5	29.7	27.9	18.8	14.9	15.6	11.0	10.7	11.1	6.5	12.4	11.5	10.6	12.3	8.4	7.2	16.2
Hispanic	22.2	33.5	39.8	29.3	24.1	22.0	22.7	18.6	16.7	16.3	18.4	14.9	17.5	11.7	14.6	7.0	7.9	34.8
Asian/Pacific Islander	5.0	7.1	7.9	6.2	6.2	6.3	6.7	4.3	3.7	1.9	1.7	1.4	2.9	2.4	3.4	0.8	0.7	2.8
American Indian/ Alaska Native	1.2	0.8	0.8	0.7	1.0	0.6	0.5	0.7	0.9	2.2	1.2	1.6	3.6	2.1	1.2	2.1	7.7	0.6
Other	0.7	0.8	0.7	1.0	0.7	0.8	0.7	1.0	1.2	0.5	0.5	0.6	0.5	0.6	0.7	0.3	0.4	1.1
Schools	98,817	25,767	13,234	5,705	6,828	27,041	22,395	2,771	1,875	13,986	1,926	7,069	4,991	31,946	13,156	11,687	7,103	77
Average school size[m]	516	578	583	582	566	642	656	583	555	447	513	462	399	388	579	308	170	13
Pupil/teacher ratio[n]	16.0	16.3	16.4	16.4	16.1	16.4	16.4	16.4	16.6	15.5	16.5	15.5	15.1	15.2	16.2	14.5	12.5	5.0
Schools (percentage distribution)	100.0	26.1	13.4	5.8	6.9	27.4	22.7	2.8	1.9	14.2	1.9	7.2	5.1	32.3	13.3	11.8	7.2	0.1
Enrollment (percentage distribution)	100.0	29.3	15.3	6.5	7.5	34.4	29.1	3.2	2.0	12.0	1.9	6.3	3.8	24.3	14.8	7.1	2.4	#
Enrollment (percentage distribution)	100.0	29.2	15.1	6.4	7.6	34.8	29.4	3.2	2.1	12.2	4.3	4.7	3.2	23.8	14.1	7.2	2.4	†
Fall 2010																		
Enrollment (in thousands)	49,178	14,425	7,545	3,186	3,694	16,872	14,290	1,580	1,001	5,841	939	3,066	1,835	12,032	7,418	3,460	1,154	8
Percentage distribution of enrollment, by race/ethnicity	100.0	100.0	100.0	100.0	100.0	100.0	100.0	100.0	100.0	100.0	100.0	100.0	100.0	100.0	100.0	100.0	0.010	100.0
White	52.5	30.3	20.4	34.1	47.0	53.5	51.7	62.8	64.7	66.3	70.0	67.6	62.5	70.8	65.7	80.3	75.3	62.1
Black	16.0	25.2	28.4	25.7	18.3	14.3	15.0	10.2	10.0	10.5	6.2	11.6	10.9	10.0	11.6	7.8	6.8	16.4
Hispanic	23.1	34.3	40.5	30.3	25.1	22.9	23.6	19.4	18.5	17.1	18.8	15.8	18.4	12.8	15.9	7.6	8.4	12.9
Asian	4.6	6.6	7.5	5.8	5.6	5.8	6.2	3.3	3.5	1.5	1.5	1.2	1.9	2.2	3.2	0.6	0.5	4.2
Pacific Islander	0.3	0.3	0.4	0.4	0.3	0.4	0.4	0.6	0.2	0.5	0.1	0.2	1.1	0.2	0.2	0.1	0.2	0.1
American Indian/ Alaska Native	1.1	0.8	0.8	0.7	0.9	0.5	0.5	0.7	0.8	2.0	1.0	1.5	3.3	2.0	1.1	2.0	7.4	0.9
Two or more races	2.4	2.5	2.0	3.1	2.8	2.6	2.5	3.1	2.3	2.2	2.4	2.2	2.1	2.0	2.3	1.6	1.4	3.4
Schools	98,817	25,879	13,279	5,737	6,863	27,108	22,425	2,805	1,878	13,838	1,906	7,004	4,928	31,952	13,348	11,593	7,011	40
Average school size[m]	517	579	584	583	568	640	655	579	555	447	511	462	400	391	583	307	170	481
Pupil/teacher ratio[n]	16.4	16.9	17.1	17.0	16.6	16.8	16.8	16.8	17.1	15.8	16.8	15.8	15.4	15.5	16.6	14.6	12.7	16.2
Enrollment (percentage distribution)	100.0	29.3	15.3	6.5	7.5	34.3	29.1	3.2	2.0	11.9	1.9	6.2	3.7	24.5	15.1	7.0	2.3	#
Schools (percentage distribution)	100.0	26.2	13.4	5.8	6.9	27.4	22.7	2.8	1.9	14.0	1.9	7.1	5.0	32.3	13.5	11.7	7.1	#

School Size

During the 2011–12 academic year the average enrollment at public schools across the United States was 520 students per school—479 in elementary schools and 690 in secondary schools. (See Table 2.3.) Overall, nearly six out of 10 (58.1%) public schools had enrollments

TABLE 2.2

Public elementary and secondary school enrollment, number of schools, racial/ethnic distribution, and other characteristics, by type of locale, 2008–09 to 2011–12 [CONTINUED]

Enrollment, number of schools, and other characteristics	Total	City				Suburban				Town				Rural				Locale unknown
		Total	Large[a]	Midsize[b]	Small[c]	Total	Large[d]	Midsize[e]	Small[f]	Total	Fringe[g]	Distant[h]	Remote[i]	Total	Fringe[j]	Distant[k]	Remote[l]	
Fall 2011																		
Enrollment (in thousands)	49,256	14,457	7,559	3,180	3,718	16,709	14,193	1,549	967	5,671	907	2,953	1,812	12,418	7,859	3,416	1,431	†
Percentage distribution of enrollment, by race/ethnicity	100.0	100.0	100.0	100.0	100.0	100.0	100.0	100.0	100.0	100.0	100.0	100.0	100.0	100.0	100.0	100.0	0.010	†
White	51.7	29.7	20.2	33.3	46.1	52.5	50.7	61.9	63.9	65.5	69.1	66.8	61.6	70.0	65.0	79.9	75.0	†
Black	15.8	24.8	27.9	25.4	18.2	14.2	14.9	9.9	9.7	10.4	6.1	11.5	10.8	10.0	11.5	7.5	6.8	†
Hispanic	23.7	34.9	41.0	31.0	25.8	23.8	24.4	20.3	19.3	17.7	19.8	16.4	19.0	13.4	16.4	8.1	8.7	†
Asian	4.7	6.7	7.5	5.9	5.6	5.9	6.4	3.4	3.5	1.5	1.6	1.2	1.9	2.2	3.2	0.6	0.5	†
Pacific Islander	0.4	0.4	0.4	0.4	0.3	0.4	0.4	0.6	0.2	0.5	0.1	0.2	1.1	0.2	0.3	0.2	0.2	†
American Indian/Alaska Native	1.1	0.8	0.8	0.6	0.9	0.5	0.4	0.6	0.8	2.0	1.0	1.5	3.4	1.9	1.1	2.0	7.3	†
Two or more races	2.6	2.7	2.2	3.3	3.1	2.8	2.7	3.3	2.7	2.4	2.3	2.5	2.3	2.2	2.5	1.8	1.6	†
English language learners (in thousands)[o]	4,389	2,035	1,211	430	394	1,604	1,439	97	68	336	63	159	114	414	294	77	42	†
English language learners as a percent of enrollment[o]	9.1	14.2	16.7	12.6	10.9	9.0	9.4	6.4	7.6	6.2	8.4	5.7	6.1	3.9	4.7	2.5	3.9	†
Schools	98,328	25,800	13,266	5,666	6,868	26,840	22,263	2,760	1,817	13,387	1,844	6,720	4,823	12,303	13,904	11,445	6,952	†
Average school size[m]	520	581	585	588	568	641	656	577	552	448	509	463	402	399	592	307	170	†
Pupil/teacher ratio[n]	16.3	16.9	17.1	17.0	16.4	16.6	16.5	16.6	17.0	15.9	16.9	15.9	15.4	15.5	16.5	14.6	12.5	†
Enrollment (percentage distribution)	100.0	29.4	15.3	6.5	7.5	33.9	28.8	3.1	2.0	11.5	1.8	6.0	3.7	25.2	16.0	6.9	2.3	†
Schools (percentage distribution)	100.0	26.2	13.5	5.8	7.0	27.3	22.6	2.8	1.8	13.6	1.9	6.8	4.9	32.9	14.1	11.6	7.1	†

†Not applicable.
#Rounds to zero.
[a]Located inside an urbanized area and inside a principal city with a population of at least 250,000.
[b]Located inside an urbanized area and inside a principal city with a population of at least 100,000, but less than 250,000.
[c]Located inside an urbanized area and inside a principal city with a population less than 100,000.
[d]Located inside an urbanized area and outside a principal city with a population of 250,000 or more.
[e]Located inside an urbanized area and outside a principal city with a population of at least 100,000, but less than 250,000.
[f]Located inside an urbanized area and outside a principal city with a population less than 100,000.
[g]Located inside an urban cluster that is 10 miles or less from an urbanized area.
[h]Located inside an urban cluster that is more than 10 but less than or equal to 35 miles from an urbanized area.
[i]Located inside an urban cluster that is more than 35 miles from an urbanized area.
[j]Located outside any urbanized area or urban cluster, but 5 miles or less from an urbanized area or 2.5 miles or less from an urban cluster.
[k]Located outside any urbanized area or urban cluster and more than 5 miles but less than or equal to 25 miles from an urbanized area, or more than 2.5 miles but less than or equal to 10 miles from an urban cluster.
[l]Located outside any urbanized area or urban cluster, more than 25 miles from an urbanized area, and more than 10 miles from an urban cluster.
[m]Average for schools reporting enrollment. Enrollment data were available for 94,820 out of 98,706 schools in 2008–09, 95,222 out of 98,817 schools in 2009–10, 95,111 out of 98,817 schools in 2010–11, and 94,743 out of 98,328 schools in 2011–12.
[n]Ratio for schools reporting both full-time-equivalent teachers and fall enrollment data.
[o]Data are based on locales of school districts rather than locales of schools as in the rest of the table. Includes imputed data for California and Vermont.
Note: Detail may not sum to totals because of rounding. Race categories exclude persons of Hispanic ethnicity. Enrollment and ratios are based on data reported by schools and may differ from data reported in other tables that reflect aggregate totals reported by states. Some data have been revised from previously published figures.

SOURCE: Thomas D. Snyder and Sally A. Dillow, "Table 214.40. Public Elementary and Secondary School Enrollment, Number of Schools, and Other Selected Characteristics, by Locale: 2008–09 through 2011–12," in *Digest of Education Statistics 2013*, U.S. Department of Education, Institute of Education Sciences, National Center for Education Statistics, May 2015, http://nces.ed.gov/pubs2015/2015011.pdf (accessed July 20, 2015)

of fewer than 500 students, and more than a quarter (27.7%) had enrollments between 300 and 499 students. Approximately 58.1% of elementary schools had smaller enrollments (fewer than 500 students), and 55.5% of regular secondary schools (excluding special education, vocational, and alternative schools) had enrollments of 500 or more students. Nearly three out of 10 (29.3%) regular secondary schools had enrollments of 1,000 or more students.

The right-hand side of Table 2.3 provides public school enrollment figures, with total enrollment shown at nearly 49.3 million students for the 2011–12 academic year. Nearly one-third (32.2%) of elementary students attended schools with enrollments of between 400 and 599 students. The majority (61.9%) of secondary students in 2011–12 attended high schools with enrollments of 1,000 or more students.

Racial and Ethnic Diversity

Public school enrollment has become more racially and ethnically diverse, reflecting the nation's changing demographics. Between the fall of 2002 and the fall of 2012 the percentage of non-Hispanic white students declined from 59.5% to 51%, whereas the percentage of Hispanic students rose from 17.8% to 24.3%, and the

TABLE 2.3

Number and percentage distribution of public elementary and secondary schools, by level, type, and enrollment size of school, 2011–12

Enrollment size of school	Number and percentage distribution of schools, by level and type						Enrollment totals and percentage distribution, by level and type of school[a]					
			Secondary[d]		Combined elementary/ secondary[e]				Secondary[d]		Combined elementary/ secondary[e]	
	Total[b]	Elementary[c]	All schools	Regular schools[g]		Other[f]	Total[b]	Elementary[c]	All schools	Regular schools[g]		Other[f]
1	2	3	4	5	6	7	8	9	10	11	12	13
2011–12												
Total	98,328	66,689	24,357	19,441	6,311	971	49,256,120	31,724,573	15,708,815	15,194,153	1,818,020	4,712
Percent[h]	100.00	100.00	100.00	100.00	100.00	100.00	100.00	100.00	100.00	100.00	100.00	100.00
Under 100	10.32	5.46	17.47	9.31	37.92	67.86	0.89	0.57	1.08	0.65	4.80	35.93
100 to 199	9.09	7.65	11.57	10.59	15.72	28.57	2.62	2.43	2.47	2.00	7.05	49.79
200 to 299	10.96	11.68	9.12	9.36	10.02	1.79	5.31	6.18	3.29	2.96	7.68	4.69
300 to 399	13.79	16.20	8.12	8.88	8.45	0.00	9.29	11.88	4.10	3.93	9.10	0.00
400 to 499	13.92	17.08	6.56	7.40	6.55	1.79	12.00	16.00	4.26	4.21	9.16	9.59
500 to 599	11.65	14.14	5.87	6.68	5.90	0.00	12.27	16.17	4.66	4.64	10.01	0.00
600 to 699	8.58	10.23	4.92	5.56	4.04	0.00	10.67	13.82	4.61	4.56	8.12	0.00
700 to 799	6.13	6.98	4.48	5.12	2.96	0.00	8.80	10.88	4.85	4.85	6.80	0.00
800 to 999	6.56	6.77	6.79	7.87	3.13	0.00	11.17	12.49	8.80	8.94	8.65	0.00
1,000 to 1,499	5.40	3.48	11.51	13.30	3.28	0.00	12.42	8.42	20.53	20.76	12.20	0.00
1,500 to 1,999	2.02	0.29	7.26	8.53	1.24	0.00	6.71	1.02	18.24	18.77	6.49	0.00
2,000 to 2,999	1.33	0.03	5.36	6.29	0.44	0.00	6.03	0.13	18.26	18.78	3.27	0.00
3,000 or more	0.25	#	0.97	1.13	0.35	0.00	1.80	0.01	4.85	4.93	6.67	0.00
Average enrollment[h]	520	479	690	78	322	84	520	479	690	788	322	84

#Rounds to zero.

[a]Totals differ from those reported in other tables because this table represents data reported by schools rather than by states or school districts. Percentage distribution and average enrollment calculations exclude data for schools not reporting enrollment.

[b]Includes elementary, secondary, combined elementary/secondary, and other schools.

[c]Includes schools beginning with grade 6 or below and with no grade higher than 8.

[d]Includes schools with no grade lower than 7.

[e]Includes schools beginning with grade 6 or below and ending with grade 9 or above.

[f]Includes special education, alternative, and other schools not reported by grade span.

[g]Excludes special education schools, vocational schools, and alternative schools.

[h]Data are for schools reporting enrollments greater than zero. Enrollments greater than zero were reported for 95,178 out of 98,817 schools in 2009–10, 95,111 out of 98,817 in 2010–11, and 94,743 out of 98,328 in 2011–12.

Note: Detail may not sum to totals because of rounding.

SOURCE: "Size of School: 2009–10, 2010–11, and 2011–12," in *Digest of Education Statistics 2013*, U.S. Department of Education, Institute of Education Sciences, National Center for Education Statistics, May 2015, http://nces.ed.gov/pubs2015/2015011.pdf (accessed July 20, 2015)

percentage of Asian or Pacific Islander students increased from 4.3% to 5.2%. (See Table 2.4.) The percentage of non-Hispanic African American students fell from 17.3% to 15.7%, as did the percentage of Native American or Alaskan Native students, from 1.2% to 1.1%.

These dramatic changes in enrollment percentages among non-Hispanic white, Hispanic, and Asian or Pacific Islander students are taking place to one degree or another in most states, with a few exceptions. One exception regards the percentage enrollment of non-Hispanic white students in public elementary and secondary schools in the District of Columbia. Although the percentage enrollment of non-Hispanic white students dropped in all states between 2002 and 2012, it nearly doubled in the District of Columbia, rising from 4.3% to 8.4% during that span. (See Table 2.4.) The percentage enrollment of non-Hispanic African American students dropped throughout the southern states, while rising slightly in a number of northern states, among them Maine, Minnesota, North Dakota, and South Dakota. The percentage enrollment of Asian or Pacific Islanders rose in all states except Hawaii, where

enrollment fell 6.4 percentage points, and to a lesser degree in Rhode Island (−0.2 of a percentage point), the District of Columbia (−0.1), and Montana (−0.1).

FINANCING THE SCHOOLS
Sources of Funding

Public schools obtain funds from three sources: local, state, and federal governments. (See Table 2.5.) Typically, local governments rely on property taxes to finance education, and state governments use revenues from state sales taxes and, in some instances, state income taxes, lotteries, motor vehicle fees, and excise taxes (fees levied on certain products, such as gasoline, alcohol, and tobacco). Local and state governments have traditionally been the primary sources of revenue for elementary and secondary schools, with the federal government contributing a relatively small percentage. Dependence on state and local revenues to fund public schools has certain ramifications for schools. When a recession occurs or businesses close or move away, tax revenues drop and property values may decline. Such events and economic cycles directly affect school funding. In these cases,

TABLE 2.4

Percentage distribution of enrollment in public elementary and secondary schools, by race/ethnicity and state, fall 2002 and fall 2012

State or jurisdiction	Percentage distribution, fall 2002						Percentage distribution, fall 2012							
	Total	White	Black	Hispanic	Asian/ Pacific Islander	American Indian/ Alaska Native	Total	White	Black	Hispanic	Asian	Pacific Islander	American Indian/ Alaska Native	Two or more races
United States	100.0	59.5	17.3	17.8	4.3	1.2	100.0	51.0	15.7	24.3	4.8	0.4	1.1	2.8
Alabama	100.0	60.2	36.3	1.8	0.9	0.8	100.0	57.6	33.9	5.1	1.3	0.1	0.8	1.2
Alaska	100.0	59.4	4.7	3.7	6.3	25.9	100.0	50.1	3.6	6.4	6.2	2.4	23.5	7.9
Arizona	100.0	50.0	4.8	36.5	2.1	6.6	100.0	41.6	5.3	43.3	2.8	0.3	4.9	1.9
Arkansas	100.0	70.5	23.2	4.8	1.0	0.5	100.0	63.9	21.0	10.6	1.5	0.5	0.7	1.8
California	100.0	34.0	8.3	45.5	11.3	0.9	100.0	25.5	6.3	52.7	11.1	0.5	0.7	3.1
Colorado	100.0	65.7	5.7	24.3	3.0	1.2	100.0	55.6	4.7	32.3	3.2	0.2	0.8	3.3
Connecticut	100.0	69.0	13.6	14.1	3.0	0.3	100.0	59.6	13.0	20.4	4.6	0.1	0.3	2.1
Delaware	100.0	58.4	31.4	7.2	2.6	0.3	100.0	48.6	31.4	13.9	3.5	0.1	0.5	2.1
District of Columbia	100.0	4.3	83.7	10.4	1.6	0.1	100.0	8.4	74.6	13.9	1.4	0.1	0.1	1.5
Florida	100.0	51.6	24.7	21.4	2.0	0.3	100.0	41.6	23.0	29.3	2.6	0.1	0.4	3.1
Georgia	100.0	53.0	38.2	6.2	2.5	0.2	100.0	43.5	36.9	12.7	3.5	0.1	0.2	3.1
Hawaii	100.0	20.4	2.4	4.6	72.2	0.5	100.0	13.9	2.2	8.3	33.0	32.8	0.5	9.3
Idaho	100.0	85.9	0.8	10.8	1.2	1.2	100.0	77.7	1.0	16.5	1.3	0.3	1.3	1.8
Illinois	100.0	58.3	21.1	16.9	3.5	0.2	100.0	50.5	17.6	24.1	4.3	0.1	0.3	3.0
Indiana	100.0	82.2	12.2	4.3	1.0	0.3	100.0	71.7	12.3	9.6	1.8	0.1	0.3	4.4
Iowa	100.0	89.0	4.3	4.4	1.8	0.5	100.0	79.8	5.2	9.3	2.1	0.2	0.4	2.9
Kansas	100.0	76.8	9.1	10.4	2.3	1.4	100.0	66.7	7.2	17.8	2.6	0.2	1.1	4.5
Kentucky	100.0	86.9	10.8	1.4	0.8	0.2	100.0	80.3	10.7	4.8	1.4	0.1	0.1	2.5
Louisiana	100.0	48.5	47.8	1.7	1.3	0.7	100.0	47.0	45.0	4.3	1.5	0.1	0.8	1.4
Maine	100.0	96.1	1.6	0.7	1.1	0.5	100.0	91.4	3.0	1.7	1.5	0.1	0.8	1.4
Maryland	100.0	51.5	37.5	5.8	4.7	0.4	100.0	41.8	35.1	12.9	6.0	0.1	0.3	3.9
Massachusetts	100.0	75.1	8.8	11.2	4.6	0.3	100.0	66.0	8.6	16.4	5.9	0.1	0.2	2.7
Michigan	100.0	72.4	20.3	3.8	2.0	1.5	100.0	68.9	18.4	6.5	2.8	0.1	0.8	2.5
Minnesota	100.0	81.1	7.4	4.2	5.3	2.1	100.0	72.0	9.4	7.7	6.3	0.1	1.8	2.8
Mississippi	100.0	47.3	50.9	1.0	0.7	0.2	100.0	45.7	49.5	2.7	1.0	#	0.2	0.9
Missouri	100.0	77.9	18.2	2.3	1.3	0.3	100.0	73.7	16.6	5.1	1.9	0.2	0.4	2.1
Montana	100.0	85.4	0.7	2.0	1.1	10.9	100.0	80.5	1.0	3.9	0.8	0.2	11.4	2.1
Nebraska	100.0	80.6	7.0	9.2	1.6	1.6	100.0	69.6	6.7	16.8	2.2	0.1	1.4	3.2
Nevada	100.0	52.7	10.5	28.7	6.4	1.7	100.0	36.8	9.7	40.0	5.7	1.3	1.1	5.4
New Hampshire	100.0	94.4	1.5	2.2	1.6	0.3	100.0	88.6	1.9	4.1	2.9	0.1	0.3	2.1
New Jersey	100.0	58.6	17.8	16.6	6.8	0.2	100.0	49.8	16.3	23.4	9.1	0.2	0.1	1.0
New Mexico	100.0	33.6	2.4	51.7	1.1	11.2	100.0	25.5	2.0	59.9	1.2	0.1	10.0	1.3
New York	100.0	54.2	20.0	19.0	6.3	0.4	100.0	47.2	18.3	24.0	8.5	0.2	0.6	1.2
North Carolina	100.0	59.2	31.4	5.9	2.0	1.5	100.0	51.9	26.2	14.2	2.6	0.1	1.4	3.6
North Dakota	100.0	88.6	1.1	1.3	0.9	8.1	100.0	82.1	2.9	3.3	1.3	0.2	9.0	1.2
Ohio	100.0	79.7	16.9	2.0	1.2	0.1	100.0	73.3	16.2	4.2	1.8	0.1	0.1	4.3
Oklahoma	100.0	62.6	10.9	7.0	1.5	17.9	100.0	52.6	9.4	14.1	1.8	0.3	15.7	6.0
Oregon	100.0	78.1	3.0	12.5	4.2	2.2	100.0	64.5	2.5	22.0	3.9	0.7	1.7	4.9
Pennsylvania	100.0	77.1	15.5	5.2	2.2	0.1	100.0	69.9	15.2	9.1	3.4	0.1	0.2	2.3
Rhode Island	100.0	72.2	8.4	15.6	3.3	0.5	100.0	62.8	8.2	22.4	2.9	0.2	0.6	2.9
South Carolina	100.0	54.4	41.5	2.7	1.1	0.3	100.0	52.9	35.4	7.0	1.4	0.1	0.3	2.9
South Dakota	100.0	85.3	1.5	1.6	1.0	10.6	100.0	77.6	2.7	4.3	1.7	0.1	11.5	2.1
Tennessee	100.0	71.3	24.8	2.4	1.2	0.2	100.0	66.3	23.0	7.3	1.7	0.1	0.2	1.4
Texas	100.0	39.8	14.3	42.7	2.9	0.3	100.0	30.0	12.7	51.3	3.6	0.1	0.4	1.8
Utah	100.0	84.1	1.1	10.4	2.9	1.5	100.0	76.9	1.3	15.7	1.7	1.5	1.2	1.7
Vermont	100.0	95.8	1.3	0.7	1.6	0.6	100.0	91.9	2.0	1.5	1.8	0.1	0.3	2.4
Virginia	100.0	61.8	27.2	6.2	4.5	0.3	100.0	52.9	23.5	12.5	6.2	0.1	0.3	4.5
Washington	100.0	72.6	5.6	11.6	7.6	2.6	100.0	59.2	4.6	20.4	7.2	0.9	1.4	6.3
West Virginia	100.0	94.4	4.5	0.5	0.6	0.1	100.0	91.4	4.9	1.3	0.7	#	0.1	1.6
Wisconsin	100.0	79.5	10.4	5.4	3.3	1.5	100.0	73.1	9.8	10.1	3.6	0.1	1.3	2.2
Wyoming	100.0	86.7	1.3	7.7	0.9	3.3	100.0	80.1	1.1	12.8	0.8	0.2	3.3	1.6
Bureau of Indian Education	100.0	0.0	0.0	0.0	0.0	100.0	—	—	—	—	—	—	—	—
DoD, overseas	100.0	56.5	19.8	12.9	9.9	0.8	—	—	—	—	—	—	—	—
DoD, domestic	100.0	49.2	24.2	22.2	3.7	0.7	—	—	—	—	—	—	—	—

states and local governments must find ways to meet revenue shortfalls to adequately fund their public schools.

AN ECONOMIC CRISIS LEADS TO GOVERNMENT STIMULUS FUNDING. Near the end of the first decade of the 21st century just such a situation arose: a severe recession put school funding in jeopardy. A financial crisis that began in late 2007 in the United States, which was linked to reckless home mortgage lending practices, was the beginning of what became a deep recession and economic crisis, not only in the United States but also around the world.

During 2008 and into 2009 real estate values tumbled, and many people who had bought homes in the few years preceding the recession began to see that

TABLE 2.4

Percentage distribution of enrollment in public elementary and secondary schools, by race/ethnicity and state, fall 2002 and fall 2012 [CONTINUED]

State or jurisdiction	Percentage distribution, fall 2002						Percentage distribution, fall 2012							
	Total	White	Black	Hispanic	Asian/ Pacific Islander	American Indian/ Alaska Native	Total	White	Black	Hispanic	Asian	Pacific Islander	American Indian/ Alaska Native	Two or more races
Other jurisdictions														
American Samoa	100.0	0.0	0.0	0.0	100.0	0.0	—	—	—	—	—	—	—	—
Guam	—	—	—	—	—	—	100.0	0.7	0.2	0.1	23.7	73.2	#	2.1
Northern Marianas	100.0	0.4	0.0	0.0	99.5	0.0	100.0	0.6	0.0	0.1	40.5	58.3	0.0	0.5
Puerto Rico	100.0	0.0	0.0	100.0	0.0	0.0	100.0	0.1	#	99.8	#	#	0.1	0.0
U.S. Virgin Islands	100.0	0.7	84.7	14.1	0.2	0.2	100.0	1.5	78.9	18.2	0.3	0.1	0.1	0.8

DoD = Department of Defense.

—Not available.

#Rounds to zero.

Note: Percentage distribution based on students for whom race/ethnicity was reported, which may be less than the total number of students in the state. Race categories exclude persons of Hispanic ethnicity. Detail may not sum to totals because of rounding.

SOURCE: "Table 203.70. Percentage Distribution of Enrollment in Public Elementary and Secondary Schools, by Race/Ethnicity and State or Jurisdiction: Fall 2002 and Fall 2012," in "Most Current Digest Tables," *Digest of Education Statistics*, U.S. Department of Education, Institute of Education Sciences, National Center for Education Statistics, November 2014, https://nces.ed.gov/programs/digest/d14/tables/xls/tabn203.70.xls (accessed July 20, 2015)

their home was worth less than what they owed on their mortgage. Unemployment rates also rose dramatically during this economic crisis, and many could no longer afford to pay their mortgage. Foreclosures soared and property tax revenues declined. In addition, people were buying less, so sales tax revenues declined as well. As a direct result, school funding declined dramatically, forcing school consolidations, slashing educational programs, cutting back or eliminating sports programs, laying off teachers, and putting more children in fewer classrooms.

In February 2009 Congress passed the American Recovery and Reinvestment Act (ARRA), which earmarked $100 billion for schools. The broad goals of this funding were to save jobs and spur innovation. Michele McNeil notes in "ARRA Brings Home Mixed Report Card" (EdWeek.org, February 9, 2011) that by early 2011 the economic stimulus package had saved or created an estimated 368,000 school-related jobs during the 2009–10 school year. This figure was compiled by the U.S. Department of Education from state and school district self-reported data. McNeil explains in "States Slow to Tap 'Edujobs' Funding" (EdWeek.org, March 2, 2011) that another fund—the Education Jobs Funds, or "edujobs"—was created and funded at $10 billion by Congress in August 2010. The fund was meant to help states and school districts pay the salaries of teachers and other school personnel when the ARRA funding ran out in September 2011. Edujobs funding was available through 2012.

However, these relief measures proved only temporary, as subsequent budget shortfalls threatened to further erode funding of the nation's schools. In August 2011, in the midst of a bitter political struggle over the nation's

debt, Congress passed the Budget Control Act. The law called for automatic, wide-ranging budget cuts to be implemented by the government in 2013. The process of establishing limits to federal spending is commonly referred to as sequestration. In "New School Year Brings Sequestration Pain for Many Districts" (NPR.org, September 7, 2013), Claudio Sanchez reports that sequestration resulted in $3 billion in cuts to federal education spending nationwide during the 2013–14 school year. Meanwhile, a number of states were cutting education budgets. Michael Leachman and Chris Mai of the Center on Budget and Policy Priorities report in *Most States Funding Schools Less than before the Recession* (May 20, 2014, http://www.cbpp.org//sites/default/files/atoms/files/9-12-13sfp.pdf) that 35 states were spending less money on education in 2013–14 than they were spending before the recession. Over that span, 14 states had cut average spending per student by over 10 percent. As Leachman and Mai note in a follow-up report, "Most States Still Funding Schools Less than before the Recession" (October 16, 2014, http://www.cbpp.org/sites/default/files/atoms/files/10-16-14sfp.pdf), by the 2014–15 school year the number of states still spending less on education than before the recession had fallen to 30; 17 states were spending more on education in 2014–15, while three states (Hawaii, Indiana, and Iowa) lacked sufficient data to make an accurate comparison. Of the states in which education spending rose after the recession, only two—Alaska (16.4%) and North Dakota (31.6%)—reported double-digit increases.

EQUITY IN SCHOOL FUNDING. In *Overview and Inventory of State Education Reforms: 1990 to 2000* (July 2003, http://nces.ed.gov/pubs2003/2003020.pdf), David Hurst

TABLE 2.5

Sources of revenue for public elementary and secondary schools, by state, 2011–12

[In current dollars]

State or jurisdiction	Total (in thousands)	Federal Amount (in thousands)	Federal Per pupil	Federal Percent of total	State Amount (in thousands)	State Percent of total	Local (including intermediate sources below the state level) Amount (in thousands)[a]	Local Percent of total	Property taxes Amount (in thousands)	Property taxes Percent of total	Private[b] Amount (in thousands)	Private Percent of total
United States	$600,488,586	$61,043,194	$1,235	10.2	$271,452,810	45.2	$267,992,581	44.6	$215,813,214	35.9	$11,813,419	2.0
Alabama	7,099,553	838,285	1,126	11.8	3,934,577	55.4	2,326,690	32.8	1,088,896	15.3	314,693	4.4
Alaska	2,496,679	353,993	2,699	14.2	1,618,975	64.8	523,711	21.0	297,730	11.9	21,069	0.8
Arizona	9,305,199	1,374,629	1,272	14.8	3,804,900	40.9	4,125,669	44.3	3,007,906	32.3	242,635	2.6
Arkansas	5,284,555	698,938	1,447	13.2	2,723,740	51.5	1,861,878	35.2	1,608,527	30.4	148,872	2.8
California	65,808,329	8,260,861	1,329	12.6	37,079,384	56.3	20,468,083	31.1	16,065,320	24.4	427,487	0.6
Colorado	8,698,810	722,810	846	8.3	3,765,940	43.3	4,210,060	48.4	3,394,918	39.0	339,720	3.9
Connecticut	10,274,602	535,208	965	5.2	3,978,525	38.7	5,760,869	56.1	5,607,191	54.6	109,351	1.1
Delaware	1,871,464	235,905	1,829	12.6	1,096,243	58.6	539,316	28.8	464,458	24.8	16,067	0.9
District of Columbia	2,073,564	208,249	2,818	10.0	†	†	1,865,315	90.0	583,315	28.1	11,295	0.5
Florida	23,988,519	3,122,488	1,170	13.0	8,702,310	36.3	12,163,720	50.7	10,191,658	42.5	999,689	4.2
Georgia	17,620,300	1,920,092	1,140	10.9	7,533,980	42.8	8,166,229	46.3	5,576,107	31.6	487,664	2.8
Hawaii	2,535,039	318,728	1,744	12.6	2,161,254	85.3	55,057	2.2	0	0.0	32,842	1.3
Idaho	2,062,254	278,914	997	13.5	1,302,949	63.2	480,391	23.3	399,952	19.4	35,389	1.7
Illinois	29,165,373	2,406,643	1,156	8.3	9,385,630	32.2	17,373,101	59.6	15,347,696	52.6	489,205	1.7
Indiana	11,940,988	1,149,521	1,104	9.6	6,510,737	54.5	4,280,730	35.8	2,886,835	24.2	338,359	2.8
Iowa	6,038,962	526,409	1,062	8.7	2,681,029	44.4	2,831,524	46.9	1,977,465	32.7	141,451	2.3
Kansas	5,796,537	485,235	998	8.4	3,209,527	55.4	2,101,775	36.3	1,584,595	27.3	140,899	2.4
Kentucky	7,086,717	971,266	1,424	13.7	3,841,443	54.2	2,274,008	32.1	1,632,734	23.0	108,175	1.5
Louisiana	8,412,167	1,458,572	2,074	17.3	3,602,717	42.8	3,350,878	39.8	1,404,203	16.7	68,960	0.8
Maine	2,556,186	233,761	1,237	9.1	1,022,269	40.0	1,300,156	50.9	1,231,367	48.2	39,813	1.6
Maryland	13,744,621	859,635	1,006	6.3	5,980,909	43.5	6,904,078	50.2	3,354,919	24.4	128,061	0.9
Massachusetts	15,835,037	1,059,639	1,111	6.7	6,206,699	39.2	8,568,699	54.1	8,060,794	50.9	214,459	1.4
Michigan	18,751,262	2,031,233	1,291	10.8	10,700,372	57.1	6,019,657	32.1	5,061,587	27.0	287,267	1.5
Minnesota	10,989,685	797,917	950	7.3	7,044,954	64.1	3,146,814	28.6	2,013,840	18.3	330,096	3.0
Mississippi	4,441,163	795,121	1,621	17.9	2,195,730	49.4	1,450,312	32.7	1,169,902	26.3	112,490	2.5
Missouri	10,221,689	1,034,047	1,128	10.1	3,275,438	32.0	5,912,203	57.8	4,623,345	45.2	349,994	3.4
Montana	1,622,721	218,297	1,534	13.5	770,180	47.5	634,244	39.1	402,736	24.8	59,287	3.7
Nebraska	3,778,749	358,930	1,245	9.5	1,167,743	30.9	2,252,076	59.6	1,918,009	50.8	161,742	4.3
Nevada	4,137,704	413,861	941	10.0	1,366,314	33.0	2,357,529	57.0	1,133,785	27.4	41,808	1.0
New Hampshire	2,864,747	188,927	985	6.6	1,031,778	36.0	1,644,043	57.4	1,571,664	54.9	48,682	1.7
New Jersey	26,590,517	1,425,761	1,051	5.4	10,507,939	39.5	14,656,818	55.1	13,818,756	52.0	561,254	2.1
New Mexico	3,611,545	540,071	1,602	15.0	2,455,787	68.0	615,688	17.0	493,780	13.7	53,220	1.5
New York	58,645,470	3,956,260	1,463	6.7	23,131,272	39.4	31,557,937	53.8	28,290,435	48.2	351,068	0.6
North Carolina	13,113,012	1,878,905	1,246	14.3	7,877,949	60.1	3,356,157	25.6	2,781,052	21.2	235,542	1.8
North Dakota	1,296,813	170,085	1,742	13.1	653,842	50.4	472,886	36.5	351,001	27.1	54,046	4.2
Ohio	22,886,511	2,186,000	1,256	9.6	10,132,936	44.3	10,567,575	46.2	8,702,819	38.0	676,160	3.0
Oklahoma	5,862,837	794,080	1,192	13.5	2,882,879	49.2	2,185,878	37.3	1,591,425	27.1	260,466	4.4
Oregon	6,172,422	618,981	1,089	10.0	3,038,044	49.2	2,515,397	40.8	2,034,939	33.0	153,561	2.5
Pennsylvania	26,807,485	2,201,593	1,243	8.2	9,594,823	35.8	15,011,068	56.0	11,973,510	44.7	434,758	1.6
Rhode Island	2,278,095	217,363	1,522	9.5	846,435	37.2	1,214,297	53.3	1,181,575	51.9	20,379	0.9
South Carolina	8,041,045	871,480	1,198	10.8	3,670,717	45.6	3,498,848	43.5	2,628,375	32.7	242,015	3.0
South Dakota	1,303,055	215,937	1,687	16.6	400,362	30.7	686,756	52.7	568,577	43.6	38,621	3.0
Tennessee	8,979,871	1,263,157	1,264	14.1	4,059,869	45.2	3,656,845	40.7	1,750,319	19.5	426,483	4.7
Texas	49,533,579	6,311,758	1,262	12.7	20,341,491	41.1	22,880,330	46.2	20,766,669	41.9	972,423	2.0
Utah	4,619,102	461,333	786	10.0	2,418,166	52.4	1,739,603	37.7	1,308,562	28.3	198,911	4.3
Vermont	1,644,282	127,644	1,420	7.8	1,451,850	88.3	64,787	3.9	961	0.1	21,862	1.3
Virginia	14,659,153	1,356,037	1,078	9.3	5,564,497	38.0	7,738,618	52.8	4,648,724	31.7	271,223	1.9
Washington	11,844,779	1,057,047	1,011	8.9	7,001,099	59.1	3,786,633	32.0	3,209,638	27.1	319,128	2.7
West Virginia	3,556,656	433,205	1,531	12.2	2,069,942	58.2	1,053,510	29.6	934,089	26.3	31,316	0.9
Wisconsin	10,879,541	953,230	1,103	8.8	4,806,328	44.2	5,119,983	47.1	4,665,016	42.9	224,611	2.1
Wyoming	1,659,641	145,148	1,620	8.7	850,339	51.2	664,154	40.0	451,537	27.2	18,852	1.1
Other jurisdictions												
American Samoa	99,334	88,536	—	89.1	10,528	10.6	271	0.3	0	0.0	58	0.1
Guam	307,591	74,850	2,396	24.3	0	0.0	232,741	75.7	0	0.0	677	0.2
Northern Marianas	65,214	33,334	3,027	51.1	31,880	48.9	0	0.0	0	0.0	0	0.0
Puerto Rico	3,374,611	1,153,166	2,547	34.2	2,221,384	65.8	62	#	0	0.0	62	#
U.S. Virgin Islands	221,673	37,899	2,412	17.1	0	0.0	183,774	82.9	0	0.0	36	#

et al. report that disparities in spending between wealthy and impoverished school districts led to legal challenges during the 1970s and 1980s. To try to resolve these disparities, many states instituted complex formulas for distributing state education funds to equalize the per-pupil expenditure statewide—that is, they gave proportionately more state funds per student to poor districts than to wealthy districts. Nonetheless, some state courts found that state education finance systems failed to deliver an acceptable level of educational services.

[In current dollars]

—Not available.
†Not applicable.
#Rounds to zero.
ªIncludes other categories of revenue not separately shown.
ᵇIncludes revenues from gifts, and tuition and fees from patrons.
Note: Excludes revenues for state education agencies. Detail may not sum to totals because of rounding.

SOURCE: "Table 235.20. Revenues for Public Elementary and Secondary Schools, by Source of Funds and State or Jurisdiction: 2011–12," in "Most Current Digest Tables," *Digest of Education Statistics*, U.S. Department of Education, Institute of Education Sciences, National Center for Education Statistics, July 2014, https://nces.ed.gov/programs/digest/d14/tables/xls/tabn235.20.xls (accessed July 20, 2015)

With the goals of improving the quality of education for all students and reducing academic achievement differences among minorities and between rich and poor students and communities, Congress enacted the No Child Left Behind (NCLB) Act of 2001. The NCLB is the reauthorization of the Elementary and Secondary Education Act, which was originally passed in 1965 to ensure educational equity by raising achievement and closing achievement gaps among students. The NCLB requires that school districts annually test students in grades three to eight to determine whether they are meeting certain student performance goals.

However, Andrew Reschovsky and Jennifer Imazeki suggest in "Financing Education So That No Child Is Left Behind: Determining the Costs of Improving Student Performance" (William J. Fowler Jr., ed., *Developments in School Finance: 2003—Fiscal Proceedings from the Annual State Data Conference of July 2003*, August 2004, http://nces.ed.gov/pubs2004/2004325.pdf) that the amount of money required for students to reach specified performance standards varies across school districts due to factors beyond the school districts' control. Some districts have to pay higher salaries to attract teachers; others have large numbers of economically disadvantaged students or have students from families where English is not the first language, and these schools ask for additional resources to fund special programs.

Besides inequities of the financial burden of the NCLB among school districts, other aspects such as national academic standards and school accountability are highly controversial. In March 2010 the Obama administration released *A Blueprint for Reform: The Reauthorization of the Elementary and Secondary Education Act* (March 2010, http://www2.ed.gov/policy/elsec/leg/blueprint/blueprint.pdf), with the aim of addressing and remedying the shortcomings of the NCLB. The NCLB, the controversy surrounding it, the Obama administration's plans for the future of education, and responses to these plans by major education organizations, including the National Education Association, are discussed in greater detail in Chapter 5.

Revenues

During the 2011–12 school year, revenues for public elementary and secondary schools totaled $600.5 billion. (See Table 2.5.) Table 2.5 shows that state (45.2%) and local (44.6%) governments provided most of the revenues for public elementary and secondary schools during the 2011–12 school year, with 10.2% coming from the federal government and 2% from private sources.

The percentages given in the previous paragraph are averages, and Table 2.5 shows that the percentages of federal, state, and local funding for education varied widely by state during the 2011–12 academic year. For example, in Vermont the state provided 88.3% of the public school revenue, the federal government provided 7.8%, and local governments provided 3.9%. By contrast, in Connecticut, Illinois, Massachusetts, Nebraska, New Hampshire, New Jersey, and Rhode Island, local property taxes accounted for more than half of all education spending. Of the states, Mississippi received the highest percentage of its funding from federal sources (17.9%), whereas Connecticut received the lowest percentage of its funding from federal sources (5.2%).

Expenditures

Expenditures for public elementary and secondary students for the 2011–12 academic year are shown in Table 2.6. On average, spending per student reached $10,667 nationwide that year. Less than two-thirds (60.8%) of these funds, or $6,495 per student, was dedicated to instruction-related expenses. The District of Columbia spent $19,847 per student in 2011–12, the most in the nation; New York was a close second at $19,396 per student. By contrast, Utah ($6,441) and Idaho ($6,626) spent the least in education funding for each student in 2011–12.

INTERNATIONAL COMPARISONS OF EXPENDITURES PER STUDENT. One method of measuring a country's commitment to education is to examine what portion of its gross domestic product (GDP; the total value of goods and services produced in a country) goes to educating its people. In 2010 governmental expenditures for education

TABLE 2.6

Expenditures per pupil for public elementary and secondary education, by type of expenditure and state or jurisdiction, 2011–12

State or jurisdiction	School year 2011–12 student membership[c]	Current expenditures[a] per pupil											
				Support services[b]									
		Total	Instruction	Total support services[g]	Student support services[d]	Instructional staff support	General administration	School administration	Operations and maintenance	Student transportation	Other support services	Food services	Enterprise operations[e]
United States[f]	49,414,846	$10,667[g]	$6,495[g]	$3,721[g]	$594[g]	$495[g]	$214[g]	$585[g]	$1,008[g]	$464[g]	$361[g]	$429[g]	$22
Alabama	744,621	8,577	4,966	3,015	495	388	195	529	781	443	185	595	0
Alaska	131,167	17,475	9,645	7,286	1,466	1,148	254	1,058	2,166	531	663	477	68
Arizona	1,080,319	7,382[g]	4,035[g]	2,970[g]	532[g]	379[g]	124[g]	385[g]	927[g]	328[g]	295[g]	375	1
Arkansas	483,114	9,536[g]	5,396[g]	3,586[g]	489[g]	799[g]	236[g]	481[g]	933[g]	372[g]	277[g]	542[g]	11
California	6,214,204	9,329[g]	5,606[g]	3,317[g]	494[g]	555[g]	90[g]	617[g]	929[g]	226[g]	406[g]	383	24
Colorado	854,265	8,594	4,948	3,297	422	475	146	583	822	258	591	307	43
Connecticut	554,437	16,855[g]	10,659[g]	5,650[g]	1,069[g]	502[g]	340[g]	976[g]	1,518[g]	853[g]	392[g]	408[g]	138
Delaware	128,946	13,580	8,659	4,466	575	246	197	711	1,418	680	640	456	0
District of Columbia	73,911	19,847	11,301	7,720	706	748	1,050	1,742	1,741	1,295	438	783	43
Florida	2,668,156	8,520[g]	5,196[g]	2,915[g]	370[g]	542[g]	75[g]	473[g]	887[g]	354[g]	215[g]	409	0
Georgia	1,685,016	9,272[g]	5,734[g]	3,009[g]	428[g]	477[g]	122[g]	557[g]	690[g]	417[g]	317[g]	503	27
Hawaii	182,706	11,973	6,861	4,431	1,125	425	58	731	1,375[g]	415	301	681	1
Idaho	279,873	6,626	3,996[g]	2,272[g]	370[g]	264[g]	153[g]	375[g]	612[g]	332[g]	166[g]	357[g]	0
Illinois	2,082,457	12,011[g]	7,233[g]	4,405[g]	802[g]	482[g]	497[g]	610[g]	1,039[g]	565[g]	409[g]	373	1
Indiana	1,040,765	9,588[g]	5,640[g]	3,517[g]	459[g]	365[g]	243[g]	562[g]	1,067[g]	582[g]	240[g]	431	0
Iowa	495,870	10,027	6,164	3,397	560	482	255	578	854	374	295	456	9
Kansas	486,108	10,021	6,090	3,457	593	419	296	576	938	394	240	475	0
Kentucky	681,987	9,327	5,401	3,347	428	510	208	530	853	580	238	556	24
Louisiana	703,390	10,726[g]	6,108[g]	4,031[g]	646[g]	567[g]	263[g]	645[g]	971[g]	630[g]	309[g]	586	#
Maine	188,969	12,335[g]	7,374[g]	4,537[g]	806[g]	622[g]	382[g]	670[g]	1,271	632	153	422	1
Maryland	854,086	13,871	8,620[g]	4,880[g]	628[g]	750[g]	125	994[g]	1,180	744	460[g]	371	0
Massachusetts	953,369	14,844	9,605[g]	4,837[g]	1,050[g]	680[g]	206[g]	604[g]	1,299[g]	634[g]	363[g]	403	0
Michigan	1,573,537	10,477	6,082	4,012	800	516	216	571	937	447	527	383	0
Minnesota	839,738	10,781[g]	7,070[g]	3,209[g]	288[g]	464[g]	334[g]	429[g]	764[g]	611[g]	318[g]	472	30
Mississippi	490,619	8,097	4,620	2,974	394	418	257	470	851	398	185	503	1
Missouri	916,584	9,514	5,670	3,389	444	412	307	551	951	498	226	454	0
Montana	142,349	10,569	6,288	3,810	653	401	325	578	1,074	522	257	453	18
Nebraska	288,389	11,640	7,427	3,395	450	371	368	573	1,005	368	260	505	312
Nevada	439,634	8,130	4,764	3,057	436	409	122	608	862	333	287	308	#
New Hampshire	191,900	13,774	8,875	4,526	1,026	416	462	753	1,133	590	145	374	0
New Jersey	1,356,431	17,982	10,779	6,608	1,782	558	364	849	1,757	897	399	403	193
New Mexico	337,225	9,013	5,151	3,431	928	253	201	539	938	299	274	425	5
New York	2,704,718	19,396[g]	13,459[g]	5,529[g]	651[g]	488[g]	370[g]	746[g]	1,684[g]	1,030[g]	560[g]	408	0
North Carolina	1,507,864	8,160	5,087	2,616	384	289	126	510	692	362	253	456	0
North Dakota	97,646	11,246	6,570	3,735	483	403	506	567	1,017	483	275	589	351
Ohio	1,740,030	11,323	6,444	4,493	720	740	345	645	990	547	508	384	1
Oklahoma	666,120	7,763	4,318	2,878	529	320	249	414	857	269	239	490	77
Oregon	568,208	9,485	5,509	3,619	673	353	127	603	783	452	629	354	3
Pennsylvania	1,771,395	13,091	7,993	4,587	694	449	405	602	1,270	671	496	452	60
Rhode Island	142,854	15,172	9,405[g]	5,376[g]	1,567[g]	534[g]	214[g]	740[g]	1,199[g]	587[g]	535[g]	386[g]	6
South Carolina	727,186	9,077	5,148	3,416	677	548	98	549	868	373	304	487	25
South Dakota	128,016	8,593	5,053	3,014	470	344	287	419	870	321	304	473	53
Tennessee	999,693	8,354	5,194	2,714	360	523	176	478	715	313	150	445	0
Texas	5,000,470	8,213	4,850	2,890	399	411	124	466	909	237	344	473	0
Utah	586,860	6,441	4,101	1,949	251	261	76	400	586	205	169	363	28
Vermont	89,908	16,651	10,434	5,746	1,278	702	341	1,079	1,390	548	408	460	12
Virginia	1,257,883	10,656	6,458	3,772	519	707	165	616	1,019	577	168	424	2
Washington	1,045,453	9,617[g]	5,609[g]	3,561	832	365	179	557	865	397	366	332	115

TABLE 2.6

Expenditures per pupil for public elementary and secondary education, by type of expenditure and state or jurisdiction, 2011–12 [CONTINUED]

| | | | | Current expenditures[a] per pupil | | | | | | | | | |
| | | | | Support services[b] | | | | | | | | | |
State or jurisdiction	Fall 2011 student membership[c]	Total	Instruction	Total support services	Student support services[d]	Instructional staff support	General administration	School administration	Operations and maintenance	Student transportation	Other support services	Food services	Enterprise operations[e]
West Virginia	282,870	11,579[g]	6,786[g]	4,140[g]	551[g]	479[g]	230[g]	616[g]	1,201[g]	862[g]	201[g]	653	0
Wisconsin	863,949	11,233[g]	6,748[g]	4,058[g]	535[g]	530[g]	313[g]	552[g]	1,027[g]	486[g]	615[g]	427	#
Wyoming	89,581	15,988	9,460	6,034	934	978	332	861	1,538	771	619	485	10
Other jurisdictions													
American Samoa	—	—	—	—	—	—	—	—	—	—	—	—	—
Guam	31,243	9,300	4,576	4,359	835	155	56	539	1,502	180	1,092	365	0
Commonwealth of the Northern Mariana Islands	11,011	6,246	2,696	2,707	599	501	228	492	416	277	194	844	0
Puerto Rico	452,740	7,403	3,266	3,086	499	374	124	345	687	296	763	1,050	0
U.S. Virgin Islands	15,711	11,669	6,092	4,873	916	329	461	594	827	448	1,298	681	23

—Not available. Data are missing for American Samoa because they did not report student membership.

Rounds to zero.

[a]Current expenditures include instruction, instruction-related, support services, and other elementary/secondary current expenditures, but exclude expenditures on capital outlay, other programs, and interest on long-term debt.

[b]Support services is an expenditure function divided into seven subfunctions: student support services, instructional staff support, general administration, school administration, operations and maintenance, student transportation, and other support services.

[c]The student membership variable is derived from the State Nonfiscal Survey. Three states (Nebraska, Utah, and Wyoming) indicated that the state fiscal data reported in National Public Education Finance Survey (NPEFS) excluded prekindergarten programs. In these three states, the NPEFS total student membership variable excludes prekindergarten membership. Illinois and Wisconsin did not report finance data for charter schools in the fiscal year NPEFS survey. National Center for Education Statistics (NCES) edited student membership for Illinois and Wisconsin by excluding students from districts where all associated schools are charter schools.

[d]Student support services include attendance and social work, guidance, health, psychological services, speech pathology, audiology, and other student support services.

[e]Enterprise operations include operations that are operated as a business and receipts from the operation are expected to fund the enterprise (e.g., school bookstores and certain after school activities).

[f]United States totals include the 50 states and the District of Columbia.

[g]Value affected by redistribution of reported expenditure values to correct for missing data items, and/or to distribute state direct support expenditures.

Note: Detail may not sum to totals because of rounding.

SOURCE: Stephen Q. Cornman, "Table 3. Student Membership and Current Expenditures per Pupil for Public Elementary and Secondary Education, by Function, Subfunction, and State or Jurisdiction: Fiscal Year 2012," in *Revenues and Expenditures for Public Elementary and Secondary Education: School Year 2011–12 (Fiscal Year 2012)*, U.S. Department of Education, Institute of Education Sciences, National Center for Education Statistics, January 2015, http://nces.ed.gov/pubs2014/2014301.pdf (accessed July 20, 2015)

FIGURE 2.3

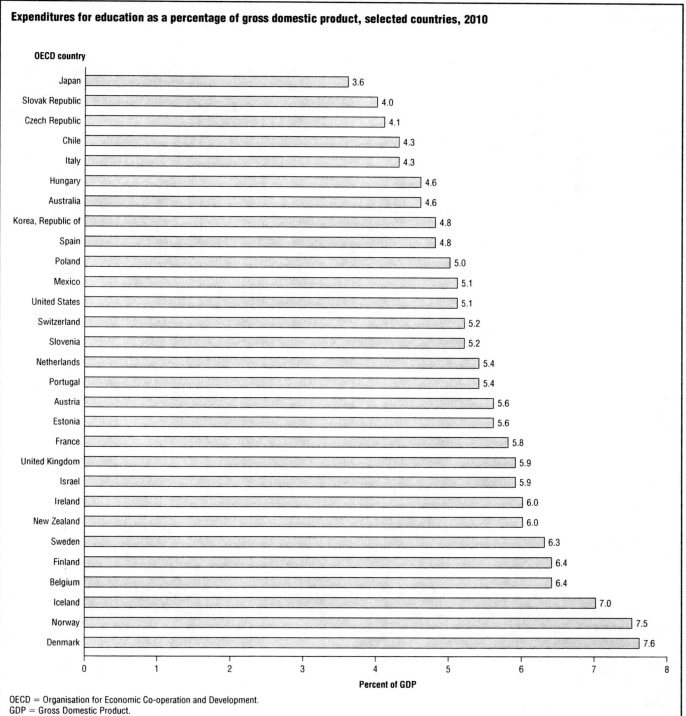

Expenditures for education as a percentage of gross domestic product, selected countries, 2010

OECD country

Country	Percent of GDP
Japan	3.6
Slovak Republic	4.0
Czech Republic	4.1
Chile	4.3
Italy	4.3
Hungary	4.6
Australia	4.6
Korea, Republic of	4.8
Spain	4.8
Poland	5.0
Mexico	5.1
United States	5.1
Switzerland	5.2
Slovenia	5.2
Netherlands	5.4
Portugal	5.4
Austria	5.6
Estonia	5.6
France	5.8
United Kingdom	5.9
Israel	5.9
Ireland	6.0
New Zealand	6.0
Sweden	6.3
Finland	6.4
Belgium	6.4
Iceland	7.0
Norway	7.5
Denmark	7.6

Percent of GDP

OECD = Organisation for Economic Co-operation and Development.
GDP = Gross Domestic Product.
Note: Includes amounts spent directly by governments to hire educational personnel and to procure other resources, as well as amounts provided by governments to public and private institutions.

SOURCE: Thomas D. Snyder and Sally A. Dillow, "Figure 29. Public Direct Expenditures on Education Institutions as a Percentage of Gross Domestic Product (GDP), by OECD Country: 2010," in *Digest of Education Statistics 2013*, U.S. Department of Education, Institute of Education Sciences, National Center for Education Statistics, May 2015, http://nces.ed.gov/pubs2015/2015011.pdf (accessed July 20, 2015)

in the United States (public direct expenditures) totaled 5.1% of the GDP. (See Figure 2.3.) This figure placed the United States roughly in the middle among countries belonging to the Organisation for Economic Co-operation and Development (OECD). As Figure 2.3 shows, Japan spent only 3.3% of its GDP on education spending in 2010, the least among the OECD nations. On the opposite end of the spectrum, Denmark devoted a greater

TABLE 2.7

Expenditures for education as a percentage of gross domestic product, by level of education and country, selected years 1995–2011

| Country | All institutions (including preprimary education and subsidies to households, not separately shown) | | | | | | | | Elementary and secondary institutions (excludes preprimary unless otherwise noted) | | | | |
| | Public direct expenditures | | | | | Direct expenditures, 2011 | | | Public direct expenditures | | | | |
	1995	2000[a]	2005[a]	2009[a]	2010[a]	Public[a]	Private	Total	1995	2000[a]	2005[a]	2009[a]	2010[a]
OECD average[b]	4.9	4.9	5.0	5.4	5.4	5.3	0.9	6.1	3.5	3.4	3.5	3.7	3.7
Australia	4.5	4.6	4.3	4.5	4.6	4.3	1.5	5.8	3.2	3.7	3.4	3.6	3.7
Austria	5.3	5.4[c]	5.2	5.7	5.6	5.5	0.2	5.7	3.8	3.7[c]	3.5	3.8	3.5
Belgium	5.0	5.1	5.8	6.4	6.4	6.4	0.2	6.6	3.4	3.4[d]	3.9	4.3	4.3
Canada	5.8	5.2	4.8	5.0	5.2	—	—	—	4.0	3.3[e]	3.3[e,f]	3.4[f]	3.6[f]
Chile	—	4.2	3.3	4.1	4.3	3.9	2.5	6.4	—	3.2	2.7	3.3	2.9
Czech Republic	4.8	4.2	4.1	4.2	4.1	4.4	0.6	5.0	3.4	2.8[d]	2.7	2.6	2.6
Denmark	6.5	6.4[c]	6.8	7.5	7.6	7.5	0.4	7.9	4.2	4.1[c]	4.4	4.7	4.7
Estonia	—	—	4.7	5.9	5.6	5.2	0.3	5.5	—	—	3.5	4.1	3.9
Finland	6.6	5.5	5.9	6.3	6.4	6.3	0.1	6.5	4.2	3.5	3.8	4.1	4.1
France	5.8	5.7	5.6	5.8	5.8	5.6	0.5	6.1	4.1	4.0	3.8	3.8	3.8
Germany	4.5	4.3	4.2	4.5	—	4.4	0.7	5.1	2.9	2.9	2.8	2.9	—
Greece	3.7	3.7[c]	4.0	—	—	—	—	—	2.8	2.7[c,f]	2.5[f]	—	—
Hungary	4.9	4.4	5.1	4.8	4.6	4.4	—	—	3.3	2.8	3.3	3.0	2.8
Iceland	4.5	5.7[c]	7.2	7.3	7.0	6.9	0.7	7.7	3.4	4.6[c]	5.2	5.0	4.7
Ireland	4.7	4.1	4.3	6.0	6.0	5.7	0.5	6.2	3.3	2.9[d]	3.3	4.6	4.6
Israel	—	6.6	6.2	5.8	5.9	5.6	1.7	7.3	—	4.5	4.2	3.8	4.0
Italy	4.5	4.5	4.3	4.5	4.3	4.2	0.4	4.6	3.2	3.2	3.2	3.3	3.1
Japan	3.6	3.5	3.4	3.6	3.6	3.6	1.6	5.1	2.8	2.7	2.6	2.7	2.8
Korea, Republic of	3.6	4.3	4.3	4.9	4.8	4.9	2.8	7.6	3.0	3.3	3.4	3.6	3.4
Luxembourg	4.3	—	—	—	—	—	—	—	4.2	—	3.7[f]	3.2	3.4
Mexico	4.6	4.7	5.3	5.0	5.1	5.0	1.1	6.2	3.4	3.3	3.7	3.3	3.4
Netherlands	4.6	4.3	4.6	5.3	5.4	5.3	0.9	6.2	3.0	3.0	3.3	3.7	3.7
New Zealand	5.3	5.8	5.2	6.1	6.0	6.3	1.2	7.5	3.8	4.6	4.0	4.5	4.4
Norway	6.8	5.8	5.7	6.1	7.5	7.3	—	—	4.1	3.6	3.8	4.2	5.1
Poland	5.2	5.2[c]	5.4	5.0	5.0	4.8	0.7	5.5	3.3	3.7[c]	3.7	3.5	3.4
Portugal	5.4	5.6[c]	5.3	5.5	5.4	5.1	0.4	5.5	4.1	4.1[c]	3.8	4.0	3.9
Slovak Republic	4.6	4.0[c]	3.7	4.1	4.0	3.8	0.5	4.4	—	2.7[c,d,h]	2.5[h]	2.7[h]	2.8[h]
Slovenia	—	—	5.3	5.3	5.2	5.3	0.7	5.9	—	—	3.9	3.6	3.6
Spain	4.8	4.3	4.1	4.9	4.8	4.7	0.8	5.5	3.5	3.1	2.7	3.1	3.0
Sweden	6.6	6.3	6.2	6.6	6.3	6.2	0.2	6.3	4.4	4.4[d]	4.2	4.2	4.0
Switzerland	5.5	5.3	5.6	5.5	5.2	5.2	0.4	5.6	4.1	3.8	3.9	3.8	3.6
Turkey	2.2	3.4[c]	—	—	—	—	—	—	1.4	2.4[c]	—	—	2.5
United Kingdom	4.6	4.5	5.0	5.3	5.9	5.6	0.8	6.4	3.8	3.4	3.8	4.5	4.8
United States	5.0	4.6[c]	4.9	5.3	5.1	4.7	2.2	6.9	3.5	3.5[e]	3.6	3.8	3.7
Other reporting countries													
Brazil	—	—	4.4	5.5	5.6	5.9	—	—	—	—	3.3	4.3	4.3
Russian Federation	3.4	3.0[c]	3.8	4.7	4.1	3.9	0.7	4.6	1.9	1.7	1.9	2.3	2.0

percentage of its GDP (7.6%) to education than any other country, followed closely by Norway (7.5%). The percentage of GDP that the United States spent on public education fell to 4.7% in 2011. (See Table 2.7.) This figure was below the OECD average public expenditures of 5.3% of GDP that year.

Another way to examine international expenditures for education is to compare how much money countries spend per student as a percentage of their per capita GDP. By a substantial margin, Luxembourg had the highest GDP per capita ($88,668) of all the OECD nations in 2011; Switzerland was second ($51,582), while the United States was third ($49,321). (See Table 2.8.) In 2011 the United States spent $11,841 per student, which was 24% of its per capita GDP. The OECD average was $8,789 spent per elementary and secondary student with a per capita GDP of $32,276, yielding an average 27.2% per capita GDP. Thus, the United States shows below average spending per capita GDP for elementary and secondary education among OECD nations.

The United States also lags behind many OECD nations in its net enrollment rates for school-age children. According to the United Nations Educational, Scientific, and Cultural Organization (UNESCO) Institute for Statistics (2014, http://www.uis.unesco.org/DataCentre/Pages/country-profile.aspx?regioncode=40500&code=USA), net enrollment refers to the "total number of pupils or students in the theoretical age group for a given level of education enrolled in that level, expressed as a percentage of the total population in that age group." In its "Global Rankings" (2014, http://www.uis.unesco.org/DataCentre/Pages/global-ranking.aspx), UNESCO reports that 16 OECD nations recorded adjusted net enrollment rates of 99% or higher in 2013. By contrast, adjusted net enrollment among school-age children was 92.8% in the United States that year.

TABLE 2.7

Expenditures for education as a percentage of gross domestic product, by level of education and country, selected years 1995–2011 [CONTINUED]

Country	Elementary and secondary institutions (excludes preprimary unless otherwise noted) Direct expenditures, 2011			Higher education institutions Public direct expenditures					Higher education institutions Direct expenditures, 2011		
	Public[a]	Private	Total	1995	2000[a]	2005[a]	2009[a]	2010[a]	Public[a]	Private	Total
OECD average[b]	3.6	0.3	3.8	0.9	1.0	1.0	1.1	1.1	1.1	0.5	1.6
Australia	3.5	0.6	4.1	1.2	0.8	0.8	0.7	0.8	0.7	0.9	1.6
Austria	3.5	0.1	3.6	0.9	1.2[c]	1.2	1.4	1.5	1.4	0.1	1.5
Belgium	4.3	0.1	4.4	0.9	1.2[d]	1.2	1.4	1.4	1.3	0.1	1.4
Canada	—	—	—	1.5	1.6[e]	1.5[e]	1.5	1.6	—	—	—
Chile	2.7	0.7	3.4	—	0.6	0.3	0.3	0.8	0.7	1.7	2.4
Czech Republic	2.6	0.3	2.9	0.7	0.8[d]	0.8	1.0	1.0	1.2	0.3	1.4
Denmark	4.3	0.1	4.4	1.3	1.5[c, g]	1.6[g]	1.8[g]	1.8[g]	1.8[g]	0.1[g]	1.9[g]
Estonia	3.3	#	3.4	—	—	0.9	1.3	1.3	1.4	0.3	1.7
Finland	4.1	#	4.1	1.7	1.7	1.7	1.8	1.9	1.9	0.1	1.9
France	3.7	0.3	3.9	1.0	1.0	1.1	1.3	1.3	1.3	0.2	1.5
Germany	2.8	0.4	3.1	1.0	1.0	0.9	1.1	—	1.1	0.2	1.3
Greece	—	—	—	0.8	0.9[c]	1.4	—	—	—	—	—
Hungary	2.6	—	—	0.8	0.9	0.9	1.0	0.8	1.0	—	—
Iceland	4.7	0.2	4.9	0.7	0.8[c]	1.1[g]	1.2	1.1	1.1	0.1	1.2
Ireland	4.4	0.2	4.6	0.9	1.2[d]	1.0	1.4	1.3	1.2	0.3	1.5
Israel	3.8	0.4	4.2	—	1.1	1.0	1.0	1.0	0.9	0.8	1.7
Italy	3.0	0.1	3.1	0.7	0.7	0.6	0.8	0.8	0.8	0.2	1.0
Japan	2.7	0.2	2.9	0.4	0.5[g]	0.5[g]	0.5[g]	0.5[g]	0.5[g]	1.0[g]	1.6[g]
Korea, Republic of	3.4	0.8	4.1	0.3	0.6	0.6	0.7	0.7	0.7	1.9	2.6
Luxembourg	3.3	0.1	3.4	0.1	—	—	—	—	—	—	—
Mexico	3.3	0.6	4.0	0.8	0.8	0.9	1.0	1.0	0.9	0.4	1.3
Netherlands	3.6	0.4	4.0	1.1	1.0	1.0	1.2	1.3	1.3	0.5	1.8
New Zealand	4.8	0.6	5.4	1.1	0.9	0.9	1.1	1.0	1.0	0.5	1.5
Norway	4.9	—	—	1.5	1.2	1.3	1.3	1.6	1.6	0.1	1.7
Poland	3.2	0.2	3.4	0.8	0.8[c]	1.2	1.1	1.0	1.0	0.3	1.3
Portugal	3.7	#	3.7	1.0	1.0[c]	0.9	1.0	1.0	1.0	0.4	1.4
Slovak Republic	2.5[h]	0.3[h]	2.8[h]	—	0.7[c, d, h]	0.7[h]	0.7[g, h]	0.7[h]	0.8[h]	0.2[h]	1.0[h]
Slovenia	3.5	0.3	3.8	—	—	1.0	1.1	1.1	1.1	0.2	1.3
Spain	2.9	0.3	3.2	0.8	0.9	0.9	1.1	1.1	1.0	0.3	1.3
Sweden	3.9	#	3.9	1.6	1.5[d]	1.5	1.6	1.6	1.6	0.2	1.7
Switzerland	3.6	0.5	4.0	1.1	1.2	1.4	1.4	1.3	1.3	—	—
Turkey	—	—	—	0.8	1.0[c]	—	—	—	—	—	—
United Kingdom	4.4	0.4	4.7	0.7	0.7	0.9	0.6	0.7	0.9	0.3	1.2
United States	3.4	0.3	3.7	1.1	0.8[e]	1.0	1.1	1.0	0.9	1.8	2.7
Other reporting countries											
Brazil	4.4	—	—	—	—	0.8	0.8	0.9	0.9	—	—
Russian Federation	2.0	0.1	2.1	0.7	0.5	0.8	1.2	1.0	0.9	0.5	1.4

—Not available.

#Rounds to zero.

[a]Unless otherwise noted, includes public subsidies to households for payments to education institutions and direct expenditures on education institutions from international sources.

[b]Refers to the mean of the data values for all reporting Organization for Economic Cooperation and Development (OECD) countries, to which each country reporting data contributes equally. The average includes all current OECD countries for which a given year's data are available, even if they were not members of OECD in that year.

[c]Public subsidies to households not included in public expenditures.

[d]Direct expenditures on education institutions from international sources exceed 1.5 percent of all public expenditures.

[e]Postsecondary non-higher-education included in higher education.

[f]Preprimary education (for children ages 3 and older) included in elementary and secondary education.

[g]Postsecondary non-higher-education included in both secondary and higher education.

[h]Occupation-specific education corresponding to that offered at the vocational associate's degree level in the United States is included in secondary education.

Note: Public direct expenditures on education include both amounts spent directly by governments to hire education personnel and to procure other resources, and amounts provided by governments to public or private institutions. Private direct expenditures exclude public subsidies that are used for payments to education institutions. Postsecondary non-higher-education is included in elementary and secondary education unless otherwise noted. Data for "all institutions" include expenditures that could not be reported by level of education. Detail may not sum to totals because of rounding.

SOURCE: "Table 605.20. Public and Private Direct Expenditures on Education Institutions as a Percentage of Gross Domestic Product, by Level of Education and Country: Selected Years, 1995 through 2011," in "Most Current Digest Tables," *Digest of Education Statistics*, U.S. Department of Education, Institute of Education Sciences, National Center for Education Statistics, August 2014, https://nces.ed.gov/programs/digest/d14/tables/xls/tabn605.20.xls (accessed July 20, 2015)

PRIVATE SCHOOLS, CHARTER SCHOOLS, AND HOME SCHOOLING

Stephanie Ewart of the U.S. Census Bureau reports in *The Decline in Private School Enrollment* (January 2013, https://www.census.gov/hhes/school/files/ewert_private _school_enrollment.pdf) that the proportion of elementary and secondary students attending private school has dropped steadily since the mid-20th century. During the

TABLE 2.8

Per student expenditures for education and per capita gross domestic product, by level of education and country, selected years 2005–11

Country	Gross domestic product per capita					Elementary and secondary education expenditures per FTE student					Higher education expenditures per FTE student				
	2005	2008	2009	2010	2011	2005	2008	2009	2010	2011	2005	2008	2009	2010	2011
						Current dollars									
OECD average[a]	$28,772	$33,886	$33,206	$33,471	$35,276	$6,751	$8,180	$8,632	$8,501	$8,789	$11,342	$13,391	$13,707	$13,211	$13,619
Australia	33,983	39,532	39,971	40,801	43,208	7,142	7,814	9,139	9,803	9,383	14,579	15,043	16,074	15,142	16,267
Austria	34,107	39,849	38,834	40,411	42,978	9,436	10,994	11,681	11,693	12,509	14,775	15,043	14,257	15,007	14,895
Belgium	32,077	36,879	36,698	37,878	40,093	7,306	9,706	9,783	10,123	10,722	11,960	15,020	15,443	15,179	15,420
Canada	—	38,522	40,136	37,480	—	7,774[b]	8,997[b]	9,774[b]	10,078[b]	—	22,810[c, d]	20,903[c]	22,475[c]	23,226[c]	
Chile	12,635	14,106	14,578	15,107	17,312	2,099	2,245	2,635	2,935	3,203	6,873	6,829	6,829	6,863	7,101
Czech Republic	20,280	25,845	25,614	25,364	27,046	4,098	5,236	5,615	5,532	6,128	6,649	8,318	8,237	7,635	9,392
Denmark[e]	33,626	39,494	38,299	40,600	41,843	8,997	10,429	11,094	11,404	10,230	14,959	17,634	18,556	18,977	21,254
Estonia	16,660	21,802	19,789	20,093	23,088	3,736	6,054	6,149	5,984	6,055	3,869	6,022[d]	6,373	6,501	7,868
Finland	30,468	37,795	35,848	36,030	38,611	6,610	8,068	8,314	8,591	9,180	12,285	15,402	16,569	16,714	18,002
France	29,644	34,233	33,724	34,395	36,391	7,456	8,559	8,861	9,070	9,329	10,995	14,079	14,642	15,067	15,375
Germany	30,496	37,171	36,048	37,661	40,990	7,039	7,859	8,534	—	9,521	12,446	15,390	15,711	—	16,723
Greece	25,472	29,920	29,381	27,539	26,622	5,493[b]	—	—	—	—	6,130	—	—	—	—
Hungary[c]	17,014	20,700	20,154	20,625	22,413	4,027	4,626	4,506	4,555	4,527	6,244	7,327	8,518	8,745	9,210
Iceland	35,571	39,029	36,718	35,509	38,224	8,815	9,745	9,309	8,592	9,326	9,474e	10,429	9,939	8,728	8,612
Ireland	38,061	42,644	39,750	41,000	42,943	6,411	8,915[c]	9,615[c]	9,638[c]	9,830[c]	10,468	16,284[c]	16,420[c]	16,008[c]	16,095[c]
Israel	21,474	27,690	27,454	26,552	30,168	5,041	5,780	5,464	5,692	6,277	10,919	12,568	11,214	10,730	11,554
Italy	27,750	33,271	32,397	32,110	33,870	7,410[c]	9,071[c]	8,943[c]	8,489[c]	8,534[c]	8,026[c]	9,553	9,562	9,580	9,990
Japan[e]	30,290	33,902	32,324	35,238	34,967	7,343	8,301	8,502	9,168	9,102	12,326	14,890	15,957	16,015	16,446
Korea, Republic of	21,342	26,877	27,171	28,829	29,035	5,638	6,723	8,122	7,396	7,652	7,606	9,081	9,513	9,972	9,927
Luxembourg	69,984	89,732	82,972	84,672	88,668	15,930[b, c]	16,909	18,018	19,050	19,600	—	—	—	—	—
Mexico	11,299	15,190	14,397	15,195	17,125	2,025	2,284	2,339	2,464	2,765	6,402	7,504	8,020	7,872	7,889
Netherlands	34,724	42,887	41,089	41,682	43,150	7,045	9,251	10,030	10,075	10,268	13,883	17,245	17,849	17,161	17,549
New Zealand	24,882	29,231	29,204	29,629	31,487	5,659	6,496	7,556	7,681	8,831	10,262	10,526	10,619	10,418	10,582
Norway	47,620	43,659	54,708	44,825	46,696	9,975	12,070	12,971	13,067	13,219	15,552	18,942	19,269	18,512	18,840
Poland[c]	13,573	18,062	18,910	20,034	21,753	3,165	4,682	5,167	5,693	6,066	5,593	7,063	7,776	8,866	9,659
Portugal[c]	19,967	24,962	24,935	25,519	25,672	5,646	6,276	7,288	7,419	7,282	8,787	10,373	10,481	10,578	9,640
Slovak Republic[f]	15,881	23,205	22,620	23,194	25,130	2,740	4,006	4,781	5,066	5,105	5,783	6,560	6,758	6,904	8,177
Slovenia	23,043	29,241	27,150	26,649	28,156	7,065	8,555	8,670	8,505	8,867	8,573	9,263	9,311	9,693	10,413
Spain	27,270	33,173	32,146	31,574	32,157	6,411	8,522	8,818	8,479	8,476	10,089	13,366	13,614	13,373	13,173
Sweden	32,770	39,321	37,192	39,251	41,761	7,861	9,524	9,709	10,044	10,548	15,946	20,014	19,961	19,562	20,818
Switzerland[c]	35,500	45,517	44,773	48,962	51,582	10,721	13,775	13,411	13,510	14,623	21,734	21,648	21,577	21,893	22,882
Turkey	—	14,963	14,442	15,775	17,781	—	—	—	2,020	2,501	—	—	—	—	8,193
United Kingdom	31,580	36,817	34,483	35,299	33,886	6,888	9,169	9,602	9,980	9,738	13,506	15,310	16,338	15,862	14,223
United States	41,674	46,901	45,087	46,548	49,321	9,771	11,107	11,818	11,826	11,841	23,435	27,499	27,066	25,576	26,021
						Constant 2013 dollars									
OECD average[a]	$34,322	$36,665	$36,057	$35,759	$36,534	$8,053	$8,850	$9,373	$9,082	$9,102	$13,529	$14,489	$14,884	$14,114	$14,104
Australia	40,537	42,774	43,403	43,590	44,748	8,519	8,454	9,924	10,473	9,717	17,391	16,276	17,454	16,177	16,847
Austria	40,685	43,116	42,168	43,172	44,510	11,256	11,895	12,684	12,492	12,955	17,625	16,277	15,482	16,033	15,426
Belgium	38,263	39,903	39,849	40,466	41,522	8,715	10,501	10,623	10,815	11,105	14,267	16,252	16,769	16,216	15,970
Canada	—	41,680	43,582	40,042	—	9,273[b]	9,734[b]	10,613[b]	10,766[b]	—	27,209[c, d]	22,617[c]	24,405[c]	24,813[c]	
Chile	15,072	15,263	15,829	16,139	17,929	2,504	2,429	2,861	3,136	3,317	8,198	7,389	7,415	7,332	7,354
Czech Republic	24,192	27,964	27,814	27,097	28,010	4,888	5,666	6,098	5,910	6,347	7,931	9,000	8,944	8,157	9,727
Denmark[e]	40,112	42,733	41,587	43,375	43,334	10,732	11,284	12,047	12,183	10,595	17,844	19,080	20,149	20,274	22,011
Estonia	19,873	23,590	21,488	21,446	23,911	4,457	6,550	6,677	6,393	6,271	4,615	6,516[d]	6,920	6,945	8,148
Finland	36,345	40,894	38,926	38,492	39,987	7,885	8,730	9,028	9,178	9,507	14,654	16,665	17,991	17,856	18,643
France	35,362	37,040	36,619	36,745	37,688	8,895	9,261	9,622	9,689	9,662	13,116	15,233	15,899	16,097	15,923
Germany	36,377	40,219	39,143	40,234	42,451	8,396	8,503	9,267	—	9,860	14,846	16,652	17,060	—	17,319
Greece	30,385	32,373	31,904	29,421	27,571	6,553[b]	—	—	—	—	7,313	—	—	—	—
Hungary[c]	20,296	22,397	21,885	22,035	23,212	4,803	5,006	4,893	4,866	4,689	7,449	7,928	9,249	9,343	9,538
Iceland	42,431	42,229	39,871	37,936	39,587	10,515	10,544	10,108	9,179	9,658	11,302[e]	11,285	10,792	9,324	8,919
Ireland	45,401	46,141	43,163	43,802	44,473	7,647	9,646[c]	10,441[c]	10,296[c]	10,180[c]	12,487	17,619[c]	17,830[c]	17,102[c]	16,669[c]
Israel	25,616	29,961	29,812	28,367	31,243	6,013	6,254	5,933	6,081	6,501	13,025	13,599	12,177	11,463	11,966
Italy	33,102	35,999	35,179	34,304	35,077	8,839[c]	9,815[c]	9,711[c]	9,069[c]	8,838[c]	9,574[c]	10,337	10,382	10,234	10,346
Japan[e]	36,132	36,682	35,100	37,646	36,213	8,760	8,981	9,231	9,794	9,427	14,703	16,111	17,327	17,109	17,032
Korea, Republic of	25,458	29,080	29,504	30,799	30,070	6,726	7,274	8,820	7,902	7,924	9,073	9,826	10,330	10,653	10,280
Luxembourg	83,482	97,090	90,096	90,458	91,829	19,003[b, c]	18,296	19,565	20,352	20,298	—	—	—	—	—

late 1950s nearly 15% of all elementary and secondary students attended private school. By 1970 this figure had fallen to roughly 10%. The proportion of private school students fluctuated over the ensuing decades. As the National Center for Education Statistics (NCES) notes in "Private School Enrollment" (January 2014, http://

nces.ed.gov/programs/coe/indicator_cgc.asp), private school enrollment actually rose during the second half of the 1990s, increasing from 5.9 million in 1995–96 to 6.3 million in 2001–02. By 2011–12, however, the number of students attending private schools had fallen to 5.3 million, or 10% of the total pre-K through grade 12 student

TABLE 2.8

Per student expenditures for education and per capita gross domestic product, by level of education and country, selected years 2005–11 [CONTINUED]

Country	Gross domestic product per capita					Elementary and secondary education expenditures per FTE student					Higher education expenditures per FTE student				
	2005	2008	2009	2010	2011	2005	2008	2009	2010	2011	2005	2008	2009	2010	2011
Mexico	13,478	16,435	15,634	16,233	17,735	2,416	2,471	2,540	2,632	2,863	7,637	8,119	8,709	8,410	8,170
Netherlands	41,421	46,404	44,617	44,530	44,688	8,404	10,010	10,892	10,764	10,634	16,560	18,659	19,382	18,334	18,175
New Zealand.	29,680	31,628	31,712	31,654	32,609	6,751	7,028	8,205	8,206	9,146	12,241	11,389	11,531	11,130	10,959
Norway	56,805	47,239	59,405	47,889	48,360	11,899	13,060	14,084	13,960	13,690	18,552	20,495	20,923	19,777	19,512
Poland[c]	16,191	19,543	20,534	21,403	22,528	3,775	5,065	5,610	6,082	6,282	6,671	7,642	8,444	9,472	10,003
Portugal[c]	23,818	27,009	27,076	27,263	26,587	6,735	6,790	7,914	7,926	7,541	10,482	11,223	11,380	11,301	9,983
Slovak Republic[f]	18,944	25,108	24,562	24,779	26,025	3,268	4,335	5,191	5,413	5,287	6,899	7,098	7,338	7,375	8,469
Slovenia	27,488	31,638	29,481	28,470	29,159	8,427	9,257	9,415	9,086	9,183	10,226	10,022	10,111	10,355	10,785
Spain	32,530	35,893	34,906	33,731	33,303	7,647	9,221	9,575	9,058	8,778	12,035	14,462	14,783	14,287	13,642
Sweden	39,090	42,546	40,385	41,934	43,250	9,378	10,305	10,543	10,731	10,924	19,022	21,655	21,675	20,899	21,560
Switzerland[c]	42,346	49,249	48,617	52,308	53,421	12,788	14,905	14,562	14,434	15,145	25,926	23,423	23,430	23,389	23,697
Turkey	—	16,189	15,682	16,853	18,415	—	—	—	2,158	2,590	—	—	—	—	8,485
United Kingdom	37,671	39,836	37,444	37,711	35,094	8,217	9,921	10,427	10,662	10,085	16,111	16,565	17,741	16,946	14,730
United States	49,712	50,747	48,959	49,729	51,079	11,655	12,018	12,832	12,634	12,263	27,955	29,754	29,390	27,324	26,949

—Not available.

[a]Refers to the mean of the data values for all reporting Organization for Economic Cooperation and Development (OECD) countries, to which each country reporting data contributes equally. The average includes all current OECD countries for which a given year's data are available, even if they were not members of OECD in that year.

[b]Includes preprimary education.

[c]Public institutions only.

[d]Excludes occupation-specific education corresponding to that offered at the vocational associate's degree level in the United States.

[e]Postsecondary non-higher-education included in both secondary and higher education.

[f]Occupation-specific education corresponding to that offered at the vocational associate's degree level in the United States is included under elementary and secondary education instead of under higher education.

Note: FTE = Full-time-equivalent students. Includes all expenditures by public and private education institutions (such as administration, instruction, ancillary services for students and families, and research and development) unless otherwise noted. Expenditures for International Standard Classification of Education (ISCED) level 4 (postsecondary non-higher-education) are included in elementary and secondary education unless otherwise noted. Data for Canada, France, Greece, Italy, Luxembourg, Portugal, and the United States do not include postsecondary non-higher-education. Data adjusted to U.S. dollars using the purchasing power parity (PPP) index. Constant dollars based on the Consumer Price Index, prepared by the Bureau of Labor Statistics, U.S. Department of Labor.

SOURCE: "Table 605.10. Gross Domestic Product per Capita and Public and Private Education Expenditures per Full-Time-Equivalent (FTE) Student, by Level of Education and Country: Selected Years, 2005 through 2011," in "Most Current Digest Tables," *Digest of Education Statistics*, U.S. Department of Education, Institute of Education Sciences, National Center for Education Statistics, August 2014, https://nces.ed.gov/programs/digest/d14/tables/xls/tabn605.10.xls (accessed July 20, 2015)

population that year. The NCES reports in *Projections of Education Statistics to 2022* (February 2014, https://nces .ed.gov/pubs2014/2014051.pdf) that enrollment in pre-K through grade 12 private schools was projected to fall below 5 million by the year 2022–23.

Meanwhile, Ewart notes that of the 40 states that funded charter schools in 2010, all but three states saw enrollment rise in this category between 2009 and 2010. California experienced the largest increase in charter school enrollment, with 47,785 more students attending charter schools between 2009 and 2010, followed by Ohio (21,707), Florida (17,445), and Texas (16,401). Overall, California had the highest number of students attending charter schools in 2010, at 365,207; Texas was a distant second with 165,471 charter school students, followed by Florida (155,233), Arizona (125,284), Ohio (114,275), and Michigan (113,481). As the NCES reports in "Charter School Enrollment" (April 2015, http://nces .ed.gov/programs/coe/indicator_cgb.asp), nationwide enrollment in public charter schools rose from roughly 300,000 in 1999–2000 to 2.3 million in 2012–13. During this span, the overall percentage of public school students attending charter schools increased from 0.7% to 4.6%. Note that as of September 2015 the NCES did not publish projections for future charter school enrollment.

At the same time, the number of students receiving their education at home has risen in a number of states. As Ewart notes, North Carolina had the largest number of home-schooled students in 2010 (83,609), followed by Florida (69,281) and Georgia (42,474). Florida experienced the largest total increase in students who were home schooled, from 62,567 in 2009 to 69,281 in 2010, a jump of 10.7%. States that saw the numbers of students attending home school decrease during this period were Ohio, which had 1,851 fewer home-schooled students in 2010 compared with 2009, and Utah, where 1,023 fewer students attended school at home.

TEACHERS AND TEACHER-PUPIL RATIOS

During the fall of 2012 there were a total of just over 3.5 million elementary and secondary teachers in grades pre-K to 12 across the United States. (See Table 2.9.) Approximately 3.1 million (88%) of all teachers were employed in public schools and a projected 414,000 (12%) were employed in private schools. The teacher-pupil ratio in public schools was one teacher per 16 students. The projected ratio was somewhat lower in private schools at one teacher for every 12.5 students. These ratios were considerably lower than they had been during the 1950s, 1960s, and 1970s.

TABLE 2.9

Public and private elementary and secondary teachers, enrollment, and pupil-teacher ratios, selected years fall 1955–fall 2024

Year	Teachers (in thousands)			Enrollment (in thousands)			Pupil/teacher ratio			Number of new teacher hires (in thousands)[a]		
	Total	Public	Private	Total	Public	Private	Total	Public	Private	Total	Public	Private
1955	1,286	1,141	145[b]	35,280	30,680	4,600[b]	27.4	26.9	31.7[b]	—	—	—
1960	1,600	1,408	192[b]	42,181	36,281	5,900[b]	26.4	25.8	30.7[b]	—	—	—
1965	1,933	1,710	223	48,473	42,173	6,300	25.1	24.7	28.3	—	—	—
1970	2,292	2,059	233	51,257	45,894	5,363	22.4	22.3	23.0	—	—	—
1975	2,453	2,198	255[b]	49,819	44,819	5,000[b]	20.3	20.4	19.6[b]	—	—	—
1980	2,485	2,184	301	46,208	40,877	5,331	18.6	18.7	17.7	—	—	—
1985	2,549	2,206	343	44,979	39,422	5,557	17.6	17.9	16.2	—	—	—
1990	2,759	2,398	361[b]	46,864	41,217	5,648[b]	17.0	17.2	15.6[b]	—	—	—
1995	2,974	2,598	376	50,759	44,840	5,918	17.1	17.3	15.7	—	—	—
2000	3,366	2,941	424[b]	53,373	47,204	6,169[b]	15.9	16.0	14.5[b]	—	—	—
2005	3,593	3,143	450	55,187	49,113	6,073	15.4	15.6	13.5	—	—	—
2010	3,529	3,099	429[b]	54,867	49,484	5,382[b]	15.5	16.0	12.5[b]	—	—	—
2012	3,523	3,109	414[c]	54,952	49,771	5,181[c]	15.6	16.0	12.5[c]	321	247	74
2013[c]	3,527	3,120	407	55,036	49,942	5,094	15.6	16.0	12.5	319	250	69
2014[c]	3,520	3,122	398	54,965	49,986	4,979	15.6	16.0	12.5	310	244	66
2015[c]	3,521	3,129	391	54,994	50,094	4,899	15.6	16.0	12.5	316	249	67
2020[c]	3,700	3,302	398	56,404	51,547	4,856	15.2	15.6	12.2	362	285	76
2024[c]	3,881	3,466	415	57,872	52,920	4,952	14.9	15.3	11.9	375	293	81

—Not available.

[a] A teacher is considered to be a new hire for a public or private school if the teacher had not taught in that control of school in the previous year. A teacher who moves from a public to private or a private to public school is considered a new teacher hire, but a teacher who moves from one public school to another public school or one private school to another private school is not considered a new teacher hire.

[b] Estimated.

[c] Projected.

Note: Data for teachers are expressed in full-time equivalents (FTE). Counts of private school teachers and enrollment include prekindergarten through grade 12 in schools offering kindergarten or higher grades. Counts of public school teachers and enrollment include prekindergarten through grade 12. The pupil/teacher ratio includes teachers for students with disabilities and other special teachers, while these teachers are generally excluded from class size calculations. Ratios for public schools reflect totals reported by states and differ from totals reported for schools or school districts. Some data have been revised from previously published figures. Detail may not sum to totals because of rounding.

SOURCE: Adapted from "Table 208.20. Public and Private Elementary and Secondary Teachers, Enrollment, Pupil/Teacher Ratios, and New Teacher Hires: Selected Years, Fall 1955 through Fall 2024," in "Most Current Digest Tables," *Digest of Education Statistics*, U.S. Department of Education, Institute of Education Sciences, National Center for Education Statistics, March 2015, https://nces.ed.gov/programs/digest/d14/tables/xls/tabn208.20.xls (accessed July 21, 2015)

STUDENT SUPPORT PROGRAMS AND SERVICES

The type of supportive programs and services that are available to schools and school districts is one indicator of the access students have to educational opportunities. Although individual schools can apply directly for these programs and services, the school district (especially in public schools) usually decides whether the programs and services will be provided in its schools.

Schools offer a variety of student services, such as free or reduced-price lunches financed by public funds, services for disabled students, remedial programs, programs for gifted and talented students, programs under Title I of the Elementary and Secondary Education Act of 1965 (federal funds for special educational programs for disadvantaged children), drug and alcohol prevention programs, English as a second language programs, and bilingual programs.

The amount spent per pupil for student support services is shown in Table 2.6. In 2011–12 an average of $594 was spent per pupil across the United States for support services, which was 5.6% of the average total per pupil expenditure of $10,667 for that year. Among the District of Columbia and the 50 states, New Jersey had the highest expenditure for support services at $1,782 per pupil. Rhode Island was second with an expenditure of $1,567 per pupil. The states with the lowest expenditures per pupil for support services were Utah ($251) and Minnesota ($288).

GRADUATING FROM HIGH SCHOOL

Over a century ago, during the 1899–1900 academic year, only 95,000 students graduated from high school. (See Table 2.10.) By 1929–30 the number of students who graduated from high school grew to 667,000 and by 1939–40 to 1.2 million.

As Table 2.10 shows, 1969–70 was the first academic year in which the Department of Education calculated the averaged freshman graduation rate for public schools, which is an estimate of the percentage of high school students who graduate. In that year 78.7% of those students who entered high school four years earlier graduated. The graduation rate fluctuated between 71% and 74% throughout much of the 1980s, 1990s, and the first decade of the 21st century, before rising again during the second decade of the century. During the 2011–12 academic year the graduation rate was 80.8%, with nearly 3.2 million students graduating from public schools and 304,680 students graduating from private schools.

TABLE 2.10

Number of high school graduates and graduation rates, selected years 1869–70 to 2023–24

| School year | Total[a] | Sex | | Control | | | | Averaged freshman graduation rate for public schools[c] | Population 17 years old[d] | Graduates as a ratio of 17-year-old population |
| | | Males | Females | Public[b] | | | Private | | | |
				Total	Males	Females	Total			
1869–70	16,000	7,064	8,936	—	—	—	—	—	815,000	2.0
1879–80	23,634	10,605	13,029	—	—	—	—	—	946,026	2.5
1889–90	43,731	18,549	25,182	21,882	—	—	21,849[e]	—	1,259,177	3.5
1899–1900	94,883	38,075	56,808	61,737	—	—	33,146[e]	—	1,489,146	6.4
1909–10	156,429	63,676	92,753	111,363	—	—	45,066[e]	—	1,786,240	8.8
1919–20	311,266	123,684	187,582	230,902	—	—	80,364[e]	—	1,855,173	16.8
1929–30	666,904	300,376	366,528	591,719	—	—	75,185[e]	—	2,295,822	29.0
1939–40	1,221,475	578,718	642,757	1,143,246	538,273	604,973	78,229[e]	—	2,403,074	50.8
1949–50	1,199,700	570,700	629,000	1,063,444	505,394	558,050	136,256[e]	—	2,034,450	59.0
1959–60	1,858,023	895,000	963,000	1,627,050	791,426	835,624	230,973	—	2,672,000	69.5
1969–70	2,888,639	1,430,000	1,459,000	2,588,639	1,285,895	1,302,744	300,000[e]	78.7	3,757,000	76.9
1974–75	3,132,502	1,542,000	1,591,000	2,822,502	1,391,519	1,430,983	310,000[e]	74.9	4,256,000	73.6
1979–80	3,042,214	1,503,000	1,539,000	2,747,678	—	—	294,536	71.5	4,262,000	71.4
1984–85	2,676,917	—	—	2,413,917	—	—	263,000[e]	74.2	3,699,000	72.4
1989–90[f]	2,574,162	—	—	2,320,337	—	—	253,825[g]	73.6	3,505,000	73.4
1994–95	2,519,084	—	—	2,273,541	—	—	245,543	71.8	3,635,803	69.3
1999–2000	2,832,844	—	—	2,553,844	1,241,631	1,312,213	279,000[e]	71.7	4,056,639	69.8
2004–05	3,106,499	—	—	2,799,250	1,369,749	1,429,501	307,249	74.7	4,120,073	75.4
2009–10	3,440,185	—	—	3,128,022	1,542,684[h]	1,585,338[h]	312,163[e]	78.2	4,311,831	79.8
2010–11	3,449,719	—	—	3,143,879	—	—	305,840	79.6	4,366,292	79.0
2011–12	3,452,470	—	—	3,147,790	—	—	304,680[e]	80.8	4,291,741	80.4
2012–13[i]	3,408,600	—	—	3,110,150	—	—	298,450	—	—	—
2013–14[i]	3,365,560	—	—	3,070,440	—	—	295,120	—	—	—
2014–15[i]	3,322,780	—	—	3,031,450	—	—	291,320	—	—	—
2019–20[i]	3,326,590	—	—	3,085,600	—	—	240,980	—	—	—
2023–24[i]	3,388,680	—	—	3,164,540	—	—	224,140	—	—	—

—Not available.

[a]Includes graduates of public and private schools.

[b]Data for 1929–30 and preceding years are from *Statistics of Public High Schools* and exclude graduates from high schools that failed to report to the Office of Education. Includes estimates for jurisdictions not reporting counts of graduates by sex.

[c]The averaged freshman graduation rate provides an estimate of the percentage of students who receive a regular diploma within 4 years of entering ninth grade. The rate uses aggregate student enrollment data to estimate the size of an incoming freshman class and aggregate counts of the number of diplomas awarded 4 years later. Averaged freshman graduation rates in this table are based on reported totals of enrollment by grade and high school graduates, rather than on details reported by race/ethnicity.

[d]Derived from Current Population Reports, Series P-25. For years 1869–70 through 1989–90, 17-year-old population is an estimate of the October 17-year-old population based on July data. Data for 1990–91 and later years are October resident population estimates prepared by the Census Bureau.

[e]Estimated.

[f]Includes imputations for nonreporting states.

[g]Projected by private schools responding to the Private School Universe Survey.

[h]Includes estimate for Connecticut, which did not report graduates by sex.

[i]Projected by the National Center for Education Statistics (NCES).

Note: Includes graduates of regular day school programs. Excludes graduates of other programs, when separately reported, and recipients of high school equivalency certificates. Some data have been revised from previously published figures. Detail may not sum to totals because of rounding.

SOURCE: Adapted from "Table 219.10. High school Graduates, by Sex and Control of School: Selected Years, 1869–70 through 2023–24," in "Most Current Digest Tables," *Digest of Education Statistics*, U.S. Department of Education, Institute of Education Sciences, National Center for Education Statistics, April 2014, https://nces.ed.gov/programs/digest/d13/tables/xls/tabn219.10.xls (accessed July 21, 2015)

Completing High School: The GED

The term *high school graduates* is not the same as *high school completers*. The latter are students who finish their high school education through alternative programs, such as the General Educational Development (GED) program. The GED program is an alternative way for young people who have left school to get equivalency credit for high school graduation and obtain a high school diploma. The GED Testing Service is provided by the American Council on Education (http://www.acenet.edu).

The number of students earning GED diplomas rose sharply from 340,000 in 1975 to 479,000 in 1980. (See Table 2.11.) The number generally dropped during the 1980s, falling to 410,000 in 1990, but by 1995 it had increased to 504,000. In 2013 a reported 816,000 people took the GED tests (one or more subtests) and 541,000 passed.

CAREER AND TECHNICAL EDUCATION

Career and technical education (CTE), also known as vocational education, includes study areas such as office administration, automotive technology, carpentry and construction, medical technology, agricultural production, culinary arts, transportation, electronics, and computer graphics. For much of the 20th century, most high schools had a two-track educational system: an academic curriculum that centered on traditional subjects and prepared students for college, and a vocational curriculum

TABLE 2.11

Number of General Education Development test takers and credentials issued, by age, 1971–2013

Year	Number of test takers (in thousands)			Percentage distribution of test passers, by age group[a]				
	Total[b]	Completing test battery[c]	Passing tests[d]	16 to 18 years old	19 to 24 years old	25 to 29 years old	30 to 34 years old	35 years old or over
1971[e]	377	—	227	—	—	—	—	—
1972[e]	419	—	245	—	—	—	—	—
1973[e]	423	—	249	—	—	—	—	—
1974	—	—	294	35[f]	27[f]	13	9	17
1975	—	—	340	33[f]	26[f]	14	9	18
1976	—	—	333	31[f]	28[f]	14	10	17
1977	—	—	330	40[f]	24[f]	13	8	14
1978	—	—	381	31[f]	27[f]	13	10	18
1979	—	—	426	37[f]	28[f]	12	13	11
1980	—	—	479	37[f]	27[f]	13	8	15
1981	—	—	489	37[f]	27[f]	13	8	14
1982	—	—	486	37[f]	28[f]	13	8	15
1983	—	—	465	34[f]	29[f]	14	8	15
1984	—	—	427	32[f]	28[f]	15	9	16
1985	—	—	413	32[f]	26[f]	15	10	16
1986	—	—	428	32[f]	26[f]	15	10	17
1987	—	—	444	33[f]	24[f]	15	10	18
1988	—	—	410	35[f]	22[f]	14	10	18
1989	632	541	357	22	37	13	—	—
1990	714	615	410	22	39	13	10	15
1991	755	657	462	20	40	13	10	16
1992	739	639	457	22	39	13	9	17
1993	746	651	469	22	38	13	10	16
1994	774	668	491	25	37	13	10	15
1995	787	682	504	27	36	13	9	15
1996	824	716	488	27	37	13	9	14
1997	785	681	460	31	36	12	8	13
1998	776	673	481	32	36	11	7	13
1999	808	702	498	32	37	11	7	13
2000	811	699	487	33	37	11	7	13
2001[g]	1,016	928	648	29	38	11	8	14
2002[g]	557	467	330	38	36	10	6	11
2003	657	552	387	35	37	10	7	11
2004	666	570	406	35	38	11	6	10
2005	681	588	424	34	37	12	7	11
2006	676	580	398	35	36	12	6	11
2007	692	600	429	35	35	12	7	11
2008	737	642	469	34	35	13	7	11
2009	748	645	448	31	36	13	8	12
2010	720	623	452	27	37	14	9	14
2011	691	602	434	27	37	13	9	14
2012	674	581	401	26	37	14	9	13
2013	816	714	541	22	35	15	11	17

—Not available.

[a]Age data for 1988 and prior years are for all test takers and may not be comparable to data for later years. For 1989 and later years, age data are only for test passers. The less than 1 percent of people who failed to report their date of birth—2,948 of the 540,535 test passers in 2013—were excluded from the calculation.

[b]All people taking the General Education Development (GED) tests (one or more subtests).

[c]People completing the entire GED battery of five tests.

[d]Data for 2002 and later years are for people passing the GED tests (i.e., earning both a passing total score on the test battery and a passing score on each individual test). Data for 2001 and prior years are for high school equivalency credentials issued by the states to GED test passers. In order to receive high school equivalency credentials in some states, GED test passers must meet additional state requirements (e.g., complete an approved course in civics or government).

[e]Includes other jurisdictions, such as Puerto Rico, Guam, and American Samoa.

[f]For 1988 and prior years, 19-year-olds are included with the 16- to 18-year-olds instead of the 19-to 24-year-olds.

[g]A revised GED test was introduced in 2002. In 2001, test takers were required to successfully complete all five components of the GED or else begin the five-part series again with the new test that was introduced in 2002.

Note: Data are for the United States only and exclude other jurisdictions, except where noted. Detail may not sum to totals because of rounding.

SOURCE: "Table 219.60. Number of People Taking the General Educational Development (GED) Test and Percentage Distribution of Those Who Passed, by Age Group: 1971 through 2013," in "Most Current Digest Tables," *Digest of Education Statistics*, U.S. Department of Education, Institute of Education Sciences, National Center for Education Statistics, November 2014, https://nces.ed.gov/programs/digest/d14/tables/xls/tabn219.60.xls (accessed July 21, 2015)

that focused on career skills and prepared students to enter the workforce. However, the high-skill job market of the 21st century requires all high school graduates to have both academic knowledge and workplace skills and training. Professional careers now demand technical skills and the ability to work in teams; technical careers require the ability to diagnose and analyze problems.

The integration of academic and vocational education, emphasizing a curriculum that makes connections between knowledge development and its application in the workplace, is mandated in the United States under the Carl D. Perkins Vocational and Applied Technology Education Act, which was originally enacted in 1990 and most recently reauthorized in 2006. This act also provides funding for the improvement of secondary and postsecondary CTE programs. According to the Department of Education's Office of Vocational and Adult Education, in *Report to Congress on State Performance Program Year 2010–11* (April 2014, https://s3.amazonaws.com/PCRN/docs/Rpt_to_Congress/Perkins_RTC_2010-11.pdf), 12.1 million students were enrolled in CTE programs during the 2010–11 academic year. Approximately 7.5 million students were in secondary-level programs in 2010–11, 4.4 million students were in postsecondary CTE programs, and 146,300 students were in adult programs. (See Table 2.12.) Although men accounted for the majority of CTE students enrolled in secondary programs in 2010–11, women outnumbered men in postsecondary-level programs.

In the face of a rapidly evolving economy, the federal government has increased its commitment to developing and expanding the nation's CTE programs. In *Investing in America's Future: A Blueprint for Transforming Career and Technical Education* (April 2012, http://www2.ed.gov/about/offices/list/ovae/pi/cte/transforming-career-technical-education.pdf), the Department of Education outlines four core principles that are aimed at preparing the U.S. workforce to confront new challenges posed by increased global competition in the technological age:

1. Alignment—effective alignment between high-quality CTE programs and labor market needs to equip students with 21st-century skills and prepare them for in-demand occupations in high-growth industry sectors

2. Collaboration—strong collaborations among secondary and postsecondary institutions, employers, and industry partners to improve the quality of CTE programs

3. Accountability—meaningful accountability for improving academic outcomes and building technical and employability skills in CTE programs for all students, based upon common definitions and clear metrics for performance

4. Innovation—increased emphasis on innovation supported by systemic reform of state policies and practices to support CTE implementation of effective practices at the local level

According to the Department of Education, the Obama administration pledged $1.1 billion toward implementing these goals during fiscal year 2012.

TABLE 2.12

Enrollment in career and technical education programs, by level of program and select demographic categories, 2010–11

CTE student[a] characteristics	Disaggregated student category	Secondary Number of students	Secondary Percentage of students	Postsecondary Number of students	Postsecondary Percentage of students	Adult Number of students	Adult Percentage of students
Gender[b] (unduplicated count)							
Total		7,494,042	100.00%	4,411,875	100.00%	146,300	100.00%
	Male	3,980,357	53.11%	2,035,339	46.13%	74,492	50.92%
	Female	3,513,685	46.89%	2,376,536	53.87%	71,808	49.08%
Race/ethnicity[c] (duplicated count)							
Total[d]		7,501,366	100.00%	4,410,663	100.00%	148,610	100.00%
	American Indian or Alaska Native	80,745	1.08%	60,645	1.37%	2571	1.73%
	Asian	288,575	3.85%	258,273	5.86%	1989	1.34%
	Black or African American	1,306,569	17.42%	625,465	14.18%	35,480	23.87%
	Hispanic/Latino	1,661,064	22.14%	644,465	14.61%	15512	10.44%
	Native Hawaiian or other Pacific Islander	34,498	0.46%	55,853	1.27%	143	0.10%
	White	3,950,199	52.66%	2,369,754	53.73%	89,987	60.55%
	Two or more races	179,716	2.40%	48,995	1.11%	1105	0.74%
	Unknown	—[e]	†	347,213	7.87%	1,823	1.23%
Special populations and other student categories (duplicated count)							
Total[d]		6,471,359	100.00%	3,066,113	100.00%	113,663	100.00%
	Individuals with disabilities (ADA[f])	—[g]	†	152,872	4.99%	4,363[h]	3.84%
	Individuals with disabilities (ESEA /IDEA)[h]	797,869	12.33%	—[h]	†	—[h]	†
	Economically disadvantaged students	3,317,572	51.27%	1,668,686	54.42%	74,186	65.27%
	Single parents	32,780	0.51%	263,868	8.61%	11,984	10.54%
	Displaced homemakers	2,038	0.03%	110,196	3.59%	4,356	3.83%
	Limited English proficient	383,800	5.93%	177,584	5.79%	7,176	6.31%
	Migrant students	53,733	0.83%	—[i]	†	—[i]	†
	Students in nontraditional programs	1,883,567	29.11%	692,907	22.60%	11,598	10.20%

†No data applicable to the cell.

—Data not applicable.

[a]Reflects unduplicated counts of all students (CTE participants and CTE concentrators) reported by each state as having taken one or more CTE courses or credits at the secondary, postsecondary, and adult levels. States report data based on their definitions of CTE participant and CTE concentrator.

[b]The sum of the totals for gender corresponds to the total for career and technical education student enrollment for program year (PY) 2010–11 in figure 1.

[c]According to the Department's Oct. 19, 2007, memorandum titled "Final Guidance on Maintaining, Collecting, and Reporting Racial and Ethnic Data" states were required beginning in PY 2010–11 to report data disaggregated by race/ethnicity using the "Revisions to the Standards for the Classification of Federal Data on Race and Ethnicity" that was issued by the Office of Management & Budget (OMB) in 1997.

[d]The totals for race/ethnicity standards and special populations and other student categories are based on data and information reported by CTE students or their parents. The sum of the totals for disaggregated categories of race/ethnicity and other special populations and other student categories do not correspond to each other or to the career and technical education student enrollment for PY 2010–11 in figure 1 because (1) a few states did not submit disaggregated data on CTE students for one or more categories; and (2) students can be included in more than one race/ethnicity category, special population category, and/or other student category.

[e]Secondary education reports are based on the 1997 race/ethnicity categories. The eepartment does not include a "race and/or ethnicity unknown" category for its aggregate elementary and secondary reporting of racial and ethnic data for the 1997 race/ethnicity categories.

[f]The Americans with Disabilities Act of 1990 (ADA) was amended by the ADA Amendments Act of 2008 (Public Law 110-325), which became effective on Jan. 1, 2009.

[g]While ADA is applicable to individuals with disabilities in secondary and postsecondary education, for reporting purposes, the states reported ADA data only for the postsecondary and adult populations.

[h]ESEA and the Individuals with Disabilities Education Act (IDEA) are applicable to only those students at the secondary level. "Individuals with disability" in ESEA refers to "disability status," as used in Sec. 1111(h)(1)(C)(i) of ESEA, and refers to a "child with a disability," which under Sec. 9101(5) of ESEA has the same meaning as the term is used in Sec. 602 of IDEA. The term an "individual with a disability" as defined in Sec. 602(3)(A) of IDEA, refers to a "child with a disability," which means a child "(i) with mental retardation, hearing impairments (including deafness), speech or language impairments, visual impairments (including blindness), serious emotional disturbance (referred to in this title as 'emotional disturbance'), orthopedic impairments, autism, traumatic brain injury, other health impairments, or specific learning disabilities; and (ii) who, by reason thereof, needs special education and related service.

[i]The category "migrant students" is applicable only to students in the migrant status category under ESEA and, therefore, does not include students at the postsecondary and adult levels.

Note: CTE means career and technical education. Perkins IV means the Carl D. Perkins Career and Technical Education Act of 2006. The total value of the cells in the race/ethnicity and special populations and other categories sections do vary because a few states did not submit disaggregated data on CTE participants for one or more categories and the data for these categories are duplicated counts. The percentage of students is by disaggregated category at the secondary, postsecondary, and adult levels. Therefore, the percentage totals are not summative horizontally.

The 50 U.S. states, the District of Columbia, the Commonwealth of Puerto Rico, and three of the outlying areas—the United States Virgin Islands, Guam, and Republic of Palau—were required to report data and information under Perkins IV for PY 2010–11. The Republic of Palau did not submit data or information because it did not have a fully approved state plan. The United States Virgin Islands received its allotted Perkins IV funds consolidated with funds allotted under other formula grant programs and used some of the funds in the consolidated grant for Perkins IV, Title I purposes. American Samoa and the Commonwealth of the Northern Mariana Islands did not submit data or information for CTE programs because they consolidated their Perkins IV, Title I, allotments with funds under other formula programs and used these funds for allowable program purposes rather than for career and technical education. Thus, the CTE data reported for PY 2010–11 represent 54 of the 57 states that received Perkins IV state grants. Florida, Louisiana, Missouri, Ohio, Oklahoma, and Tennessee provided performance levels and report data for their adult-level CTE, concentrators using the Perkins IV Sec. 113(b)(2)(B) postsecondary core indicators.

SOURCE: "Table 4. Enrollment of CTE students in CTE Programs, by Disaggregated Student Category: Program Year 2010–11," in Carl D. Perkins Career and Technical Education Act of 2006, Report to Congress on State Performance Program Year 2010–11, U.S. Department of Education, Office of Vocational and Adult Education, Division of Academic and Technical Education, April 2014, https://s3.amazonaws.com/PCRN/docs/Rpt_to_Congress/Perkins_RTC_2010-11.pdf (accessed July 21, 2015)

CHAPTER 3
EDUCATION FOR SPECIAL NEEDS STUDENTS

The right to a free, public education is guaranteed to all children in the United States. For many children, however, having access to education requires adaptations that are suited to their special needs. In general, the term "special needs" is used to refer to a broad range of physical, mental, and emotional conditions that might impair or delay a student's ability to learn. Special needs students can include (but are not limited to) children who suffer from cognitive or physical disabilities, who contend with learning impairments such as dyslexia or attention deficit/hyperactivity disorder (ADHD), or who have endured psychological or emotional trauma. For school districts it can be challenging to meet the myriad special needs that are presented in a sizable student population.

INDIVIDUALS WITH DISABILITIES EDUCATION ACT

In 1975 Congress passed the Education for All Handicapped Children Act, which required schools to develop programs for disabled children. The law was modified in 1983, and in 1986 Congress highlighted the importance of the preschool years by lowering to age three the age at which children were eligible for special education and related services. The amendments also established the Handicapped Infants and Toddlers Program to assist children and their families from birth to age three. Having children with special needs receive educational services at younger ages builds the foundation for learning the skills they will need in elementary school. For many disabled children, early education programs can reduce or even eliminate the need for intensive services as they get older.

In 1992 the Education for All Handicapped Children Act was renamed the Individuals with Disabilities Education Act (IDEA). The act was reauthorized and amended most recently in 2004 by the Individuals with Disabilities Education Improvement Act, commonly referred to as IDEA 2004. IDEA 2004 regulations took effect in October 2006.

IDEA 2004 defines the term *child with a disability* as one:

(i) with mental retardation, hearing impairments (including deafness), speech or language impairments, visual impairments (including blindness), serious emotional disturbance (referred to in this title as "emotional disturbance"), orthopedic impairments, autism, traumatic brain injury, other health impairments, or specific learning disabilities; and

(ii) who, by reason thereof, needs special education and related services.

The purposes of IDEA 2004 as described in the law are:

(1)(A) to ensure that all children with disabilities have available to them a free appropriate public education that emphasizes special education and related services designed to meet their unique needs and prepare them for further education, employment, and independent living;

(B) to ensure that the rights of children with disabilities and parents of such children are protected; and

(C) to assist States, localities, educational service agencies, and Federal agencies to provide for the education of all children with disabilities;

(2) to assist States in the implementation of a statewide, comprehensive, coordinated, multidisciplinary, interagency system of early intervention services for infants and toddlers with disabilities and their families;

(3) to ensure that educators and parents have the necessary tools to improve educational results for children with disabilities by supporting system improvement activities; coordinated research and

personnel preparation; coordinated technical assistance, dissemination, and support; and technology development and media services; and

(4) to assess, and ensure the effectiveness of, efforts to educate children with disabilities.

Over time a number of advocacy groups have emerged that provide vital support for special needs students. Notable organizations include the Federation for Children with Special Needs (http://fcsn.org), which serves as an educational resource and community liaison for special needs students, and the Special Needs Alliance (http://www.specialneedsalliance.org), which provides legal counsel to special needs individuals and their families on a range of issues, including education.

Trends in the Number of Children Served

As Table 3.1 displays, approximately 6.4 million disabled children and youth aged three to 21 years were served during the 2012–13 academic year, compared with 3.7 million in 1976–77. Children with specific learning disabilities make up the category that includes the largest number of children served. During the 2012–13 academic year nearly 2.3 million students with specific learning disabilities, or 35.4% of all disabled students, were served in federally supported programs. That number was down considerably from 2000–01, when nearly 2.9 million students with specific disabilities (45.4% of all disabled students) participated in federal programs.

Children with speech or language impairment made up the category of disability that includes the next-largest number of children served, as shown in Table 3.1. In 2012–13 nearly 1.4 million students with speech or language impairments, or 21.1% of all special needs students, were served. This percentage was much lower than in 1976–77, when 35.2% of special needs students were identified as having speech or language impairments. In 2012–13 this category of special needs student accounted for 2.7% of all students enrolled in public school in grades prekindergarten to 12.

The number of autistic students served has grown dramatically in the 21st century. In 2000–01, 93,000 students with autism were served by special needs programs; by 2012–13, this figure had risen to 498,000, an increase of more than 535%. (See Table 3.1.) The proportion of students with autism also rose during this span, from 1.5% of all special needs students in 2000–01 to 7.8% of all special needs students in 2012–13. In 2012–13 autistic students made up 1% of all students enrolled in public school in grades prekindergarten to 12.

What Are Learning Disabilities?

As mentioned in the previous section, children with specific learning disabilities make up the category that

includes the greatest number of special needs children served. IDEA 2004 defines a *specific learning disability* as "a disorder in 1 or more of the basic psychological processes involved in understanding or in using language, spoken or written, which ... may manifest itself in the imperfect ability to listen, think, speak, read, write, spell, or do mathematical calculations."

In the category of specific learning disabilities, the law includes perceptual disabilities, brain injury, attention deficit disorder, dyslexia (a type of reading disability), and developmental aphasia (the inability to use words) as learning disabilities. The learning disability category does not include "a learning problem that is primarily the result of visual, hearing, or motor disabilities, of mental retardation, of emotional disturbance, or of environmental, cultural, or economic disadvantage." To be categorized as learning disabled, a student must also show a severe discrepancy between potential, as measured by intelligence quotient (IQ), and current ability level, as measured by achievement tests. A student who has problems in school and needs remedial education but does not fit into any other category may be labeled as having a learning disability.

Racial, Ethnic, and Geographic Characteristics of Special Education Students

As the National Center for Education Statistics (NCES) reports in *Digest of Education Statistics* (October 2014, https://nces.ed.gov/programs/digest/d14/tables/xls/tabn204.40.xls), over half (52.8%) of students aged three to 21 years who were being served under IDEA in 2012–13 were non-Hispanic white. A little over one-fifth (21.9%) were Hispanic and slightly under one-fifth (18.5%) were non-Hispanic African American. The percentages served of Asian or Pacific Islander students was 2.6% and of Native American or Alaskan Native students was 1.4%.

Table 3.2 provides a breakdown of students served under IDEA by state. Massachusetts had the highest proportion of students served under IDEA in 2012–13, with 17.4% of all public school students between the ages of three and 21 years served by the law. Other states with substantial proportions of students served by IDEA that year included Maine (17.3% of all public school students) and Rhode Island (17%). States with low proportions of public school students served under IDEA in 2012–13 included Texas (8.7%), Idaho (9.5%), and Colorado (10.3%).

Individualized Education Programs

The original Education for All Handicapped Children Act of 1975 provided for the development of an individualized education program (IEP) for each child who receives special education services, and the IEP concept was incorporated into the IDEA laws that followed,

TABLE 3.1

Students aged 3–21 served in federally supported programs for the disabled, by type of disability, selected years 1976–77 to 2012–13

Type of disability	1976–77	1980–81	1990–91	2000–01	2005–06	2009–10	2011–12	2012–13
				Number served (in thousands)				
All disabilities	**3,694**	**4,144**	**4,710**	**6,296**	**6,718**	**6,481**	**6,401**	**6,429**
Autism	—	—	—	93	223	378	455	498
Deaf-blindness	—	3	1	1	2	2	2	1
Developmental delay	—	—	—	213	339	368	393	402
Emotional disturbance	283	347	389	480	477	407	373	362
Hearing impairment	88	79	58	77	79	79	78	77
Intellectual disability	961	830	534	624	556	463	435	430
Multiple disabilities	—	68	96	131	141	131	132	133
Orthopedic impairment	87	58	49	82	71	65	61	59
Other health impairment[a]	141	98	55	303	570	689	743	779
Preschool disabled[b]	†	†	390	†	†	†	†	†
Specific learning disability	796	1,462	2,129	2,860	2,740	2,431	2,303	2,277
Speech or language impairment	1,302	1,168	985	1,388	1,468	1,416	1,373	1,356
Traumatic brain injury	—	—	—	16	24	25	26	26
Visual impairment	38	31	23	29	29	29	28	28
				Percentage distribution of children served				
All disabilities	**100.0**	**100.0**	**100.0**	**100.0**	**100.0**	**100.0**	**100.0**	**100.0**
Autism	—	—	—	1.5	3.3	5.8	7.1	7.8
Deaf-blindness	—	0.1	#	#	#	#	#	#
Developmental delay	—	—	—	3.4	5.0	5.7	6.1	6.2
Emotional disturbance	7.7	8.4	8.3	7.6	7.1	6.3	5.8	5.6
Hearing impairment	2.4	1.9	1.2	1.2	1.2	1.2	1.2	1.2
Intellectual disability	26.0	20.0	11.3	9.9	8.3	7.1	6.8	6.7
Multiple disabilities	—	1.6	2.0	2.1	2.1	2.0	2.1	2.1
Orthopedic impairment	2.4	1.4	1.0	1.3	1.1	1.0	1.0	0.9
Other health impairment[a]	3.8	2.4	1.2	4.8	8.5	10.6	11.6	12.1
Preschool disabled[b]	†	†	8.3	†	†	†	†	†
Specific learning disability	21.5	35.3	45.2	45.4	40.8	37.5	36.0	35.4
Speech or language impairment	35.2	28.2	20.9	22.0	21.8	21.8	21.4	21.1
Traumatic brain injury	—	—	—	0.2	0.4	0.4	0.4	0.4
Visual impairment	1.0	0.7	0.5	0.5	0.4	0.4	0.4	0.4
				Number served as a percent of total enrollment[c]				
All disabilities	**8.3**	**10.1**	**11.4**	**13.3**	**13.7**	**13.1**	**12.9**	**12.9**
Autism	—	—	—	0.2	0.5	0.8	0.9	1.0
Deaf-blindness	—	#	#	#	#	#	#	#
Developmental delay	—	—	—	0.5	0.7	0.7	0.8	0.8
Emotional disturbance	0.6	0.8	0.9	1.0	1.0	0.8	0.8	0.7
Hearing impairment	0.2	0.2	0.1	0.2	0.2	0.2	0.2	0.2
Intellectual disability	2.2	2.0	1.3	1.3	1.1	0.9	0.9	0.9
Multiple disabilities	—	0.2	0.2	0.3	0.3	0.3	0.3	0.3
Orthopedic impairment	0.2	0.1	0.1	0.2	0.1	0.1	0.1	0.1
Other health impairment[a]	0.3	0.2	0.1	0.6	1.2	1.4	1.5	1.6
Preschool disabled[b]	†	†	0.9	†	†	†	†	†
Specific learning disability	1.8	3.6	5.2	6.1	5.6	4.9	4.7	4.6
Speech or language impairment	2.9	2.9	2.4	2.9	3.0	2.9	2.8	2.7
Traumatic brain injury	—	—	—	#	#	0.1	0.1	0.1
Visual impairment	0.1	0.1	0.1	0.1	0.1	0.1	0.1	0.1

—Not available.

†Not applicable.

#Rounds to zero.

[a]Other health impairments include having limited strength, vitality, or alertness due to chronic or acute health problems such as a heart condition, tuberculosis, rheumatic fever, nephritis, asthma, sickle cell anemia, hemophilia, epilepsy, lead poisoning, leukemia, or diabetes.

[b]For 1990–91, preschool children are not included in the counts by disability condition but are separately reported. For other years, preschool children are included in the counts by disability condition.

[c]Based on the total enrollment in public schools, prekindergarten through 12th grade.

Note: Prior to October 1994, children and youth with disabilities were served under Chapter 1 of the Elementary and Secondary Education Act as well as under the Individuals with Disabilities Education Act (IDEA), Part B. Data reported in this table for years prior to 1994–95 include children ages 0–21 served under Chapter 1. Data are for the 50 states and the District of Columbia only. Increases since 1987–88 are due in part to new legislation enacted in fall 1986, which added a mandate for public school special education services for 3- to 5-year-old children with disabilities. Detail may not sum to totals because of rounding.

SOURCE: Adapted from "Table 204.30. Children 3 to 21 Years Old Served under Individuals with Disabilities Education Act (IDEA), Part B, by Type of Disability: Selected Years, 1976–77 through 2012–13," in "Most Current Digest Tables," *Digest of Education Statistics*, U.S. Department of Education, Institute of Education Sciences, National Center for Education Statistics, October 2014, https://nces.ed.gov/programs/digest/d14/tables/xls/tabn204.30.xls (accessed July 21, 2015)

including IDEA 2004. An IEP must include a statement of the student's current performance as well as short-term objectives and long-term (annual) goals. It must also describe the nature and duration of the instructional services that have been designed to meet the goals. Finally, it must describe the methods of evaluation that will be used

TABLE 3.2

Number and percentage of children aged 3–21 served under the Individuals with Disabilities Education Act, by age group and state, selected years 1990–91 to 2012–13

State or jurisdiction	3- to 21-year-olds served						As a percent of public school enrollment, 2012–13*	Percent change in number served, 2000–01 to 2012–13	3- to 5-year-olds served					
	1990–91	2000–01	2005–06	2010–11	2011–12	2012–13			1990–91	2000–01	2005–06	2010–11	2011–12	2012–13
United States	**4,710,089**	**6,295,816**	**6,712,605**	**6,434,916**	**6,401,238**	**6,429,331**	**12.9**	**2.1**	**389,751**	**592,087**	**698,608**	**723,738**	**730,558**	**735,890**
Alabama	94,601	99,828	92,635	82,286	80,149	79,705	10.7	-20.2	7,154	7,554	8,218	7,492	7,355	7,344
Alaska	14,390	17,691	17,997	18,048	18,055	17,959	13.7	1.5	1,458	1,637	2,082	2,104	2,166	2,116
Arizona	56,629	96,442	124,504	125,816	127,198	128,281	11.8	33.0	4,330	9,144	14,062	14,756	15,235	15,386
Arkansas	47,187	62,222	67,314	64,881	64,790	64,698	13.3	4.0	4,626	9,376	10,286	13,034	13,275	12,789
California	468,420	645,287	676,318	672,174	679,269	688,346	10.9	6.7	39,627	57,651	66,653	72,404	73,720	75,285
Colorado	56,336	78,715	83,498	84,710	87,233	89,280	10.3	13.4	4,128	8,202	10,540	11,797	12,348	12,799
Connecticut	63,886	73,886	71,968	68,167	68,280	69,730	12.7	-5.6	5,466	7,172	7,881	7,933	7,956	8,025
Delaware	14,208	16,760	18,857	18,608	19,166	19,224	14.9	14.7	1,493	1,652	2,073	2,123	2,230	2,304
District of Columbia	6,290	10,559	11,738	11,947	12,536	12,585	16.5	19.2	411	374	507	957	1,431	1,550
Florida	234,509	367,335	398,916	368,808	358,922	354,352	13.2	-3.5	14,883	30,660	34,350	36,027	37,445	37,470
Georgia	101,762	171,292	197,596	177,544	179,423	185,037	10.9	8.0	7,098	16,560	20,728	15,911	16,539	17,395
Hawaii	12,705	23,951	21,963	19,716	19,605	19,696	10.7	-17.8	809	1,919	2,423	2,398	2,449	2,554
Idaho	21,703	29,174	29,021	27,388	26,864	27,086	9.5	-7.2	2,815	3,591	4,043	3,596	3,379	3,283
Illinois	236,060	297,316	323,444	302,830	292,956	292,430	14.1	-1.6	22,997	28,787	35,454	36,488	36,943	37,211
Indiana	112,949	156,320	177,826	166,073	164,147	168,815	16.2	8.0	7,243	15,101	19,228	18,725	18,172	18,476
Iowa	59,787	72,461	72,457	68,501	67,990	65,882	13.2	-9.1	5,421	5,580	6,118	7,378	7,467	7,109
Kansas	44,785	61,267	65,595	66,873	65,809	67,369	13.8	10.0	3,881	7,728	9,267	10,604	10,598	10,850
Kentucky	78,853	94,572	108,798	102,370	98,785	97,555	14.2	3.2	10,440	16,372	21,317	17,963	17,422	17,455
Louisiana	72,825	97,938	90,453	82,943	82,301	81,238	11.4	-17.1	6,703	9,957	10,597	10,427	11,206	11,209
Maine	27,987	35,633	36,522	32,261	32,078	32,194	17.3	-9.7	2,895	3,978	4,348	3,824	3,831	3,793
Maryland	88,017	112,077	110,959	103,490	103,563	103,429	12.0	-7.7	7,163	10,003	12,148	12,875	13,114	13,062
Massachusetts	149,743	162,216	162,654	167,526	166,236	166,437	17.4	2.6	12,141	14,328	15,195	16,662	16,491	16,583
Michigan	166,511	221,456	243,607	218,957	210,034	203,427	13.1	-8.1	14,547	19,937	24,290	23,183	21,086	20,831
Minnesota	79,013	109,880	116,511	122,850	123,353	123,785	14.6	12.7	8,646	11,522	13,402	15,076	15,361	15,289
Mississippi	60,872	62,281	68,099	64,038	64,334	64,860	13.1	4.1	5,642	6,944	8,319	10,191	10,498	10,244
Missouri	101,166	137,381	143,204	127,164	125,075	123,655	13.5	-10.0	4,100	11,307	15,268	15,891	15,984	16,040
Montana	16,955	19,313	19,259	16,761	16,032	16,450	11.5	-14.8	1,751	1,635	1,925	1,656	1,696	1,697
Nebraska	32,312	42,793	45,239	44,299	44,829	45,564	15.0	6.5	2,512	3,724	4,665	5,050	5,175	5,379
Nevada	18,099	38,160	47,794	48,148	49,117	50,332	11.3	31.9	1,401	3,676	5,492	6,947	7,598	8,047
New Hampshire	19,049	30,077	31,782	29,920	29,422	29,329	15.5	-2.5	1,468	2,387	2,902	3,135	3,158	3,227
New Jersey	178,870	221,715	249,385	232,002	223,935	232,317	16.9	4.8	14,741	16,361	19,329	17,073	16,925	17,954
New Mexico	36,000	52,256	50,322	46,628	46,555	46,498	13.7	-11.0	2,210	4,970	6,441	5,224	5,021	4,494
New York	307,366	441,333	447,422	454,542	452,319	450,794	16.6	2.1	26,266	51,665	58,297	64,923	64,082	65,031
North Carolina	122,942	173,067	192,820	185,107	187,767	190,098	12.5	9.8	10,516	17,361	20,543	18,433	18,787	18,665
North Dakota	12,294	13,652	13,883	13,170	13,093	13,234	13.1	-3.1	1,164	1,247	1,520	1,714	1,791	1,804
Ohio	205,440	237,643	266,447	259,454	259,064	255,953	14.8	7.7	12,487	18,664	22,702	22,454	23,904	23,401
Oklahoma	65,457	85,577	96,601	97,250	98,960	100,893	15.0	17.9	5,163	6,393	8,149	8,298	8,480	8,500
Oregon	54,422	75,204	77,376	81,050	81,718	82,183	14.0	9.3	2,854	6,926	8,167	9,392	9,913	10,052
Pennsylvania	214,254	242,655	288,733	295,080	294,963	295,502	16.8	21.8	17,982	21,477	25,964	31,072	32,722	33,041
Rhode Island	20,646	30,727	30,681	25,332	24,826	24,165	17.0	-21.4	1,682	2,614	2,815	2,945	2,984	2,910
South Carolina	77,367	105,922	110,219	100,289	99,624	99,530	13.5	-6.0	7,948	11,775	11,603	11,083	10,862	10,626
South Dakota	14,726	16,825	17,631	18,026	18,005	18,316	14.0	8.9	2,105	2,286	2,747	2,738	2,726	2,659
Tennessee	104,853	125,863	122,122	120,263	124,070	127,407	12.8	1.2	7,487	10,699	12,008	13,096	13,381	13,067
Texas	344,529	491,642	507,405	442,019	439,675	439,635	8.7	-10.6	24,848	36,442	40,236	41,494	40,756	43,981
Utah	46,606	53,921	60,526	70,278	71,233	78,270	12.8	45.2	3,424	5,785	7,462	8,990	8,856	9,890
Vermont	12,160	13,623	13,917	13,936	13,833	13,873	15.5	1.8	1,097	1,237	1,556	1,762	1,752	1,831
Virginia	112,072	162,212	174,640	162,338	161,198	161,498	12.8	-0.4	9,892	14,444	17,480	17,081	16,677	16,611
Washington	83,545	118,851	124,498	127,978	129,346	130,778	12.4	10.0	9,558	11,760	13,429	14,275	14,588	14,763
West Virginia	42,428	50,333	49,677	45,007	44,259	44,487	15.7	-11.6	2,923	5,445	5,833	5,607	5,488	5,483
Wisconsin	85,651	125,358	130,076	124,722	123,825	123,287	14.1	-1.7	10,934	14,383	16,077	16,079	16,106	16,325

TABLE 3.2

Number and percentage of children aged 3–21 served under the Individuals with Disabilities Education Act, by age group and state, selected years 1990–91 to 2012–13 [CONTINUED]

State or jurisdiction	3- to 21-year-olds served						As a percent of public school enrollment, 2012–13*	Percent change in number served, 2000–01 to 2012–13	3- to 5-year-olds served					
	1990–91	2000–01	2005–06	2010–11	2011–12	2012–13			1990–91	2000–01	2005–06	2010–11	2011–12	2012–13
Wyoming	10,852	13,154	13,696	15,348	15,419	11,883	13.0	−9.7	1,221	1,695	2,469	3,398	3,429	—
Bureau of Indian Education	6,997	8,448	7,795	6,801	—	6,504	—	−23.0	1,092	338	330	396	—	305
Other jurisdictions	**38,986**	**70,670**	**93,256**	**1,31,847**	**1,34,600**	**1,35,431**	**—**	**91.6**	**3,892**	**8,168**	**5,149**	**14,505**	**15,396**	**13,785**
American Samoa	363	697	1,211	935	932	870	—	33.7	48	48	80	142	161	102
Guam	1,750	2,267	2,480	2,003	2,013	2,017	6.5	−11.2	198	205	171	165	179	161
Northern Marianas	411	569	750	944	931	895	8.4	63.6	211	53	70	104	104	86
Palau	—	131	—	—	—	119	—	—	—	10	—	—	—	9
Puerto Rico	35,129	65,504	87,125	1,26,560	1,29,314	1,30,212	30.0	97.4	3,345	7,746	4,677	13,952	14,791	13,276
U.S. Virgin Islands	1,333	1,502	1,690	1,405	1,410	1,318	8.7	−6.1	90	106	151	142	161	151

—Not available.

*Based on the total enrollment in public schools, prekindergarten through 12th grade.

Note: Prior to October 1994, children and youth with disabilities were served under Chapter 1 of the Elementary and Secondary Education Act as well as under the Individuals with Disabilities Education Act. Data reported in this table for 1990–91 include children ages 0–21 served under Chapter 1.

SOURCE: "Table 204.70 Number and Percentage of Children Served under Individuals with Disabilities Education Act (IDEA), Part B, by Age Group and State or Jurisdiction: Selected Years, 1990–91 through 2012–13," in "Most Current DigestTables," *Digest of Education Statistics*, U.S. Department of Education, Institute of Education Sciences, National Center for Education Statistics, October 2014, https://nce.sed.gov/programs/digest/d14/tables/xls/tabn204.70.xls (accessed July 21, 2015)

to monitor the child's progress and to determine whether the objectives are being met.

Patrick Keaton of the NCES notes in *Documentation to the NCES Common Core of Data Local Education Agency Universe Survey: School Year 2010–11* (September 2012, http://nces.ed.gov/ccd/pdf/pau102agen.pdf) that during the 2010–11 academic year there were approximately 6.3 million students in the United States who had an IEP. Rhode Island had the highest percentage (17.6%) of students with an IEP, followed closely by Massachusetts (17.5%); Vermont had the lowest, at 8.6%. The average percentage of students across the United States who had an IEP was 12.8%.

Inclusive Education

Before the passage of the Education for All Handicapped Children Act of 1975, not all students with disabilities were educated, and those who were educated were often schooled at home, in special classrooms, or in special schools. This law not only required all school districts to develop and provide a free, appropriate public education for all children and youth with disabilities but also required all school districts to educate children with disabilities in the least restrictive environment possible. Although this law did not mandate that special needs children be educated in regular classrooms, it opened the door to such an educational approach.

Educating students with disabilities in regular classrooms is called inclusive education or mainstreaming. In most situations the special education student spends part of the day in the regular classroom and the rest of the day in a resource room with a special education teacher. There the student receives help in subjects such as reading or mathematics. Figure 3.1 shows how the percentage of students served under IDEA and who spend 80% or more of their time in general classes has increased, from 33% during the 1990–91 school year to 61% during the 2012–13 school year. Students served under IDEA who spend less than that amount of time in general classes decreased during this period. Those who spend 40% to 79% of their time in general classes decreased from 36% in 1990–91 to 20% in 2012–13. Those who spend less

FIGURE 3.1

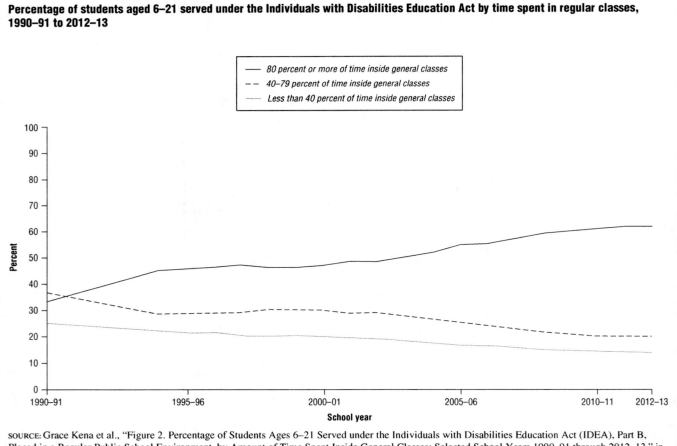

Percentage of students aged 6–21 served under the Individuals with Disabilities Education Act by time spent in regular classes, 1990–91 to 2012–13

SOURCE: Grace Kena et al., "Figure 2. Percentage of Students Ages 6–21 Served under the Individuals with Disabilities Education Act (IDEA), Part B, Placed in a Regular Public School Environment, by Amount of Time Spent Inside General Classes: Selected School Years 1990–91 through 2012–13," in *The Condition of Education 2015*, U.S. Department of Education, Institute of Education Sciences, National Center for Education Statistics, May 2015, http://nces.ed.gov/pubs2015/2015144.pdf (accessed July 21, 2015)

than 40% of their time in general classes decreased from about 25% in 1990–91 to 14% in 2010–11.

In 2012, 94.8% of disabled students aged six to 21 years participated in inclusive education programs, in which they received at least part of their educational and related services in school settings with nondisabled students. The remaining students received their educational and related services in separate public or private school facilities, in public or private residential facilities, at homes, in hospitals, or in correctional facilities. Of all special needs (disabled) students, 61.2% spent 80% or more of their time in regular classrooms in 2012. (See Table 3.3.) An additional 19.7% of disabled students received special education and related services while spending between 40% and 79% of the school day in regular classes. Another 13.9% spent less than 40% of the school day in regular classes.

Looking at individual disabilities helps show which students can be most easily included in regular classroom settings. In 2012, 86.8% of speech- or language-impaired children were educated primarily in regular classrooms, being in regular class 80% or more of the time. (See Table 3.3.) Nearly half or more of students with hearing impairments, orthopedic impairments, visual impairments, traumatic brain injuries, specific learning

disabilities, and developmental delays were educated primarily in regular classrooms as well. However, only 12.9% of students with multiple disabilities experienced inclusion most of the time.

Common Core State Standards and Special Needs

As special needs students have become increasingly integrated into mainstream classrooms, educators have attempted to introduce new academic expectations for students served under IDEA. During the first decade of the 21st century, the National Governors Association, in collaboration with the Council of Chief State School Officers, set out to create new national standards for the instruction of mathematics and English language arts. The result of this initiative, the Common Core State Standards, was officially released in 2010. The new guidelines included a set of provisions for measuring academic performance in special needs students. In "Application to Students with Disabilities" (2015, http://www.corestandards.org/assets/application-to-students-with-disabilities.pdf), the National Governors Association and Council of Chief State School Officers outline a set of academic goals for special need students who attend schools that follow Common Core standards. While the application acknowledges that special needs students will continue to receive specific

TABLE 3.3

Students with disabilities aged 6–21 receiving educational services, by educational environment and by type of disability, 2012

Type of disability	All environments	Regular school, time inside general class			Separate school for students with disabilities	Separate residential facility	Parentally placed in regular private schools[a]	Home-bound/ hospital placement	Correctional facility
		Less than 40 percent	40–79 percent	80 percent or more					
2012									
All students with disabilities	**100.0**	**13.9**	**19.7**	**61.2**	**3.0**	**0.3**	**1.2**	**0.4**	**0.3**
Autism	100.0	33.3	18.1	39.5	7.7	0.5	0.7	0.3	#
Deaf-blindness	100.0	34.7	11.4	21.0	19.8	8.2	1.5	2.7	0.7
Developmental delay	100.0	16.6	19.5	62.3	0.8	0.1	0.6	0.2	#
Emotional disturbance	100.0	20.4	17.8	44.0	13.0	1.8	0.2	1.1	1.7
Hearing impairment	100.0	12.6	16.4	57.6	8.3	3.4	1.4	0.2	0.1
Intellectual disability	100.0	49.1	27.0	16.5	6.1	0.4	0.3	0.5	0.2
Multiple disabilities	100.0	46.4	16.3	12.9	19.1	1.7	0.4	3.1	0.1
Orthopedic impairment	100.0	21.8	16.2	54.6	4.5	0.2	0.9	1.7	0.1
Other health impairment[b]	100.0	9.8	22.4	63.7	1.7	0.2	1.1	0.8	0.3
Specific learning disability	100.0	6.4	25.0	66.7	0.5	0.1	0.9	0.1	0.3
Speech or language impairment	100.0	4.3	5.4	86.8	0.3	#	3.0	#	#
Traumatic brain injury	100.0	20.1	22.4	49.0	5.3	0.6	0.8	1.8	0.1
Visual impairment	100.0	11.3	13.3	64.0	6.0	3.6	1.2	0.6	0.1

#Rounds to zero.

[a]Students who are enrolled by their parents or guardians in regular private schools and have their basic education paid through private resources, but receive special education services at public expense. These students are not included under "Regular school, time inside general class."

[b]Other health impairments include having limited strength, vitality, or alertness due to chronic or acute health problems such as a heart condition, tuberculosis, rheumatic fever, nephritis, asthma, sickle cell anemia, hemophilia, epilepsy, lead poisoning, leukemia, or diabetes.

Note: Data are for the 50 states, the District of Columbia, and the Bureau of Indian Education schools. Detail may not sum to totals because of rounding.

SOURCE: Adapted from "Table 204.60. Percentage Distribution of Students 6 to 21 Years Old Served under Individuals with Disabilities Education Act (IDEA), Part B, by Educational Environment and Type of Disability: Selected Years, Fall 1989 through Fall 2012," in "Most Current Digest Tables," *Digest of Education Statistics*, U.S. Department of Education, Institute of Education Sciences, National Center for Education Statistics, October 2014, https://nces.ed.gov/programs/digest/d14/tables/xls/tabn204.60.xls (accessed July 21, 2015)

"accommodations and supports" in order to keep pace with their peers, it also asserts that students served under IDEA "must be challenged to excel within the general curriculum and be prepared for success in their post-school lives." By 2015, 42 states and the District of Columbia had adopted Common Core.

Despite this effort to challenge students with disabilities to achieve high academic standards, some critics maintained that the Common Core failed to address the unique educational needs of students served under IDEA. As Katharine Beals writes in "The Common Core Is Tough on Kids with Special Needs" (Atlantic.com, February 21, 2014), the Common Core fell short of providing adequate supports and accommodations for certain groups of special needs students, notably those suffering from severe cognitive disabilities. In particular, Beals criticizes the Common Core for requiring special needs students to read the same texts as students without disabilities, even when cognitive impairments might impede a special needs student's ability to comprehend certain vocabulary or syntax. Beals asserts that the Common Core's fundamental goal, to achieve "success for all students," must take account of the "cognitive diversity" of certain members of the classroom. As Beals concludes, such a measure of success is not "so easily standardized."

In order to confront this challenge, educators have continued to explore ways to adapt academic standards to address the specific needs of students served under IDEA. In "Top 10 Trends in Special Education" (Sci-Learn.com, January 6, 2015), Will J. Gordillo discusses several possible approaches to achieving broader inclusivity for special needs students. Among the proposals outlined by Gordillo include the establishment of a multi-tiered system of support, one based on "specially designed instruction," in order to evaluate and educate special needs students with greater flexibility and precision. At the same time, Gordillo suggests that new technologies will play a vital role in improving special education programs, allowing students with disabilities to use electronic devices that cater to their specific needs while they are in the classroom. Perhaps most important, Gordillo writes, educators must focus on implementing "evidence-based practices and interventions" that will enable students with IEPs to meet the academic standards established by the Common Core.

Exiting from Special Education

The Office of Special Education Programs within the U.S. Department of Education has been collecting data since the 1984–85 academic year on special needs students aged 14 years and older who leave the education system. These data are presented for the 2011–12 academic year in Table 3.4. During that academic year, 386,385 disabled students aged 14 to 21 years exited school. Of this number, 247,763 (64.1%) exiting students with disabilities graduated with diplomas; 53,575 (13.9%) received attendance certificates; 5,505 (1.4%) reached the maximum age for services, which varies by state; and 77,986 (20.2%) dropped out, which includes students who may have moved. A small percentage (0.4%, or 1,556) died.

GIFTED AND TALENTED STUDENTS

For more than a century, researchers, scientists, and educators have tried to define the term *gifted*. Historically, the term was closely associated with the concept of genius. After IQ tests were developed, students who scored extremely well were considered geniuses and gifted. In the 21st century some observers criticize the use of IQ tests as the single measure of intelligence. They believe the tests are biased in favor of white, middle- and upper-class individuals and penalize those from different cultural backgrounds. Also, many researchers and educators believe giftedness is more than high intellectual ability. It also involves creativity, memory, motivation, physical dexterity, social adeptness, and aesthetic sensitivity—qualities that reflect particular talents or skills that can help make a student successful in life, but are not measured by IQ tests.

Howard Gardner of the Harvard Graduate School of Education challenges long-held ideas about intelligence and IQ in the landmark book *Frames of Mind: The Theory of Multiple Intelligences* (1993). He identifies seven intelligences:

- Linguistic—the ability to employ language as a means of understanding and expressing complex ideas

- Logical-mathematical—a proficiency with mathematical concepts and abstract thought

- Musical—a talent for distinguishing elements of music such as pitch, tone, and timbre

- Spatial—the ability to imagine and analyze three-dimensional imagery

- Bodily-kinesthetic—the ability to link thought with physical activity, as exemplified in an athlete or dancer

- Interpersonal—a skill for communicating with others

- Intrapersonal—a knowledge of the self, particularly emotions and qualities of empathy

Gardner has since identified two more intelligences: naturalist (a sensitivity to aspects of the physical world) and existential (a capacity for pondering deep metaphysical questions). Gardner suggests that there is not one type of intelligence, such as measured by IQ tests, but that several types of intelligence exist and work together within the individual. He asserts that multiple intelligences explain

TABLE 3.4

Number and percentage distributions of students with disabilities aged 14–21 exiting special education, by exit reason, age, and disability type, 2011–12

| Year, age, and type of disability | Total | Exiting school | | | | | Transferred to regular education[c] | Moved, known to be continuing[d] |
		Graduated with diploma	Received a certificate of attendance	Reached maximum age[a]	Dropped out[b]	Died		
2011–12								
Total number	386,385	247,763	53,575	5,505	77,986	1,556	64,063	174,960
Percentage distribution of total	100.0	64.1	13.9	1.4	20.2	0.4	†	†
Number by age								
14	—	—	—	†	—	—	—	—
15	—	—	—	†	—	—	—	—
16	—	—	—	†	—	—	—	—
17	—	—	—	†	—	—	—	—
18	—	—	—	—	—	—	—	—
19	—	—	—	—	—	—	—	—
20	—	—	—	—	—	—	—	—
21	—	—	—	—	—	—	—	—
Number by type of disability								
Autism	16,714	10,802	3,791	840	1,217	64	1,815	4,947
Deaf-blindness	82	39	15	12	12	4	6	27
Emotional disturbance	40,634	20,909	3,671	362	15,538	154	6,050	32,485
Hearing impairment	4,692	3,443	696	60	479	14	726	1,504
Intellectual disability	37,989	15,421	13,248	2,163	6,914	243	2,176	14,098
Multiple disabilities	8,669	4,220	2,118	708	1,363	260	334	3,038
Orthopedic impairment	3,731	2,305	731	183	422	90	502	1,181
Other health impairment[e]	54,117	37,868	5,431	268	10,270	280	9,688	24,977
Specific learning disability	205,606	142,240	22,352	760	39,850	404	33,695	87,031
Speech or language impairment	9,815	7,365	907	49	1,483	11	8,682	4,625
Traumatic brain injury	2,583	1,771	412	60	319	21	204	671
Visual impairment	1,727	1,337	220	40	119	11	185	453

—Not available.

†Not applicable.

[a]Students may exit special education services due to maximum age beginning at age 18, depending on state law or practice or order of any court.

[b]"Dropped out" is defined as the total who were enrolled at some point in the reporting year, were not enrolled at the end of the reporting year, and did not exit for any of the other reasons described. Includes students previously categorized as "moved, not known to continue."

[c]"Transferred to regular education" was previously labeled "no longer receives special education."

[d]"Moved, known to be continuing" is the total number of students who moved out of the administrative area or transferred to another district and are known to be continuing in an educational program.

[e]Other health impairments include having limited strength, vitality, or alertness due to chronic or acute health problems such as a heart condition, tuberculosis, rheumatic fever, nephritis, asthma, sickle cell anemia, hemophilia, epilepsy, lead poisoning, leukemia, or diabetes.

Note: Data are for the 50 states, the District of Columbia, and the Bureau of Indian Education schools. Detail may not sum to totals because of rounding.

SOURCE: Adapted from "Table 219.90. Number and Percentage Distribution of 14- through 21-Year-Old Students Served under Individuals with Disabilities Education Act (IDEA), Part B, Who Exited School, by Exit Reason, Age, and Type of Disability: 2010–11 and 2011–12," in "Most Current Digest Tables," *Digest of Education Statistics*, U.S. Department of Education, Institute of Education Sciences, National Center for Education Statistics, November 2014, https://nces.ed.gov/programs/digest/d14/tables/xls/tabn219.90.xls (accessed July 21, 2015)

---

how and why people learn in ways different from one another and have different skills and talents.

In "Assumptions Underlying the Identification of Gifted and Talented Students" (*Gifted Child Quarterly*, vol. 49, no. 1, Winter 2005), Scott W. Brown et al. suggest that the traditional view that a student was either gifted or not gifted is inconsistent with current research. They posit that "varying degrees of gifted behaviors [can] be developed in certain people at certain times under certain circumstances." The researchers conclude that "almost total reliance on test scores" to determine giftedness is no longer appropriate and that "the research in favor of a more flexible approach is so overwhelming that it no longer needs to be argued."

Joseph S. Renzulli, the director of the National Research Center on the Gifted and Talented at the University of Connecticut, explains in "A Practical System for Identifying Gifted and Talented Students" (January 8, 2009, http://www.gifted.uconn.edu/sem/semart04.html) that he has developed a research-based system for identifying gifted and talented students. The interlocking three-ring conception of giftedness considers well-above-average ability as well as creativity and task commitment.

There is no federal legislation requiring states to provide special education to gifted and talented students. Therefore, states make their own decisions as to the education of those who are identified as gifted and talented, and most have developed their own definitions of gifted and talented students. Many states base their definition on one that was developed by a team of people in 1972 for the U.S. commissioner of education Sidney Marland (1914–1992) or from the updated, yet similar, 1993 definition from the Department of Education.

The Marland definition, as it has become known, identified gifted and talented children as those with demonstrated achievement or potential in the areas of general intellectual ability, specific academic aptitude, creative or productive thinking, leadership ability, visual and performing artistic talent, and psychomotor ability. The updated Department of Education definition was released in *National Excellence: A Case for Developing America's Talent* (October 1993, https://www.ocps.net/cs/ese/programs/gifted/Documents/National%20Excellence_%20A%20Case%20for%20Developing%20America's%20Talent_%20Introduction.pdf) and contains some phrasing from the Marland definition. It describes gifted and talented qualities as:

> Children and youth with outstanding talent perform or show the potential for performing at remarkably high levels of accomplishment when compared with others of their age, experience, or environment.

> These children and youth exhibit high performance capability in intellectual, creative, and/or artistic areas, possess an unusual leadership capacity, or excel in specific academic fields. They require services or activities not ordinarily provided by the schools.

> Outstanding talents are present in children and youth from all cultural groups, across all economic strata, and in all areas of human endeavor.

DISADVANTAGED STUDENTS

Disadvantaged students include children from families with very low incomes; children who are linguistically isolated or have limited English proficiency, usually because they are members of immigrant families; and children who change schools frequently (for example, children of seasonal farm workers or homeless parents).

Title I Funding

Title I is the major federal program that provides funding for remedial education programs for disadvantaged children in public schools and in some private programs. Title I originated as part of the Elementary and Secondary Education Act of 1965 and was amended by the Improving America's Schools Act of 1994. It is now part of the No Child Left Behind Act of 2001, which reauthorized the Elementary and Secondary Education Act.

States and school districts can apply for Title I funds for a variety of programs that are aimed at improving the performance of disadvantaged students. Title I funds are allocated to states and school districts on a formula basis, but states with higher numbers of poor, immigrant, and/or migrant students are typically eligible for, apply for, and receive more federal funds.

In *Selected Statistics from the Public Elementary and Secondary Education Universe: School Year 2012–13* (October 2014, http://nces.ed.gov/pubs2014/2014098.pdf), Keaton notes that during the 2012–13 academic year there were 68,140 Title I–eligible schools in the nation. (See Table 3.5 under "Title I"; "Title I schoolwide" is a subset of Title I schools and has a higher percentage of Title I–eligible students than other Title I schools.) During the 2012–13 academic year California had the most Title I–eligible schools (7,155), followed by Texas (6,970).

Appropriations for Title I in fiscal year (FY) 2014 were $15.3 billion, up from $14.7 billion in FY 2013. (See Table 3.6.) Combined, California ($1.9 billion), Texas ($1.4 billion), and New York ($1.1 billion) accounted for 29% of the available Title I funding in FY 2014. By contrast, the five states receiving the least amount of Title I funding in FY 2014—New Hampshire ($45 million), South Dakota ($44.5 million), Wyoming ($36 million), Vermont ($35.5 million), and North Dakota ($34.7 million)—together received only 1.3% of available Title I funding.

Table 3.6 also shows the relative funding for various Title I programs. Roughly 94.1% ($14.4 billion) of the Title I funding for FY 2014 went to local education agencies, which are school districts. Put simply, the Title I monies primarily funded schools' requests for resources for remedial education programs for disadvantaged children in their district. The remaining 5.9% funded particular programs, such as state-run programs for neglected and delinquent children or for children of migrant workers; the Even Start Program, which offers grants to support local family literacy projects; and Turnaround grants, which provide money for school districts that are committed to improving their low-performing schools.

LEP Students

Students with limited English proficiency (LEP) are those for whom English is not their first language, and they cannot speak English well or at all. They are served by English as a second language (ESL) programs, which are sometimes known as English language learner (ELL) programs. The primary purpose of ESL programs is to teach students English so they can be taught and learn in English. These programs are funded by a variety of state and federal sources, including Title I funds. According to Keaton, in *Documentation to the NCES Common Core of Data Local Education Agency Universe Survey*, during the 2010–11 academic year there were just under 3 million (6% of all public school students) students in the United States receiving ELL services.

TABLE 3.5

Number of operating public elementary and secondary schools, by school type, 2012–13

State or jurisdiction	Total number of operating schools[a]	School type				Charter	Magnet[b]	Title I[c]	Title I schoolwide[c]
		Regular	Special education	Vocational education	Alternative education				
Reporting states[d]	98,454	89,031	2,034	1,403	5,986	6,079	3,151	68,140	51,529
Alabama	1,637	1,402	44	72	119	†	32	906	884
Alaska	509	436	3	3	67	27	17	367	347
Arizona	2,267	1,955	22	225	65	542	19	1,794	1,318
Arkansas	1,102	1,061	4	26	11	45	38	938	867
California	10,315	8,786	149	87	1,293	1,085	421	7,155	5,295
Colorado	1,825	1,725	7	6	87	187	25	658	493
Connecticut	1,148	1,035	47	16	50	17	69	572	218
Delaware	224	191	21	6	6	22	3	183	175
District of Columbia	230	208	7	3	12	102	34	180	175
Florida	4,269	3,609	185	51	424	581	494	2,697	2,587
Georgia	2,387	2,253	59	1	74	93	86	1,575	1,478
Hawaii	286	284	1	0	1	32	†	228	210
Idaho	719	629	11	10	69	47	19	570	517
Illinois	4,266	3,978	140	0	148	58	108	3,330	1,734
Indiana	1,925	1,860	29	27	9	72	32	1,497	1,194
Iowa	1,390	1,354	6	0	30	3	†	960	548
Kansas	1,351	1,338	10	1	2	16	33	1,057	858
Kentucky	1,568	1,301	6	126	135	†	42	1,116	1,069
Louisiana	1,407	1,218	28	9	152	104	77	1,181	1,139
Maine	617	587	3	27	0	2	1	529	398
Maryland	1,449	1,327	39	26	57	52	92	385	337
Massachusetts	1,854	1,774	21	39	20	77	—	1,053	547
Michigan	3,550	3,057	193	6	294	346	435	2,347	1,475
Minnesota	2,403	1,626	279	11	487	176	82	867	322
Mississippi	1,063	908	4	90	61	0	17	721	710
Missouri	2,406	2,173	64	64	105	57	29	1,842	1,503
Montana	824	818	2	0	4	†	†	708	424
Nebraska	1,090	1,011	26	0	53	†	†	498	356
Nevada	664	599	12	1	52	40	37	171	168
New Hampshire	481	481	0	0	0	22	†	419	137
New Jersey	2,598	2,360	59	62	117	86	—	1,640	478
New Mexico	877	829	8	1	39	94	2	782	752
New York	4,822	4,644	123	29	26	211	†	4,429	1,927
North Carolina	2,557	2,444	25	7	81	108	106	2,120	2,004
North Dakota	517	472	33	12	0	†	†	275	109
Ohio	3,685	3,555	54	70	6	368	†	2,935	2,709
Oklahoma	1,784	1,776	4	0	4	23	†	1,251	1,114
Oregon	1,251	1,211	2	0	38	123	†	574	466
Pennsylvania	3,127	3,021	8	87	11	175	46	2,372	1,525
Rhode Island	304	285	2	12	5	18	†	228	137
South Carolina	1,239	1,166	10	42	21	55	100	1,054	1,013
South Dakota	697	651	9	3	34	†	†	615	360
Tennessee	1,817	1,764	16	16	21	51	132	1,504	1,439
Texas	8,731	7,710	22	0	999	628	242	6,970	6,707
Utah	995	897	69	3	26	88	23	297	217
Vermont	318	302	0	15	1	†	2	241	189
Virginia	2,182	1,874	54	58	196	4	136	740	503
Washington	2,370	1,932	98	18	322	†	†	1,579	1,326
West Virginia	755	692	3	30	30	†	†	338	336
Wisconsin	2,238	2,125	10	5	98	238	4	1,519	639
Wyoming	364	337	3	0	24	4	†	173	96
Department of Defense dependents schools, Bureau of Indian Education, and other jurisdictions									
Department of Defense (DoDEA)	191	191	0	0	0	—	—	—	—
Bureau of Indian Education	174	174	0	0	0	†	—	169	169
American Samoa	28	27	0	1	0	—	—	—	—
Guam	39	39	0	0	0	—	—	—	—
Commonwealth of the Northern Mariana Islands	29	29	0	0	0	†	†	0	0
Puerto Rico	1,457	1,395	23	30	9	†	†	1,439	1,356
U.S. Virgin Islands	31	30	0	1	0	†	1	—	—

Migrant Children

With frequent moves and usually limited English skills, migrant children are at high risk for developing school-related problems. They often live in substandard housing and are frequently poor and alienated from other children at school. They may experience exposure to harmful agricultural chemicals and receive inadequate health care. These factors can make getting an education

TABLE 3.5

Number of operating public elementary and secondary schools, by school type, 2012–13 [CONTINUED]

—Not available.
† Not applicable. Some states/jurisdictions do not have charter school authorization and some states/jurisdictions do not designate magnet schools.
‡ Reporting standards not met. Data missing for more than 20 percent of schools in the state or jurisdiction.
aTotal number of operating schools excludes schools also reported by the Bureau of Indian Education (BIE). The number of operating schools shared with the BIE includes two in Arizona, one in Michigan, and eight in North Dakota.
bMassachusetts and New Jersey have magnet schools but were not able to provide data that indicate the magnet status of each school.
cSchools eligible for Title I schoolwide programs are also included in the count of all Title I eligible schools. A Title I eligible school is one in which the percentage of children from low-income families is at least 35 percent of children from low-income families served by the local education agency (LEA) as a whole. A schoolwide Title I eligible school has a percentage of low-income students that is at least 40 percent.
dA reporting states total is shown if data for any item in the table were missing for some, but reported for at least 85 percent of all schools in the United States.
Note: Every school is assigned only one school type based on its instructional emphasis. Independent of school type, every school is assigned a separate charter status, magnet status, and Title 1 status. Numbers and types of schools may differ from those published by states.

SOURCE: Patrick Keaton, "Table 3. Number of Operating Public Elementary and Secondary Schools, by School Type, Charter, Magnet, Title I, and Title I Schoolwide Status, and State or Jurisdiction: School Year 2012–13," in *Selected Statistics from the Public Elementary and Secondary Education Universe: School Year 2012–13*, U.S. Department of Education, Institute of Education Sciences, National Center for Education Statistics, October 2014, http://nces.ed.gov/pubs2014/2014098.pdf (accessed July 22, 2015)

---

difficult. The Title I Migrant Education Program (MEP), which was authorized under the Hawkins-Stafford Elementary and Secondary School Improvement Amendments of 1988, provides funding for state education agencies to meet the special needs of migrant children.

The term *migrant children* may refer to independent children who move often, perhaps from family to family, or to children of migrant workers who move frequently to secure jobs in the farming, fishing, timber, or dairy industries. The MEP serves current and former (for up to three years) migrant children aged three to 21 years. The MEP includes preschool services, testing, regular academic or remedial instruction, bilingual education, vocational education, guidance and counseling, and health services.

Jennifer Sable, Christopher Plotts, and Chen-Su Chen indicate in *Documentation to the NCES Common Core of Data Local Education Agency Universe Survey: School Year 2007–08* (August 2010, http://nces.ed.gov/ccd/pdf/pau071bgen.pdf), the most recent data available as of September 2015, that California (94,172) and Texas (10,246) had the largest numbers of students receiving migrant services during the 2007–08 school year—well beyond those of any other state that had data available. The states with the fewest numbers of students receiving migrant services during the 2007–08 school year were Delaware (40), Nevada (41), and Maryland (137). Many states had no data available.

Homeless Children

The McKinney-Vento Homeless Assistance Act of 1986, which was reauthorized under the No Child Left Behind Act of 2001, provides funding to facilitate the enrollment, attendance, and success in school of homeless children and youth. The law also requires school districts to keep students in the same school, which the parents can choose, even if the family is not located in that district and even when the parents move to various

temporary housing situations, such as the homes of relatives or friends, homeless shelters, hotels/motels, or unsheltered situations. In addition, the school district must provide free transportation to school for the student if needed. This act also ensures children free breakfast and lunch at school.

The National Center for Homeless Education reports in *Education for Homeless Children and Youth (EHCY) Program Profile* (January 2015, http://center.serve.org/nche/downloads/ehcy_profile.pdf) that more than 1.2 million homeless students attended U.S. schools in 2012–13. Of these, three-quarters (75%) regularly slept in "doubled-up" households, or households consisting of more than one family; another 16% slept in homeless shelters, and 6% were residing in motels or hotels. In 2012–13, 3% of all homeless students had no access to shelter. Homelessness puts students at a clear disadvantage in the classroom. According to the National Association for the Education of Homeless Children and Youth (NAEHCY), in *Homelessness through the Eyes of Children: A Special Needs Perspective* (November 2013, http://www.naehcy.org/sites/default/files/dl/conf-2013/h1/popp-sped-intro.pptx), 21% of all homeless students repeat a grade in school because of excessive absences, compared with 5% of students who are not homeless.

At the same time, the emotional and psychological strain of living without reliable shelter can take a toll on a homeless student's ability to learn. In "Improving Special Education Services for Homeless Students with Disabilities" (*The American Almanac of Family Homelessness 2013*, http://www.icphusa.org/index.asp?page=55&americanalmanac=2&story=85&pg=348), the Institute for Children, Poverty & Homelessness reports that only 21.5% of homeless elementary students demonstrated proficiency in math during the 2009–10 school year, compared to 39.6% of their housed classmates. A more dramatic gap existed in high school, with only 11.4% of homeless secondary school students

TABLE 3.6

Title I appropriations, by program and state, 2013 and 2014

[In thousands of current dollars]

State or jurisdiction	Title I total, 2013	Title I, 2014 Total	Grants to local education agencies[a]	State agency programs Neglected and delinquent	Migrant	Turnaround grants	Assessing achievement, 2014	Improving teacher quality state grants, 2014
1	2	3	4	5	6	7	8	9
Total, 50 states and D.C.[b]	$14,036,475	$14,670,761	$13,796,419	$45,801	$364,751	$463,789	$359,992	$2,196,200
Total, 50 states, D.C., other activities, and other jurisdictions	14,686,340	15,306,917	14,378,796	47,614	374,751	505,756	378,000	2,348,898
Alabama	225,529	231,483	221,466	678	2,038	7,301	6,138	36,401
Alaska	46,353	47,015	38,380	274	6,895	1,467	3,511	10,864
Arizona	329,674	343,741	325,037	1,541	6,506	10,658	7,566	35,624
Arkansas	157,668	169,704	158,732	437	5,218	5,317	4,992	22,098
California	1,727,173	1,879,397	1,689,214	1,565	128,658	59,960	28,691	255,264
Colorado	152,054	165,061	152,377	458	6,965	5,261	6,479	25,582
Connecticut	112,738	120,110	115,076	1,220	0	3,814	5,287	21,636
Delaware	44,783	46,329	44,036	555	289	1,448	3,567	10,864
District of Columbia	45,653	44,788	43,228	168	0	1,392	3,272	10,864
Florida	751,054	828,405	777,790	1,489	22,495	26,631	14,361	103,321
Georgia	506,861	534,297	508,022	1,594	7,809	16,872	10,018	60,114
Hawaii	50,528	56,130	53,163	361	794	1,812	3,834	10,864
Idaho	59,646	64,157	58,158	422	3,532	2,045	4,211	10,899
Illinois	653,520	671,485	646,908	1,203	1,887	21,488	11,571	93,923
Indiana	262,763	274,461	259,785	527	5,437	8,712	7,490	38,966
Iowa	88,449	89,682	84,913	349	1,591	2,829	5,040	17,870
Kansas	111,858	121,697	106,047	368	11,413	3,871	5,018	18,313
Kentucky	226,133	237,193	221,318	1,058	7,310	7,508	5,848	35,960
Louisiana	293,035	305,595	291,923	1,700	2,443	9,529	6,101	52,193
Maine	51,870	55,009	51,908	209	1,156	1,735	3,756	10,864
Maryland	190,390	205,842	197,275	1,435	500	6,632	6,766	33,300
Massachusetts	215,360	224,142	213,005	2,397	1,591	7,148	6,963	41,942
Michigan	537,523	547,089	521,188	795	8,459	16,647	9,444	91,567
Minnesota	152,797	152,302	145,020	418	2,046	4,817	6,590	31,295
Mississippi	184,137	194,567	186,626	905	1,024	6,012	5,077	34,127
Missouri	235,151	248,856	238,060	1,539	1,499	7,758	6,934	39,564
Montana	45,562	47,324	44,750	110	995	1,469	3,627	10,864
Nebraska	73,022	78,641	70,737	370	5,032	2,503	4,288	11,141
Nevada	105,776	119,842	115,346	397	234	3,865	4,863	11,474
New Hampshire	41,800	45,043	42,952	539	144	1,408	3,792	10,864
New Jersey	290,966	320,160	306,501	1,641	1,938	10,079	8,737	52,350
New Mexico	117,062	115,290	110,471	336	910	3,573	4,421	18,091
New York	1,127,026	1,136,001	1,087,574	2,780	9,764	35,884	14,816	188,531
North Carolina	400,326	433,586	413,385	732	5,567	13,902	9,448	49,995
North Dakota	33,887	34,704	33,277	103	231	1,093	3,439	10,864
Ohio	578,184	589,653	567,409	1,030	2,621	18,593	10,549	86,106
Oklahoma	154,913	162,053	155,106	351	1,515	5,081	5,630	26,302
Oregon	162,663	163,660	146,982	1,371	10,121	5,185	5,418	22,199
Pennsylvania	560,204	578,222	550,543	510	8,946	18,222	10,706	93,787
Rhode Island	49,299	50,567	48,499	494	0	1,573	3,614	10,864
South Carolina	214,796	223,916	214,667	1,559	554	7,136	6,034	28,601
South Dakota	43,888	44,507	42,116	163	827	1,401	3,570	10,864
Tennessee	274,366	286,771	276,465	542	568	9,196	7,207	38,950
Texas	1,417,811	1,424,442	1,319,477	2,108	58,218	44,639	22,656	187,495
Utah	90,701	94,371	88,478	1,038	1,823	3,033	5,477	14,983
Vermont	34,285	35,503	33,553	206	626	1,118	3,355	10,864
Virginia	230,231	243,176	233,413	1,275	784	7,704	8,211	40,841
Washington	227,582	239,255	215,320	1,454	14,921	7,560	7,436	37,519
West Virginia	94,138	92,171	88,259	996	0	2,916	4,077	19,693
Wisconsin	220,873	217,322	208,484	1,353	627	6,858	6,712	37,811
Wyoming	34,415	36,043	33,999	679	230	1,135	3,383	10,864
Other activities/jurisdictions								
Indian Tribe Set-Aside	96,451	95,688	92,597	0	0	3,091	1,845	11,686
Other nonstate allocations	45,255	45,462	8,984	1,190	10,000	25,288	8,949	58,722
American Samoa	10,939	11,221	10,859	0	0	362	359	2,671
Guam	11,632	16,769	16,228	0	0	542	809	4,494
Northern Marianas	4,289	7,171	6,939	0	0	232	262	1,643
Puerto Rico	467,547	447,436	434,644	623	0	12,169	5,369	70,605
U.S. Virgin Islands	13,751	12,409	12,125	0	0	284	415	2,877

TABLE 3.6

Title I appropriations, by program and state, 2013 and 2014 [CONTINUED]

[In thousands of current dollars]

aIncludes Basic, Concentration, Targeted, and Education Finance Incentive Grants.
bTotal excludes other activities and other jurisdictions.
Note: Detail may not sum to totals because of rounding. Estimates for fiscal year 2014 are preliminary.

SOURCE: "Table 401.70. Appropriations for Title I and Selected Other Programs under the No Child Left Behind Act of 2001, by Program and State or Jurisdiction: Fiscal Years 2013 and 2014," in "Most Current Digest Tables," *Digest of Education Statistics*, U.S. Department of Education, Institute of Education Sciences, National Center for Education Statistics, October 2014, https://nces.ed.gov/programs/digest/d14/tables/xls/tabn401.70.xls (accessed July 22, 2015)

demonstrating mathematics proficiency, compared to 32.2% of housed high school students. As the NAEHCY notes, homeless students are four times more likely than their peers to suffer from delayed development, while roughly a third of all homeless children are diagnosed with severe mental disorders by the time they are eight years old. Furthermore, the NAEHCY also reports that homeless children tend to be dramatically underserved by special needs programs when compared to housed children. According to data included in *Homelessness through the Eyes of Children*, 38% of homeless children with disabilities have received treatment for their disorders, and only 9% are enrolled in special needs classes. By contrast, 75% of housed disabled students have received treatment, and 24% attend special needs classes.

Head Start

The Head Start program, which was established as part of the Economic Opportunity Act of 1964, has been one of the longest-lasting federal programs for at-risk children. Because disadvantaged children tend to be less prepared for an academic environment, Head Start operates when it is needed most: in early childhood, up to age five. Most children enter the program at ages three or four. Initially, not many children under the age of three were served by Head Start projects, but the 1994 reauthorization of Head Start established a companion program, Early Head Start, to serve infants and toddlers.

Head Start provides grants to public and private and to nonprofit and for-profit agencies to conduct the Head Start program. The purpose of the program is to provide child development services to economically disadvantaged children and families. Families are a key to the Head Start philosophy: they are involved in the program, helping their children learn while being helped themselves to attain their literacy and employment goals. The goal for the children is to ready them for school by developing early reading and math skills. Head Start programs also provide health, nutritional, social, and other services to enrolled children and families.

As Figure 3.2 shows, Head Start enrollment rose substantially between 1990 and 2013, from under 600,000 to more than 900,000. According to the U.S. Department of Health and Human Services, in *Head Start Program Facts Fiscal Year 2014* (April 2015, http://eclkc.ohs.acf.hhs.gov/hslc/data/factsheets/docs/hs-program-fact-sheet-2014.pdf), 927,275 children were enrolled in Head Start preschool programs in FY 2014. That year, total funding of Head Start programs topped $7.8 billion. (See Table 3.7.) California received the most money of all the states, garnering $979.8 million. Other states with high levels of Head Start funding were Texas, at $570.5 million, and New York, at $505.5 million. Together, these three states received 26.4% of the total Head Start allocations for FY 2014.

FIGURE 3.2

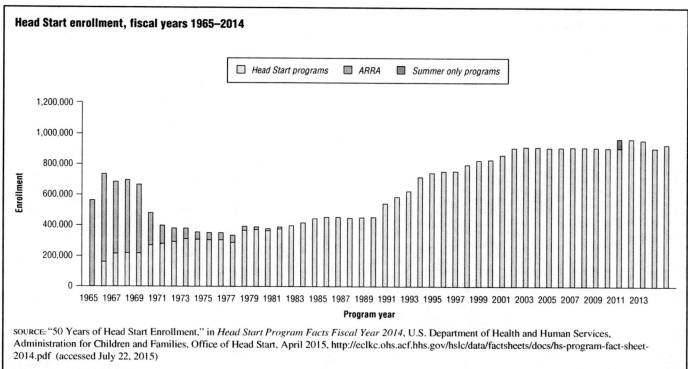

Head Start enrollment, fiscal years 1965–2014

SOURCE: "50 Years of Head Start Enrollment," in *Head Start Program Facts Fiscal Year 2014*, U.S. Department of Health and Human Services, Administration for Children and Families, Office of Head Start, April 2015, http://eclkc.ohs.acf.hhs.gov/hslc/data/factsheets/docs/hs-program-fact-sheet-2014.pdf (accessed July 22, 2015)

TABLE 3.7

Funding and enrollment for Head Start and Native American and Alaska Native programs, by state, fiscal year 2014

State/Territory	Federal funding by state/territory	Funded enrollment by state/territory	Federal funding for AIAN*	Funded enrollment for AIAN*
Alabama	$124,377,203	16,606		
Alaska	$14,677,625	1,632	$20,367,652	1,645
Arizona	$121,586,377	14,065	$40,216,130	3,936
Arkansas	$73,063,664	10,034		
California	$979,754,551	101,189	$8,214,838	632
Colorado	$83,043,878	10,538	$2,311,376	191
Connecticut	$62,589,568	6,701		
Delaware	$15,172,449	2,209		
District of Columbia	$27,977,602	3,106		
Florida	$318,389,657	37,609		
Georgia	$203,399,319	24,191		
Hawaii	$26,060,039	3,152		
Idaho	$26,697,173	3,111	$3,456,600	319
Illinois	$321,387,029	40,898		
Indiana	$113,430,566	15,179		
Iowa	$60,129,449	7,680		
Kansas	$60,237,400	8,556	$1,145,185	84
Kentucky	$128,035,469	15,960		
Louisiana	$166,131,337	21,772		
Maine	$32,208,621	3,237	$757,275	60
Maryland	$91,807,269	10,273		
Massachusetts	$124,459,511	12,501		
Michigan	$271,485,932	32,708	$6,928,707	596
Minnesota	$85,086,710	11,288	$10,737,229	932
Mississippi	$182,885,459	26,782	$2,218,116	268
Missouri	$141,473,617	17,527		
Montana	$24,385,336	3,055	$15,311,257	1,692
Nebraska	$42,962,702	5,204	$1,942,332	226
Nevada	$28,416,227	2,852	$3,513,542	362
New Hampshire	$15,739,084	1,650		
New Jersey	$156,698,017	15,074		
New Mexico	$61,861,561	7,672	$16,682,165	1,689
New York	$505,464,030	50,216	$1,331,753	143
North Carolina	$171,279,580	20,278	$2,853,094	230
North Dakota	$20,359,378	2,378	$10,094,047	1,000
Ohio	$291,584,452	39,293		
Oklahoma	$99,351,062	13,986	$24,030,953	2,822
Oregon	$71,691,114	12,741	$3,598,471	400
Pennsylvania	$270,312,578	36,626		
Rhode Island	$25,484,182	2,811		
South Carolina	$101,263,106	12,860	$953,479	80
South Dakota	$21,988,051	2,890	$16,293,892	1,690
Tennessee	$136,892,761	16,841		
Texas	$570,538,533	71,465	$434,688	34
Utah	$48,418,043	6,080	$1,789,758	215
Vermont	$15,535,073	1,448		
Virginia	$117,220,586	14,590		
Washington	$123,638,128	12,423	$14,125,023	1,415
West Virginia	$59,476,634	7,978		
Wisconsin	$105,704,455	14,218	$10,471,303	1,032
Wyoming	$13,750,805	1,658	$2,943,488	295
Subtotal States:	**$6,955,562,952**	**834,791**		
Subtotal Indian tribes:			**$222,722, 353**	**21,988**
Migrant program	$332,402,268	30,276		
American Samoa	$2,339,933	1,332		
Guam	$2,558,825	534		
No. Marianas	$1,859,836	462		
Palau	$1,460,671	400		
Puerto Rico	$278,608,717	36,478		
Virgin Islands	$9,628,366	1,014		
Total	**$7,807,143,921**	**927,275**		

*AIAN funding is awarded to American Indian and Alaska Native tribes. For reference, the funding and enrollment has been split out by the state in which the tribe is headquartered. Some tribes serve children across state lines.

SOURCE: "Federal Funding and Funded Enrollment by State, FY 2014," in *Head Start Program Facts Fiscal Year 2014*, U.S. Department of Health and Human Services, Administration for Children and Families, Office of Head Start, April 2015, http://eclkc.ohs.acf.hhs.gov/hslc/data/factsheets/docs/hs-program-fact-sheet-2014.pdf (accessed July 22, 2015)

CHAPTER 4
TESTING AND ACHIEVEMENT

NATIONAL ASSESSMENT OF EDUCATIONAL PROGRESS

The National Assessment of Educational Progress (NAEP) is the only regular national survey of educational achievement at the elementary, middle, and high school levels. Federally funded, the NAEP has conducted assessments of U.S. students since 1969. It is authorized by Congress and administered by the National Center for Education Statistics (NCES). The NAEP also has a National Assessment Governing Board to formulate policy guidelines.

Designed to measure the effectiveness of the nation's educational system, the NAEP has two major goals: to determine what U.S. students know and can do in key subject areas and to measure educational progress over long periods. The key subject areas the NAEP assesses are reading, writing, mathematics, science, U.S. history, civics, economics, and geography. The tests are given periodically to randomly selected samples of public and private school students in grades four, eight, and 12 for the national, state, and Trial Urban District Assessment (TUDA) assessments. Launched in 2002, the TUDA program originally targeted six urban districts nationwide, with the aim of evaluating reading and writing skills among urban students. By 2013, the TUDA program had expanded to include 21 urban areas. In addition, NAEP tests are periodically administered to randomly selected samples of students aged nine, 13, and 17 years for the long-term trend assessments.

The National, State, TUDA, and Long-Term NAEP Assessments

Table 4.1 shows the schedule between 2007 and 2017 for assessing individual subjects on the national, state, and TUDA levels and for administering the long-term trend assessments. Random samples of students (not all students) take the NAEP assessments and results are reported for groups of students.

The national NAEP assessments report information for the nation as well as for geographic regions of the country. The state NAEP assessments report information for individual states and are identical to the national assessments. The TUDA assessments encompass a multiyear feasibility study for the district-level NAEP in selected urban districts. Because the TUDA assessments are the same as the national and state assessments, they can show how students in participating urban school districts are performing compared with students across the United States. In addition, they show how students in participating urban districts are performing compared with students in other participating urban districts.

The national, state, and TUDA assessments can measure change over time only for assessment years in which testing methods are the same. However, it should be noted that these assessments change every so often based on changes in curricula or in educational practices that reflect results of research in educational tests and measurement and changes in teaching methods that employ more hands-on, real-world work. For example, rather than just using multiple-choice, true-false, or fill-in-the-blank questions, the most recent NAEP national, state, and TUDA assessments include a large percentage of constructed-response questions. These are open-ended short-answer questions that are scored by using a rubric (scoring guide), which allows for giving no credit, partial credit, or full credit for an answer. Constructed-response questions test not only content knowledge but also students' higher-order thinking skills, such as application, analysis, and synthesis. In addition, national, state, and TUDA questions often require the use of calculators or other materials and may ask students to complete hands-on tasks.

TABLE 4.1

Schedule of National Assessment of Educational Progress assessments, 2007–17

Year	National grades 4, 8, and 12 unless indicated	State (also TUDA, since 2002) grades 4 and 8 only, unless indicated	Long-term trend ages 9, 13, and 17
2017	Mathematics Reading Writing	Mathematics (4, 8, 12) Reading (4, 8, 12) Writing (4, 8, 12)	
2016	Arts (8)		
2015	Mathematics Reading Science	Mathematics (4, 8, 12) Reading (4, 8, 12) Science (4, 8, 12)	
2014	Civics (8) Geography (8) Technology and Engineering Literacy (8)[a] U.S. History (8)		
2013	Mathematics Reading	Mathematics (4, 8, 12) Reading (4, 8, 12)	
2012	Economics (12)		Mathematics, Reading
2011	Mathematics (4, 8) Reading (4, 8) Science (8) Writing (8, 12)[a]	Mathematics Reading Science (8; state only)	
2010	Civics Geography U.S. History		
2009	Mathematics[a] Reading[a] Science[a] High School Transcript Study[c]	Mathematics (4, 8, 12)[a, b] Reading (4, 8, 12)[a, b] Science[a]	
2008	Arts (8)		Mathematics, Reading
2007	Mathematics (4, 8) Reading (4, 8) Writing (4, 8)	Mathematics Reading Writing (8)	

[a]An updated or new framework is planned for implementation in this subject. In the case of subjects for which frameworks are already adopted, the board will decide whether a new or updated framework is needed for this assessment year. Note: The new framework for Mathematics 2009 was adopted for grade 12 only.
[b]For 2009, there was a pilot study of twelfth-grade state-level results, for which eleven states volunteered.
[c]The High School Transcript Study collects high school transcripts of high school seniors who graduated the year that the study was conducted.
Note: TUDA = Trial Urban District Assessment.

SOURCE: Adapted from "NAEP Assessment Schedule 1969–2017," in *Timeline for National Assessment of Education Progress (NAEP) Assessments from 1969 to 2017*, U.S. Department of Education, Institute of Education Sciences, National Center for Education Statistics, July 29, 2014, https://nces.ed.gov/nationsreportcard/about/assessmentsched.aspx (accessed July 22, 2015)

How Results Are Reported

LONG-TERM TREND ASSESSMENTS. Student performance on the NAEP long-term trend assessments use scale scores (average scores for groups of students) of 0 to 500, with descriptive performance levels within the scale. The long-term trend assessment scale has five performance levels: 150, 200, 250, 300, and 350. Each performance level is described for each content area, which explains what it means to score at that level and content area. These descriptors are discussed in more detail by the NCES in "NAEP Long-Term Trend Assessments" (March 3, 2015, http://nces.ed.gov/nationsreportcard/ltt).

NATIONAL, STATE, AND TUDA ASSESSMENTS. The national, state, and TUDA assessments use scale scores on either a 0 to 300 or 0 to 500 scale, depending on the subject. (These scale scores are different from the scale scores on the long-term trend assessments and cannot be compared.) Descriptive "achievement levels" accompany the scale scores for the national, state, and TUDA assessments and correspond to ranges of scores on the scale.

The NCES indicates in "NAEP Achievement Levels" (July 12, 2012, http://nces.ed.gov/nationsreportcard/achievement.aspx) that the three achievement levels are basic, proficient, and advanced. They are reported as percentages of students who attain each of the three achievement levels. Basic level means "partial mastery of prerequisite knowledge and skills that are fundamental for proficient work at each grade." Proficient level means "solid academic performance for each grade assessed. Students reaching this level have demonstrated competency over challenging subject matter, including subject-matter knowledge, application of such knowledge to real-world situations, and analytical skills appropriate to the subject matter." Levels are cumulative; that is, students who have attained the proficient level can do basic level work as well. Advanced level means "superior performance." A student at the advanced level can do basic, proficient, and advanced work.

READING ASSESSMENT
Comparing National Reading Scores

Comparisons can be made between the 1992 and 2007 national average reading scores (scale scores) because the assessment framework was the same over those years. The NAEP frameworks provide the underlying theory for its assessments; in other words, they act like blueprints. They describe the types of questions that should be used, how they should be designed, and how they should be scored. The framework for the reading assessments changed in 2009. Table 4.2 is a summary table that shows the differences in the framework of the assessments. Because assessments conducted between 2009 and 2015 differ from previous assessments, the National Assessment Governing Board conducted special analyses and determined that the 2009–15 reading assessments could be compared with those from earlier assessment years. Thus, comparisons can be made between the 1992 and 2015 average reading scores.

Overall Trends in the Average Reading Scores by Age

Figure 4.1 shows the national trends in the average reading scores for fourth- and eighth-grade students for selected years between 1990 and 2013. During this span eighth graders made slightly better gains than fourth graders. The NCES reveals in *A First Look: 2013 Mathematics and Reading Trial Urban District Assessment* (December 2013, http://nces.ed.gov/nationsreportcard/subject/publications/main2013/pdf/2014466.pdf) that the average reading scores of fourth graders remained statistically unchanged in 18 of 21 participating cities between 2011 and 2013. During this period the District of Columbia and Los Angeles, California, recorded average gains of five and four points, respectively, whereas Houston, Texas, recorded an average decline of five points. The average reading scores of eighth graders remained statistically the same in 16 of 21 participating cities between 2011 and 2013, and five cities recorded modest gains.

Reading Score Trends by Select Student Characteristics

Table 4.3 provides an overview of NAEP reading score trends among fourth, eighth, and 12th graders between 1992 and 2013 and provides detailed trend information for selected years between 1998 and 2013. During this time fourth graders attending schools with the highest proportion of students eligible for free or reduced-price lunches showed the largest gains in average reading scores of any group. In 1998 fourth graders from high-poverty schools recorded an average NAEP reading score of 187; by 2013 this score had risen to 203, a gain of

TABLE 4.2

Comparison of National Assessment of Educational Progress reading frameworks, 1992–2007 and 2009–15

	1992–2007 NAEP reading framework		2009–2015 NAEP reading framework	
Content	Content of assessment: • Literary • Informational • Document	Contexts for reading: • For literary experience • For information • To perform task	• Literary text • Fiction • Literary nonfiction • Poetry	• Informational text • Exposition • Argumentation and persuasive text • Procedural text and documents
Cognitive processes	Stances/aspects of reading: • Forming general understanding. • Developing interpretation. • Making reader/text connections. • Examining content and structure.		Cognitive targets distinguished by text type Locate/recall Integrate/interpret Critique/evaluate	
Vocabulary	Vocabulary as a *target* of item development, with no information reported on students' use of vocabulary knowledge in comprehending what they read.		Systematic approach to vocabulary assessment with potential for a vocabulary subscore.	
Poetry	Poetry included as stimulus material at grades 8 and 12.		Poetry included as stimulus material at all grades.	
Passage source	Use of intact, authentic stimulus material.		Use of authentic stimulus material plus some flexibility in excerpting stimulus material.	
Passage length	Grade 4: 250–800 Grade 8: 400–1,000 Grade 12: 500–1,500		Grade 4: 200–800 Grade 8: 400–1,000 Grade 12: 500–1,500	
Passage selection	Expert judgment as criterion for passage selection.		Expert judgment and use of at least two research-based readability formulas for passage selection.	
Item type	Multiple-choice and constructed-response items included at all grades.		Multiple-choice and constructed-response items included at all grades.	

NAEP = National Assessment of Educational Progress.

SOURCE: "Exhibit 2. Similarities and Differences: 1992–2007 and 2009–2015 NAEP Reading Frameworks," in *Reading Framework for the 2015 National Assessment of Educational Progress*, U.S. Department of Education, National Assessment Governing Board, January 2015, http://www.nagb.org/content/nagb/assets/documents/publications/frameworks/reading/2015-reading-framework.pdf (accessed July 22, 2015)

FIGURE 4.1

Trends in average reading scores for fourth- and eighth-grade students, 1992–2013

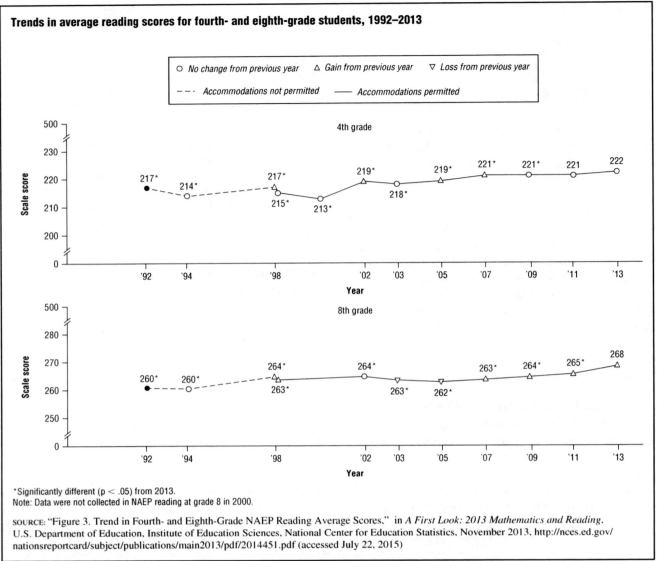

○ *No change from previous year*   △ *Gain from previous year*   ▽ *Loss from previous year*

--- *Accommodations not permitted*   —— *Accommodations permitted*

*Significantly different (p < .05) from 2013.
Note: Data were not collected in NAEP reading at grade 8 in 2000.

SOURCE: "Figure 3. Trend in Fourth- and Eighth-Grade NAEP Reading Average Scores," in *A First Look: 2013 Mathematics and Reading*, U.S. Department of Education, Institute of Education Sciences, National Center for Education Statistics, November 2013, http://nces.ed.gov/nationsreportcard/subject/publications/main2013/pdf/2014451.pdf (accessed July 22, 2015)

16 points. Despite this progress, fourth graders from high-poverty schools still lagged considerably behind their more-advantaged peers in 2013. That year, fourth graders from schools with the lowest proportion of students eligible for free or reduced-price lunches recorded an average NAEP reading score of 240, 37 points higher than students living at the highest poverty levels.

Table 4.3 also compares average reading scores among disabled and nondisabled fourth, eighth, and 12th graders between 1998 and 2013. For example, in 2000 fourth-grade students without disabilities recorded an average reading score of 217. By contrast, fourth-grade students with disabilities recorded average reading scores of 167 that year, a difference of 50 points. Disabled fourth graders narrowed the gap over the next half-decade. In 2007 fourth graders with disabilities recorded an average reading score of 191, 33 points lower than the average reading score of 224 recorded by their

nondisabled peers. Following these gains, the discrepancy between reading scores of disabled and nondisabled fourth graders grew wider in subsequent years. In 2013 average reading scores of disabled fourth graders fell to 184, whereas average reading scores of nondisabled fourth graders increased slightly to 227, a difference of 43 points.

Table 4.4 offers a breakdown of NAEP reading scores among fourth and eighth graders in 2013, by state and English language learner (ELL) status. Nationwide, ELL fourth graders recorded an average reading score of 187 in 2013, and ELL eighth graders posted an average score of 225. By comparison, non-ELL fourth graders posted an average reading score of 225 (the same score as ELL eighth graders), and non-ELL eighth graders posted an average reading score of 268. As Table 4.4 shows, ELL fourth graders scored highest in Maryland (207), South Carolina (206), and Ohio (205) in 2013.

TABLE 4.3

Average National Assessment of Educational Progress reading scores and achievement levels, by grade and select student characteristics, selected years 1992–2013

Grade and year	Percent of students in school eligible for free or reduced-price lunch — Average reading scale score[b]					English language learner (ELL) status			Disability status[a]			Percent of all students attaining reading achievement levels		
	0–25 percent eligible (low poverty)	26–50 percent eligible	51–75 percent eligible	76–100 percent eligible (high poverty)	Gap between low-poverty and high-poverty score	Average reading scale score — ELL	Average reading scale score — Non-ELL	Gap between non-ELL and ELL score	Average reading scale score[b] — Identified as student with disability (SD)	Not identified as SD	Gap between non-SD and SD score	Below Basic[c]	At or above basic[c]	At or above proficient[d]
Grade 4														
1992[e]	—	—	—	—	—	‡	‡	‡	‡	‡	‡	38	62	29
1994[e]	—	—	—	—	—	‡	‡	‡	‡	‡	‡	40	60	30
1998	231	218	205	187	44	174	217	43	176	217	41	40	60	29
2000	231	218	205	184	48	167	216	49	167	217	50	41	59	29
2002	233	221	210	196	37	183	221	38	187	221	34	36	64	31
2003	233	221	211	194	39	186	221	35	185	222	36	37	63	31
2005	234	221	211	197	37	187	222	35	190	224	32	36	64	31
2007	235	223	212	200	35	188	224	36	191	224	33	33	67	33
2009	237	223	215	202	35	188	224	36	190	224	35	33	67	33
2011	238	226	217	203	35	188	225	36	186	225	39	33	67	34
2013	240	227	218	203	37	187	226	38	184	227	42	32	68	35
Grade 8														
1992[e]	—	—	—	—	—	‡	‡	‡	‡	‡	‡	31	69	29
1994[e]	—	—	—	—	—	‡	‡	‡	‡	‡	‡	30	70	30
1998	273	262	252	240	33	218	264	46	224	266	42	27	73	32
2000	—	—	—	—	—	—	—	—	—	—	—	—	—	—
2002	276	264	254	240	36	224	266	42	228	268	39	25	75	33
2003	275	263	253	239	36	222	265	43	225	267	42	26	74	32
2005	274	262	252	240	34	224	264	40	227	266	39	27	73	31
2007	275	263	253	241	34	223	265	42	227	266	39	26	74	31
2009	277	265	256	243	34	219	266	47	230	267	37	25	75	32
2011	279	268	258	247	32	224	267	44	231	269	38	24	76	34
2013	282	270	261	249	33	225	270	45	232	272	39	22	78	36
Grade 12														
1992[e]	—	—	—	—	—	‡	‡	‡	‡	‡	‡	20	80	40
1994[e]	—	—	—	—	—	‡	‡	‡	‡	‡	‡	25	75	36
1998	296	284	275	272	23	244	291	46	244	292	48	24	76	40
2000	—	—	—	—	—	—	—	—	—	—	—	—	—	—
2002	293	282	275	268	25	245	288	43	247	289	42	26	74	36
2003	—	—	—	—	—	247	288	40	244	289	45	—	—	—
2005	292	282	273	266	26	247	288	40	244	289	45	27	73	35
2007	—	—	—	—	—	—	—	—	—	—	—	—	—	—

TABLE 4.3

Average National Assessment of Educational Progress reading scores and achievement levels, by grade and select student characteristics, selected years 1992–2013 [CONTINUED]

| Grade and year | Percent of students in school eligible for free or reduced-price lunch — Average reading scale score[b] | | | | | English language learner (ELL) status — Average reading scale score | | | Disability status[a] — Average reading scale score[b] | | Gap between non-SD and SD score | Percent of all students attaining reading achievement levels | | |
	0–25 percent eligible (low poverty)	26–50 percent eligible	51–75 percent eligible	76–100 percent eligible (high poverty)	Gap between low-poverty and high-poverty score	ELL	Non-ELL	Gap between non-ELL and ELL score	Identified as student with disability (SD)	Not identified as SD		Below Basic[c]	At or above basic[c]	At or above proficient[d]
2009	299	286	276	266	33	240	290	50	253	291	38	26	74	38
2011	—	—	—	—	—	—	—	—	—	—	—	—	—	—
2013	302	289	280	268	35	237	290	53	252	292	40	25	75	38

—Not available.

‡Reporting standards not met (too few cases for a reliable estimate).

[a]The student with disability (SD) variable used in this table includes students who have a 504 plan, even if they do not have an Individualized Education Plan (IEP).

[b]Scale ranges from 0 to 500.

[c]Basic denotes partial mastery of the knowledge and skills that are fundamental for proficient work at a given grade.

[d]Proficient represents solid academic performance. Students reaching this level have demonstrated competency over challenging subject matter.

[e]Accommodations were not permitted for this assessment.

Note: Includes public and private schools. For 1998 and later years, includes students tested with accommodations (1 to 11 percent of all students, depending on grade level and year); excludes only those students with disabilities and English language learners who were unable to be tested even with accommodations (2 to 6 percent of all students).

SOURCE: Adapted from "Table 221.12. Average National Assessment of Educational Progress (NAEP) Reading Scale Score and Percentage of Students Attaining Selected NAEP Reading Achievement Levels, by Selected School and Student Characteristics and Grade: Selected Years, 1992 through 2013," in "Most Current Digest Tables," *Digest of Education Statistics*, U.S. Department of Education, Institute of Education Sciences, National Center for Education Statistics, September 2014, https://nces.ed.gov/programs/digest/d14/tables/xls/tabn221.12.xls (accessed July 31, 2015)

TABLE 4.4

Average National Assessment of Educational Progress reading scores among fourth- and eighth-grade students, by state and English-language learner status, 2013

State	4th-graders English language learners — Percent of all students assessed	Average scale score[a]	Percent At or above basic[b]	Percent At or above proficient[c]	Not English language learners Average scale score[a]	Percent At or above basic[b]	Percent At or above proficient[c]	8th-graders English language learners — Percent of all students assessed	Average scale score[a]	Percent At or above basic[b]	Percent At or above proficient[c]	Not English language learners Average scale score[a]	Percent At or above basic[b]	Percent At or above proficient[c]
United States	**10**	**187**	**31**	**7**	**225**	**71**	**37**	**5**	**225**	**30**	**3**	**268**	**79**	**36**
Alabama	2	‡	‡	‡	219	66	31	1	‡	‡	‡	258	69	25
Alaska	14	154	10	1	218	65	32	11	214	16	1	267	78	35
Arizona	7	159	8	1	217	63	30	1	‡	‡	‡	261	73	28
Arkansas	8	202	47	17	220	68	33	6	245	55	12	263	74	31
California	25	182	26	5	223	69	34	12	220	23	2	267	79	33
Colorado	14	192	37	8	232	80	46	8	232	37	3	274	85	43
Connecticut	5	181	25	4	232	79	45	3	222	27	1	276	85	47
Delaware	2	184	24	4	227	74	39	1	‡	‡	‡	267	77	34
District of Columbia	6	182	23	5	207	51	24	5	218	25	2	249	59	18
Florida	10	199	41	10	230	79	42	4	226	30	3	268	79	35
Georgia	3	189	29	8	223	68	35	2	220	21	4	265	76	32
Hawaii	7	166	14	3	219	65	32	10	224	29	3	264	76	31
Idaho	4	170	17	3	222	70	34	3	222	21	2	272	84	39
Illinois	8	174	18	3	222	68	36	5	219	23	1	269	80	38
Indiana	6	203	48	13	227	75	39	3	236	40	6	268	81	36
Iowa	5	195	41	11	225	73	39	2	226	27	2	270	83	38
Kansas	13	203	49	17	226	75	41	8	245	55	13	269	80	38
Kentucky	2	197	41	11	225	72	37	1	237	43	5	270	80	38
Louisiana	2	202	47	10	211	57	23	1	‡	‡	‡	258	68	24
Maine	2	190	35	9	226	72	38	2	‡	‡	‡	270	79	39
Maryland	4	207	51	18	233	78	46	1	‡	‡	‡	274	83	43
Massachusetts	10	192	40	12	237	83	51	5	224	28	4	280	87	50
Michigan	8	194	39	9	219	66	32	3	232	41	8	267	78	34
Minnesota	8	188	33	8	230	78	44	5	231	40	6	273	84	42
Mississippi	1	‡	‡	‡	209	54	21	1	‡	‡	‡	253	64	20
Missouri	2	197	37	6	223	70	36	1	‡	‡	‡	267	79	36
Montana	3	174	16	2	225	72	36	2	‡	‡	‡	273	85	41
Nebraska	7	190	34	7	226	74	39	2	‡	‡	‡	270	82	37
Nevada	22	185	30	6	222	71	33	7	217	21	2	265	76	33
New Hampshire	2	196	34	10	233	81	45	2	‡	‡	‡	275	85	44
New Jersey	3	188	33	9	230	76	43	1	‡	‡	‡	277	86	47
New Mexico	18	168	16	3	214	60	25	13	224	29	2	261	73	25
New York	7	182	25	4	227	74	40	6	215	20	1	270	80	37
North Carolina	6	183	23	4	225	72	37	4	232	41	7	266	77	34
North Dakota	2	‡	‡	‡	225	74	34	2	‡	‡	‡	269	82	35
Ohio	3	205	51	19	224	71	38	1	251	60	20	269	79	39
Oklahoma	6	186	30	6	219	68	31	4	229	39	6	263	76	30
Oregon	13	183	29	6	225	71	38	3	218	23	1	270	81	38
Pennsylvania	2	181	27	5	227	74	41	2	222	26	3	273	83	43
Rhode Island	6	168	17	4	226	73	40	4	216	20	3	269	79	37
South Carolina	6	206	54	18	214	61	29	3	242	54	10	262	73	30
South Dakota	3	160	20	5	220	67	33	2	‡	‡	‡	269	82	36
Tennessee	3	174	19	2	221	69	35	1	‡	‡	‡	266	77	33
Texas	22	194	36	9	223	70	34	7	227	32	2	267	79	33
Utah	5	159	9	2	226	74	39	3	220	21	3	272	83	40

TABLE 4.4

Average National Assessment of Educational Progress reading scores among fourth- and eighth-grade students, by state and English-language learner status, 2013 [CONTINUED]

	4th-graders							8th-graders						
	English language learners				Not English language learners			English language learners				Not English language learners		
			Percent			Percent				Percent			Percent	
State	Percent of all students assessed	Average scale score[a]	At or above basic[b]	At or above proficient[c]	Average scale score[a]	At or above basic[b]	At or above proficient[c]	Percent of all students assessed	Average scale score[a]	At or above basic[b]	At or above proficient[c]	Average scale score[a]	At or above basic[b]	At or above proficient[c]
Vermont	2	‡	‡	‡	229	76	43	1	‡	‡	‡	275	84	45
Virginia	7	186	28	5	232	77	46	5	242	51	7	269	79	38
Washington	9	179	20	3	229	77	43	5	222	26	3	275	84	44
West Virginia	1	‡	‡	‡	215	62	27	#	‡	‡	‡	257	70	25
Wisconsin	8	190	34	9	223	70	37	5	242	51	9	269	79	38
Wyoming	3	196	37	9	227	76	38	2	‡	‡	‡	272	85	38
Department of Defense dependents schools	5	216	63	20	233	83	44	3	244	52	6	278	91	46

#Rounds to zero.

‡Reporting standards not met (too few cases for a reliable estimate).

[a]Scale ranges from 0 to 500.

[b]Basic denotes partial mastery of the knowledge and skills that are fundamental for proficient work at a given grade.

[c]Proficient represents solid academic performance. Students reaching this level have demonstrated competency over challenging subject matter.

Note: The results for English language learners are based on students who were assessed and cannot be generalized to the total population of such students. Although testing accommodations were permitted, some English language learners did not have a sufficient level of English proficiency to participate in the 2013 Reading Assessment.

SOURCE: Adapted from "Table 221.70. Average National Assessment of Educational Progress (NAEP) Reading Scale Scores of 4th- and 8th-Graders in Public Schools and Percentage Scoring at or above Selected Reading Achievement Levels, by English Language Learner (ELL) Status and State: 2013," in "Most Current Digest Tables," *Digest of Education Statistics,* U.S. Department of Education. Institute of Education Sciences. National Center for Education Statistics, November 2013. https://nces.ed.gov/programs/digest/d14/tables/xls/tabn221.70.xls (accessed July 31, 2015)

That year, Ohio (251), Kansas (245), and Arkansas (244) recorded the highest average reading scores among ELL eighth graders.

Reading Score Gaps between White, African American, and Hispanic Students

Table 4.5 provides a breakdown of reading scores for fourth- and eighth-grade students in 2009, 2011, and 2013; it also shows scores by race and ethnicity for 2011 and 2013. Among fourth graders, Asian Americans (237) recorded the highest average reading scores in 2013, followed by non-Hispanic whites (231). Hispanic fourth graders recorded an average reading score of 207 that year, and African American fourth graders posted an average score of 205. This gap remained roughly the same among eighth graders in 2013. As Table 4.5 shows, Asian American eighth graders scored highest in reading, recording an average reading score of 280. Non-Hispanic white eighth graders recorded average reading scores of 275 in 2013, followed by Hispanics (255) and African Americans (250).

Reading Achievement-Level Performance

Figure 4.2 provides a glimpse into reading gains achieved by fourth- and eighth-grade students between 1992 and 2013. In 1992, 34% of fourth graders were reading at a basic level, and 38% were reading below the basic level; another 22% tested as proficient in reading, and 6% were advanced. As Figure 4.2 shows, by 2013 fourth graders had shown notable improvement in reading. That year, 33% of fourth-grade students were reading at a basic level, whereas 27% were proficient, and 8% were advanced. Meanwhile, the proportion of fourth graders reading at below basic levels had fallen to 32% in 2013. Eighth graders saw comparable gains during these years. In 1992, 31% of eighth-grade students were reading at a below basic level; 40% were reading at a basic level, 26% at a proficient level, and 3% at advanced. By 2013 the proportion of eighth graders reading below basic levels had fallen to 22%, whereas the percentages of eighth graders reading at basic (42%), proficient (32%), and advanced (4%) levels had all increased.

In 2013, 14 states reported that the percentages of fourth and eighth graders who were reading at or above proficient levels was higher than the national average. (See Figure 4.3.) In addition, nine states reported that the percentage of fourth graders reading at or above proficient levels was higher than the national average, while three states (Montana, Idaho, and Kentucky) reported that the percentage of eighth graders reading at or above proficient exceeded the national average. By contrast, 13 states and the District of Columbia reported that the percentage of both fourth and eighth graders reading at or above proficient levels was lower than the national average in 2013.

In 2013, 38% of 12th graders in the U.S. were reading at or above proficient levels. (See Figure 4.4.) A higher proportion of Asian or Pacific Islanders (47%) and non-Hispanic whites (47%) in the 12th grade were reading at or above proficient levels that year, compared with 12th graders who identified as Native American or Alaskan Native (38%), Hispanic (23%), or African American (16%). Overall, 12th graders whose parents had graduated from college (49%) were twice as likely as 12th graders whose parents had only graduated from high school (24%) to read at or above proficient levels in 2013. (See Figure 4.4.)

Table 4.6 provides an overview of reading-level trends for fourth, eighth, and 12th graders between 1998 and 2013, by race/ethnicity, sex, and eligibility for free or reduced-price school lunches. As Table 4.6 shows, between 1998 and 2013 female students have consistently outperformed male students in reading at all three grade levels. In 2013, 72% of fourth-grade girls were reading at or above the basic level, compared with 65% of fourth-grade boys. This gender gap grew slightly wider among older students. For example, 82% of eighth-grade girls were reading at or above the basic level in 2013, eight percentage points higher than the proportion of boys (74%) reading at or above the basic level. That year, 79% of 12th-grade girls were reading at or above the basic level, compared with 70% of 12th-grade boys.

Vocabulary Score Trends

Between 2009 and 2013, fourth graders of Asian or Pacific Islander descent consistently produced the highest NAEP vocabulary scores, followed closely by non-Hispanic white fourth graders. (See Figure 4.5.) Among eighth graders, non-Hispanic whites scored slightly higher than Asian or Pacific Islanders on NAEP vocabulary testing during this span, although the gap had narrowed by 2013. (See Figure 4.6.) Meanwhile, Hispanic and Native American/Alaskan Native eighth graders scored roughly the same on NAEP vocabulary testing in 2013, followed by African American eighth graders. As Figure 4.7 shows, non-Hispanic white and Native American/Alaskan Native 12th graders showed modest gains in NAEP vocabulary test scores between 2009 and 2013; Asian or Pacific Islanders in the same grade recorded a steady decline over the same period, and vocabulary scores among Hispanic and African American 12th graders remained roughly the same.

MATHEMATICS ASSESSMENT

The national, state, and TUDA mathematics assessments for grades four, eight, and 12 were conducted in 2015. (See Table 4.1.) The results shown in this chapter

TABLE 4.5

Average National Assessment of Educational Progress reading scores and achievement levels among fourth- and eighth-grade students, by race/ethnicity and selected urban districts, 2009, 2011, and 2013

Grade level and jurisdiction or specific urban district	2009	2011					2013					Percent of students 2013	
	All students	All students	White	Black	Hispanic	Asian	All students	White	Black	Hispanic	Asian	At or above basic[b]	At or above proficient[c]
4th grade													
United States	220	220	230	205	205	236	221	231	205	207	237	67	34
All large cities	210	211	232	202	203	225	212	235	202	204	229	57	26
Selected urban districts													
Albuquerque	—	209	231	‡	201	‡	207	232	‡	199	‡	54	24
Atlanta	209	212	251	203	215	‡	214	252	204	208	‡	57	27
Austin	220	224	249	215	210	‡	221	250	206	208	‡	65	36
Baltimore City	202	200	221	198	‡	‡	204	233	201	‡	‡	45	14
Boston	215	217	241	211	214	226	214	237	205	210	234	61	26
Charlotte	225	224	244	211	212	233	226	245	215	212	238	72	40
Chicago	202	203	229	197	201	228	206	239	198	203	235	51	20
Cleveland	194	193	209	187	196	‡	190	206	185	191	‡	33	9
Dallas	204	204	237	204	200	‡	205	231	201	204	‡	49	16
Detroit	187	191	‡	190	199	‡	190	‡	188	199	‡	30	7
District of Columbia	203	201	255	191	204	‡	206	260	192	211	‡	49	25
Fresno	197	194	216	191	190	195	196	218	187	192	199	39	13
Hillsborough County (FL)	211	213	242	218	223	245	228	237	214	223	247	75	40
Houston	219	223	243	207	209	256	208	238	202	204	245	52	19
Jefferson County (KY)	197	201	230	208	221	226	221	233	203	221	‡	66	33
Los Angeles	221	221	225	196	196	‡	205	237	204	199	222	50	19
Miami-Dade	196	221	240	210	222	206	223	239	209	225	‡	70	35
Milwaukee	196	195	216	187	198	206	199	223	190	200	201	42	15
New York City	217	216	235	209	207	230	216	231	210	208	233	62	28
Philadelphia	195	199	217	195	191	212	200	214	196	193	215	44	14
San Diego	213	215	240	205	201	225	218	240	205	204	229	64	33
8th grade													
United States	262	264	272	248	251	277	266	275	250	255	280	77	34
All large cities	252	255	273	245	249	271	258	276	246	253	273	68	26
Selected urban districts													
Albuquerque	—	254	271	‡	248	‡	256	275	‡	250	‡	66	23
Atlanta	250	253	287	249	‡	‡	255	294	249	254	‡	63	22
Austin	261	261	285	246	251	‡	261	286	245	251	‡	70	31
Baltimore City	245	246	267	242	‡	‡	252	275	249	‡	‡	61	16
Boston	257	255	281	246	245	280	257	281	247	250	278	66	28
Charlotte	259	265	283	253	256	264	266	286	253	259	‡	76	36
Chicago	249	253	271	245	255	262	253	279	244	255	278	64	21
Cleveland	242	240	260	234	241	‡	239	250	235	241	‡	49	11
Dallas	—	248	276	244	246	‡	251	‡	244	253	‡	63	15
Detroit	232	237	‡	235	244	‡	239	‡	239	242	‡	46	9
District of Columbia	240	237	290	231	232	‡	245	301	237	247	‡	53	18
Fresno	240	238	257	230	234	241	245	265	236	241	247	54	13
Hillsborough County (FL)	—	264	276	247	258	‡	267	277	252	263	‡	77	35
Houston	252	252	283	247	249	‡	252	284	245	250	284	63	19
Jefferson County (KY)	259	260	269	245	‡	‡	261	271	243	258	‡	69	29

TABLE 4.5

Average National Assessment of Educational Progress reading scores and achievement levels among fourth- and eighth-grade students, by race/ethnicity and selected urban districts, 2009, 2011, and 2013 [CONTINUED]

Grade level and jurisdiction or specific urban district	Average reading scale score[a]												Percent of students 2013	
	2009	2011					2013							
	All students	All students	White	Black	Hispanic	Asian	All students	White	Black	Hispanic	Asian		At or above basic[b]	At or above proficient[c]
Los Angeles	244	246	273	242	241	269	250	276	240	245	272		60	19
Miami-Dade	261	260	275	246	262	‡	259	278	245	261	‡		71	27
Milwaukee	241	238	255	232	243	248	242	262	232	253	‡		51	13
New York City	252	254	271	248	246	273	256	274	253	249	271		67	25
Philadelphia	247	247	264	244	239	258	249	261	244	243	265		58	16
San Diego	254	256	275	238	245	268	260	281	244	247	266		70	29

—Not available.

‡ Reporting standards not met (too few cases for a reliable estimate).

[a]Scale ranges from 0 to 500.

[b]Basic denotes partial mastery of prerequisite knowledge and skills that are fundamental for proficient work at a given grade.

[c]Proficient represents solid academic performance. Students reaching this level have demonstrated competency over challenging subject matter.

Note: Race categories exclude persons of Hispanic ethnicity. Totals include racial/ethnic groups not shown separately.

SOURCE: Adapted from "Table 221.80. Average National Assessment of Educational Progress (NAEP) Reading Scale Scores of 4th- and 8th-Grade Public School Students and Percentage Attaining Achievement Levels, by Race/Ethnicity and Jurisdiction or Specific Urban District: 2009, 2011, and 2013," in "Most Current Digest Tables," Digest of Education Statistics, U.S. Department of Education, Institute of Education Sciences, National Center for Education Statistics, December 2013, https://nces.ed.gov/programs/digest/d14/tables/xls/tabn221.80.xls (accessed July 31, 2015)

FIGURE 4.2

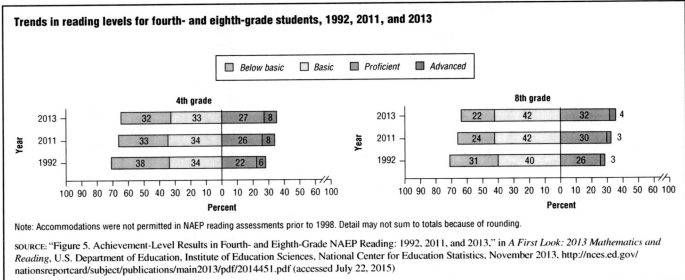

Trends in reading levels for fourth- and eighth-grade students, 1992, 2011, and 2013

Note: Accommodations were not permitted in NAEP reading assessments prior to 1998. Detail may not sum to totals because of rounding.

SOURCE: "Figure 5. Achievement-Level Results in Fourth- and Eighth-Grade NAEP Reading: 1992, 2011, and 2013," in *A First Look: 2013 Mathematics and Reading*, U.S. Department of Education, Institute of Education Sciences, National Center for Education Statistics, November 2013, http://nces.ed.gov/nationsreportcard/subject/publications/main2013/pdf/2014451.pdf (accessed July 22, 2015)

for mathematics are from *A First Look: 2013 Mathematics and Reading* (November 2013, http://nces.ed.gov/nationsreportcard/subject/publications/main2013/pdf/2014451.pdf); from *2013 Mathematics Grade 12 Assessment Report Card: Summary Data Tables with Additional Detail for National and Pilot State Average Scores and Achievement Level Results* (2013, http://www.nationsreportcard.gov/reading_math_g12_2013/files/Results_Appendix_Math_G12.pdf); and from *Are the Nation's 12th-Graders Making Progress in Math and Reading?* (2013, http://nces.ed.gov/nationsreportcard/subject/publications/main2013/pdf/2014087.pdf). Additional data have been taken from select tables published by the NCES in the *Digest of Education Statistics* (https://nces.ed.gov/programs/digest). In reviewing the following tables, it is important to note that NAEP mathematics assessments score fourth and eighth graders on a scale of 0 to 500, whereas 12th graders are evaluated on a scale of 0 to 300.

For the 2013 national, state, and TUDA assessments, the NAEP assessed proficiency in five content areas of mathematics: number properties and operations, measurement, geometry, data analysis and probability, and algebra. For each of these content areas, the NAEP focused not only on the content but also on the ways of knowing and doing mathematics.

Overall Trends in the Average Mathematics Scores by Age

Figure 4.8 shows the national trends in the average mathematics scores for fourth- and eighth-grade students for selected years between 1990 and 2013. Improvement among fourth graders was somewhat more substantial, with the average test scores rising 29 points over that span, compared with a 22-point rise among eighth graders. The NCES reports in *2013 Mathematics Grade*

12 Assessment Report Card that the nation's 12th graders saw modest gains in average mathematics scores during the early 21st century, rising from 150 to 153 between 2005 and 2013. Among different races/ethnicities, Asian or Pacific Islander 12th graders produced the highest average mathematics score (172) in 2013, followed by non-Hispanic whites (162), Native Americans and Alaskan Natives (142), Hispanics (141), and African Americans (132). On the whole, male 12th graders (155) performed slightly better on average than female 12th graders (152) on the 2013 NAEP mathematics assessment.

Mathematics Score Results by Select Student Characteristics

As Table 4.7 shows, there appears to be a correlation between a student's poverty level and his or her performance on the NAEP mathematics assessment. For example, in 2013 fourth graders attending schools where between 76% to 100% of the students were eligible for free or reduced-price lunches produced an average mathematics score of 226. By contrast, fourth graders attending schools where 25% or less of the student body was eligible for free or reduced-price lunches produced average scores of 257, a difference of 31 points. The discrepancies between high-poverty and low-poverty students was even more substantial among eighth and 12th graders. Whereas eighth graders attending schools with the lowest poverty levels produced average mathematics scores of 301 in 2013, their counterparts at schools with the highest poverty levels produced average scores of 265, a 36-point difference. Among 12th graders that year, a 35-point gap separated students attending schools with the lowest poverty levels (169) and those attending schools with the highest poverty levels (134).

Student attitudes toward mathematics can also influence performance on NAEP testing. As Table 4.8 shows,

FIGURE 4.3

Reading levels for fourth- and eighth-grade students, by state, 2013

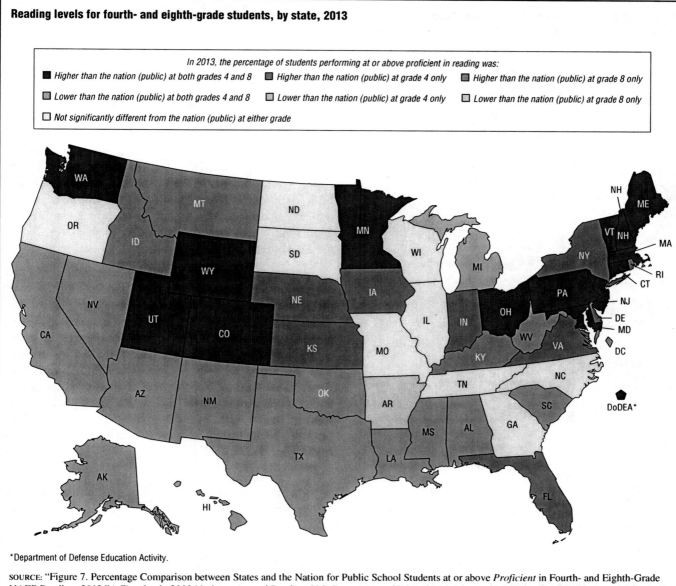

In 2013, the percentage of students performing at or above proficient in reading was:

■ *Higher than the nation (public) at both grades 4 and 8*   ■ *Higher than the nation (public) at grade 4 only*   ■ *Higher than the nation (public) at grade 8 only*

■ *Lower than the nation (public) at both grades 4 and 8*   ☐ *Lower than the nation (public) at grade 4 only*   ☐ *Lower than the nation (public) at grade 8 only*

☐ *Not significantly different from the nation (public) at either grade*

*Department of Defense Education Activity.

SOURCE: "Figure 7. Percentage Comparison between States and the Nation for Public School Students at or above *Proficient* in Fourth- and Eighth-Grade NAEP Reading: 2013,"*A First Look: 2013 Mathematics and Reading*, U.S. Department of Education, Institute of Education Sciences, National Center for Education Statistics, November 2013, http://nces.ed.gov/nationsreportcard/subject/publications/main2013/pdf/2014451.pdf (accessed July 22, 2015)

eighth graders who always or almost always found mathematics to be engaging or interesting produced average math scores of 287 in 2013, whereas students who were never or hardly ever interested in math produced average scores of 280. This discrepancy was far more pronounced among 12th graders. In 2013, 12th-grade students who always or almost always found mathematics engaging produced an average score of 166 on NAEP testing, while those who never or hardly ever found math engaging produced an average score of only 145. (See Table 4.9.) Overall, 12th graders who believed that studying math in school would prove valuable later in life performed better than those who believed studying mathematics had little or no value for their futures. On average, 12th graders

who strongly disagreed with the notion that studying math would help them in the future scored 140 on NAEP mathematics testing in 2013, whereas those who strongly agreed with the idea that math would prove valuable later in their lives produced an average score of 165 on the NAEP math assessment that year. (See Figure 4.9.)

Mathematics Achievement-Level Performance

As explained at the beginning of this chapter, descriptive achievement levels accompany the average scale scores for the national, state, and TUDA assessments and correspond to ranges of scores on the scale. The three achievement levels are basic, proficient, and advanced. As Figure 4.10 shows, fourth and eighth

FIGURE 4.4

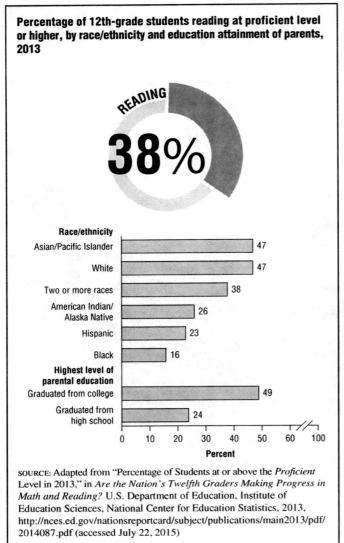

Percentage of 12th-grade students reading at proficient level or higher, by race/ethnicity and education attainment of parents, 2013

SOURCE: Adapted from "Percentage of Students at or above the *Proficient* Level in 2013," in *Are the Nation's Twelfth Graders Making Progress in Math and Reading?* U.S. Department of Education, Institute of Education Sciences, National Center for Education Statistics, 2013, http://nces.ed.gov/nationsreportcard/subject/publications/main2013/pdf/2014087.pdf (accessed July 22, 2015)

graders demonstrated considerable improvement in mathematics between 1990 and 2013. For example, in 1990 half (50%) of all fourth graders were rated at below basic in mathematics achievement. Another 37% were at a basic level, whereas 12% were proficient in math; only 1% of all fourth graders demonstrated advanced mathematics ability in 1990. By 2013 the proportion of fourth graders with below basic math abilities had fallen to 17%, and the percentage of fourth graders who demonstrated proficiency in math rose to 34%. In addition, 8% of the nation's fourth graders exhibited advanced mathematics ability in 2013. Similarly, nearly half (48%) of eighth graders were assessed as having mathematics abilities that were below basic in 1990; by 2013 this figure had fallen to 26 percent. During this time, the proportion of eighth graders demonstrating proficiency or advanced ability in math more than doubled, from 15% (13% proficient, 2% advanced) in 1990 to 36% (27% proficient, 9% advanced) in 2013.

Figure 4.11 provides an overview of fourth and eighth graders who tested at proficient or higher in mathematics in 2013, by state. In 18 states that year, the percentages of both fourth and eighth graders who tested at proficient or better in math exceeded the national average. Conversely, in 10 states and the District of Columbia, the percentages of both fourth and eighth graders who were proficient or advanced at math were below the national average in 2013. As Figure 4.11 shows, there appear to be distinct regional differences in mathematics performance among fourth and eighth graders in the United States. In general, fourth- and eighth-grade students in New England, the Midwest and Mid-Atlantic, the Great Plains, and the Rocky Mountain region performed at a higher level in mathematics in 2013 than fourth and eighth graders in the Deep South, the Southwest, and California.

Among 12th graders in 2013, a considerably higher proportion of Asian or Pacific Islanders (47%) were proficient or higher in math than any other race or ethnicity. (See Figure 4.12.) Roughly one-third (33%) of non-Hispanic white 12th graders demonstrated proficiency or better in math that year, followed by students who belonged to two or more races (26%), Native Americans/Alaskan Natives and Hispanics (12% each), and African Americans (7%). In 2013 a higher proportion of male 12th graders (28%) than female 12th graders (24%) tested at a proficient level or higher in math. (See Table 4.10.)

SCIENCE ASSESSMENT

The 2009 national, state, and TUDA science assessments were based on a new science framework. This new framework was developed to reflect the goals and objectives of the National Research Council, in *National Science Education Standards* (1996, http://www.nap.edu/openbook.php?record_id=4962), and the American Association for the Advancement of Science, in *Benchmarks for Science Literacy* (1993, http://www.project2061.org/publications/bsl/online/index.php). The new science framework was also developed to reflect advances in research in science and cognition, national and international science assessments, and innovative assessment approaches. Appropriate accommodations were incorporated for students who needed them. Due to these extensive changes, the results of the 2009 and subsequent science assessments cannot be compared with assessments from previous years.

In "What Does the NAEP Science Assessment Measure?" (March 31, 2012, https://nces.ed.gov/nationsreportcard/science/whatmeasure.aspx), the NCES compares the 1996–2005 science framework with the 2009 framework. The 2009 framework requires testing in three major areas of science: physical, life, and earth and space science.

TABLE 4.6

Percentage of students at or above National Assessment of Educational Progress reading achievement levels, by grade, race/ethnicity, and eligibility for free or reduced-price school lunches, selected years 1998–2013

Grade and selected student characteristic	1998 At or above basic[a]	1998 At or above proficient[b]	2000 At or above basic[a]	2000 At or above proficient[b]	2003 At or above basic[a]	2003 At or above proficient[b]	2005 At or above basic[a]	2005 At or above proficient[b]	2007 At or above basic[a]	2007 At or above proficient[b]	2009 At or above basic[a]	2009 At or above proficient[b]	2011 At or above basic[a]	2011 At or above proficient[b]	2013 At or above basic[a]	2013 At or above proficient[b]
4th grade, all students	**60**	**29**	**59**	**29**	**63**	**31**	**64**	**31**	**67**	**33**	**67**	**33**	**67**	**34**	**68**	**35**
Sex																
Male	57	27	55	25	60	28	61	29	64	30	64	30	64	31	65	32
Female	62	32	64	34	67	35	67	34	70	36	70	36	71	37	72	38
Race/ethnicity																
White	70	37	70	38	75	41	76	41	78	43	78	42	78	44	79	46
Black	36	10	35	10	40	13	42	13	46	14	48	16	49	17	50	18
Hispanic	37	13	37	13	44	15	46	16	50	17	49	17	51	18	53	20
Asian/Pacific Islander	58	30	70	41	70	38	73	42	77	46	80	49	80	49	80	51
Asian	—	—	—	—	—	—	—	—	—	—	—	—	81	50	82	53
Pacific Islander	—	—	—	—	—	—	—	—	—	—	—	—	61	28	57	27
American Indian/Alaska Native	‡	‡	63	28	47	16	48	18	49	18	50	20	47	18	51	21
Two or more races	—	—	—	—	—	—	—	—	—	—	—	—	50	20	73	40
Eligibility for free or reduced-price lunch																
Eligible	39	13	38	13	45	15	46	16	50	17	51	17	52	18	53	20
Not eligible	73	40	73	39	76	42	77	42	79	44	80	45	82	48	83	51
Unknown	69	37	71	40	76	43	77	45	80	46	81	50	82	48	83	51
8th grade, all students	**73**	**32**	**—**	**—**	**74**	**32**	**73**	**31**	**74**	**31**	**75**	**32**	**76**	**34**	**78**	**36**
Sex																
Male	67	26	—	—	69	27	68	26	69	26	71	28	72	29	74	31
Female	80	39	—	—	79	38	78	36	79	36	79	37	80	38	82	42
Race/ethnicity																
White	81	39	—	—	83	41	82	39	84	40	84	41	85	43	86	46
Black	53	13	—	—	54	13	52	12	55	13	57	14	59	15	61	17
Hispanic	53	14	—	—	56	15	56	15	58	15	61	17	64	19	68	22
Asian/Pacific Islander	75	33	—	—	79	40	80	40	80	41	83	45	83	47	86	52
Asian	—	—	—	—	—	—	—	—	—	—	—	—	84	49	87	54
Pacific Islander	—	—	—	—	—	—	—	—	—	—	—	—	63	24	70	27
American Indian/Alaska Native	‡	‡	—	—	57	17	59	17	56	18	62	21	63	22	62	19
Two or more races	—	—	—	—	—	—	—	—	—	—	—	—	79	39	81	40
Eligibility for free or reduced-price lunch																
Eligible	56	14	—	—	57	16	57	15	58	15	60	16	63	18	66	20
Not eligible	80	38	—	—	82	40	81	39	83	40	85	42	86	45	87	48
Unknown	80	43	—	—	81	42	84	45	86	48	89	51	90	54	92	59

TABLE 4.6

Percentage of students at or above National Assessment of Educational Progress reading achievement levels, by grade, race/ethnicity, and eligibility for free or reduced-price school lunches, selected years 1998–2013 [CONTINUED]

Grade and selected student characteristic	1998 At or above basic[a]	1998 At or above proficient[b]	2000 At or above basic[a]	2000 At or above proficient[b]	2003 At or above basic[a]	2003 At or above proficient[b]	2005 At or above basic[a]	2005 At or above proficient[b]	2007 At or above basic[a]	2007 At or above proficient[b]	2009 At or above basic[a]	2009 At or above proficient[b]	2011 At or above basic[a]	2011 At or above proficient[b]	2013 At or above basic[a]	2013 At or above proficient[b]
12th grade, all students	76	40	—	—	—	—	73	35	—	—	74	38	—	—	75	38
Sex																
Male	70	32	—	—	—	—	67	29	—	—	69	32	—	—	70	33
Female	83	48	—	—	—	—	78	41	—	—	80	43	—	—	79	42
Race/ethnicity																
White	82	47	—	—	—	—	79	43	—	—	81	46	—	—	83	47
Black	57	17	—	—	—	—	54	16	—	—	57	17	—	—	56	16
Hispanic	62	24	—	—	—	—	60	20	—	—	61	22	—	—	64	23
Asian/Pacific Islander	74	38	—	—	—	—	74	36	—	—	81	49	—	—	80	47
Asian	—	—	—	—	—	—	—	—	—	—	—	—	—	—	80	48
Pacific Islander	—	—	—	—	—	—	—	—	—	—	—	—	—	—	75	39
American Indian/Alaska Native	‡	‡	—	—	—	—	67	26	—	—	70	29	—	—	65	26
Two or more races	—	—	—	—	—	—	—	—	—	—	—	—	—	—	77	38

—Not available.

‡Reporting standards not met (too few cases for a reliable estimate).

[a]Basic denotes partial mastery of the knowledge and skills that are fundamental for proficient work at a given grade.

[b]Proficient represents solid academic performance. Students reaching this level have demonstrated competency over challenging subject matter.

Note: Includes public and private schools. Includes students tested with accommodations (1 to 12 percent of all students, depending on grade level and year); excludes only those students with disabilities and English language learners who were unable to be tested even with accommodations (2 to 6 percent of all students). Race categories exclude persons of Hispanic ethnicity. Prior to 2011, separate data for Asians, Pacific Islanders, and those of two or more races were not collected.

SOURCE: Adapted from "Table 221.20. Percentage of Students at or above Selected National Assessment of Educational Progress (NAEP) Reading Achievement Levels, by Grade and Selected Student Characteristics: Selected Years, 1998 through 2013," in "Most Current Digest Tables," *Digest of Education Statistics*, U.S. Department of Education, Institute of Education Sciences, National Center for Education Statistics, June 2014, https://nces.ed.gov/programs/digest/d14/tables/xls/tabn221.20.xls (accessed July 31, 2015)

FIGURE 4.5

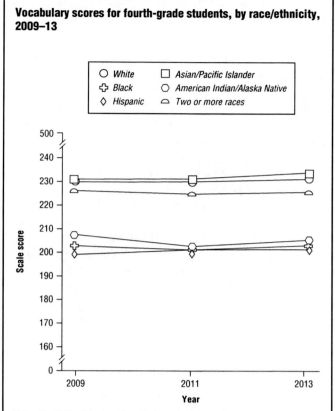

Vocabulary scores for fourth-grade students, by race/ethnicity, 2009–13

Legend:
○ White
✚ Black
◇ Hispanic
□ Asian/Pacific Islander
○ American Indian/Alaska Native
⌒ Two or more races

Notes: The National Assessment of Educational Progress (NAEP) reading vocabulary scale ranges from 0–500. Numerical differences of the same magnitude may or may not be statistically significant depending on the size of the standard errors of the estimates. Results are not shown for data points with insufficient sample sizes to permit reliable estimates. Black includes African American, Hispanic includes Latino, and Pacific Islander includes Native Hawaiian. Race categories exclude Hispanic origin. NSLP = National School Lunch Program (i.e., eligibility for free/reduced-price school lunch). Students with disabilities includes students identified as having either an Individualized Education Program or protection under Section 504 of the Rehabilitation Act of 1973. The results for students with disabilities and English language learners are based on students who were assessed and cannot be generalized to the total population of such students.

SOURCE: "Trend in Fourth-Grade NAEP Vocabulary Scores, by Race/Ethnicity," in "Scores by Student Group," *The Nation's Report Card 2013: Vocabulary*, U.S. Department of Education, Institute of Education Sciences, National Center for Education Statistics, 2013, http://www.nationsreportcard.gov/reading_2013/vocabulary/#student-groups (accessed July 22, 2015)

FIGURE 4.6

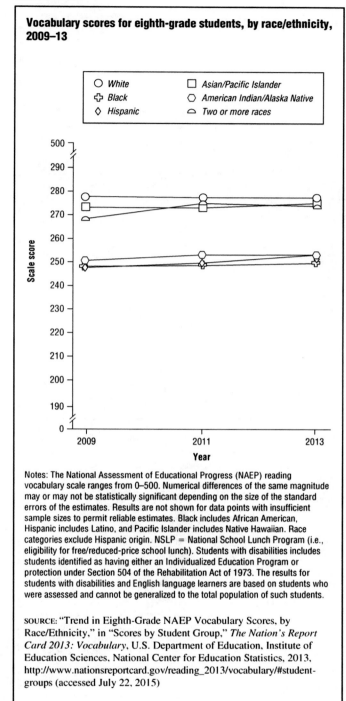

Vocabulary scores for eighth-grade students, by race/ethnicity, 2009–13

Legend:
○ White
✚ Black
◇ Hispanic
□ Asian/Pacific Islander
○ American Indian/Alaska Native
⌒ Two or more races

Notes: The National Assessment of Educational Progress (NAEP) reading vocabulary scale ranges from 0–500. Numerical differences of the same magnitude may or may not be statistically significant depending on the size of the standard errors of the estimates. Results are not shown for data points with insufficient sample sizes to permit reliable estimates. Black includes African American, Hispanic includes Latino, and Pacific Islander includes Native Hawaiian. Race categories exclude Hispanic origin. NSLP = National School Lunch Program (i.e., eligibility for free/reduced-price school lunch). Students with disabilities includes students identified as having either an Individualized Education Program or protection under Section 504 of the Rehabilitation Act of 1973. The results for students with disabilities and English language learners are based on students who were assessed and cannot be generalized to the total population of such students.

SOURCE: "Trend in Eighth-Grade NAEP Vocabulary Scores, by Race/Ethnicity," in "Scores by Student Group," *The Nation's Report Card 2013: Vocabulary*, U.S. Department of Education, Institute of Education Sciences, National Center for Education Statistics, 2013, http://www.nationsreportcard.gov/reading_2013/vocabulary/#student-groups (accessed July 22, 2015)

(Space science was added in the 2009 framework.) The NCES also outlines areas of science practice in which students were assessed in 2009 and compares these areas to those that were used in the 1996–2005 assessments. The 2009 science practice area focuses on science principles, the nature of science, conceptual understanding, and the application of science knowledge and skills to problem solving.

Science Achievement-Level Performance

Table 4.11 shows the average NAEP science scores for fourth, eighth, and 12th graders in 2009; because eighth graders were assessed again in 2011, data for that year are also included for that grade level. All three grades were scheduled to be assessed again in 2015. (See Table 4.1.) Table 4.11 includes a breakdown of performance levels, by race, ethnicity, and gender, as well as by education level of parents, school type, and other demographic categories.

FOURTH GRADERS. In 2009 nearly three-quarters (72%) of fourth-grade students performed at or above basic achievement levels in science. (See Table 4.11.)

FIGURE 4.7

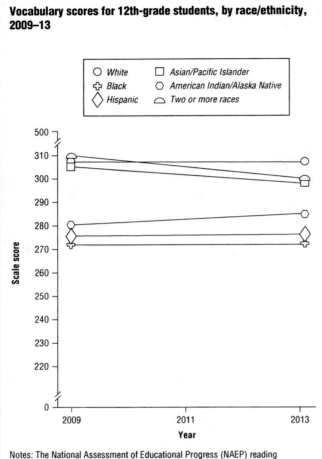

Vocabulary scores for 12th-grade students, by race/ethnicity, 2009–13

○ White   □ Asian/Pacific Islander
✚ Black   ○ American Indian/Alaska Native
◇ Hispanic   △ Two or more races

Notes: The National Assessment of Educational Progress (NAEP) reading vocabulary scale ranges from 0–500. Numerical differences of the same magnitude may or may not be statistically significant depending on the size of the standard errors of the estimates. Results are not shown for data points with insufficient sample sizes to permit reliable estimates. Black includes African American, Hispanic includes Latino, and Pacific Islander includes Native Hawaiian. Race categories exclude Hispanic origin. NSLP = National School Lunch Program (i.e., eligibility for free/reduced-price school lunch). Students with disabilities includes students identified as having either an Individualized Education Program or protection under Section 504 of the Rehabilitation Act of 1973. The results for students with disabilities and English language learners are based on students who were assessed and cannot be generalized to the total population of such students.

SOURCE: "Trend in Twelfth-Grade NAEP Vocabulary Scores, by Race/Ethnicity," in "Scores by Student Group," *The Nation's Report Card 2013: Vocabulary*, U.S. Department of Education, Institute of Education Sciences, National Center for Education Statistics, 2013, http://www.nationsreportcard.gov/reading_2013/vocabulary/#student-groups (accessed July 22, 2015)

Approximately one-third (34%) of fourth graders scored at or above proficient in science that year, and 1% reached advanced achievement levels. More than a quarter (28%) of fourth-grade students scored below basic achievement levels in science in 2009. White fourth graders performed highest among all racial and ethnic groups, with an average NAEP science scale score of 163. Asian or Pacific Island fourth graders scored second highest in science testing, with an average score of 160, followed by Native American or Alaskan Native fourth

graders (135), Hispanic fourth graders (131), and African American fourth graders (127). Accounting for gender, male fourth graders (151) scored slightly higher than female fourth graders (149).

EIGHTH GRADERS. In 2011, 65% of eighth-grade students scored at or above basic achievement levels in science, 32% scored at or above proficient, and 2% performed at an advanced level. (See Table 4.11.) As with fourth-grade students in 2009, white eighth graders performed highest in science among all racial and ethnic groups in 2011, with an average score of 163, followed by Asian or Pacific Islander students (159), Native American or Alaskan Native students (141), Hispanic students (137), and African American students (129). On average, private school eighth graders (163) scored higher than public school eighth graders (151) in science achievement in 2011. Table 4.11 also shows a direct correlation between eighth graders' science scores and the highest education level attained by their parents. For example, on average, eighth graders whose parents never completed high school scored 132 on the NAEP science achievement tests in 2011. By contrast, eighth graders whose parents graduated from college posted an average score of 162.

12TH GRADERS. In 2009, 60% of 12th-grade students performed at or above basic achievement levels in science. (See Table 4.11.) Asian or Pacific Islander 12th graders performed highest on the science achievement tests in 2009, with an average score of 164; they were followed by white (159), Native American or Alaskan Native (144), Hispanic (134), and African American (125) 12th graders. On average, male 12th graders (153) scored higher than female 12th graders (147) on the science achievement tests in 2009.

HISTORY ASSESSMENT

Figure 4.13 shows trends in history achievement among eighth graders between 1994 and 2014. Over that two-decade span, the proportion of eighth-grade students testing at proficient in history rose by four percentage points, from 13% in 1994 to 17% in 2014. During that same period, the proportion of eighth graders who demonstrated below basic ability in history fell by 10 points, from 39% in 1994 to 29% in 2014. Among different races and ethnic groups, Asian or Pacific Islander eighth graders showed the most significant improvement in history between 1994 and 2014. As Figure 4.14 reveals, the proportion of Asian or Pacific Islander eighth graders who tested as proficient in history nearly doubled over that period, rising from 16% in 1994 to 30% in 2014. Overall, one-third of Asian or Pacific Islander eighth graders tested as proficient or advanced in 2014, compared with one-quarter of non-Hispanic whites, 8% of Hispanics, and 6% of African Americans.

FIGURE 4.8

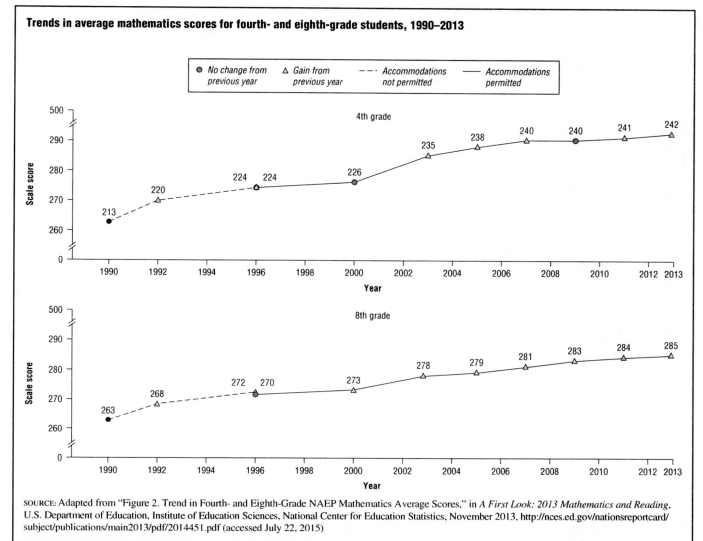

Trends in average mathematics scores for fourth- and eighth-grade students, 1990–2013

● No change from previous year   △ Gain from previous year   – – · Accommodations not permitted   —— Accommodations permitted

SOURCE: Adapted from "Figure 2. Trend in Fourth- and Eighth-Grade NAEP Mathematics Average Scores," in *A First Look: 2013 Mathematics and Reading*, U.S. Department of Education, Institute of Education Sciences, National Center for Education Statistics, November 2013, http://nces.ed.gov/nationsreportcard/subject/publications/main2013/pdf/2014451.pdf (accessed July 22, 2015)

INTERNATIONAL COMPARISONS IN READING, SCIENCE, AND MATHEMATICS ACHIEVEMENT

The International Association for the Evaluation of Educational Achievement (IEA), an independent international cooperative of national research institutions and governmental research agencies, publishes the Progress in International Reading Literary Study (PIRLS), a research report that is dedicated to analyzing reading achievement worldwide. In addition, the IEA uses the Trends in International Mathematics and Science Study (TIMSS) to measure students' mathematics and science achievement. Overall, the IEA has conducted more than 25 research studies of cross-national achievement, such as the PIRLS and TIMSS, in an effort to identify comparative strengths and weaknesses of educational systems. These data can help countries learn from one another.

International Comparisons in Reading

In *Progress in International Reading Literacy Study (PIRLS) 2011 International Results in Reading* (2012, http://timssandpirls.bc.edu/pirls2011/downloads/P11_IR_FullBook.pdf), Ina V. S. Mullis et al. provide an overview of reading achievement by country. Figure 4.15 shows the average scores of fourth-grade students on a combined reading literacy scale, by country, for 2011. Fourth graders in Hong Kong ranked highest that year, with an average score of 571, followed by the Russian Federation (568), Finland (568), and Singapore (567). The average reading literacy score for U.S. students was 556, which was well above the PIRLS scale center point of 500.

International Comparisons in Mathematics

Mullis et al. assess in *Trends in International Mathematics and Science Study (TIMSS) 2011 International Results in Mathematics* (2012, http://timssandpirls.bc.edu/timss2011/downloads/T11_IR_Mathematics_FullBook.pdf) mathematics achievement worldwide. Figure 4.16 shows the average mathematics literacy scale scores

TABLE 4.7

Average National Assessment of Educational Progress mathematics scores and achievement levels, by grade and select student characteristics, selected years 1990–2013

Grade and year	Percent of students in school eligible for free or reduced-price lunch — Average mathematics scale score[b]					English language learner (ELL) status			Disability status[a] — Average mathematics scale score[b]			Percent of all students attaining mathematics achievement levels		
	0–25 percent eligible (low poverty)	26–50 percent eligible	51–75 percent eligible	76–100 percent eligible (high poverty)	Gap between low-poverty and high-poverty score	ELL (Average mathematics)	Non-ELL	Gap between non-ELL and ELL score	Identified as student with disability (SD)	Not identified as SD	Gap between non-SD and SD score	Below basic[c]	At or above basic[c]	At or above proficient[d]
Grade 4														
1990[e]	—	—	—	—	—	†	†	†	†	†	†	50	50	13
1992[e]	—	—	—	—	—	†	†	†	†	†	†	41	59	18
1996	—	—	—	—	—	201	225	24	204	225	22	37	63	21
2000	239	227	216	205	34	199	227	28	198	228	30	35	65	24
2003	247	237	229	216	31	214	237	23	214	237	23	23	77	32
2005	250	240	232	220	30	216	240	24	219	240	22	20	80	36
2007	252	242	234	222	30	217	242	25	220	242	22	18	82	39
2009	254	242	234	223	31	218	242	24	221	242	21	18	82	39
2011	255	245	237	226	29	219	243	24	218	244	26	18	82	40
2013	257	246	238	226	31	219	244	25	218	245	26	17	83	42
Grade 8														
1990[e]	—	—	—	—	—	†	†	†	†	†	†	48	52	15
1992[e]	—	—	—	—	—	†	†	†	†	†	†	42	58	21
1996	—	—	—	—	—	226	272	46	231	273	42	39	61	23
2000	287	270	260	246	41	234	274	40	230	276	47	37	63	26
2003	291	278	266	251	40	242	279	38	242	282	39	32	68	29
2005	293	280	268	254	38	244	281	37	245	283	38	31	69	30
2007	296	282	271	259	37	246	283	38	246	285	38	29	71	32
2009	298	284	274	260	38	243	285	42	249	287	38	27	73	34
2011	300	287	276	264	36	244	286	42	250	288	38	27	73	35
2013	301	289	277	265	36	246	287	41	249	289	40	26	74	35
Grade 12														
1990[e]	—	—	—	—	—	†	†	†	†	†	†	—	—	—
1992[e]	—	—	—	—	—	†	†	†	†	†	†	—	—	—
1996	—	—	—	—	—	—	—	—	—	—	—	—	—	—
2000	—	—	—	—	—	—	—	—	—	—	—	—	—	—
2003	—	—	—	—	—	—	—	—	—	—	—	—	—	—
2005	158	147	136	122	36	120	151	31	114	153	39	39	61	23
2007	—	—	—	—	—	—	—	—	—	—	—	—	—	—
2009	166	150	140	130	36	117	154	38	120	156	36	36	64	26
2011	—	—	—	—	—	—	—	—	—	—	—	—	—	—
2013	169	155	143	134	35	109	155	46	119	157	38	35	65	26

TABLE 4.7

Average National Assessment of Educational Progress mathematics scores and achievement levels, by grade and select student characteristics, selected years 1990–2013 [CONTINUED]

—Not available.

†Not applicable.

[a]The student with disability (SD) variable used in this table includes students who have a 504 plan, even if they do not have an Individualized Education Plan (IEP).

[b]For the grade 4 and grade 8 assessments, scale ranges from 0 to 500. For the grade 12 assessment scale ranges from 0 to 300.

[c]Basic denotes partial mastery of the knowledge and skills that are fundamental for proficient work at a given grade.

[d]Proficient represents solid academic performance. Students reaching this level have demonstrated competency over challenging subject matter.

[e]Accommodations were not permitted for this assessment.

[f]Because of major changes to the framework and content of the grade 12 assessment, results from 2005 and later assessment years cannot be compared with results from earlier assessment years. Therefore, this table does not include results from the earlier grade 12 assessment years (1990, 1992, 1996, and 2000).

Note: Includes public and private schools. For 1996 and later years, includes students tested with accommodations (1 to 12 percent of all students, depending on grade level and year); excludes only those students with disabilities and English language learners who were unable to be tested even with accommodations (1 to 4 percent of all students).

SOURCE: Adapted from "Table 222.12. Average National Assessment of Educational Progress (NAEP) Mathematics Scale Score and Percentage of Students Attaining Selected NAEP Mathematics Achievement Levels, by Selected school and Student Characteristics and Grade: Selected Years, 1990 through 2013," in "Most Current Digest Tables," *Digest of Education Statistics*, U.S. Department of Education, Institute of Education Sciences, National Center for Education Statistics, September 2014. https://nces.ed.gov/programs/digest/d14/tables/xls/tabn222.12.xls (accessed July 31, 2015)

TABLE 4.8

Average National Assessment of Educational Progress mathematics scores among eighth-grade students, by attitudes toward mathematics and selected student characteristics, 2013

Student characteristic	Math work is engaging and interesting				Math work is challenging				Math work is too easy			
	Never or hardly ever	Sometimes	Often	Always/ almost always	Never or hardly ever	Sometimes	Often	Always/ almost always	Never or hardly ever	Sometimes	Often	Always/ almost always
	Average scale score[a]											
All students	**280**	**284**	**289**	**287**	**295**	**286**	**284**	**275**	**285**	**283**	**287**	**290**
Sex												
Male	281	285	290	287	297	287	284	274	284	284	289	292
Female	279	284	289	288	293	285	284	277	286	283	286	288
Race/ethnicity												
White	286	294	300	300	303	295	294	286	292	293	297	299
Black	260	263	267	266	273	265	263	255	264	262	266	269
Hispanic	268	271	275	275	279	273	271	264	272	270	275	277
Asian	303	306	314	311	324	310	303	296	311	307	310	316
Pacific Islander	269	278	273	277	289	278	271	265	277	274	275	283
American Indian/Alaska Native	270	269	272	271	281	270	271	262	268	268	277	276
Two or more races	281	285	290	302	299	290	285	277	286	285	293	299
Eligibility for free or reduced-price lunch												
Eligible	267	270	274	272	280	272	269	260	268	269	274	277
Not eligible	289	297	303	303	306	298	296	289	296	296	300	304
Unknown	284	297	306	305	308	299	295	292	296	297	304	302
Highest education level of either parent[b]												
Did not finish high school	263	266	270	271	276	269	266	257	263	266	271	275
Graduated high school	268	271	273	272	280	272	270	261	269	269	274	277
Some education after high school	281	286	289	288	295	286	283	278	282	284	288	295
Graduated college	289	296	301	299	305	297	295	287	296	295	298	301
	Percent of students											
All students	**22**	**35**	**28**	**15**	**12**	**45**	**32**	**11**	**17**	**55**	**21**	**7**
Sex												
Male	21	33	29	16	12	45	33	10	15	54	23	8
Female	22	37	27	14	11	45	32	12	20	55	19	6
Race/ethnicity												
White	25	36	27	12	12	45	32	11	20	54	19	6
Black	18	33	27	21	11	44	32	14	15	54	22	8
Hispanic	19	36	30	16	10	46	33	11	13	56	23	8
Asian	14	37	31	18	14	50	28	8	9	52	27	12
Pacific Islander	15	36	28	21	11	46	33	11	9	57	28	7
American Indian/Alaska Native	20	36	28	16	11	44	32	13	16	57	21	7
Two or more races	22	37	28	14	13	44	32	12	18	52	22	8
Eligibility for free or reduced-price lunch												
Eligible	20	35	28	16	11	45	32	12	14	55	23	8
Not eligible	23	36	28	13	12	45	32	10	19	54	20	7
Unknown	22	33	28	16	11	45	33	11	23	56	16	5
Highest education level of either parent[b]												
Did not finish high school	22	35	28	15	10	45	33	12	14	57	22	8
Graduated high school	22	36	27	15	10	45	32	12	16	55	22	7
Some education after high school	23	35	28	14	12	45	33	10	17	55	21	7
Graduated college	22	35	29	15	13	44	32	11	19	53	20	7

TABLE 4.8

Average National Assessment of Educational Progress mathematics scores among eighth-grade students, by attitudes toward mathematics and selected student characteristics, 2013 [CONTINUED]

[a]Scale ranges from 0 to 500.

[b]Based on student reports. The category of students whose parents have an unknown level of education is not shown, although data for these students is included in table totals.

Note: Includes public and private schools. Includes students tested with accommodations (12 percent of all 8th-grade students); excludes only those students with disabilities and English language learners who were unable to be tested even with accommodations (1 percent of all 8th-grade students). Race categories exclude persons of Hispanic ethnicity. Detail may not sum to totals because of rounding.

SOURCE: Adapted from "Table 222.30. Average National Assessment of Educational Progress (NAEP) Mathematics Scale Score of 8th-Graders with Various Attitudes toward Mathematics and Percentage Reporting These Attitudes, by Selected Student Characteristics: 2013," in "Most Current Digest Tables," *Digest of Education Statistics*, U.S. Department of Education, Institute of Education Sciences, National Center for Education Statistics, October 2014, https://nces.ed.gov/programs/digest/d14/tables/xls/tabn222.30.xls (accessed July 31, 2015)

TABLE 4.9

Average National Assessment of Educational Progress mathematics scores among 12th-grade students, by attitudes toward mathematics and selected student characteristics, 2013

Student characteristic	Math work is engaging and interesting				Math work is challenging				Math work is too easy			
	Never or hardly ever	Sometimes	Often	Always/almost always	Never or hardly ever	Sometimes	Often	Always/almost always	Never or hardly ever	Sometimes	Often	Always/almost always
	Average scale score[a]											
All students	**145**	**155**	**165**	**166**	**158**	**157**	**158**	**154**	**156**	**156**	**158**	**162**
Sex												
Male	146	158	167	169	161	160	158	155	157	157	163	165
Female	145	153	163	164	154	153	157	154	156	154	152	157
Race/ethnicity												
White	152	164	175	179	165	165	166	163	163	165	168	169
Black	127	133	139	135	136	134	134	129	133	132	134	136
Hispanic	135	142	147	154	141	144	144	141	144	142	144	150
Asian	167	173	182	187	188	179	174	176	181	174	176	185
Pacific Islander	‡	‡	‡	‡	‡	‡	‡	‡	‡	‡	‡	‡
American Indian/Alaska Native	137	149	140	‡	‡	140	145	‡	145	141	‡	‡
Two or more races	145	156	168	‡	‡	159	158	153	158	153	160	‡
Eligibility for free or reduced-price lunch												
Eligible	133	139	146	148	143	142	141	137	139	139	143	149
Not eligible	151	164	175	177	166	165	166	163	163	165	167	169
Unknown	155	165	175	183	174	169	166	165	166	167	169	‡
Highest education level of either parent[b]												
Did not finish high school	131	136	144	148	137	139	140	136	136	137	141	147
Graduated high school	134	141	147	152	147	142	142	137	140	141	142	150
Some education after high school	141	153	161	162	156	152	153	152	151	152	155	159
Graduated college	155	166	177	178	169	168	169	166	167	167	171	171
	Percent of students											
All students	**26**	**36**	**27**	**11**	**7**	**35**	**37**	**21**	**32**	**47**	**15**	**6**
Sex												
Male	25	35	28	12	8	36	37	18	27	48	18	7
Female	27	37	25	11	6	34	36	23	36	47	13	4
Race/ethnicity												
White	28	35	27	10	8	35	37	21	34	45	14	6
Black	27	37	24	13	8	37	34	22	32	48	14	6
Hispanic	24	35	28	13	6	35	39	20	25	52	18	6
Asian	13	37	32	17	6	36	36	21	24	49	20	8
Pacific Islander	20	42	18	20	7	32	31	31	36	41	19	4
American Indian/Alaska Native	27	40	22	11	10	30	38	22	30	50	11	10
Two or more races	28	40	22	10	6	36	37	21	35	46	13	6
Eligibility for free or reduced-price lunch												
Eligible	25	35	27	12	7	36	35	21	27	50	17	6
Not eligible	27	36	26	11	7	35	37	21	34	46	15	6
Unknown	25	37	28	10	6	33	40	21	38	44	14	4
Highest education level of either parent[b]												
Did not finish high school	25	35	26	14	7	38	35	20	24	49	20	7
Graduated high school	29	36	26	10	8	36	37	19	29	49	15	6
Some education after high school	27	38	25	9	8	35	36	21	32	47	15	5
Graduated college	25	35	28	12	7	35	37	21	34	46	14	6

TABLE 4.9

Average National Assessment of Educational Progress mathematics scores among 12th-grade students, by attitudes toward mathematics and selected student characteristics, 2013 [CONTINUED]

‡Reporting standards not met (too few cases for a reliable estimate).
ªScale ranges from 0 to 300.
ᵇBased on student reports. The category of students whose parents have an unknown level of education is not shown, although data for these students is included in table totals.
Note: Includes public and private schools. Includes students tested with accommodations (9 percent of all 12th-grade students); excludes only those students with disabilities and English language learners who were unable to be tested even with accommodations (2 percent of all 12th-grade students). Race categories exclude persons of Hispanic ethnicity. Detail may not sum to totals because of rounding.

SOURCE: Adapted from "Table 222.35. Average National Assessment of Educational Progress (NAEP) Mathematics Scale Score of 12th-Graders with Various Attitudes toward Mathematics and Percentage Reporting These Attitudes, by Selected Student Characteristics: 2013," in "Most Current Digest Tables," *Digest of Education Statistics*, U.S. Department of Education, Institute of Education Sciences, National Center for Education Statistics, October 2014. https://nces.ed.gov/programs/digest/d14/tables/xls/tabn222.35.xls (accessed July 31, 2015)

of fourth graders, by country, for 2011. Asian countries dominated the top rankings for mathematics achievement that year, with Singapore (606), the Republic of Korea (South Korea; 605), Hong Kong (602), Chinese Taipei (591), and Japan (585) occupying the first five spots on the list. Fourth graders from the United States scored an average of 541 in mathematics achievement, one point behind England (542) and the Russian Federation (542), and 11th overall.

International Comparisons in Science

In *Trends in International Mathematics and Science Study (TIMSS) 2011 International Results in Science*

(2012, http://timssandpirls.bc.edu/timss2011/downloads/T11_IR_Science_FullBook.pdf), Michael O. Martin et al. measure achievement in science for 2011. Figure 4.17 shows the average science literacy scale scores of fourth-grade students, by country, for that year. Fourth graders from South Korea ranked first worldwide, with an average score of 587, followed closely by fourth graders from Singapore (583). Other top countries included Finland (570), Japan (559), and the Russian Federation (552). Fourth graders from the United States ranked seventh overall on the list, with an average science achievement score of 544.

STANDARDIZED TESTING AT THE STATE LEVEL

Individual states administer their own tests at the elementary, middle, and high school levels. In "Standardized Testing State by State" (2015, http://www.time4learning.com/testprep), Time4Learning.com provides a breakdown of tests state by state. All but three states administer a single standardized testing format, such as the West Virginia Educational Standards Test or Louisiana's LEAP Alternate Assessment. Connecticut and Iowa administer two standardized tests, while Maine administers three separate tests: the New England Common Assessment Program, which also serves as the standardized test in New Hampshire, Rhode Island, and Vermont; the Maine Educational Assessment; and the Maine High School Assessment.

HIGH SCHOOL GRADUATION REQUIREMENTS

According to Lauren Stillman and Rolf K. Blank of the Council of Chief State School Officers, in *Key State Education Policies on PK–12 Education: 2008* (2009, http://www.ccsso.org/Documents/2008/Key_State

FIGURE 4.9

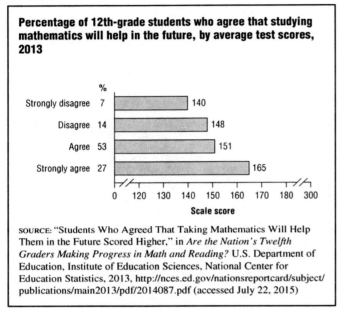

Percentage of 12th-grade students who agree that studying mathematics will help in the future, by average test scores, 2013

SOURCE: "Students Who Agreed That Taking Mathematics Will Help Them in the Future Scored Higher," in *Are the Nation's Twelfth Graders Making Progress in Math and Reading?* U.S. Department of Education, Institute of Education Sciences, National Center for Education Statistics, 2013, http://nces.ed.gov/nationsreportcard/subject/publications/main2013/pdf/2014087.pdf (accessed July 22, 2015)

FIGURE 4.10

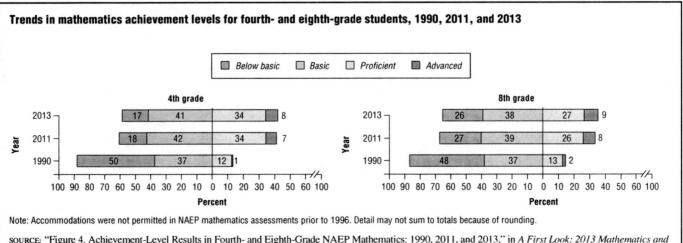

Trends in mathematics achievement levels for fourth- and eighth-grade students, 1990, 2011, and 2013

Note: Accommodations were not permitted in NAEP mathematics assessments prior to 1996. Detail may not sum to totals because of rounding.

SOURCE: "Figure 4. Achievement-Level Results in Fourth- and Eighth-Grade NAEP Mathematics: 1990, 2011, and 2013," in *A First Look: 2013 Mathematics and Reading*, U.S. Department of Education, Institute of Education Sciences, National Center for Education Statistics, November 2013, http://nces.ed.gov/nationsreportcard/subject/publications/main2013/pdf/2014451.pdf (accessed July 22, 2015)

FIGURE 4.11

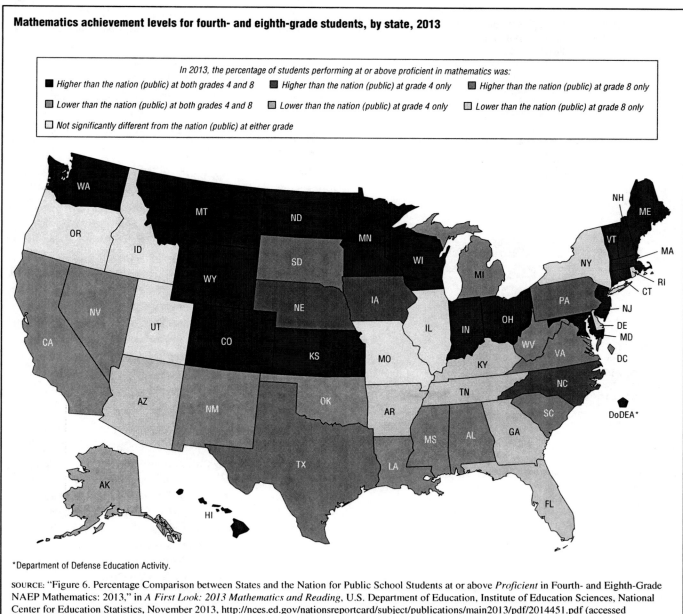

Mathematics achievement levels for fourth- and eighth-grade students, by state, 2013

In 2013, the percentage of students performing at or above proficient in mathematics was:

■ Higher than the nation (public) at both grades 4 and 8 ■ Higher than the nation (public) at grade 4 only ■ Higher than the nation (public) at grade 8 only

■ Lower than the nation (public) at both grades 4 and 8 □ Lower than the nation (public) at grade 4 only □ Lower than the nation (public) at grade 8 only

□ Not significantly different from the nation (public) at either grade

*Department of Defense Education Activity.

SOURCE: "Figure 6. Percentage Comparison between States and the Nation for Public School Students at or above *Proficient* in Fourth- and Eighth-Grade NAEP Mathematics: 2013," in *A First Look: 2013 Mathematics and Reading*, U.S. Department of Education, Institute of Education Sciences, National Center for Education Statistics, November 2013, http://nces.ed.gov/nationsreportcard/subject/publications/main2013/pdf/2014451.pdf (accessed July 22, 2015)

_Education_Policies_2008.pdf), the most recent report on this topic as of September 2015, of the 50 states and the District of Columbia, 45 states had a state policy on the minimum Carnegie credits (units) that were required for high school graduation in 2008. One Carnegie credit equals an academic-year-long course of two semesters. Most states require a certain number of credits within each subject area necessary for graduation.

HIGH SCHOOL EXIT EXAMS

School accountability became a major issue of school reform during the first decade of the 21st century. Many states mandated what should be taught in each grade, developed assessments to measure student achievement, designed school report cards, rated their schools and publicly identified failing schools, assisted low-performing schools with additional funding, and even closed or took over failing schools. Included in the various accountability measures was the high school exit examination. According to Shelby McIntosh of the Center on Education Policy, in *State High School Exit Exams: A Policy in Transition* (September 2012, http://www.cep-dc .org/cfcontent_file.cfm?Attachment=McIntosh_Report _HSEE2012_9.19.12.pdf), there were 26 states that required students to take and pass a high school exit

FIGURE 4.12

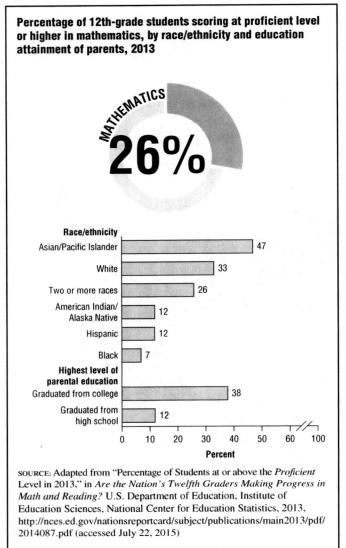

Percentage of 12th-grade students scoring at proficient level or higher in mathematics, by race/ethnicity and education attainment of parents, 2013

MATHEMATICS

26%

Race/ethnicity

Asian/Pacific Islander	47
White	33
Two or more races	26
American Indian/Alaska Native	12
Hispanic	12
Black	7

Highest level of parental education

Graduated from college	38
Graduated from high school	12

Percent

SOURCE: Adapted from "Percentage of Students at or above the *Proficient Level* in 2013," in *Are the Nation's Twelfth Graders Making Progress in Math and Reading?* U.S. Department of Education, Institute of Education Sciences, National Center for Education Statistics, 2013, http://nces.ed.gov/nationsreportcard/subject/publications/main2013/pdf/2014087.pdf (accessed July 22, 2015)

exam during the 2011–12 academic year. Three additional states required students to take end-of-course exams, although they were not required to pass these exams to receive their diplomas. Connecticut planned to implement an exit exam beginning in 2020, although it had not yet determined whether or not passing the exam would be a requirement for graduation.

Proponents of high school exit exams believe standardized tests are the best way to ensure high standards and accountability. They maintain that tests can communicate what is expected of students and teachers and assess whether progress is being made. Supporters believe that if tests are aligned to a rigorous curriculum, they are the best chance that low-performing students have to get the education they need and to narrow the minority achievement gap.

Those who oppose these tests point out that a single test is not an accurate measure of a student's performance. Opponents claim that these tests put poor and minority students at a disadvantage. A further criticism of "high-stakes" tests is that they push teachers to "teach to" the test, taking too much time away from classroom practices that support true learning.

COLLEGE ENTRANCE TESTS: THE SAT AND THE ACT

Most students applying for admission to colleges and universities in the United States take either the Scholastic Aptitude Test (SAT) or the American College Test (ACT) as part of their admission requirements. According to Melissa E. Clinedinst of the National Association for College Admission Counseling, in *State of College Admission Report 2014* (2015, http://www.nxtbook.com/ygsreprints/NACAC/2014SoCA_nxtbk), 87.8% of U.S. colleges and universities placed "considerable or moderate importance" on standardized test scores in making admissions decisions. Other important factors are high school grades and the student's level of interest in attending the college. Clinedinst also notes that between 1993 and 2013 a student's class rank became less important as a factor in the college admissions process.

There are two types of SAT tests: the SAT Reasoning Test and the SAT Subject Matter Tests. The SAT Reasoning Test assesses students' ability to think critically. It consists of 10 parts that focus on mathematics, writing, and critical reading. The SAT Subject Matter Tests assess students' knowledge and skills in particular subject areas, such as English, history, mathematics, science, and language. In addition, these tests measure students' ability to apply their knowledge. Both types of SAT tests are scored on a scale of 200 to 800. In *2015 College-Bound Seniors Total Group Profile Report* (2015, https://secure-media.collegeboard.org/digitalServices/pdf/sat/total-group-2015.pdf), the College Board indicates that the average scores of college-bound high school seniors in the class of 2014 were 495 for critical reading, 511 for mathematics, and 484 for writing, for a combined total of 1,490. This combined score fell more than 50 points below the SAT benchmark of 1,550 for that year. The College Board reveals in *2015 College Board Program Results* (2015, https://www.collegeboard.org/program-results/performance) that only 41.9% of high school seniors met the SAT benchmark for college and career readiness in 2015. According to the College Board, students who fall below the 1,550 threshold are not as prepared to tackle the academic challenges posed by college coursework. Indeed, students who performed below the SAT benchmark were proven to have less than a 65% chance of achieving a B− grade point average or above during their first year in college.

TABLE 4.10

Percentage of students at or above National Assessment of Educational Progress mathematics achievement levels, by grade, race/ethnicity, and eligibility for free or reduced-price school lunches, selected years 1996–2013

Grade and selected student characteristic	1996		2000		2003		2005		2007		2009		2011		2013	
	At or above basic[a]	At or above proficient[b]	At or above basic[a]	At or above proficient[b]	At or above basic[a]	At or above proficient[b]	At or above basic[a]	At or above proficient[b]	At or above basic[a]	At or above proficient[b]	At or above basic[a]	At or above proficient[b]	At or above basic[a]	At or above proficient[b]	At or above basic[a]	At or above proficient[b]
4th grade, all students	**63**	**21**	**65**	**24**	**77**	**32**	**80**	**36**	**82**	**39**	**82**	**39**	**82**	**40**	**83**	**42**
Sex																
Male	63	22	67	26	78	35	81	38	82	41	82	41	83	42	82	43
Female	63	20	64	22	76	30	80	34	82	37	82	37	82	39	83	41
Race/ethnicity																
White	76	27	78	31	87	43	90	47	91	51	91	51	91	52	91	54
Black	27	3	36	5	54	10	60	13	64	15	64	16	66	17	66	18
Hispanic	40	7	42	7	62	16	68	19	70	22	71	22	72	24	73	26
Asian/Pacific Islander	67	27	‡	‡	87	48	90	55	91	58	92	60	91	62	91	64
Asian	—	—	—	—	—	—	—	—	—	—	—	—	93	64	92	66
Pacific Islander	—	—	—	—	—	—	—	—	—	—	—	—	77	34	77	33
American Indian/Alaska Native	57	‡	40	8	64	17	68	21	70	25	66	21	66	22	68	23
Two or more races	—	—	—	—	—	—	—	—	—	—	—	—	87	45	85	46
Eligibility for free or reduced-price lunch																
Eligible	40	8	43	8	62	15	67	19	70	22	70	22	72	24	73	25
Not eligible	76	27	78	32	88	45	90	49	91	53	91	54	92	57	93	59
Unknown	72	28	80	36	84	41	87	45	90	48	88	47	90	52	90	52
8th grade, all students	**61**	**23**	**63**	**26**	**68**	**29**	**69**	**30**	**71**	**32**	**73**	**34**	**73**	**35**	**74**	**35**
Sex																
Male	62	25	64	27	69	30	70	31	72	34	73	36	73	36	74	36
Female	60	22	63	24	67	27	69	28	71	30	72	32	73	34	74	35
Race/ethnicity																
White	73	30	76	34	80	37	80	39	82	42	83	44	84	44	84	45
Black	25	4	31	5	39	7	42	9	47	11	50	12	51	13	52	14
Hispanic	39	8	41	8	48	12	52	13	55	15	57	17	61	20	62	21
Asian/Pacific Islander	‡	‡	75	41	78	43	81	47	83	50	85	54	86	55	87	60
Asian	—	—	—	—	—	—	—	—	—	—	—	—	88	58	89	63
Pacific Islander	—	—	—	—	—	—	—	—	—	—	—	—	59	22	67	24
American Indian/Alaska Native	‡	‡	47	‡	52	15	53	14	53	16	56	18	55	17	59	21
Two or more races	—	—	—	—	—	—	—	—	—	—	—	—	78	39	76	38
Eligibility for free or reduced-price lunch																
Eligible	38	8	41	9	48	12	51	13	55	15	57	17	59	19	60	20

TABLE 4.10

Percentage of students at or above National Assessment of Educational Progress mathematics achievement levels, by grade, race/ethnicity, and eligibility for free or reduced-price school lunches, selected years 1996–2013 [CONTINUED]

Grade and selected student characteristic	1996 At or above basic[a]	1996 At or above proficient[b]	2000 At or above basic[a]	2000 At or above proficient[b]	2003 At or above basic[a]	2003 At or above proficient[b]	2005 At or above basic[a]	2005 At or above proficient[b]	2007 At or above basic[a]	2007 At or above proficient[b]	2009 At or above basic[a]	2009 At or above proficient[b]	2011 At or above basic[a]	2011 At or above proficient[b]	2013 At or above basic[a]	2013 At or above proficient[b]
Not eligible	69	28	74	34	79	37	79	39	81	42	83	45	84	47	86	49
Unknown	70	30	67	29	75	36	79	40	81	43	83	48	85	48	84	50
12th grade, all students	c	c	c	c	—	—	**61**	**23**	—	—	**64**	**26**	—	—	**65**	**26**
Sex																
Male	c	c	c	c	—	—	62	25	—	—	65	28	—	—	66	28
Female	c	c	c	c	—	—	60	21	—	—	63	24	—	—	64	24
Race/ethnicity																
White	c	c	c	c	—	—	70	29	—	—	75	33	—	—	75	33
Black	c	c	c	c	—	—	30	6	—	—	37	6	—	—	38	7
Hispanic	c	c	c	c	—	—	40	8	—	—	45	11	—	—	50	12
Asian/Pacific Islander	c	c	c	c	—	—	73	36	—	—	84	52	—	—	81	47
Asian	c	c	c	c	—	—	—	—	—	—	—	—	—	—	83	49
Pacific Islander	c	c	c	c	—	—	—	—	—	—	—	—	—	—	65	16
American Indian/Alaska Native	c	c	c	c	—	—	42	6	—	—	56	12	—	—	54	12
Two or more races	c	c	c	c	—	—	—	—	—	—	—	—	—	—	67	26

—Not available.

c Reporting standards not met (too few cases for a reliable estimate).

a Basic denotes partial mastery of the knowledge and skills that are fundamental for proficient work.

b Proficient represents solid academic performance. Students reaching this level have demonstrated competency over challenging subject matter.

c Because of major changes to the framework and content of the grade 12 assessment, results from 2005 and later assessment years cannot be compared with results from earlier assessment years. Therefore, this table excludes grade 12 results from 1996 and 2000.

Note: Includes public and private schools. Includes students tested with accommodations (1 to 13 percent of all students, depending on grade level and year); excludes only those students with disabilities and English language learners who were unable to be tested even with accommodations (1 to 6 percent of all students). Race categories exclude persons of Hispanic ethnicity. Prior to 2011, separate data for Asians, Pacific Islanders, and those of two or more races were not collected.

SOURCE: Adapted from "Table 222.20. Percentage of Students at or above Selected National Assessment of Educational Progress (NAEP) Mathematics Achievement Levels, by Grade and Selected Student Characteristics: Selected Years, 1996 through 2013," in "Most Current Digest Tables," *Digest of Education Statistics*, U.S. Department of Education, Institute of Education Sciences, National Center for Education Statistics, June 2014, https://nces.ed.gov/programs/digest/d14/tables/xls/tabn222.20.xls (accessed July 31, 2015)

TABLE 4.11

Average science scores for 4th-, 8th-, and 12th-graders, by grade, race/ethnicity, school type, and other characteristics, 2009 and 2011

Selected characteristic, percentile, and achievement level	Grade 4 2009 Total, all students	Grade 4 2009 Male	Grade 4 2009 Female	Grade 8 2009 Total, all students	Grade 8 2009 Male	Grade 8 2009 Female	Grade 8 2011 Total, all students	Grade 8 2011 Male	Grade 8 2011 Female	Grade 12 2009 Total, all students	Grade 12 2009 Male	Grade 12 2009 Female
					Average science scale score[a]							
All students	**150**	**151**	**149**	**150**	**152**	**148**	**152**	**154**	**149**	**150**	**153**	**147**
Race/ethnicity												
White	163	164	162	162	164	160	163	166	161	159	162	156
Black	127	126	128	126	125	126	129	130	128	125	127	123
Hispanic	131	132	130	132	134	130	137	140	134	134	138	130
Asian/Pacific Islander	160	159	160	160	162	158	159	161	157	164	161	166
American Indian/Alaska Native	135	135	135	137	141	133	141	143	139	144	†	†
Highest education level of either parent												
Did not finish high school	—	—	—	131	135	128	132	136	130	131	136	128
Graduated high school	—	—	—	139	141	137	140	143	138	138	140	136
Some education after high school	—	—	—	152	154	150	153	156	151	147	150	144
Graduated college	—	—	—	161	162	159	162	164	160	161	163	159
Eligibility for free or reduced-price lunch												
Eligible	134	134	133	133	135	131	137	139	135	132	135	130
Not eligible	163	164	163	161	163	159	164	166	161	157	159	154
Unknown	162	163	161	164	167	161	164	168	159	156	156	156
School type												
Public	149	149	148	149	151	147	151	153	148	—	—	—
Private	163	165	162	164	167	161	163	168	158	—	—	—
School locale												
City	142	142	142	142	144	141	144	146	142	146	148	144
Suburban	154	154	153	154	155	152	155	158	153	154	157	150
Town	150	151	149	149	152	147	153	155	150	150	153	146
Rural	155	156	154	154	156	152	156	159	153	150	153	146
Percentile[b]												
10th	104	103	104	103	103	103	106	107	105	104	106	103
25th	128	128	128	128	130	127	131	133	129	126	128	125
50th	153	154	152	153	156	151	155	158	152	151	154	148
75th	175	176	174	175	178	172	176	179	173	174	178	171
90th	192	194	191	192	195	188	193	196	189	194	198	190
					Standard deviation of the science scale score[c]							
All students	**35**	**36**	**34**	**35**	**36**	**34**	**34**	**35**	**33**	**35**	**36**	**34**
Achievement level					Percent of students attaining science achievement levels							
Below basic	28	27	28	37	35	38	35	32	37	40	37	42
At or above basic[d]	72	73	72	63	65	62	65	68	63	60	63	58
At or above proficient[e]	34	35	32	30	34	27	32	35	28	21	24	18
At advanced[f]	1	1	1	2	2	1	2	2	1	1	2	1

TABLE 4.11

Average science scores for 4th-, 8th-, and 12th-graders, by grade, race/ethnicity, school type, and other characteristics, 2009 and 2011 [CONTINUED]

—Not available.

[1] Reporting standards not met (too few cases for a reliable estimate).

[a] Scale ranges from 0 to 300 for all three grades, but scores cannot be compared across grades. For example, the average score of 163 for white 4th-graders does not denote higher performance than the score of 159 for white 12th-graders.

[b] The percentile represents a specific point on the percentage distribution of all students ranked by their science score from low to high. For example, 10 percent of students scored at or below the 10th percentile score, while 90 percent of students scored above it.

[c] The standard deviation provides an indication of how much the test scores varied. The lower the standard deviation, the closer the scores were clustered around the average score. About two-thirds of the student scores can be expected to fall within the range of one standard deviation above and one standard deviation below the average score. For example, the average score for all 4th-graders was 150, and the standard deviation was 35. This means that we would expect about two-thirds of the students to have scores between 185 (one standard deviation above the average) and 115 (one standard deviation below).

[d] Basic denotes partial mastery of the knowledge and skills that are fundamental for proficient work.

[e] Proficient represents solid academic performance. Students reaching this level have demonstrated competency over challenging subject matter.

[f] Advanced signifies superior performance.

Note: In 2011, only 8th-grade students were assessed in science. Includes students tested with accommodations (7 to 11 percent of all students, depending on grade level and year); excludes only those students with disabilities and English language learners who were unable to be tested even with accommodations (2 to 3 percent of all students). Race categories exclude persons of Hispanic ethnicity.

SOURCE: Adapted from "Table 168. Average National Assessment of Educational Progress (NAEP) Science Scale Score, Standard Deviation, and Percentage of Students Attaining Science Achievement Levels, by Grade Level, Selected Student and School Characteristics, and Percentile: 2009 and 2011," in *Advance Release of Selected 2012 Digest Tables*, U.S. Department of Education, Institute of Education Sciences, National Center for Education Statistics, August 2012, https://nces.ed.gov/programs/digest/d12/tables/dt12_168.asp (accessed July 22, 2015)

FIGURE 4.13

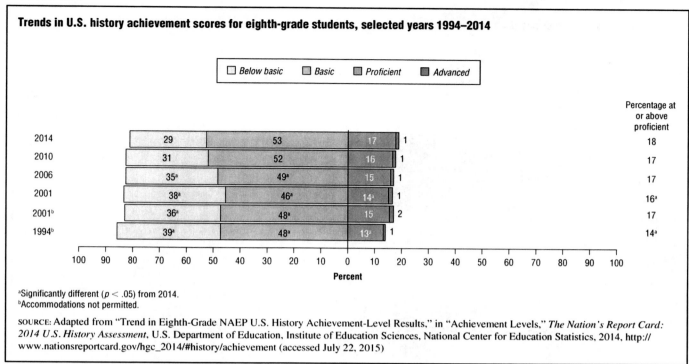

Trends in U.S. history achievement scores for eighth-grade students, selected years 1994–2014

□ Below basic   ▨ Basic   ▨ Proficient   ▨ Advanced

				Percentage at or above proficient
2014	29	53	17	1	18
2010	31	52	16	1	17
2006	35ª	49ª	15	1	17
2001	38ª	46ª	14ª	1	16ª
2001ᵇ	36ª	48ª	15	2	17
1994ᵇ	39ª	48ª	13ª	1	14ª

Percent

ªSignificantly different (*p* < .05) from 2014.
ᵇAccommodations not permitted.

SOURCE: Adapted from "Trend in Eighth-Grade NAEP U.S. History Achievement-Level Results," in "Achievement Levels," *The Nation's Report Card: 2014 U.S. History Assessment*, U.S. Department of Education, Institute of Education Sciences, National Center for Education Statistics, 2014, http://www.nationsreportcard.gov/hgc_2014/#history/achievement (accessed July 22, 2015)

The composite ACT measures students' ability in English, mathematics, reading, and science. The optional writing test measures students' ability to plan and write a short essay. The ACT results are measured on a scale of 1 to 36. The College Board indicates in *ACT Profile Report—National: Graduating Class 2015* (2015, http://www.act.org/newsroom/data/2015/pdf/profile/National 2015.pdf) that the 2015 average composite ACT score was 21. This figure was identical to the 21 average composite score recorded in 2014, and slightly higher than the average composite score of 20.9 recorded in 2013.

Trends in Scores by Race and Ethnicity

The College Board reveals in *2015 College-Bound Seniors Total Group Profile Report* that in 2015 white students scored the highest in critical reading, with a mean (average) of 529, while Asian or Pacific Islander students scored the second highest, at 525, and Native American or Alaskan Native students scored the third highest, at 481.

For mathematics and writing, Asian or Pacific Islander students scored the highest, at 598 and 531, respectively, and white students scored the second highest, at 534 and 513, respectively. Native American or Alaskan Native students scored the third highest in both mathematics (482) and writing (460).

In *ACT Profile Report—National: Graduating Class 2015*, the College Board shows composite ACT scores by race and ethnicity. Between 2011 and 2015 the average ACT composite scores rose slightly for Asian American students, from 23.6 in 2011 to 23.9 in 2015. Asian American students consistently scored the highest among the racial and ethnic groups during this span. White students showed no change during these years, averaging a score of 22.4 in both 2011 and 2015. Comparing performance levels in 2011 and 2015, scores also remained stable for Hispanic students (18.7 and 18.9, respectively) and African American students (17 and 17.1, respectively).

FIGURE 4.14

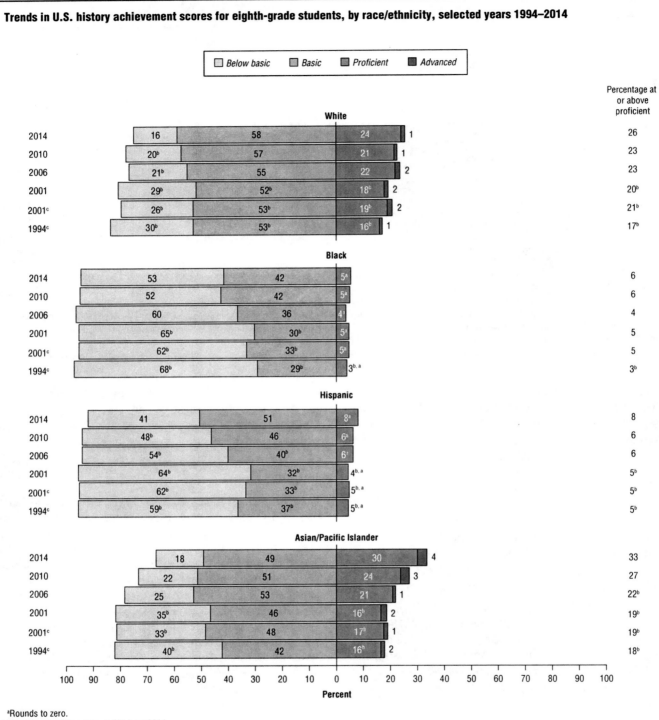

Trends in U.S. history achievement scores for eighth-grade students, by race/ethnicity, selected years 1994–2014

☐ Below basic ☐ Basic ▨ Proficient ▨ Advanced

ªRounds to zero.
ᵇSignificantly different (p < .05) from 2014.
ᶜAccommodations not permitted.

SOURCE: Adapted from "Trend in Eighth-Grade NAEP U.S. History Achievement-Level Results, by Race/Ethnicity," in "Achievement Levels," *The Nation's Report Card: 2014 U.S. History Assessment*, U.S. Department of Education, Institute of Education Sciences, National Center for Education Statistics, 2014, http://www.nationsreportcard.gov/hgc_2014/#history/achievement (accessed July 22, 2015)

FIGURE 4.15

Average scores of fourth-grade students on reading literacy scale, with performance percentile breakdowns, by country, 2011

▲ Country average significantly higher than the centerpoint of the PIRLS scale
▼ Country average significantly lower than the centerpoint of the PIRLS scale

Country	Average scale score		Reading achievement distribution
Hong Kong SAR	571	▲	
Russian Federation	568	▲	
Finland	568	▲	
Singapore	567	▲	
Northern Ireland	558	▲	
United States	556	▲	
Denmark	554	▲	
Croatia	553	▲	
Chinese Taipei	553	▲	
Ireland	552	▲	
England	552	▲	
Canada	548	▲	
Netherlands	546	▲	
Czech Republic	545	▲	
Sweden	542	▲	
Italy	541	▲	
Germany	541	▲	
Israel	541	▲	
Portugal	541	▲	
Hungary	539	▲	
Slovak Republic	535	▲	
Bulgaria	532	▲	
New Zealand	531	▲	
Slovenia	530	▲	
Austria	529	▲	
Lithuania	528	▲	
Australia	527	▲	
Poland	526	▲	
France	520	▲	
Spain	513	▲	
Norway	507	▲	
Belgium (French)	506	▲	
Romania	502		
PIRLS scale centerpoint	**500**		
Georgia	488	▼	
Malta	477	▼	
Trinidad and Tobago	471	▼	
Azerbaijan	462	▼	
Iran, Islamic Rep. of	457	▼	
Colombia	448	▼	
United Arab Emirates	439	▼	
Saudi Arabia	430	▼	
Indonesia	428	▼	
Qatar	425	▼	
Oman[a]	391	▼	
Morocco[b]	310	▼	

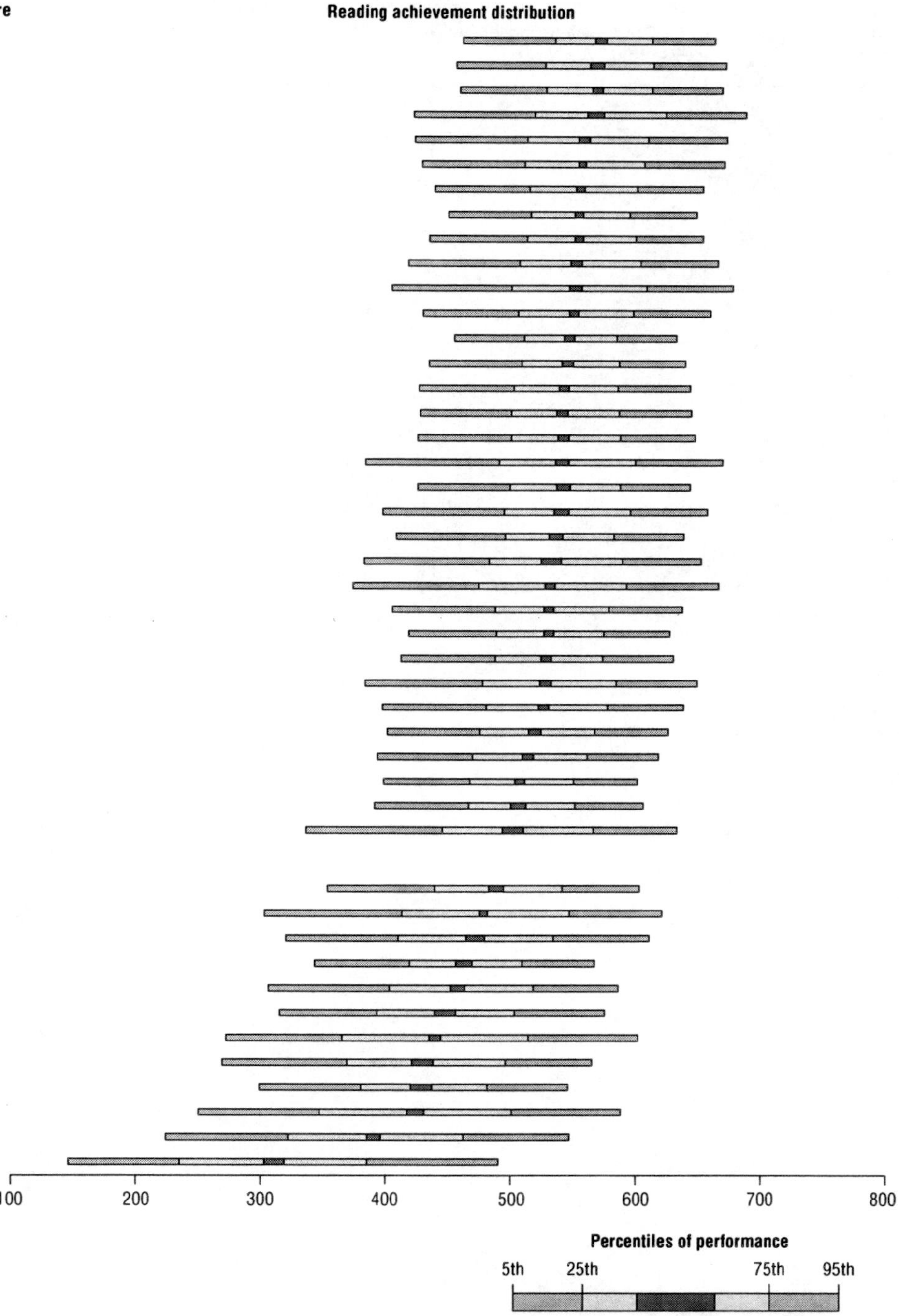

100   200   300   400   500   600   700   800

Percentiles of performance

5th   25th   75th   95th

FIGURE 4.15

Average scores of fourth-grade students on reading literacy scale, with performance percentile breakdowns, by country, 2011 [CONTINUED]

PIRLS = Progress in International Reading Literacy Study.
[a]Reservations about reliability of average achievement because the percentage of students with achievement too low for estimation does not exceed 25% but exceeds 15%.
[b]Average achievement not reliably measured because the percentage of students with achievement too low for estimation exceeds 25%.

SOURCE: Ina V. S. Mullis et al., "Exhibit 1.1. Distribution of Reading Achievement," in *Progress in International Reading Literacy Study (PIRLS) 2011 International Results in Reading*, International Association for the Evaluation of Educational Achievement (IEA) and TIMSS and PIRLS International Study Center, Lynch School of Education, Boston College, 2012, http://timssandpirls.bc.edu/pirls2011/downloads/ P11_IR_FullBook.pdf (accessed July 22, 2015)

FIGURE 4.16

Average mathematics scores of fourth-grade students, with performance percentile breakdowns, by country, 2011

▲ *Country average significantly higher than the centerpoint of the TIMSS 4th grade scale*
▼ *Country average significantly lower than the centerpoint of the TIMSS 4th grade scale*

Country	Average scale score		Mathematics achievement distribution
Singapore	606	▲	
Korea, Rep. of	605	▲	
Hong Kong SAR	602	▲	
Chinese Taipei	591	▲	
Japan	585	▲	
Northern Ireland	562	▲	
Belgium (Flemish)	549	▲	
Finland	545	▲	
England	542	▲	
Russian Federation	542	▲	
United States	541	▲	
Netherlands	540	▲	
Denmark	537	▲	
Lithuania	534	▲	
Portugal	532	▲	
Germany	528	▲	
Ireland	527	▲	
Serbia	516	▲	
Australia	516	▲	
Hungary	515	▲	
Slovenia	513	▲	
Czech Republic	511	▲	
Austria	508	▲	
Italy	508	▲	
Slovak Republic	507		
Sweden	504		
Kazakhstan	501		
TIMSS scale centerpoint	**500**		
Malta	496	▼	
Norway	495		
Croatia	490	▼	
New Zealand	486	▼	
Spain	482	▼	
Romania	482	▼	
Poland	481	▼	
Turkey	469	▼	
Azerbaijan	463	▼	
Chile	462	▼	
Thailand	458	▼	
Armenia	452	▼	
Georgia	450	▼	
Bahrain	436	▼	
United Arab Emirates	434	▼	
Iran, Islamic Rep. of	431	▼	
Qatar	413	▼	
Saudi Arabia	410	▼	
Oman[b]	385	▼	
Tunisia[b]	359	▼	
Kuwait[a]	342	▼	
Morocco[a]	335	▼	
Yemen[a]	248	▼	

100   200   300   400   500   600   700   800

FIGURE 4.16

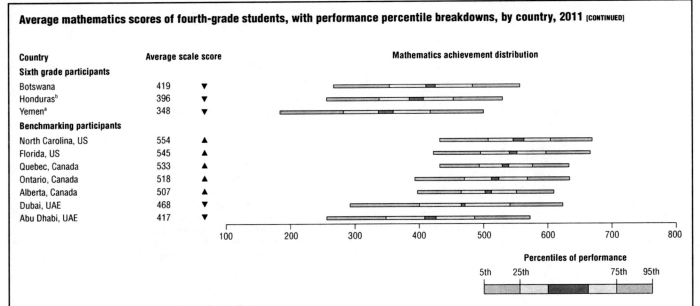

Average mathematics scores of fourth-grade students, with performance percentile breakdowns, by country, 2011 [CONTINUED]

TIMSS = Trends in International Mathematics and Science Study.
[a]Average achievement not reliably measured because the percentage of students with achievement too low for estimation exceeds 25%.
[b]Reservations about reliability of average achievement because the percentage of students with achievement too low for estimation does not exceed 25% but exceeds 15%.

SOURCE: Ina V. S. Mullis et al., "Exhibit 1.1. Distribution of Mathematics Achievement," in *Trends in International Mathematics and Science Study (TIMSS) 2011 International Results in Mathematics*, International Association for the Evaluation of Educational Achievement (IEA) and TIMSS and PIRLS International Study Center, Lynch School of Education, Boston College, 2012, http://timssandpirls.bc.edu/timss2011/downloads/T11_IR_Mathematics_FullBook.pdf (accessed July 22, 2015)

FIGURE 4.17

Average science scores of fourth-grade students, with performance percentile breakdowns, by country, 2011

▲ Country average significantly higher than the centerpoint of theTIMSS 4th grade scale
▼ Country average significantly lower than the centerpoint of theTIMSS 4th grade scale

Country	Average scale score		Science achievement distribution
Korea, Rep. of	587	▲	
Singapore	583	▲	
Finland	570	▲	
Japan	559	▲	
Russian Federation	552	▲	
Chinese Taipei	552	▲	
United States	544	▲	
Czech Republic	536	▲	
Hong Kong SAR	535	▲	
Hungary	534	▲	
Sweden	533	▲	
Slovak Republic	532	▲	
Austria	532	▲	
Netherlands	531	▲	
England	529	▲	
Denmark	528	▲	
Germany	528	▲	
Italy	524	▲	
Portugal	522	▲	
Slovenia	520	▲	
Northern Ireland	517	▲	
Ireland	516	▲	
Croatia	516	▲	
Australia	516	▲	
Serbia	516	▲	
Lithuania	515	▲	
Belgium (Flemish)	509	▲	
Romania	505		
Spain	505		
Poland	505		
TIMSS scale centerpoint	**500**		
New Zealand	497		
Kazakhstan	495		
Norway	494	▼	
Chile	480	▼	
Thailand	472	▼	
Turkey	463	▼	
Georgia	455	▼	
Iran, Islamic Rep. of	453	▼	
Bahrain	449	▼	
Malta	446	▼	
Azerbaijan	438	▼	
Saudi Arabia	429	▼	
United Arab Emirates	428	▼	
Armenia	416	▼	
Qatar	394	▼	
Oman	377	▼	
Kuwait[b]	347	▼	
Tunisia[b]	346	▼	
Morocco[a]	264	▼	
Yemen[a]	209	▼	

100   200   300   400   500   600   700   800

FIGURE 4.17

Average science scores of fourth-grade students, with performance percentile breakdowns, by country, 2011 [CONTINUED]

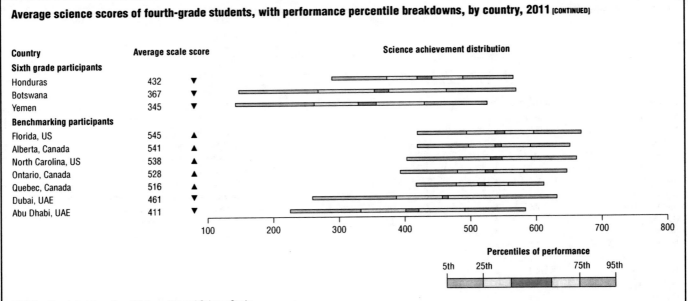

Country	Average scale score		Science achievement distribution
Sixth grade participants			
Honduras	432	▼	
Botswana	367	▼	
Yemen	345	▼	
Benchmarking participants			
Florida, US	545	▲	
Alberta, Canada	541	▲	
North Carolina, US	538	▲	
Ontario, Canada	528	▲	
Quebec, Canada	516	▲	
Dubai, UAE	461	▼	
Abu Dhabi, UAE	411	▼	

Percentiles of performance

5th   25th   75th   95th

TIMSS = Trends in International Mathematics and Science Study.

[a]Average achievement not reliably measured because the percentage of students with achievement too low for estimation exceeds 25%.

[b]Reservations about reliability of average achievement because the percentage of students with achievement too low for estimation does not exceed 25% but exceeds 15%.

SOURCE: Michael O. Martin et al., "Exhibit 1.1. Distribution of Science Achievement," in *Trends in International Mathematics and Science Study (TIMSS) 2011 International Results in Science*, International Association for the Evaluation of Educational Achievement (IEA) and TIMSS and PIRLS International Study Center, Lynch School of Education, Boston College, 2012, http://timssandpirls.bc.edu/timss2011/downloads/T11_IR_Science_FullBook.pdf (accessed July 22, 2015)

CHAPTER 5
NATIONAL POLICIES FOR IMPROVEMENT

A CALL TO REFORM

The National Commission on Excellence in Education report *A Nation at Risk: The Imperative for Educational Reform* (April 1983, http://www.ed.gov/pubs/NatAtRisk/index.html) proved to be a "wake-up call" on the state of the U.S. educational system. It warned of a "rising tide of mediocrity that threatens our very future as a Nation and a people." As a result, educators, lawmakers, and governors began earnest efforts to improve schools. The commission recommended, among other things, a longer school year, a tougher curriculum, and stronger teacher-training programs. It specifically expressed alarm at the deterioration of academics at the secondary school level.

To improve the situation, the commission recommended that no student should graduate from high school without completing four years of English; three years each of mathematics, science, and social studies; half a year of computer science; and, for college-bound students, two years of a foreign language. *A Nation at Risk* was the beginning of an education reform movement that has continued into the 21st century. This document has maintained its relevance through several presidential administrations and remains pertinent more than 30 years after its publication.

THE NATIONAL EDUCATION GOALS FOR 2000

One response to the National Commission on Excellence in Education's message in *A Nation at Risk* was the first Education Summit, which was held in Charlottesville, Virginia, in 1989. President George H. W. Bush (1924–) and the nation's state governors established six National Education Goals to be achieved by 2000. A bipartisan National Education Goals Panel was created in 1990 to oversee and report on the progress toward these national goals. The panel was made up of governors, members of Congress, state legislators, and members appointed by the president. In March 1994,

expressing the continued concern of the nation, Congress passed and President Bill Clinton (1946–) signed the Goals 2000: Educate America Act. This act reemphasized the National Education Goals and added two more goals.

The eight goals were:

1. Prepare children so they are ready to learn by the time they start school

2. Raise high school graduation rates to at least 90%

3. Have all students leaving grades four, eight, and 12 demonstrating competency over challenging subject matter

4. Provide full access to teacher education and professional development programs

5. Ensure that U.S. students are first in the world in mathematics and science

6. Increase adult literacy and lifelong learning

7. Provide safe, disciplined, and alcohol- and drug-free schools

8. Promote parental participation in the schools

Were the Goals Reached?

Although many schools responded to the challenge that was first issued in 1989, the National Education Goals Panel concluded in *The National Education Goals Report: Building a Nation of Learners 1993* (September 1993, http://www2.ed.gov/pubs/goals/report/goalsrpt.txt) that "the findings continue to reveal how far we are from achieving the Goals. They show modest progress in some areas (mathematics achievement, school safety), but stagnation or movement in the wrong direction in others (high school completion, adult literacy)." The panel concluded that "the current rate of progress is wholly inadequate if we are to achieve the National Education Goals by the year 2000."

In 1999, on the 10th anniversary of the first national education summit, the results discussed by the National Education Goals Panel in *The National Education Goals Report: Building a Nation of Learners 1999* (http://govinfo .library.unt.edu/negp/reports/99rpt.pdf) were still mixed. Young children had made gains in school readiness, and student achievement had improved in reading at the eighth-grade level and in mathematics at the fourth-, eighth-, and 12th-grade levels. However, teacher support and training goals were not met, student achievement was below desired levels in math and science, and schools were still not free of drugs, alcohol, and violence.

SCIENCE, TECHNOLOGY, ENGINEERING, AND MATH EDUCATION

In many respects, the nation's current commitment to educational achievement in math and science dates to 1957, when the Soviet Union launched the world's first artificial satellite, *Sputnik I*, into orbit around the earth. Fearing it would quickly fall behind other countries in the fields of engineering and technology, the United States promptly dedicated itself to increasing the number of university graduates from these areas of study, while also devoting federal and state resources to promoting scientific innovation. To help the nation meet these goals, President Dwight D. Eisenhower (1890–1969) ordered the creation of the National Aeronautics and Space Administration (NASA) in 1958. Karen Woodruff, the associate director of NASA's Endeavor Science Teaching Certificate Project, notes in "A History of STEM—Reigniting the Challenge with NGSS and CCSS" (March 12, 2013, http:// www.us-satellite.net/STEMblog/?p=31) that by the 1980s U.S. colleges and universities were producing 80,000 graduates annually in engineering alone.

In spite of these advances, by the 1990s U.S. students still lagged behind their overseas counterparts in the fields of math and science. To foster further improvements in these areas, the National Science Foundation began promoting a more holistic method of teaching these subjects in schools. This integrated approach was embodied in the acronym STEM, which stands for science, technology, engineering, and math. "After years of research," Woodruff writes, "we understand that subjects cannot and should not be taught in isolation, just as they do not exist in isolation in the workforce." In the ensuing years, STEM has become a key component of education reform initiatives on both the state and federal levels. In "Science, Technology, Engineering, & Math (STEM) Education" (2011, http://www.nga.org/cms/stem), the National Governors Association asserts that its Center for Best Practices works with individual states to develop policies that promote STEM educational initiatives. In *Prepare and Inspire: K–12 Education in Science, Technology, Engineering, and Math (STEM) for America's Future* (September 2010, http://www.whitehouse.gov/

sites/default/files/microsites/ostp/pcast-stemed-report .pdf), President Barack Obama's (1961–) Council of Advisers on Science and Technology cites STEM educational initiatives as vital to the United States' continued leadership role worldwide, as well as the cornerstone of the nation's efforts to "solve immense challenges in such areas as energy, health, environmental protection, and national security." According to *Preparing Americans with 21st Century Skills* (March 2014, https:// www.whitehouse.gov/sites/default/files/microsites/ostp/ fy_2015_stem_ed.pdf), the Obama administration allocated $2.9 billion to promote STEM educational programs in 2015.

THE NO CHILD LEFT BEHIND ACT

In January 2002 President George W. Bush (1946–) signed into law the No Child Left Behind (NCLB) Act, which was a major reform of the Elementary and Secondary Education Act (ESEA) of 1965. The ESEA authorized various school initiatives that were considered appropriate at the time. Over the years this federal legislation was reviewed, revised, and reauthorized by Congress and by several presidents to meet changing needs. The NCLB focused on two new national goals: achieving proficiency in reading and mathematics for all students by the 2013–14 academic year and narrowing the achievement gap among subgroups of students, including disadvantaged students. To reach these goals, the legislation demanded comprehensive reforms, including strong assessment and accountability, teacher support for achieving and maintaining a high level of competence, more choices for students and parents, a new emphasis on school improvement, and the use of research-based instructional practices. The law also placed a layer of federal governmental involvement in and control of education, which is generally considered to be a state and local matter.

The NCLB and Student Achievement

The NCLB requires the states to develop and implement academic standards and assessments in reading/ language arts and math for each of grades three to eight; academic standards and assessments in science for elementary, middle, and high schools; and assessments of English language proficiency. In addition, the states must participate in National Assessment of Educational Progress assessments for reading and mathematics every other year. (See Table 4.1 in Chapter 4.)

Under the NCLB, statewide report cards present performance data that are classified by race, ethnicity, gender, and other criteria to demonstrate overall student achievement and to chart progress in closing the achievement gap between disadvantaged students and other groups of students. Each state develops its own accountability system based on its standards and assessments and defines the adequate yearly progress (AYP) that students and subgroups of students should achieve to make sufficient progress toward the long-term NCLB goals. The state accountability system has to meet certain minimum requirements set down by the NCLB, which are outlined in a policy letter (July 24, 2002, http://www.ed.gov/print/policy/elsec/guid/secletter/020724.html) by the U.S. secretary of education Rod Paige (1933–). In addition, the state accountability system has to include annual targets for academic achievement, participation in assessments, graduation rates for high schools, and at least one other academic indicator for elementary and middle schools.

The state and local educational agencies must annually review the status of every school and must identify schools that have not met the definition of AYP for two consecutive years. Schools that have not made AYP but have made at least a 10% reduction from the previous year in the percentage of students who are not proficient are deemed to have made sufficient progress. Otherwise, the schools are identified as needing improvement. The NCLB provides options for schools needing improvement for each consecutive year that they do not make AYP. These school improvement options are outlined in Paige's policy letter and include proposals such as offering supplemental educational services to students, changing school personnel and management, and hiring a consultant to work with the school on its AYP plan.

The situation regarding AYP and understanding what AYP really means for schools across the nation is more complex, however, than it may seem. Alexandra Usher of the Center on Education Policy notes in *Update with 2009–10 Data and Five-Year Trends: How Many Schools Have Not Made Adequate Yearly Progress?* (April 2011, http://www.cep-dc.org/cfcontent_file.cfm?Attachment=Usher%5FReport%5FAYP%5F042811%2Epdf) that "the performance targets and the tests used to measure student achievement vary greatly among states. For that reason, AYP results are not comparable between states, and a state with a high percentage of schools failing to make AYP should not be assumed to have a weak educational system." Usher observes that 38% of schools across the United States did not make AYP in 2010 and that their distribution was not evenly spread across the nation.

Assessing the NCLB

The Center on Education Policy (CEP), an independent advocate for public education and for more effective public schools, has studied the NCLB and its effects since its implementation. In *Compendium of Key Studies of the No Child Left Behind Act* (April 23, 2009, http://files.eric.ed.gov/fulltext/ED505036.pdf), the CEP provides summaries of key studies that were conducted by itself as well as by various organizations.

CURRICULUM AND INSTRUCTION. Student assessment is a major component of the NCLB. However, it should be noted that if more time is taken during the school year to assess students' proficiency in reading and math and if more time is spent on instruction in these subjects to improve student scores, then less time is available for other subjects in the curriculum unless the school day is lengthened. Jennifer McMurrer of the CEP discusses this issue in *Choices, Changes, and Challenges: Curriculum and Instruction in the NCLB Era* (December 2007, http://www.cep-dc.org/cfcontent_file.cfm?Attachment=McMurrer%5FFullReport%5FCurricAndInstruction%5F072407%2Epdf).

According to McMurrer, 62% of school districts reported to the CEP that they had increased their instructional time for English language arts and/or math in the elementary schools since the implementation of the NCLB. Forty-four percent of the districts reported that they had taken the time for this additional English and/or math instruction from other subjects, such as social studies, science, art, music, and physical education (a practice called curriculum narrowing), or they had taken it from lunch and recess. CEP data show an average reduction of 31% in the total instructional time that was devoted to other subjects. Districts with schools needing improvement were more likely to have made such changes than districts with schools not needing improvement. In *Compendium of Major NCLB Studies: Curriculum and Instruction* (April 2009, http://www.cep-dc.org/documents/RFR-CompendiumNCLB/CurriculumandInstruction.pdf), the CEP describes these curricular and instructional changes in more detail.

Data pointing to curriculum narrowing leads the CEP to suggest that the current testing framework promotes an unbalanced curriculum and to recommend that NCLB testing include assessments of proficiency in other academic subjects. It also recommends that states give adequate emphasis to art and music and that schools include more cross-curricular work, such as incorporating the teaching of reading and math skills into instruction in other subjects.

TEACHER QUALITY. The NCLB requires that highly qualified teachers be in every public school classroom. To be considered "highly qualified," a teacher must hold a bachelor's degree, have certification or licensure to teach in the state of his or her employment, and have proven knowledge in the subject he or she teaches. The CEP notes in *Compendium of Major NCLB Studies: Teacher Quality* (April 2009, http://www.cep-dc.org/documents/RFR-CompendiumNCLB/TeacherQuality.pdf) that most teachers already meet these qualifications and that these requirements "had minimal or no impact on teacher effectiveness."

Many school officials think the NCLB definition of a highly qualified teacher is too narrow and too focused on content expertise. They believe the definition should be broadened to incorporate other characteristics of good teachers, such as their ability to relate to students and be effective in the classroom. The CEP agrees and recommends that states be encouraged to develop their own definitions of teacher effectiveness and their own methods of measuring teacher competence.

STUDENT ACHIEVEMENT. Two overarching reports by the CEP are *Has Student Achievement Increased since No Child Left Behind?* (June 2007, http://hub.mspnet.org/index.cfm/14328) and *Compendium of Major NCLB Studies: Achievement and Related Issues.* These reports point to mixed results that may or may not be due to the NCLB. Nonetheless, the reports note that some gains in student achievement in reading and math have occurred since the NCLB was enacted and that there has been some narrowing of achievement gaps. In 2009 these gains seemed enough for a reauthorization of the NCLB. Even so, senators and representatives did not discuss whether to reauthorize the NCLB, but how to improve the legislation to respond to concerns that had been raised. However, with the country in a serious recession, reauthorizing and reforming the NCLB was not a top priority, so a vote never occurred that year or the next.

Status of Congressional Reauthorization of the NCLB

In 2007, five years after the initial implementation of the NCLB during the 2002–03 school year, the legislation was poised for renewal. However, the congressional process stalled, so automatic one-year extensions of the law went into effect. No reauthorization of this law occurred before President Obama took office in January 2009. After he took office, President Obama intended to work with Congress to reform and reauthorize the NCLB, but reform and reauthorization was delayed because Congress was focused on other issues regarding the economy, health care, and, by 2011, the national debt ceiling.

In August 2011 President Obama announced that the U.S. Department of Education would grant waivers to the states from the NCLB because Congress had not acted to reauthorize the act, with or without reform. According to the Department of Education, in "U.S. Department of Education Approves ESEA Flexibility Renewal for Pennsylvania" (September 8, 2015, http://www.ed.gov/news/press-releases/us-department-education-approves-esea-flexibility-renewal-pennsylvania), as of September 2015, 42 states and the District of Columbia had been approved for waiver status.

Public Opinion on Federal Government Involvement in Education

With the passage and implementation of the NCLB in 2003, the federal government's role in education increased from previous years. By 2014, however, public opinion on the federal government's role in education reform had

TABLE 5.1

Public opinion on federal, state, and local influence on education policy, by political affiliation, 2014

IN YOUR OPINION, WHO SHOULD HAVE THE GREATEST INFLUENCE IN DECIDING WHAT IS TAUGHT IN THE PUBLIC SCHOOLS HERE—THE FEDERAL GOVERNMENT, THE STATE GOVERNMENT, OR THE LOCAL SCHOOL BOARD?

	All Americans	Democrats	Independents	Republicans
	%	%	%	%
Federal government	15	28	16	3
State government	28	26	28	28
Local school board	56	44	55	68
Don't know/refused	1	1	1	*

*Less than 0.5%.

SOURCE: Valerie J. Calderon, "In your opinion, who should have the greatest influence in deciding what is taught in the public schools here—the federal government, the state government, or the local school board?" in *Americans Wary of Federal Influence on Public Schools*, The Gallup Organization, August 20, 2014, http://www.gallup.com/poll/175181/americans-wary-federal-influence-public-schools.aspx?utm_source=public%20schools&utm_medium=search&utm_campaign=tiles (accessed July 22, 2015). Copyright © 2015 Gallup, Inc. All rights reserved. The content is used with permission; however, Gallup retains all rights of republication.

gradually shifted. Table 5.1 reveals various attitudes toward this issue, both in general and according to political affiliation. Overall, more than half (56%) of Americans felt that local school boards should exert the most influence over educational policy in their communities. Slightly more than one-quarter (28%) believed that state governments were best qualified to determine what should be taught in public schools, while only 15% believed that education policy should be left to the federal government. Democrats (28%) were considerably more likely than Republicans (3%) to entrust the federal government to play a leading role in public education policies. Conversely, slightly more than two-thirds (68%) of Republicans believed that local school boards should have the greatest influence over issues affecting public schools, compared to 55% of independents and 44% of Democrats.

Thus, by 2015 the American people seemed increasingly uncomfortable with the involvement of the federal government in primary and secondary education. How do they rate the leader of the federal government and his performance in support of public schools? In "Try It Again, Uncle Sam: The 46th Annual PDK/Gallup Poll of the Public's Attitudes toward the Public Schools" (*Phi Delta Kappan*, vol. 96, no. 1, September 2014, http://www.pdkintl.org/noindex/PDK_Poll46_2014.pdf), William J. Bushaw and Valerie J. Calderon examine public opinion of President Obama's handing of education between 2011 and 2014. The survey asks respondents to use letter grades to evaluate the president's performance, with "A" representing excellent, "B" good, "C" average, "D" poor, and "F" failing. As Bushaw and Calderon report, between 2011 and 2014 the percentage of

Americans who rated President Obama's performance in education as an A or a B fell from 41% to 27 percent. In 2014, 61% of Democrats gave him an A or a B, whereas only 3% of Republicans concurred. Independents trended closer to Republicans on this issue, with only 24% grading his performance in education as an A or a B.

On the whole, public opinion on the value of standardized testing has also shifted during the years since the NCLB became law. According to Bushaw and Calderon, in 2014 a majority of all Americans (54%) believed that standardized testing does not actually help students learn. Among parents of public school children, this attitude was even more pronounced, with just over two-thirds (68%) of all public school parents expressing a negative view of standardized testing that year.

THE OBAMA ADMINISTRATION'S PLAN FOR REFORMING THE NCLB

A Stimulus to Help Jump-Start Reform

When President Obama took office in January 2009, the country was in a deep recession that had begun in December 2007. Through the American Recovery and Reinvestment Act (ARRA) of 2009, an economic stimulus package passed by Congress, the federal government provided $100 billion for education. The Department of Education explains in the press release "President Obama, U.S. Secretary of Education Duncan Announce National Competition to Advance School Reform" (July 24, 2009, http://www.ed.gov/news/press-releases/president-obama-us-secretary-education-duncan-announce-national-competition-advance-school-reform) that of these funds, $10 billion were Title I (Improving the Academic Achievement of the Disadvantaged) funds. In addition, schools were encouraged to vie for grants from the Race to the Top Fund, a one-time $4.4 billion competition. The grant money was to be used to implement reform activities that were expected to dramatically improve student achievement. Other programs under the ARRA umbrella were also designed to infuse money into schools for needed reform, such as $650 million for the Investing in Innovation Fund. This fund was intended to "support local efforts by school districts and partnerships with nonprofits to start or expand research-based innovative programs that help close the achievement gap and improve outcomes for students."

A Blueprint for Reform of the NCLB: The Reauthorization of the ESEA

In March 2010 the Obama administration released its plan for the restructuring of the NCLB. In the preface of *A Blueprint for Reform: The Reauthorization of the Elementary and Secondary Education Act* (http://www2.ed.gov/policy/elsec/leg/blueprint/blueprint.pdf), President Obama calls the NCLB a "flawed law" that needs repair. He also notes that the *Blueprint for Reform* is "an outline for a reenvisioned federal role in education."

The framework for reforming the NCLB builds on initiatives that began with the ARRA and focuses on the following priorities:

- Preparing college- and career-ready students—this priority focuses on preparing all students to graduate from high school ready to attend college or begin a career. Schools will be asked to develop college- and career-ready standards in English and mathematics along with new assessments that are designed to determine whether students have developed the skills they need. Although there will be a focus in these two areas, this priority also mandates a well-rounded education.

- Fostering great teachers and leaders—this priority seeks to elevate the teaching profession by rewarding excellence and supporting teacher development. It also aims to strengthen teacher and principal preparation and recruitment.

- Promoting equity and opportunity—this priority includes all students "in an accountability system that builds on college- and career-ready standards, rewards progress and success, and requires rigorous interventions in the lowest-performing schools." This priority also focuses on encouraging states to equalize resources among schools.

- Raising the bar and rewarding excellence—this priority encourages school choice and the expansion of high-performing schools. It also encourages the development of accelerated courses in high school that will help students become ready for college. The Race to the Top incentives for systemic reform, which began with the ARRA stimulus funding at the state level, will be expanded "to school districts that are willing to take on bold, comprehensive reforms."

- Promoting innovation—this priority focuses on using the strengths in the surrounding community—including families and community members—to help students learn and grow. The Investing in Innovation Fund will assist local leaders in building programs that will help students develop ideas. New models of learning will help "keep students safe, supported, and healthy both in and out of school."

The federal budget also gives some idea of the plans to reform the NCLB, because federal money pays for the development and implementation of the NCLB assessments. In *Fiscal Year 2016 Budget: Summary and Background Information* (February 2, 2015, http://www2.ed.gov/about/overview/budget/budget16/summary/16summary.pdf), the Department of Education mentions NCLB only once, describing the law as "outdated and obsolete." The budget subsequently reports that $378 million was appropriated for state assessments in 2014 and 2015, with the aim of helping "ensure that all students graduate from high school with the knowledge and skills they need to be successful in college and the workplace." According to *Fiscal Year 2016 Budget*, the total amount allocated for state assessments in 2016 was projected to top $403 million.

REACTIONS TO THE *BLUEPRINT FOR REFORM*

A few days after the *Blueprint for Reform* was released and the heads of various educational organizations had an opportunity to respond to the plan, Greg Toppo remarked in "Education Groups Laud, Criticize Obama 'No Child' Overhaul Plan" (USAToday.com, March 15, 2010) that the reaction among the educational community was mixed. Toppo noted that "teachers unions complained that teachers are being scapegoated by the overhaul; a school board leader praised it but called for more flexibility; and an administrators group said it was just glad to see NCLB go away." The following are some of the opinions of various educational leaders who represent the United States' top educational organizations, all of which reflect Toppo's comment.

National Education Association

Cynthia McCabe reports in "NEA President: Reauthorization 'Blueprint' Disappointing" (March 13, 2010, http://www.nea.org/home/38526.htm) that Dennis Van Roekel, the president of the National Education Association (NEA), thought the reform plan of the NCLB still has a focus on standardized testing that puts students and schools in "winning" and "losing" categories. In addition, it forces states to compete for funding and resources. As a result, he indicated that the NEA does not back the plan.

Van Roekel told McCabe, "We were expecting school turnaround efforts to be research-based and fully collaborative. Instead, we see too much top-down scapegoating of teachers and not enough collaboration." Van Roekel added, "The public knows that struggling schools need a wide range of targeted actions to ensure they succeed, and yet the administration's plan continues to call for prescriptions before the actual problems are diagnosed. We need proven answers along with the deep insight of the experienced professionals who actually work in schools."

According to McCabe, the NEA offers the following principles for reauthorizing the NCLB:

- The federal government should serve as a partner to support state efforts to transform public schools.

- A revamped accountability system must correctly identify schools in need of assistance and provide a system of effective interventions to help them succeed.

- The federal government should respect the profession of teachers and education [and should] support professionals by providing supports and resources to help students succeed.

- The federal government should require states to detail how they will remedy inequities in educational tools, opportunities and resources.

- State and local collective bargaining for school employees must be respected.

- Targeted programs that support students and schools with unique needs—such as English Language Acquisition, Impact Aid [funds and technical help for schools that are burdened by federal activities], rural schools and Indian education—should be maintained and expanded.

- The federal government should serve as a research clearinghouse, making available to educators a wealth of knowledge about how best to teach students and help schools improve practices.

American Federation of Teachers

In "Teachers Skeptical of Obama's Education Plan" (NPR.org, March 17, 2010), Melissa Block interviewed Randi Weingarten, the president of the American Federation of Teachers, who echoed Van Roekel's belief that the prescriptions for cures of failing and struggling schools are being put forth before diagnoses are made. According to Block, Weingarten indicated that a reform effort needs to include a research-backed turnaround program. Weingarten stated, "It's time to actually start using what works, not simply talk about what sounds good." She also noted that the reform plan places all the burden of turning schools around on the teachers, but does not supply them with the resources and support systems they need.

American Association of School Administrators

Dan Domenech, the executive director of the American Association of School Administrators, had a more positive approach to the *Blueprint for Reform* than Van Roekel or Weingarten. In "Statement by Dan Domenech on the Blueprint for a New Federal Education Law" (March 15, 2010, http://www.aasa.org/BlueprintBlog .aspx?terms=blueprint+for+reform), he expressed his opinion that President Obama's reform ideas are a "significant improvement" over the NCLB and praised him for "setting a clear and obtainable goal that the United States will lead the world in college completion by 2020." In addition, Domenech was pleased that school districts would be given time to develop better assessments than those that are used with the NCLB, but remarked that districts should not be compelled to use the old assessments during a transition period.

National Association of Elementary School Principals

Gail Connelly, the executive director of the National Association of Elementary School Principals, was also looking forward to further explanation of what she called "a broad overview of proposals" in the *Blueprint for Reform*. Connelly made this comment in "NAESP Statement on Obama Administrations' Blueprint for ESEA" (March 15, 2010, http://www.naesp.org/naesp-statement-obama-administration%E2%80%99s-blueprint-esea), in which she expressed concern about "required models of reform that put principals on the firing line without providing adequate resources and support, including significant training to develop transformational leadership skills that are essential for sustainable improvement." Connelly was concerned that research-based standards would not be used for evaluating instructional leadership, concerns that were raised by others, such as by Van Roekel and Weingarten, in other contexts.

National Association of Secondary School Principals

The comments of both Gerald N. Tirozzi, the executive director of the National Association of Secondary School Principals (NASSP), and Amanda Karhuse, the director of government relations of the NASSP, regarding the *Blueprint for Reform* in the May 2010 issue of *News-Leader* (vol. 57, no. 9), had a recurrent theme: a lack of research-based solutions to school problems, including problems of low-performing schools. Tirozzi explained in "A Misguided Path to School Improvement" that school improvement "requires digging into data, crunching numbers, and discovering deficiencies; then identifying, implementing, and measuring the effect of appropriate interventions. And then it has to be done all again." He emphasized that using preplanned interventions without evaluating specific situations were ineffective ways to solve problems.

THE COMMON CORE STATE STANDARDS INITIATIVE

Even before President Obama introduced the Race to the Top program, a number of states were already in the process of developing a comprehensive education reform movement. In *The Common Core Standards: History and Fact Sheet* (2015, http://tncore.org/sites/www/Uploads/Family/Common_Core_Facts_History.pdf), the Tennessee Department of Education explains that the concept of a state-driven education reform initiative first emerged in 1996, when a coalition of state governors and business leaders founded Achieve, a bipartisan organization that was aimed at developing a uniform, collaborative set of academic standards that could be implemented in school systems throughout the United States. After more than a decade of research and assessment, the National Governors Association and the Council of Chief State School Officers formally launched the Common Core State

Standards Initiative (CCSSI). The CCSSI indicates in "Read the Standards" (2015, http://www.corestandards.org/read-the-standards) that the initiative was designed to help U.S. students achieve "success in college, career, and life in today's global economy." The Common Core standards were focused on two specific areas of study: mathematics and English language arts.

According to the Tennessee Department of Education, a draft of the new Common Core requirements was released to the public in March 2010; a final report appeared in June of that year. By year's end more than half of the states in the country had agreed to implement the new standards. In "Standards in Your State" (2015, http://www.corestandards.org/standards-in-your-state), the CCSSI notes that as of 2015, 42 states and the District of Columbia had adopted the common core standards. Kentucky was the first state to implement the new standards, during the 2011–12 school year. Four states and the District of Columbia implemented the standards in 2012–13, and the remaining states implemented them in 2013–14 and 2014–15.

Despite this widespread implementation of Common Core standards, a sizable majority of Americans remained opposed to the initiative. According to a Gallup poll conducted in May to June 2014, nearly six in 10 (59%) Americans did not want teachers in their communities to follow Common Core State Standards; by contrast, only one-third (33%) of respondents favored the use of Common Core standards in local schools. (See Table 5.2.) Among opponents of Common Core, many believed that the standards would impose undue limitations on how teachers would be able to teach, with 87% saying that this factor was a "very important" (65%) or "somewhat important" (22%) reason for opposing the

TABLE 5.2

Percentage of Americans who support or oppose Common Core State Standards, by political affiliation, 2014

DO YOU FAVOR OR OPPOSE HAVING THE TEACHERS IN YOUR COMMUNITY USE THE COMMON CORE STATE STANDARDS TO GUIDE WHAT THEY TEACH?

	All Americans	Democrats	Independents	Republicans
	%	%	%	%
Favor	33	53	34	17
Oppose	59	38	60	76
Don't know/refused	7	9	6	7

SOURCE: Valerie J. Calderon, "Do you favor or oppose having the teachers in your community use the Common Core State Standards to guide what they teach?" in *Americans Wary of Federal Influence on Public Schools*, The Gallup Organization, August 20, 2014, http://www.gallup.com/poll/175181/americans-wary-federal-influence-public-schools.aspx?utm_source=public%20schools&utm_medium=search&utm_campaign=tiles (accessed July 22, 2015). Copyright © 2015 Gallup, Inc. All rights reserved. The content is used with permission; however, Gallup retains all rights of republication.

guidelines. (See Table 5.3.) Another 77% of opponents felt that it was "very important" (51%) or "somewhat important" (26%) to oppose the standards because the teachers at their local schools also opposed them, while 62% of opponents believed that the fact that the standards were initiated by the federal government was either a "very important" (40%) or "somewhat important" (22%) factor in shaping their negative opinion of Common Core. By contrast, 96% of Common Core supporters believed that it was "very important" (73%) or "somewhat important" (23%) that the standards would guarantee that students would learn what they needed to learn in order to succeed, regardless of where they attended school. (See Table 5.4.)

THE ONGOING EFFORT TO REFORM U.S. SCHOOLS

Strengthening America's Schools Act of 2013

In June 2013, amid ongoing debate in Congress over the reauthorization of the NCLB, the U.S. senator Tom Harkin (1939–; D-IA) introduced the Strengthening America's Schools Act. Joy Resmovits reports in "No

TABLE 5.3

Reasons for opposing the Common Core State Standards, by level of importance, 2014

WOULD YOU SAY THAT EACH OF THE FOLLOWING IS A VERY IMPORTANT, SOMEWHAT IMPORTANT, NOT VERY IMPORTANT, OR A NOT AT ALL IMPORTANT REASON THAT YOU OPPOSE THE USE OF THE COMMON CORE STATE STANDARDS TO GUIDE WHAT TEACHERS IN YOUR COMMUNITY TEACH? HOW ABOUT [ITEMS ROTATED]?

[Among those who have heard a great deal, a fair amount, or only a little about the Common Core State Standards and who oppose having teachers use Common Core to guide what they teach]

	Very important	Somewhat important	Not very important	Not at all important	Don't know/ refused
	%	%	%	%	%
The Common Core State Standards will limit the flexibility that teachers have to teach what they think is best.	65	22	6	5	3
The teachers in our community do not support the Common Core State Standards.	51	26	13	8	2
The federal government initiated the Common Core State Standards.	40	22	18	20	1
The Common Core State Standards will result in a national curriculum and national tests.	38	30	18	14	1

SOURCE: Valerie J. Calderon, "Would you say that each of the following is a very important, somewhat important, not very important, or not at all important reason that you oppose the use of the Common Core State Standards to guide what teachers in your community teach? How about [ITEMS ROTATED]?" in *Americans Wary of Federal Influence on Public Schools*, The Gallup Organization, August 20, 2014, http://www.gallup.com/poll/175181/americans-wary-federal-influence-public-schools.aspx?utm_source=public%20schools&utm_medium=search&utm_campaign=tiles (accessed July 22, 2015). Copyright © 2015 Gallup, Inc. All rights reserved. The content is used with permission; however, Gallup retains all rights of republication.

TABLE 5.4

Reasons for supporting the Common Core State Standards, by level of importance, 2014

WOULD YOU SAY THAT EACH OF THE FOLLOWING IS A VERY IMPORTANT, SOMEWHAT IMPORTANT, NOT VERY IMPORTANT, OR A NOT AT ALL IMPORTANT REASON THAT YOU FAVOR THE USE OF THE COMMON CORE STATE STANDARDS TO GUIDE WHAT TEACHERS IN YOUR COMMUNITY TEACH? HOW ABOUT [ITEMS ROTATED]?

[Among those who have heard a great deal, a fair amount, or only a little about the Common Core State Standards and who favor having teachers use Common Core to guide what they teach]

	Very important	Somewhat important	Not very important	Not at all important	Don't know/ refused
	%	%	%	%	%
The Common Core State Standards will help more students learn what they need to know regardless of where they go to school.	73	23	2	1	*
Common Core State Standards will yield student tests that give parents a better understanding of what students have learned.	53	28	14	5	*
The Common Core State Standards are more challenging than other academic standards used in the past.	42	42	12	2	2*
Teachers in our community support the Common Core State Standards.	40	47	11	2	*

*Less than 0.5%.

SOURCE: Valerie J. Calderon, "Would you say that each of the following is a very important, somewhat important, not very important, or not at all important reason that you favor the use of the Common Core State Standards to guide what teachers in your community teach? How about [ITEMS ROTATED]?" in *Americans Wary of Federal Influence on Public Schools*, The Gallup Organization, August 20, 2014, http://www.gallup.com/poll/175181/americans-wary-federal-influence-public-schools.aspx?utm_source=public%20schools&utm_medium=search&utm_campaign=tiles (accessed July 22, 2015). Copyright © 2015 Gallup, Inc. All rights reserved. The content is used with permission; however, Gallup retains all rights of republication.

Child Left Behind Reauthorization Revived by Harkin Bill" (HuffingtonPost.com, June 4, 2013) that the new bill aimed to provide teachers and school systems greater flexibility in complying with the requirements of the NCLB, while reducing pressure to "teach to the test" to help students reach the NCLB's benchmarks. Furthermore, Harkin's proposed bill included a greater emphasis on early education by requiring low-performing states to broaden their prekindergarten (pre-K) programs. As of September 2015, the bill had yet to be put to a vote in the U.S. Senate.

Moving beyond NCLB: Universal Pre-K and Reauthorizing the ESEA

In his February 12, 2013, State of the Union address (https://www.whitehouse.gov/the-press-office/2013/02/12/remarks-president-state-union-address), President Obama unveiled a proposal to create a universal preschool program. The proposal was aimed specifically at lower- and middle-class families, who could not otherwise afford to enroll their children in pre-K education. Citing studies demonstrating the vital importance of early learning in a child's future academic performance, President Obama called on lawmakers at both the state and federal levels to help him "make high-quality preschool available to every single child in America." In his remarks, the president argued that every dollar invested in early education had the potential to save more than $7 over time, both by improving a child's chances of graduating from high school, thus boosting their long-term job prospects, and by reducing the costs involved with such social issues as teenage pregnancy, juvenile delinquency, and violent crime. Justin Sink notes in "Obama Campaigns for Universal Pre-K" (Hill.com, February 14, 2013) that in presenting his case to the American public President Obama hailed the success of a state-funded preschool program in Georgia, which had enrolled 83,000 four-year-old students between the program's inception in 1995 and 2013. "The size of your paycheck shouldn't determine your child's future," Sink quotes the president telling teachers during a visit to Decatur, Georgia. "So let's fix this. Let's make sure none of our kids start out the race of life a step behind."

President Obama's push for universal pre-K soon became a cornerstone of his plan to overhaul the ESEA. The administration's sweeping proposal to reform the nation's schools was unveiled by the U.S. secretary of education Arne Duncan (1964–) during a January 12, 2015, press conference. In the address "America's Educational Crossroads: Making the Right Choice for Our Children's Future" (January 12, 2015, http://www.ed.gov/news/speeches/americas-educational-crossroads-making-right-

choice-our-children%E2%80%99s-future), Duncan laid out the president's case for providing disadvantaged children with equal access to high-quality education, describing such an opportunity as both a "civil right" and a "moral imperative." At the same time, Duncan called for new limits on the amount of time devoted to standardized testing in the public schools. Although the Obama administration acknowledged the continued importance of the assessment process in measuring student performance, Duncan asserted that the assessment process should not take away from "actual classroom instruction." Other features of the proposed overhaul included greater funding for teacher salaries and school resources, as well as a greater emphasis on teaching art, history, foreign languages, and other subjects sometimes viewed as "luxuries" during a time when math, science, and reading had become the focal points of standardized testing. In his remarks, Duncan expressed strong criticism of No Child Left Behind, calling it "prescriptive" and "out-of-date." "No Child Left Behind created dozens of ways for schools to fail and very few ways to help them succeed, or to reward success," Duncan declared. "We need to do exactly the opposite."

By July 2015 both the Senate and the House of Representatives had drafted new laws aimed at reforming ESEA. As Lauren Camera reports in "Collision Alert: House, Senate ESEA Rewrites" (*Education Week*, August 5, 2015, vol. 34, no. 37), the Senate proposal, known as the Every Child Achieves Act, managed to pass with strong bipartisan support, even as Democrats and Republicans continued to argue over the role of the federal government in such areas as funding and assessments. Although the Democrats believed that strong federal oversight was essential to ensuring that minority and low-income students had equal access to quality education, Republicans balked at an increased government role in education policy, asserting that student assessments were best handled at the state and local level. As Camera notes, the House version of the law, dubbed the Student Success Act, involved several conservative proposals that were likely to prompt a veto from President Obama. Key points of contention in the House law included a provision that granted disadvantaged students the right to use Title I funding at a school of their choice, a concept known as "portability," as well as a provision granting students in certain districts the right to opt out of annual testing. In the end, the Student Success Act passed without a single Democratic vote. As of September 2015, representatives of the Senate and the House were scheduled to enter into the conference process in order to negotiate a compromise, with the aim of delivering a final bill before the end of the year.

CHAPTER 6

STUDENTS AT RISK

ACADEMIC RISK FACTORS

In *America's Children: Key National Indicators of Well-Being, 2015* (July 2015, http://www.childstats.gov/pdf/ac2015/ac_15.pdf), the Federal Interagency Forum on Child and Family Statistics describes factors that are involved in putting children at risk (in danger) for underachievement and failure in school. These factors involve the family and home social environment, economic circumstances, health, behavior, and physical environment and safety.

Thomas D. Snyder and Sally A. Dillow show in *Digest of Education Statistics, 2013* (May 2015, http://nces.ed.gov/pubs2015/2015011.pdf) that students who do not complete high school, on average, have much lower median annual earnings (the middle value; half of all households earned more and half earned less) than those who do. Furthermore, if a student does not complete high school, he or she cannot continue to higher levels of education and thereby gain a better chance of earning an even higher annual income while pursuing a career he or she enjoys. Although money is not the only value that comes from being educated and is not the only measure of success in life, money is important and basic for the support of oneself and one's family. In addition, being successful in other ways—and being happy—generally arise only if a person has sufficient food and shelter; is able to read, write, and reason; and has an education that is sufficient to achieve life's dreams—whatever those dreams may be.

FAMILY AND HOME SOCIAL ENVIRONMENT
Family Composition

Figure 6.1 shows the percentage of children from birth through age 17 years living in various family arrangements in 2014. Most children, adolescents, and teens (69%) lived in a household with two parents. Most of the rest (27%) lived with one parent, and most often

this parent was their mother. A small percentage (4%) of children lived with a grandparent, other relatives, nonrelatives, or foster parents.

The family arrangement within which a child lives bears heavily on his or her risk of poverty. Children living in poverty are more likely to be undernourished, subject to frequent illnesses, and generally much less ready for learning. The Federal Interagency Forum on Child and Family Statistics notes in *America's Children: Key National Indicators of Well-Being, 2015* that children living in poverty "are more likely to complete fewer years of school and experience more years of unemployment" than their peers who are not living in poverty.

Table 6.1 shows that 11.2% of all U.S. families lived below the poverty line in 2013 ($23,550 for a family of four in 2013). Nearly one-third (30.6%) of all families headed by single female householders were living under the poverty line that year, compared with 15.9% of families headed by single male householders and 5.8% of married-couple families. As Jennifer Calfas reports in "More Children Living in Poverty Now than during Recession" (USAToday.com, July 21, 2015), more than one in five (22%) of all American children lived below the poverty line in 2013. Poverty levels were worst among African Americans, with nearly two-fifths (39%) of all African American children living below the poverty line that year. The proportions of Native American (37%) and Hispanic (33%) children living below the poverty line were also higher than the national average in 2013, whereas poverty levels among Asian American or Pacific Islander (14%) and white (14%) children were considerably lower.

Figure 6.2 tracks poverty rates in the United States between 1959 and 2013 by age. In 1959 roughly 35% of all Americans aged 65 years and older lived in poverty. In the ensuing decades this rate among the country's elderly population fell steadily, and by 2013, 9.5% of

FIGURE 6.1

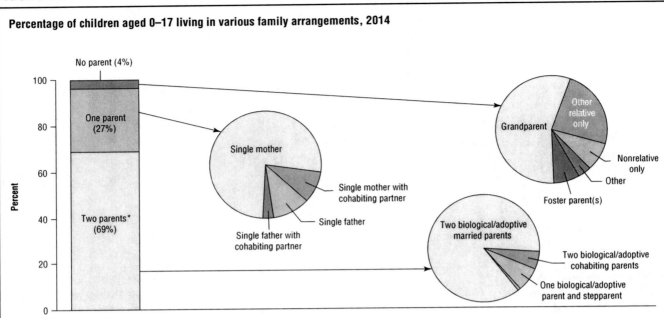

Percentage of children aged 0–17 living in various family arrangements, 2014

*Includes children living with two stepparents.

Notes: Data for 2014 exclude about 229,000 household residents under age 18 who were listed as family reference persons or spouses.

The 2014 Annual Social and Economic Supplement (ASEC) of the Current Population Survey (CPS) included redesigned questions for income and health insurance coverage. All of the approximately 98,000 addresses were selected to receive the improved set of health insurance coverage items. The improved income questions were implemented using a split panel design. Approximately 68,000 addresses were selected to receive a set of income questions similar to those used in the 2013 CPS ASEC. The remaining 30,000 addresses were selected to receive the redesigned income questions.

SOURCE: "Indicator FAM1.B. Percentage of Children Ages 0–17 Living in Various Family Arrangements, 2014," in *America's Children: Key National Indicators of Well-Being, 2015*, Federal Interagency Forum on Child and Family Statistics, July 2015, http://www.childstats.gov/pdf/ac2015/ac_15.pdf (accessed July 23, 2015)

TABLE 6.1

Families in poverty, by family type, 2012 and 2013

Characteristic	2012 Total	2012 Below poverty Number	2012 Below poverty Percent	2013[a] Total	2013[a] Below poverty Number	2013[a] Below poverty Percent	Change in poverty (2012 less 2013)[b] Number	Change in poverty (2012 less 2013)[b] Percent
Families								
Total	80,944	9,520	11.8	81,217	9,130	11.2	−390	−0.5
Type of family								
Married-couple	59,224	3,705	6.3	59,692	3,476	5.8	−228	−0.4
Female householder, no husband present	15,489	4,793	30.9	15,195	4,646	30.6	−147	−0.4
Male householder, no wife present	6,231	1,023	16.4	6,330	1,008	15.9	−15	−0.5

CPS, ASEC = Current Population Survey, Annual Social and Economic Supplement.

[a]Data are based on the CPS ASEC sample of 68,000 addresses. The 2014 CPS ASEC included redesigned questions for income and health insurance coverage. All of the approximately 98,000 addresses were eligible to receive the redesigned set of health insurance coverage questions. The redesigned income questions were implemented to a subsample of these 98,000 addresses using a probability split panel design. Approximately 68,000 addresses were eligible to receive a set of income questions similar to those used in the 2013 CPS ASEC and the remaining 30,000 addresses were eligible to receive the redesigned income questions. The soure of the 2013 data for this table is the portion of the CPS ASEC sample which received the income questions consistent with the 2013 CPS ASEC, approximately 68,000 addresses.

[b]Details may not sum to totals because of rounding.

SOURCE: Carmen DeNavas-Walt and Bernadette D. Proctor, "Table 4. Families in Poverty by Type of Family: 2012 and 2013," in *Income and Poverty in the United States: 2013*, U.S. Census Bureau, September 2014, http://www.census.gov/content/dam/Census/library/publications/2014/demo/p60-249.pdf (accessed July 23, 2015)

adults aged 65 years and older were living in poverty. By contrast, the poverty rate for Americans under the age of 18 years fluctuated dramatically during this span. In 1959 approximately 27% of all Americans in this age group

were living in poverty. This percentage decreased significantly over the next decade and a half, dipping below 15% in 1969. The proportion of Americans under the age of 18 years who were living in poverty then began to

FIGURE 6.2

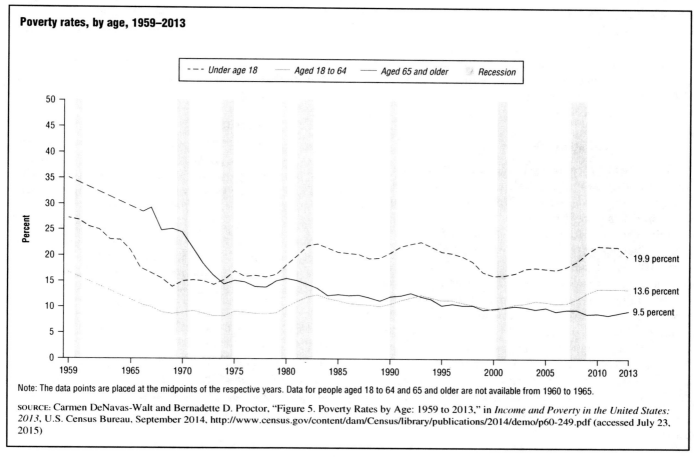

Poverty rates, by age, 1959–2013

- - - Under age 18   ⋯⋯ Aged 18 to 64   ⋯⋯ Aged 65 and older   ░ Recession

19.9 percent
13.6 percent
9.5 percent

Note: The data points are placed at the midpoints of the respective years. Data for people aged 18 to 64 and 65 and older are not available from 1960 to 1965.

SOURCE: Carmen DeNavas-Walt and Bernadette D. Proctor, "Figure 5. Poverty Rates by Age: 1959 to 2013," in *Income and Poverty in the United States: 2013*, U.S. Census Bureau, September 2014, http://www.census.gov/content/dam/Census/library/publications/2014/demo/p60-249.pdf (accessed July 23, 2015)

climb over the next 10 years, exceeding 20% by 1981. Although the poverty rate among Americans in this age group dropped to just above 15% by 2000, it soon began to rise again. By 2013 the poverty rate for Americans under the age of 18 years reached 19.9%, which was significantly higher than the poverty rates for adults aged 18 to 64 years (13.6%) and seniors (9.5%). (See Figure 6.2.)

Nonmarital and Teen Births

In *America's Children: Key National Indicators of Well-Being, 2015*, the Federal Interagency Forum on Child and Family Statistics reports that children of unmarried mothers are more likely to live in poverty than children of married mothers. In addition, the forum suggests that the emotional, financial, and social resources that are available to unmarried mothers may be limited compared with married mothers. However, the demographics of unmarried mothers in the early 21st century differ from the demographics of unmarried mothers in the late 20th century.

According to the Federal Interagency Forum on Child and Family Statistics, 40.6% of all births in 2013 were to unmarried women, up from 18% in 1980. Stephanie J. Ventura of the Centers for Disease Control and Prevention (CDC) lists in *Changing Patterns of Nonmarital*

Childbearing in the United States (May 2009, http://www.cdc.gov/nchs/data/databriefs/db18.pdf) a variety of reasons for this dramatic change, including greater societal acceptance of unmarried mothers, delayed marriage among cohabiting unmarried couples having children, unmarried single women choosing to have children, and changed patterns of sexual activity and contraceptive use. She also notes that the term *unmarried mother* is no longer synonymous with the term *teenage mother*. Ventura reports that in 2007 nearly one out of three births to women aged 25 to 29 years was nonmarital and that almost one out of five births to women aged 30 to 39 years was nonmarital. However, the risk of poverty for unmarried mothers is still higher than for married mothers, even if they are in their 20s or 30s.

Bearing a child as a teenager carries risks in addition to poverty, whether the teenage mother is married, has a cohabiting partner, or is unmarried. Babies born to teenage mothers are at a higher risk for low birth weight (under 5 pounds, 8 ounces [2.5 kilograms]) than are babies born to older mothers. Low birth weight puts babies at risk for health problems, disability, and even death. The Federal Interagency Forum on Child and Family Statistics reports that babies born to teenage mothers are also more likely to grow up in homes with less emotional support and cognitive stimulation than are babies born to older mothers. In addition, fewer babies born to teens graduate from high school than babies born to older mothers. Teen mothers are at risk as well. They find it difficult to complete their education, which reduces their chances not only of finding a job but also of finding a job that will pay them enough to support themselves and their child.

Language Spoken at Home

The Federal Interagency Forum on Child and Family Statistics indicates in *America's Children: Key National Indicators of Well-Being, 2013* (July 2013, http://www.childstats.gov/pdf/ac2013/ac_13.pdf) that in 2012 one-third (33%) of foreign-born children of foreign-born parents lived in poverty, compared with just over one-fourth (27%) of native-born children of foreign-born parents and less than one-fifth (19%) of native-born children of native-born parents. The risk of poverty is not the only problem for foreign-born students. If they have difficulty speaking English, then they may encounter significant challenges in school and later in the workplace. According to Grace Kena et al., in *The Condition of Education 2015* (May 2015, http://nces.ed.gov/pubs2015/2015144.pdf), the percentage of students who

were English language learners (ELL) rose to 9.2% in 2012–13, up from 8.7% in 2002–03. On average, ELL fourth graders scored 38 points lower than non-ELL fourth graders on reading achievement tests in 2012–13. Among older students the gap was even wider, as ELL eighth graders scored 45 points lower on average than non-ELL eighth graders.

Child Maltreatment

Child maltreatment within the family can involve neglect as well as physical, psychological, and sexual abuse. According to the Federal Interagency Forum on Child and Family Statistics, in *America's Children: Key National Indicators of Well-Being, 2015*, child maltreatment is associated with a variety of negative outcomes, including lower academic achievement, juvenile delinquency, substance abuse, and mental health problems. Figure 6.3 shows that the younger the child, the higher the rate of maltreatment.

ECONOMIC CIRCUMSTANCES: THE PREVALENCE OF POOR SCHOOL-AGED CHILDREN

Figure 6.4 shows the percentage of children living in poverty by selected family characteristics. This chapter

FIGURE 6.3

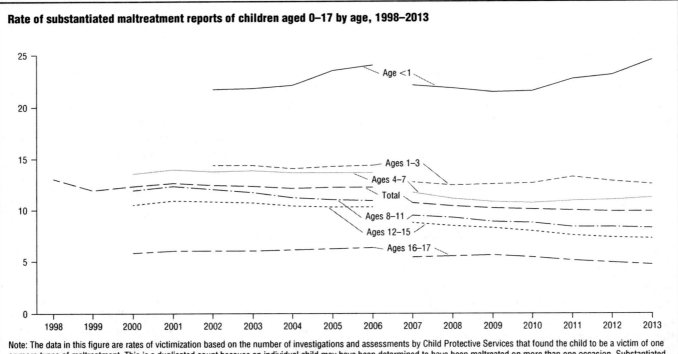

Rate of substantiated maltreatment reports of children aged 0–17 by age, 1998–2013

Note: The data in this figure are rates of victimization based on the number of investigations and assessments by Child Protective Services that found the child to be a victim of one or more types of maltreatment. This is a duplicated count because an individual child may have been determined to have been maltreated on more than one occasion. Substantiated maltreatment includes the dispositions of substantiated, indicated, or alternative response victim. The number of states reporting varies from year to year. States vary in their definition of abuse and neglect. Data since 2007 are not directly comparable with prior years as differences may be partially attributed to changes in one state's procedures for determination of maltreatment.

SOURCE: "Indicator FAM7. Rate of Substantiated Maltreatment Reports of Children Ages 0–17 by Age, 1998–2013," in *America's Children: Key National Indicators of Well-Being, 2015*, Federal Interagency Forum on Child and Family Statistics, July 2015, http://www.childstats.gov/pdf/ac2015/ac_15.pdf (accessed July 23, 2015)

FIGURE 6.4

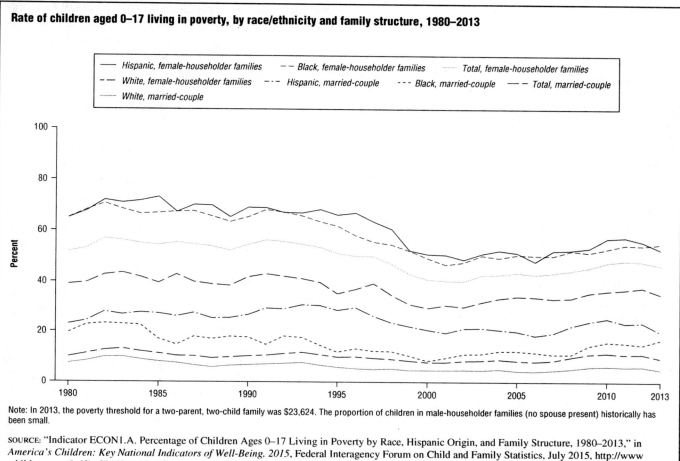

Rate of children aged 0–17 living in poverty, by race/ethnicity and family structure, 1980–2013

Note: In 2013, the poverty threshold for a two-parent, two-child family was $23,624. The proportion of children in male-householder families (no spouse present) historically has been small.

SOURCE: "Indicator ECON1.A. Percentage of Children Ages 0–17 Living in Poverty by Race, Hispanic Origin, and Family Structure, 1980–2013," in *America's Children: Key National Indicators of Well-Being, 2015*, Federal Interagency Forum on Child and Family Statistics, July 2015, http://www.childstats.gov/pdf/ac2015/ac_15.pdf (accessed July 23, 2015)

has already discussed that children living in families headed by a single parent rather than by two parents are at a higher risk for living in poverty. Figure 6.4 reiterates this fact, showing that 46% of children living in female-headed households were living in poverty in 2013, compared with 10% of children living in married-couple households. Families of African American female householders were the most likely to be living in poverty in 2013, followed closely by families of Hispanic female householders. Among married-couple families, Hispanics were the most likely to be living in poverty.

Help for Poor School-Aged Children

Parents, educators, and government officials generally agree that poor children often need help to prepare them for school and improve their performance in school. Title I is the major federal program that provides funding for remedial education programs for disadvantaged children in public schools and in some private programs. (Because many Title I programs are for children with disabilities and other special needs, Chapter 3 describes Title I programs in more detail.) States and school districts can apply for Title I funds for a variety of programs that are aimed at improving the performance of disadvantaged students. Title I funds are allocated to states and school districts on a formula basis, but states with higher numbers of poor, immigrant, and/or migrant students are typically eligible for, apply for, and receive more federal funds.

Besides Title I programs, there are a number of national and state organizations dedicated to assisting children from low-income families. One notable entity is the Children's Defense Fund (http://www.childrensdefense.org), an organization that seeks to improve the lives of underprivileged children through youth leadership programs, affordable health care initiatives, and family outreach campaigns. Headquartered at Columbia University's Mailman School of Public Health, the National Center for Children in Poverty (http://www.nccp.org) partners with individual states to provide a range of educational and community resources to children living in poverty. Meanwhile, a number of organizations devoted to alleviating child poverty have emerged on the state level, such as Children at Risk (http://children atrisk.org), a nonprofit group based in Texas that works to shape public policy through a range of educational and research programs.

ADOLESCENT AND TEEN HEALTH AND HEALTH RISK BEHAVIORS

The behavioral choices that adolescents and teens make can put their health and their ability to succeed in school at risk, which can affect their quality of life, their life span, and their success in life. Teen health and health risk behaviors are monitored regularly by various national studies. The CDC monitors teen risk behaviors with the biannual Youth Risk Behavior Surveillance study. The National Institute on Drug Abuse funds the Institute for Social Research at the University of Michigan to conduct an annual survey of substance use among students. Its report is called *Monitoring the Future*. Another major study that contributes useful information to this topic is the annual National Survey on Drug Use and Health published by the Substance Abuse and Mental Health Services Administration (SAMHSA).

According to the CDC's National Center for Injury Prevention and Control, in "WISQARS Leading Causes of Death Reports, National and Regional, 1999–2013" (June 24, 2015, http://webappa.cdc.gov/sasweb/ncipc/leadcaus10_us.html), 12,393 young people between the ages of 10 and 19 years died in 2013. The leading cause of death was "unintentional injury," with 35.7% of all deaths in this age range from this cause. Of these deaths, 62.2% were from motor vehicle–related incidents, 13.7% were from accidental poisoning, and 7.5% were from drowning. The second- and third-leading causes of death for those aged 10 to 19 years were suicide (17.2%) and homicide (12.6%), respectively. The remainder of deaths were due to disease processes, such as cancer, heart disease, and pneumonia.

In addition, death and various social and educational problems result from teen pregnancy and from the transmission of sexually transmitted infections (STIs; also called sexually transmitted diseases [STDs]) among young people. Health risk behaviors that are associated with these leading causes of death, STIs, and unintended pregnancies in school-aged youth include alcohol and other drug use, tobacco use, risky sexual behaviors, carrying weapons, and behaving in a violent or uncontrolled manner. Moreover, some youth consider taking their own life instead of trying to work through the serious issues they might face.

Perception of the Risk of Drug Use

In *Monitoring the Future: National Survey Results on Drug Use, 1975–2014. Volume 1, Secondary School Students* (June 2015, http://www.monitoringthefuture.org/pubs/monographs/mtf-vol1_2014.pdf), Richard A. Miech et al. of the University of Michigan's Institute for Social Research state that "beliefs and attitudes about drugs have been important determinants of trends, both upwards and downward, in the use of many drugs." Inverse relationships are usually found between the level of reported use of a drug and the level of its perceived risk; that is, if the perceived risk involved in taking a drug is low, the likelihood of it being used is high. With their data, Miech et al. show that in 2014 a smaller percentage of eighth-, 10th-, and 12th-grade students considered substance use to be a great risk than they did in 1991, which was a peak year for percentages of students perceiving great risk in drug taking. However, there were a few exceptions.

For 10th graders, the percentage who saw great risk in trying inhalants once or twice rose from 37.8% in 1991 to a high of 47.2% in 1996, then decreased to 43.1% in 2014. (See Table 6.2.) The percentage of 10th graders who saw great risk in trying one or two drinks of an alcoholic beverage rose as well, from 9% in 1991 to 11.6% in 2014. Among 12th graders, the perception of risk associated with taking one or two drinks of alcohol rose from 9.1% in 1991 to 10.8% in 2010, before dropping to 8.6% in 2014. (See Table 6.3.) Compared with the percentages of 10th and 12th graders in 2014 who saw great risk in trying one or two drinks, there were much higher percentages among the groups who saw great risk in consuming one or two drinks nearly every day, four or five drinks nearly every day, or five or more drinks once or twice each weekend. However, the percentages of those who perceived these risks dropped since 1991.

Miech et al. also report that a higher proportion of eighth, 10th, and 12th graders in 2014 perceived the great risks of smoking cigarettes and of using smokeless tobacco than did students in those grades in 1991. In 2014, 62.1% of eighth graders, 72% of 10th graders, and 78% of 12th graders said it was a great risk to smoke one or more packs of cigarettes per day, up from 51.6%, 60.3%, and 69.4%, respectively, in 1991. (See Table 6.2, Table 6.3, and Table 6.4.) On the other hand, in 2014, 34.5% of eighth graders and 39.9% of 10th graders said it was a great risk to use smokeless tobacco regularly, down from 35.1% and 40.3%, respectively, in 1991. By contrast, 40.7% of 12th graders perceived great risk in using smokeless tobacco regularly in 2014, up from 37.4% in 1991.

A higher percentage of 12th graders in 2014 than in 1991 perceived a great risk in trying heroin once or twice and crystal methamphetamine once or twice. In 1991, 55.2% of high school seniors perceived great risk in trying heroin once or twice, and 61.6% perceived great risk in trying crystal methamphetamine once or twice. (See Table 6.3.) In 2014 the percentages had risen to 62.8% and 70.2%, respectively. In contrast, between 1991 and 2014 the perceived risk of trying lysergic acid diethylamide (LSD) once or twice, cocaine once or twice, and crack cocaine once or twice fell among 12th graders. In 1991, 46.6% of 12th-grade students perceived great risk in trying LSD once or twice, compared with 35.5% who perceived the same risk in 2014. The perceived risk

TABLE 6.2

Trends in harmfulness of drugs as perceived by 10th-graders, selected years 1991–2014

[Percentage saying great risk[a]]

How much do you think people risk harming themselves (physically or in other ways), if they...	1991	1995	1996	2000	2005	2010	2013	2014	2013–2014 change
Try marijuana once or twice[b]	30.0	21.5	20.0	18.5	22.3	19.9	15.7	15.2	−0.5
Smoke marijuana occasionally[b]	48.6	35.4	32.8	32.4	36.6	30.9	25.1	23.9	−1.2
Smoke marijuana regularly[b]	82.1	67.9	65.9	64.7	65.5	57.2	46.5	45.4	−1.1
Try synthetic marijuana once or twice[c]	—	—	—	—	—	—	24.1	25.0	+1.0
Take synthetic marijuana occasionally[c]	—	—	—	—	—	—	32.8	30.7	−2.1
Try inhalants once or twice[d]	37.8	41.6	47.2	46.6	45.7	42.5	43.0	43.1	+0.1
Take inhalants regularly[d]	69.8	71.8	75.8	75.0	71.2	67.1	65.9	64.7	−1.2
Take LSD once or twice[e]	—	44.7	45.1	43.0	40.3	33.9	34.7	34.5	−0.2
Take LSD regularly[e]	—	75.5	75.3	72.0	60.8	56.1	55.9	54.8	−1.1
Try ecstasy (MDMA) once or twice[c]	—	—	—	—	51.4	36.3	36.0	36.8	+0.8
Take ecstasy (MDMA) occasionally[c]	—	—	—	—	72.8	59.2	58.6	58.0	−0.6
Try salvia once or twice[c]	—	—	—	—	—	—	10.7	—	—
Take salvia occasionally[c]	—	—	—	—	—	—	17.1	—	—
Try crack once or twice[d]	70.4	60.9	60.9	56.1	57.0	58.1	60.2	61.4	+1.1
Take crack occasionally[d]	87.4	81.2	80.3	76.9	76.9	76.2	77.8	76.4	−1.4
Try cocaine powder once or twice[d]	59.1	53.5	53.6	48.8	51.3	52.9	54.5	54.1	−0.4
Take cocaine powder occasionally[d]	82.2	75.6	75.0	70.9	72.4	72.2	72.8	71.7	−1.1
Try heroin once or twice without using a needle[e]	—	70.7	72.1	71.7	72.4	73.0	73.2	72.6	−0.6
Take heroin occasionally without using a needle[e]	—	85.1	85.8	85.2	85.2	84.8	84.0	82.5	−1.5
Try OxyContin once or twice[c]	—	—	—	—	—	—	29.4	29.7	+0.4
Take OxyContin occasionally[c]	—	—	—	—	—	—	44.7	44.4	−0.3
Try Vicodin once or twice[c]	—	—	—	—	—	—	21.0	22.5	+1.4
Take Vicodin occasionally[c]	—	—	—	—	—	—	36.0	36.4	+0.3
Try Adderall once or twice[c]	—	—	—	—	—	—	17.6	22.2	+4.7 sss
Take Adderall occasionally[c]	—	—	—	—	—	—	30.5	37.0	+6.5 sss
Try bath salts (synthetic stimulants) once or twice[c]	—	—	—	—	—	—	50.1	49.6	−0.5
Take bath salts (synthetic stimulants) occasionally[c]	—	—	—	—	—	—	61.8	61.1	−0.7
Try cough/cold medicine once or twice[c]	—	—	—	—	—	—	21.6	22.9	+1.3
Take cough/cold medicine occasionally[c]	—	—	—	—	—	—	37.3	38.3	+1.0
Try one or two drinks of an alcoholic beverage (beer, wine, liquor)[b]	9.0	9.3	8.9	9.6	11.5	11.9	11.3	11.6	+0.4
Take one or two drinks nearly every day[b]	36.1	31.7	31.2	32.3	32.6	33.1	30.6	31.3	+0.7
Have five or more drinks once or twice each weekend[b]	54.7	52.0	50.9	51.0	53.3	54.6	52.3	54.0	+1.7
Smoke one to five cigarettes per day[c]	—	—	—	30.2	41.0	41.4	47.7	52.0	+4.4 s
Smoke one or more packs of cigarettes per day[f]	60.3	57.0	57.9	65.9	68.1	67.2	70.8	72.0	+1.3
Use electronic cigarettes (e-cigarettes) regularly[b]	—	—	—	—	—	—	—	14.1	—
Smoke little cigars or cigarillos regularly[c]	—	—	—	—	—	—	—	31.0	—
Use smokeless tobacco regularly	40.3	38.2	41.0	46.7	46.1	43.7	40.0	39.9	−0.1
Take dissolvable tobacco regularly[c]	—	—	—	—	—	—	31.3	32.0	+0.7
Take snus regularly[c]	—	—	—	—	—	—	38.9	38.8	−0.1
Take steroids[h]	67.1	—	—	—	—	—	—	—	—
Approximate weighted population =	14,700	17,000	15,700	14,300	16,200	15,200	12,900	13,000	

[a]Answer alternatives were: (1) No risk, (2) Slight risk, (3) Moderate risk, (4) Great risk, and (5) Can't say, drug unfamiliar.
[b]Beginning in 2012 data based on two thirds of population indicated.
[c]Data based on one third of population indicated.
[d]Beginning in 1997, data based on two thirds of population indicated due to changes in questionnaire forms.
[e]Data based on one of two forms in 1993–1996; population is one half of population indicated. Beginning in 1997, data based on one third of population indicated due to changes in questionnaire forms.
[f]Beginning in 1999, data based on two thirds of population indicated due to changes in questionnaire forms.
[g]E-cigarette data based on two thirds of population indicated. Little cigars or cigarillos data based on one third population indicated.
[h]Data based on two forms in 1991 and 1992. Data based on one of two forms in 1993 and 1994; population is one half of population indicated.
Notes: Level of significance of difference between the two most recent classes: s = .05, ss = .01, sss = .001.
' — ' indicates data not available. Any apparent inconsistency between the change estimate and the prevalence estimates for the two most recent years is due to rounding.

SOURCE: Adapted from Richard A. Miech et al., "Table 8-2. Trends in Harmfulness of Drugs as Perceived by 10th Graders," in *Monitoring the Future: National Survey Results on Drug Use, 1975–2014. Volume I, Secondary School Students*, University of Michigan, Institute for Social Research, June 2015, http://www.monitoringthefuture.org/pubs/monographs/mtf-vol1_2014.pdf (accessed July 23, 2015).

among high school seniors of trying cocaine once or twice fell from 59.4% in 1991 to 53.7% in 2014, and the perceived risk of smoking crack fell from 60.6% to 54.5% during this same span.

According to SAMHSA, in *Results from the 2014 National Survey on Drug Use and Health: Detailed Tables* (September 10, 2015, http://www.samhsa.gov/data/sites/default/files/NSDUH-DetTabs2014/NSDUH-DetTabs2014.pdf), marijuana was the most commonly used illicit drug in 2014. (Illicit drugs are both illegal drugs and controlled substances that are used illegally.) Long-term use of marijuana can cause short-term memory loss, lung damage, adverse effects on reproductive

TABLE 6.3

Trends in harmfulness of drugs as perceived by 12th-graders, selected years 1991–2014

[Percentage saying great risk][a]

How much do you think people risk harming themselves (physically or in other ways), if they...	1991	1995	2000	2005	2010	2013	2014	2013–2014 change
Try marijuana once or twice	27.1	16.3	13.7	16.1	17.1	14.5	12.5	−2.0
Smoke marijuana occasionally	40.6	25.6	23. 4	25.8	24.5	19.5	16.4	−3.1 s
Smoke marijuana regularly	78.6	60.8	58. 3	58.0	46.8	39.5	36.1	−3.4
Try synthetic marijuana once or twice	—	—	—	—	—	25.9	32.5	+6.6 sss
Take synthetic marijuana occasionally	—	—	—	—	—	36.2	39.4	+3.3
Try LSD once or twice	46.6	36.4	34.3	36.5	35.6	34.9	35.5	+0.6
Take LSD regularly	84.3	78.1	75.9	69.9	65.3	66.8	62.7	−4.1 s
Try PCP once or twice	51.7	49.1	45.0	46.6	52.4	53.9	53.8	−0.1
Try ecstasy (MDMA) once or twice[b]	—	—	37.9	60.1	50.6	47.5	47.8	+0.4
Try salvia once or twice[c]	—	—	—	—	39.8	12.9	14.1	+1.2
Take salvia occasionally	—	—	—	—	—	21.3	20.0	−1.3
Try cocaine once or twice	59.4	53.7	51.1	50.5	52.8	54.4	53.7	−0.7
Take cocaine occasionally	75.5	70.8	69.5	66.7	67.8	70.2	68.1	−2.1
Take cocaine regularly	90.4	87.9	86.2	82.8	81.7	83.3	80.6	−2.6
Try crack once or twice	60.6	54.6	48.4	48.4	50.2	55.6	54.5	−1.0
Take crack occasionally	76.5	72.8	65.8	63.8	64.3	69.5	68.5	−0.9
Take crack regularly	90.1	88.6	85.3	83.3	83.8	85.4	82.0	−3.4 s
Try cocaine powder once or twice	53.6	52.0	47.0	46.2	48.2	49.9	49.9	0.0
Take cocaine powder occasionally	69.8	69.1	64.7	60.8	62.6	65.4	64.8	−0.5
Take cocaine powder regularly	88.9	87.8	85.5	82.7	81.8	83.9	81.5	−2.4
Try heroin once or twice	55.2	50.9	54.2	55.2	58.3	61.7	62.8	+1.1
Take heroin occasionally	74.9	71.0	74.6	76.0	74.8	78.2	77.9	−0.2
Take heroin regularly	89.6	87.2	89.2	87.5	85.5	87.6	85.7	−1.9
Try heroin once or twice without using a needle	—	55.6	61.6	60.5	63.8	64.5	65.3	+0.7
Take heroin occasionally without using a needle	—	71.2	74.7	73.3	76.2	76.4	73.6	−2.8
Try any narcotic other than heroin (codeine, Vicodin, OxyContin, Percocet, etc.) once or twice	—	—	—	—	40.4	43.1	42.7	−0.4
Take any narcotic other than heroin occasionally	—	—	—	—	54.3	57.3	59.0	+1.7
Take any narcotic other than heroin regularly	—	—	—	—	74.9	75.8	72.7	−3.1
Try amphetamines once or twice[d]	36.3	28.8	32.6	37.7	40.6‡	36.3	34.1	−2.2
Take amphetamines regularly[d]	74.1	65.9	66.3	67.1	63.6‡	59.5	55.1	−4.4 s
Try Adderall once or twice[e]	—	—	—	—	33.3	31.8	33.6	+1.8
Try Adderall occasionally[e]	—	—	—	—	41.6	38.8	41.5	+2.7
Try crystal methamphetamine (ice) once or twice	61.6	54.4	51.3	54.6	64.9	72. 2	70.2	−2.0
Try bath salts (synthetic stimulants) once or twice	—	—	—	—	—	59.5	59.2	−0.4
Take bath salts (synthetic stimulants) occasionally	—	—	—	—	—	69.9	68. 8	−1.0
Try sedatives (barbiturates) once or twice[f]	35.1	26.3	25.0	24.7	28.0	29.4	29.6	+0.2
Take sedatives (barbiturates) regularly[f]	70.5	61.6	52.3	54.1	52.1	53.3	50.5	−2.8
Try one or two drinks of an alcoholic beverage (beer, wine, liquor)	9.1	5.9	6.4	8.5	10.8	9.9	8.6	−1.3
Take one or two drinks nearly every day	32.7	24.8	21.7	23.7	25.4	23.1	21.1	−2.0
Take four or five drinks nearly every day	69.5	62.8	59.9	61.8	61.1	62.4	61.2	−1.3
Have five or more drinks once or twice each weekend	48.6	45.2	42.7	45.0	46.3	45.8	45.4	−0.4
Smoke one or more packs of cigarettes per day	69.4	65.6	73.1	76.5	75.0	78. 2	78.0	−0.2
Use electronic cigarettes (e-cigarettes) regularly[g]	—	—	—	—	—	—	14.2	—
Smoke little cigars or cigarillos regularly	—	—	—	—	—	—	38.3	—
Use smokeless tobacco regularly	37.4	33.2	42.2	43.6	41.2	41.6	40.7	−0.9
Take steroids	65.6	66.4	57.9	56.8	59.2	54.2	54.6	+0.4
Approximate weighted population =	**2,549**	**2,603**	**2,130**	**2,512**	**2,440**	**2,098**	**2,067**	

Notes: Level of significance of difference between the two most recent classes: s = .05, ss = .01, sss = .001.

' — ' indicates data not available. ' ‡ ' indicates some change in the question. See relevant footnote for that drug.

Any apparent inconsistency between the change estimate and the prevalence estimates for the two most recent years is due to rounding.

[a]Answer alternatives were: (1) No risk, (2) Slight risk, (3) Moderate risk, (4) Great risk, and (5) Can't say, drug unfamiliar.

[b]In 2014 "molly" was added to the question on perceived risk of using MDMA once or twice.

[c]In 2011 the question on perceived risk of using salvia once or twice appeared at the end of a form. In 2012 the question was moved to an earlier section of the same form. A question on perceived risk of using salvia occasionally was also added following the question on perceived risk of trying salvia once or twice. These changes likely explain the discontinuity in the 2012 results.

[d]In 2011 the list of examples was changed from uppers, pep pills, bennies, speed to uppers, speed, Adderall, Ritalin, etc. These changes likely explain the discontinuity in the 2011 results.

[e]In 2014 "(without a doctor's orders)" added to the questions on perceived risk of using Adderall.

[f]In 2004 the question text was changed from barbiturates to sedatives/barbiturates and the list of examples was changed from downers, goofballs, reds, yellows, etc. to just downers. These changes likely explain the discontinuity in the 2004 results.

[g]Based on two of six forms; N is two times the N indicated.

SOURCE: Adapted from Richard A. Miech et al., "Table 8-3. Trends in Harmfulness of Drugs as Perceived by 12th Graders," in *Monitoring the Future: National Survey Results on Drug Use, 1975–2014. Volume I, Secondary School Students*, University of Michigan, Institute for Social Research, June 2015, http://www .monitoringthefuture.org/pubs/monographs/mtf-vol1_2014.pdf (accessed July 23, 2015)

function, suppression of the immune system, apathy, impairment of judgment, and loss of interest in personal appearance and pursuit of goals. In spite of these long-term health risks, the proportion of eighth, 10th, and

TABLE 6.4

Trends in harmfulness of drugs as perceived by eighth-graders, selected years 1991–2014

[Percentage saying great risk[a]]

How much do you think people risk harming themselves (physically or in other ways), if they	1991	1995	2000	2005	2010	2013	2014	2013–2014 change
Try marijuana once or twice[b]	40.4	28.9	29.0	31.4	29.5	24.1	23.0	−1.1
Smoke marijuana occasionally[b]	57.9	45.9	47.4	48.9	44.1	37.2	36.7	−0.5
Smoke marijuana regularly[b]	83.8	73.0	74.8	73.9	68.0	61.0	58.9	−2.1
Try synthetic marijuana once or twice[c]	—	—	—	—	—	24.2	23.9	−0.3
Take synthetic marijuana occasionally[c]	—	—	—	—	—	36.2	32.4	−3.8 s
Try inhalants once or twice[d]	35.9	36.4	41.2	37.5	35.5	33.7	34.5	+0.8
Take inhalants regularly[d]	65.6	64.8	69.9	64.1	60.6	56.7	55.3	−1.4
Take LSD once or twice[e]	—	36.7	34.0	25.8	23.6	19.6	20.0	+0.4
Take LSD regularly[e]	—	64.4	57.5	44.0	38.6	34.5	33.7	−0.8
Try ecstasy (MDMA) once or twice[c]	—	—	—	40.0	27.0	24.1	24.3	+0.2
Take ecstasy (MDMA) occasionally[c]	—	—	—	60.8	45.0	42.1	39.4	−2.7
Try salvia once or twice[c]	—	—	—	—	—	8.5	—	—
Take salvia occasionally[c]	—	—	—	—	—	14.6	—	—
Try crack once or twice[d]	62.8	50.8	48.5	49.6	49.6	47.1	48.3	+1.2
Take crack occasionally[d]	82.2	72.1	70.1	69.4	68.4	66.5	65.5	−1.1
Try cocaine powder once or twice[d]	55.5	44.9	43.3	44.2	45.7	43.5	43.9	+0.4
Take cocaine powder occasionally[d]	77.0	66.4	65.5	65.3	64.2	62.7	61.8	−0.9
Try heroin once or twice without using a needle[e]	—	60.1	62.0	61.4	62.3	59.8	60.9	+1.0
Take heroin occasionally without using a needle[e]	—	76.8	78.6	76.8	76.7	73.4	73.2	−0.1
Try OxyContin once or twice[c]	—	—	—	—	—	19.9	22.1	+2.2
Take OxyContin occasionally[c]	—	—	—	—	—	32.6	34.4	+1.8
Try Vicodin once or twice[c]	—	—	—	—	—	15.0	18.4	+3.4 ss
Take Vicodin occasionally[c]	—	—	—	—	—	26.2	28.2	+2.0
Try Adderall once or twice[c]	—	—	—	—	—	16.5	20.7	+4.2 sss
Take Adderall occasionally[c]	—	—	—	—	—	28.3	32.5	+4.2 sss
Try bath salts (synthetic stimulants) once or twice[c]	—	—	—	—	—	39.3	36.8	−2.5 s
Take bath salts (synthetic stimulants) occasionally[c]	—	—	—	—	—	51.9	49.1	−2.8 s
Try cough/cold medicine once or twice[c]	—	—	—	—	—	20.1	22.9	+2.7 s
Take cough/cold medicine occasionally[c]	—	—	—	—	—	37.3	37.9	+0.6
Try one or two drinks of an alcoholic beverage (beer, wine, liquor)[b]	11.0	11.6	11.9	13.9	14.9	13.7	14.8	+1.0
Take one or two drinks nearly every day[b]	31.8	30.5	30.4	31.4	32.3	30.6	31.0	+0.3
Have five or more drinks once or twice each weekend[b]	59.1	54.1	55.9	57.2	57.2	55.7	54.3	−1.4
Smoke one to five cigarettes per day[c]	—	—	28.9	37.5	38.2	42.8	41.9	−0.9
Smoke one or more packs of cigarettes per day[f]	51.6	49.8	58.8	61.5	60.9	62.4	62.1	−0.3
Use electronic cigarettes (e-cigarettes) regularly[b]	—	—	—	—	—	—	14.5	—
Smoke little cigars or cigarillos regularly[c]	—	—	—	—	—	—	28.8	—
Use smokeless tobacco regularly[c]	35.1	33.5	39.0	40.8	41.8	36.2	34.5	−1.7
Take dissolvable tobacco regularly[c]	—	—	—	—	—	32.2	33.5	+1.3
Take snus regularly[c]	—	—	—	—	—	38.9	38.3	−0.5
Take steroids[h]	64.2	—	—	—	—	—	—	—
Approximate weighted population =	**17,400**	**17,500**	**16,700**	**16,800**	**15,300**	**14,600**	**14,600**	

[a]Answer alternatives were: (1) No risk, (2) Slight risk, (3) Moderate risk, (4) Great risk, and (5) Can't say, drug unfamiliar.
[b]Beginning in 2012 data based on two thirds of population indicated.
[c]Data based on one third of population indicated.
[d]Beginning in 1997, data based on two thirds of population indicated due to changes in questionnaire forms.
[e]Data based on one of two forms in 1993–1996; population is one half of population indicated. Beginning in 1997, data based on one third of population indicated due to changes in questionnaire forms.
[f]Beginning in 1999, data based on two thirds of population indicated due to changes in questionnaire forms.
[g]E-cigarette data based on two thirds of population indicated. Little cigars or cigarillos data based on one third population indicated.
[h]Data based on two forms in 1991 and 1992. Data based on one of two forms in 1993 and 1994; population is one half of population indicated.
Notes: Level of significance of difference between the two most recent classes: s = .05, ss = .01, sss = .001. ' — ' indicates data not available. Any apparent inconsistency between the change estimate and the prevalence estimates for the two most recent years is due to rounding.

SOURCE: Adapted from Richard A. Miech et al., "Table 8-1. Trends in Harmfulness of Drugs as Perceived by 8th Graders," in *Monitoring the Future: National Survey Results on Drug Use, 1975–2014. Volume I, Secondary School Students,* University of Michigan, Institute for Social Research, June 2015, http://www.monitoringthefuture.org/pubs/monographs/mtf-vol1_2014.pdf (accessed July 23, 2015)

12th graders who saw great risk in the regular use of marijuana decreased significantly between 1991 and 2014. In 2014, 58.9% of eighth graders, 45.4% of 10th graders, and 36.1% of 12th graders saw great risk in smoking marijuana regularly, down from 83.8%, 82.1%, and 78.6%, respectively, in 1991. (See Table 6.2, Table 6.3, and Table 6.4.)

Trends in Annual Prevalence of Drug Use

Figure 6.5 shows the trends in annual prevalence of drug use for college students, young adults, and eighth, 10th, and 12th graders. Miech et al. report that in 2014, 38.7% of 12th graders, 29.9% of 10th graders, and 14.6% of eighth graders responded that they had used an illicit drug during the previous 12 months. These percentages were down from peak levels of drug use during the mid-1990s, but the decline has been slow and a slight upturn has occurred since about 2007.

FIGURE 6.5

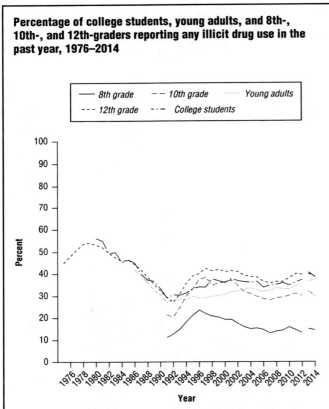

Percentage of college students, young adults, and 8th-, 10th-, and 12th-graders reporting any illicit drug use in the past year, 1976–2014

Note: Illicit drug use index includes any use of marijuana, LSD, other hallucinogens, crack, other cocaine, or heroin; or any use of narcotics other than heroin which is not under a doctor's orders, stimulants, sedatives (barbiturates), methaqualone (excluded since 1990), or tranquilizers. Beginning in 1982, the question about stimulant use (i.e., amphetamines) was revised to get respondents to exclude the inappropriate reporting of nonprescription stimulants. The prevalence rate dropped slightly as a result of this methodological change. In 2013, the question on use of amphetamines was changed. Data for any illicit drug were affected by this change.

SOURCE: Richard A. Miech et al., "Figure 2-1. Trends in Annual Prevalence of an Illicit Drug Use Index across 5 Populations," in *Monitoring the Future: National Survey Results on Drug Use, 1975–2014. Volume I, Secondary School Students*, University of Michigan, Institute for Social Research, June 2015, http://www .monitoringthefuture.org/pubs/monographs/mtf-vol1_2014.pdf (accessed July 23, 2015)

One risk factor for dropping out of school is having few friends who expect to go to college. College expectations of students also correlate with the level of annual prevalence of drug use in high school. These data are shown in Table 6.5. In 2014 students who had plans to complete four years of college had a much lower annual prevalence of illicit drug use than students who had no college plans or plans for attending less than four years of college. For eighth graders the annual prevalence of illicit drug use for students intending to graduate from a four-year college was 13.3%, compared with 29% for students with either no college plans or who did not plan on attending a four-year school; for 10th graders it was 28.4% for four-year college-bound students and 44.4% for students not intending to attend a four-year college; and for 12th graders it was 36.7% for students intending to graduate from a four-year school, and 44.5% for those who were not.

There was an inverse relationship between parental education and annual prevalence of illicit drug use among eighth, 10th, and 12th graders in 2014. That is, students with more highly educated parents (and therefore likely to be of higher socioeconomic status) were less likely to have used illicit drugs in the 12 months preceding the survey. In 2014 this inverse relationship was strong with eighth graders: 22.9% of those having parents with the lowest level of education reported having used illicit drugs in the past year, compared with 10.5% of those having parents with the highest level of education. (See Table 6.5.) As the education level of the parents went up, the prevalence of illicit drug use went down. This pattern was also noticeable with 10th and 12th graders in 2014.

The influence of gender on annual prevalence of illicit drug use varies by grade level. In 2014, 10th- and 12th-grade males typically had a higher annual prevalence than females of illicit drug use. (See Table 6.5.) By contrast, in 2014 a slightly higher percentage of eighth-grade girls (14.5%) than eighth-grade boys (14.1%) reported having used illicit drugs in the past year.

In 2014 the influence of race on annual prevalence of illicit drug use varied among eighth, 10th, and 12th graders. Among eighth graders, Hispanics had the highest annual prevalence of illicit drug use (18.5%), African Americans had the next highest annual prevalence (15.4%), and whites had the lowest annual prevalence (11.3%). (See Table 6.5.) Among 10th graders, Hispanics still had the highest annual prevalence of illicit drug use (35.2%), followed by African Americans (32.9%) and whites (28.9%). At the 12th-grade level the gap between the three groups narrowed considerably, as the annual prevalence of illicit drug use in 2014 was 40.3% for Hispanics, 39.6% for African Americans, and 38.8% for whites.

Drug Availability at School

Table 6.6 shows that in 2013, 22.1% of high school students reported that illegal drugs were offered, sold, or

TABLE 6.5

Annual prevalence of any illicit drug use by 8th-, 10th-, and 12th-graders, by demographic characteristics, 2014

[Entries in percents]

	Approximate weighted population[a]			Any illicit drug[b]			Any illicit drug other than marijuana[b]			Marijuana			Alcohol		
	8th	10th	12th	8th	10th	12th	8th	10th	12th	8th	10th	12th	8th	10th	12th
Total	14,600	13,000	12,400	14.6	29.9	38.7	6.4	11.2	15.9	11.7	27.3	35.1	20.8	44.0	60.2
Gender															
Male	6,800	6,200	5,700	14.1	30.3	39.8	5.3	10.4	16.9	11.9	28.3	37.0	19.1	42.5	58.7
Female	7,200	6,400	6,100	14.5	29.4	36.9	7.1	11.8	14.2	11.0	26.0	33.0	22.0	45.4	61.7
College plans															
None or under 4 years	1,000	1,200	2,000	29.0	44.4	44.5	14.7	21.9	19.8	24.1	41.4	40.8	33.8	58.5	62.8
Complete 4 years	13,000	11,500	9,600	13.3	28.4	36.7	5.7	10.1	14.5	10.6	25.7	33.1	19.8	42.5	59.7
Region															
Northeast	2,400	2,500	2,400	12.9	29.5	43.0	4.3	9.8	13.9	10.3	27.4	39.6	18.8	46.9	64.1
Midwest	3,200	3,000	2,500	13.4	26.6	38.3	5.6	11.8	16.2	10.7	24.5	34.6	21.2	41.5	63.7
South	5,600	4,400	4,700	14.7	31.1	37.7	7.1	11.9	17.2	11.5	27.6	33.6	21.3	45.5	58.0
West	3,400	3,100	2,800	16.7	31.8	37.0	7.5	10.9	15.1	14.0	29.4	34.3	20.9	41.9	57.4
Population density															
Large MSA	4,700	4,500	3,500	16.0	30.0	38.8	5.7	10.2	14.6	13.6	27.5	35.8	20.4	42.9	60.0
Other MSA	6,800	6,000	6,300	14.1	30.5	41.2	6.9	11.3	17.7	10.8	28.0	36.9	20.6	45.2	61.4
Non-MSA	3,100	2,500	2,600	13.7	28.5	32.3	6.4	12.7	13.0	10.9	25.1	29.7	21.8	42.9	57.3
Parental education[c]															
1.0–2.0 (Low)	1,300	1,100	1,200	22.9	35.0	40.7	9.4	14.1	14.7	19.3	31.5	37.3	25.8	50.6	57.4
2.5–3.0	2,400	2,300	2,400	19.6	34.8	41.4	7.6	12.4	16.8	16.7	32.0	37.5	26.3	46.8	63.6
3.5–4.0	3,100	3,100	3,400	16.4	33.6	39.1	7.0	13.2	15.7	12.9	30.6	35.9	23.9	47.1	60.4
4.5–5.0	3,600	3,600	3,200	10.4	25.5	36.5	4.9	9.2	15.1	8.0	23.3	32.9	18.3	41.8	61.2
5.5–6.0 (High)	2,300	2,100	1,300	10.5	24.3	37.1	5.4	9.0	16.8	7.9	21.6	32.9	16.0	41.5	60.4
Race/ethnicity (2-year average)[d]															
White	13,100	13,900	14,100	11.3	28.9	38.8	5.3	11.4	17.3	8.9	26.7	35.1	20.7	47.6	65.0
African American	4,100	2,900	2,800	15.4	32.9	39.6	4.6	7.2	11.7	13.2	30.6	35.9	17.8	37.3	47.9
Hispanic	5,700	4,300	4,000	18.5	35.2	40.3	7.4	11.4	15.1	16.0	32.6	37.1	25.4	49.6	60.1

[a]Subgroup populations may vary depending on the number of forms in which the use of each drug was asked about.

[b]Use of any illicit drug includes any use of marijuana, LSD, other hallucinogens, crack, other cocaine, or heroin; or any use of narcotics other than heroin, amphetamines, sedatives (barbiturates), or tranquilizers not under a doctor's orders. For 8th and 10th graders, the use of narcotics other than heroin and sedatives (barbiturates) has been excluded because these younger respondents appear to overreport use (perhaps because they include the use of nonprescription drugs in their answers).

[c]Parental education is an average score of mother's education and father's education reported on the following scale: (1) Completed grade school or less, (2) Some high school, (3) Completed high school, (4) Some college, (5) Completed college, (6) Graduate or professional school after college. Missing data were allowed on one of the two variables.

[d]To derive percentages for each racial subgroup, data for the specified year and the previous year have been combined to increase subgroup sample sizes and thus provide more stable estimates.

Notes. '—' indicates data not available. '*' indicates less than 0.05% but greater than 0%. MSA = metropolitan service area.

SOURCE: Adapted from Richard A. Miech et al., "Table 4-6. Annual Prevalence of Use of Various Drugs by Subgroups for 8th, 10th, and 12th Graders, 2014," in *Monitoring the Future: National Survey Results on Drug Use, 1975–2014. Volume I. Secondary School Students*, University of Michigan, Institute for Social Research, June 2015, http://www.monitoringthefuture.org/pubs/monographs/mtf-vol1_2014.pdf (accessed July 23, 2015)

TABLE 6.6

Percentage of students in grades 9–12 who reported that drugs were made available to them on school property during the previous 12 months, by selected student and school characteristics, selected years 1993–2013

Student characteristic	1993	1995	1997	1999	2001	2003	2005	2007	2009	2011	2013
Total	24.0	32.1	31.7	30.2	28.5	28.7	25.4	22.3	22.7	25.6	22.1
Sex											
Male	28.5	38.8	37.4	34.7	34.6	31.9	28.8	25.7	25.9	29.2	24.5
Female	19.1	24.8	24.7	25.7	22.7	25.0	21.8	18.7	19.3	21.7	19.7
Race/ethnicity[a]											
White	24.1	31.7	31.0	28.8	28.3	27.5	23.6	20.8	19.8	22.7	20.4
Black	17.5	28.5	25.4	25.3	21.9	23.1	23.9	19.2	22.2	22.8	18.6
Hispanic	34.1	40.7	41.1	36.9	34.2	36.5	33.5	29.1	31.2	33.2	27.4
Asian[b]	—	—	—	25.7	25.7	22.5	15.9	21.0	18.3	23.3	22.6
Pacific Islander[b]	—	—	—	46.9	50.2	34.7	41.3	38.5	27.6	38.9	27.7
American Indian/Alaska Native	20.9	22.8	30.1	30.6	34.5	31.3	24.4	25.1	34.0	40.5	25.5
Two or more races[b]	—	—	—	36.0	34.5	36.6	31.6	24.6	26.9	33.3	26.4
Grade											
9th	21.8	31.1	31.4	27.6	29.0	29.5	24.0	21.2	22.0	23.7	22.4
10th	23.7	35.0	33.4	32.1	29.0	29.2	27.5	25.3	23.7	27.8	23.2
11th	27.5	32.8	33.2	31.1	28.7	29.9	24.9	22.8	24.3	27.0	23.2
12th	23.0	29.1	29.0	30.5	26.9	24.9	24.9	19.6	20.6	23.8	18.8
Urbanicity[c]											
Urban	—	—	31.2	30.3	32.0	31.1	—	—	—	—	—
Suburban	—	—	34.2	29.7	26.6	28.4	—	—	—	—	—
Rural	—	—	22.7	32.1	28.2	26.2	—	—	—	—	—

—Not available.

[†]Not applicable.

[a]Race categories exclude persons of Hispanic ethnicity.

[b]Before 1999, Asian students and Pacific Islander students were not categorized separately, and students were not given the option of choosing two or more races. Because the response categories changed in 1999, caution should be used in comparing data on race from 1993, 1995, and 1997 with data from later years.

[c]Refers to the Standard Metropolitan Statistical Area (MSA) status of the respondent's household as defined in 2000 by the U.S. Census Bureau. Categories include "central city of an MSA (Urban)," "in MSA but not in central city (Suburban)," and "not MSA (Rural)."

Note: "On school property" was not defined for survey respondents.

SOURCE: Simone Robers et al., "Table 9.1. Percentage of Students in Grades 9–12 Who Reported that Illegal Drugs Were Made Available to Them on School Property during the Previous 12 Months, by Selected Student Characteristics: Selected Years, 1993 through 2013," in *Indicators of School Crime and Safety: 2014*, U.S. Department of Education, National Center for Education Statistics, and U.S. Department of Justice, Office of Justice Programs, Bureau of Justice Statistics, July 2015, http://nces.ed.gov/pubs2015/2015072.pdf (accessed July 23, 2015)

given to them on school property, down from the 1995 peak of 32.1% of high school students. Male high school students (24.5%) were more likely than female high school students (19.7%) to report that drugs were made available to them on school property during the previous 12 months. Tenth and 11th graders were slightly more likely than other student groups to have drugs made available to them on school property in 2013.

In 2013 there was a difference among races and ethnicities in the percentages of students who were offered, sold, or given drugs on school property. Pacific Islander students (27.7%) were the most likely to report that drugs were made available to them at school, followed by Hispanic students (27.4%), students of two or more races (26.4%), Native American or Alaskan Native students (25.5%), Asian American students (22.6%), white students (20.4%), and African American students (18.6%). (See Table 6.6.)

Tobacco and Drug Use on School Property

Table 6.7 and Table 6.8 provide data from the biannual Youth Risk Behavior Surveillance survey conducted by the CDC. The results show that in 2013, 3.8% of high school students smoked cigarettes on school property, and

22.1% were offered, sold, or given illicit drugs on school property. As Table 6.7 shows, the prevalence of smoking on school grounds peaked among 11th graders (5.3%) in 2013. Tenth and 11th graders (23.2%) were the most likely to be offered, sold, or given illicit drugs on school property in 2013, followed by ninth graders (22.4%) and high school seniors (18.8%). (See Table 6.8.)

Besides grade-level differences in health risk behaviors, racial and ethnic differences were also apparent in 2013. African American students (1.6%) were much less likely to smoke cigarettes on school grounds than were Hispanic students (2.9%) or white students (4.9%). (See Table 6.7.) Hispanic students (27.4%) were considerably more likely than white students (20.4%) or African American students (18.6%) to be offered, sold, or given illicit drugs on school property. (See Table 6.8.)

Sexual Activity

SEXUAL BEHAVIORS AND PREGNANCY. Sexual activity at an early age brings with it not only the risk of pregnancy in young girls but also STIs. Earlier in this chapter teen pregnancy was discussed in the context of the wider issue of pregnancy among unmarried women

TABLE 6.7

Percentage of high school students who smoked cigarettes on school property, by sex, race/ethnicity, and grade, 2013

| | Smoked cigarettes on school property | | |
| | Female | Male | Total |
Category	%	%	%
Race/ethnicity			
White*	5.0	4.7	4.9
Black*	0.9	2.3	1.6
Hispanic	2.7	3.2	2.9
Grade			
9	2.6	2.3	2.5
10	2.7	3.1	2.9
11	4.9	5.7	5.3
12	4.6	4.9	4.7
Total	**3.7**	**3.9**	**3.8**

*Non-Hispanic.

Notes: Pertains to students who smoked cigarettes on school property on at least 1 day during the 30 days before the survey.

SOURCE: Adapted from Laura Kann et al., "Table 35. Percentage of High School Students Who Smoked Cigarettes on School Property and Who Usually Obtained Their Own Cigarettes by Buying Them in a Store or Gas Station, by Sex, Race/Ethnicity, and Grade–United States, Youth Risk Behavior Survey, 2013," in "Youth Risk Behavior Surveillance–United States, 2013," *MMWR*, vol. 63, no. 4, June 13, 2014, http://www.cdc.gov/mmwr/pdf/ss/ss6304.pdf?utm_source=rss&utm_medium=rss&utm_campaign=youth-risk-behavior-surveillance-united-states-2013-pdf (accessed July 23, 2015)

TABLE 6.8

Percentage of high school students who were offered, given, or sold illegal drugs on school property, by sex, race/ethnicity, and grade, 2013

| | Offered, sold, or given an illegal drug on school property | | |
| | Female | Male | Total |
Category	%	%	%
Race/ethnicity			
White*	17.5	23.1	20.4
Black*	15.6	21.7	18.6
Hispanic	26.7	28.1	27.4
Grade			
9	21.9	22.9	22.4
10	21.7	24.6	23.2
11	20.2	26.4	23.2
12	13.7	24.0	18.8
Total	**19.7**	**24.5**	**22.1**

* Non-Hispanic.

Note: Pertains to students who were offered, sold, or given an illegal drug by someone on school property during the 12 months before the survey.

SOURCE: Adapted from Laura Kann et al., "Table 61. Percentage of High School Students Who Injected Illegal Drugs and Who Were Offered, Sold, or Given an Illegal Drug by Someone on School Property, by Sex, Race/Ethnicity, and Grade—United States, Youth Risk Behavior Survey, 2013," in "Youth Risk Behavior Surveillance—United States, 2013," *MMWT*, vol. 63, no. 4, June 13, 2014, http://www.cdc.gov/mmwr/pdf/ss/ss6304.pdf?utm_source=rss&utm_medium= rss&utm_campaign=youth-risk-behavior-surveillance-united-states-2013-pdf (accessed July 27, 2015)

and the increased risk of poverty and associated issues if unmarried mothers do not have a cohabiting partner. These risks are heightened in young women who still have their education to complete and may have little means to support themselves and their child. Here, teen pregnancy will be discussed in the context of teen sexual behaviors.

Although all girls who become pregnant during their teens face the risk of adverse pregnancy outcomes, the youngest teenage mothers (those younger than the age of 16 years) have the highest risk of miscarriage and giving birth to low birth weight and/or premature babies. They also have more of their schooling to finish than older teen mothers and less of a chance to support their child on their own because they are too young to work at many jobs in the United States.

In 2013 there was a low prevalence of girls having sexual intercourse before the age of 13 years, and the adolescent birth rate was low as well. Laura Kann et al. of the CDC report in "Youth Risk Behavior Surveillance—United States, 2013" (*Morbidity and Mortality Weekly Report*, vol. 63, no. 4, June 13, 2014) that in 2013, 5.6% of students reported having their first sexual intercourse before the age of 13 years. However, the prevalence was lower among females (3.1%) than males (8.3%). In "Births: Preliminary Data for 2014" (*National Vital Statistics Reports*, vol. 64, no. 6, June 17, 2015), Brady E. Hamilton et al. of the CDC reveal that birth rates for girls aged 10 to 14 years declined over the last 50 years and in 2013 and 2014 was the lowest ever reported, at 0.3 births per 1,000 girls aged 10 to 14 years for each year. The birth rate for teenagers aged 15 to 19 years was also the lowest ever in 2014, at 24.2 births per 1,000 teen girls. Figure 6.6 shows the dramatic decline in teenage birth rates between 1990 and 2014.

Thus, as a population, teenage girls are putting themselves less at risk for pregnancy; a change in sexual behaviors has helped realize some of this change. According to the CDC, in "Trends in the Prevalence of Sexual Behaviors and HIV Testing National YRBS: 1991–2013" (May 2015, http://www.cdc.gov/healthyyouth/data/yrbs/pdf/trends/us_sexual_trend_yrbs.pdf), the percentage of high school students reporting that they have ever had sexual intercourse declined between 1991 and 2013, from 54.1% to 46.8%. Furthermore, high school students reporting condom use during the last sexual intercourse increased from 46.2% in 1991 to 59.1% in 2013.

SEXUALLY TRANSMITTED INFECTIONS. STIs are spread from person to person by the intimate contact that occurs during sexual activity, primarily sexual intercourse. The greater the number of sexual partners a person has, the greater the risk of contracting an STI. When sexual activity begins at a young age, a person is more likely to have more sexual partners over a lifetime

FIGURE 6.6

Birth rates among teenage mothers aged 15–19, by age group, 1990–2014

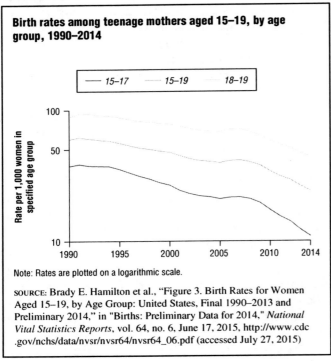

Note: Rates are plotted on a logarithmic scale.

SOURCE: Brady E. Hamilton et al., "Figure 3. Birth Rates for Women Aged 15–19, by Age Group: United States, Final 1990–2013 and Preliminary 2014," in "Births: Preliminary Data for 2014," *National Vital Statistics Reports*, vol. 64, no. 6, June 17, 2015, http://www.cdc.gov/nchs/data/nvsr/nvsr64/nvsr64_06.pdf (accessed July 27, 2015)

and thus have a greater risk of contracting STIs than if he or she began sexual activity at a later age. The CDC indicates in *Incidence, Prevalence, and Cost of Sexually Transmitted Infections in the United States* (February 2013, http://www.cdc.gov/std/stats/sti-estimates-fact-sheet-feb-2013.pdf) that young people aged 15 to 24 years account for nearly half (49%) of the nearly 20 million new STIs reported each year in the United States.

STIs caused by viruses are extremely serious because they cannot be cured. Certain medications ease the discomfort of viral STI symptoms, but virus particles remain in the tissues and can cause recurrent symptoms. Also, they can be passed continually from chronically infected individuals to others during sexual activity. STIs that are caused by viruses include genital warts, which are produced by the human papillomavirus (HPV), and human immunodeficiency virus (HIV) infection.

The incidence of HPV infection in females is highest for those aged 20 to 24 years and second highest for those aged 25 to 29 years. In *Sexually Transmitted Disease Surveillance 2013* (December 2014, http://www.cdc.gov/std/stats13/surv2013-print.pdf), the CDC notes that between 2007 and 2010 nearly 20% of women aged 20 to 24 years were infected with HPV.

HPV infection is particularly serious because it is associated with the development of cervical cancer. The U.S. Food and Drug Administration (FDA) notes in the press release "FDA Licenses New Vaccine for Prevention of Cervical Cancer and Other Diseases in Females Caused by Human Papillomavirus" (June 8, 2006, http://www.fda.gov/NewsEvents/Newsroom/PressAnnouncements/2006/

ucm108666.htm) that in June 2006 it approved a new vaccine (Gardasil) that protects against four major types of HR-HPV viruses: two types that cause about 70% of cervical cancers and two types that cause about 90% of genital warts. The vaccine is recommended for adolescent girls and boys who have not yet had sex because they have not yet been exposed to HPV. The vaccine cannot protect against an infection that has already occurred.

In 2010 the scope of the use of the Gardasil vaccine was increased. The FDA indicates in the press release "Gardasil Approved to Prevent Anal Cancer" (December 22, 2010, http://www.fda.gov/newsevents/newsroom/pressannouncements/ucm237941.htm) that in December 2010 the vaccine was approved for use in both males and females aged nine to 26 years to prevent anal cancer. HPV is responsible for approximately 90% of all anal cancers.

Although public health officials and medical professionals largely view Gardasil as an effective weapon against the spread of HPV, the vaccine has also sparked controversy. Richard Knox reports in "HPV Vaccine: The Science behind the Controversy" (NPR.com, September 19, 2011) that some parents have expressed discomfort at the idea that prepubescent girls should be injected with a vaccine aimed at preventing an STI. For example, Julie Stewart, the mother of an 11-year-old girl, told Knox that she was "shocked" when her daughter's pediatrician recommended that she be vaccinated with Gardasil. "My daughter is so not sexually active that it seems very premature to even think about protecting her from cervical cancer," Stewart said. Still, Stewart conceded that her concerns had more to do with her own uneasiness about the subject than the medical basis of the vaccine. "I realize it's probably more about my squeamishness with the thought of her becoming sexually active than the vaccination itself," she added. "It's not the science. I think it's my own issues around her developing sexually."

HIV infection is another STI that is caused by a virus and is particularly serious because it leads to acquired immunodeficiency syndrome (AIDS) and death. Globally, HIV infection is a widespread pandemic disease. Table 6.9 shows that the number of young people aged 15 to 19 years living with HIV/AIDS in the United States has declined every year between 2009 and 2012, from 2,700 to 1,972. The group at highest risk for becoming infected with HIV—as demonstrated by the highest number of people living with HIV/AIDS—is made up of those engaging in male-to-male sexual contact (224,666 were living with HIV/AIDS in 2012). Other high-risk behaviors leading to HIV are injection drug use and women engaging in high-risk heterosexual contact (females having sex with male partners known to have or be at risk for HIV infection). In addition, pregnant women infected with HIV may pass their infection onto their babies before, during, or after birth (via breastfeeding).

STIs are also caused by bacteria. Chlamydia is an STI caused by a bacterium that primarily infects the

TABLE 6.9

Estimated number of persons living with HIV/AIDS, by year and selected characteristics, 2009–12

| | 2009 | | | 2010 | | | 2011 | | | 2012 | | |
| | | Estimated[a] | | | Estimated[a] | | | Estimated[a] | | | Estimated[a] | |
	No.	No.	Rate	No.	No.	Rate	No.	No.	Rate	No.	No.	Rate
Age at end of year												
<13	539	543	1.0	448	452	0.8	366	370	0.7	305	309	0.6
13–14	472	475	5.7	325	328	3.9	253	255	3.1	192	194	2.3
15–19	2,700	2,721	12.4	2,555	2,582	11.6	2,297	2,330	10.6	1,972	2,009	9.3
20–24	7,023	7,114	32.6	7,616	7,753	35.3	8,106	8,297	37.0	8,292	8,539	37.3
25–29	15,664	15,856	72.1	16,008	16,273	76.0	16,344	16,693	77.5	16,683	17,138	79.2
30–34	27,900	28,165	139.5	28,164	28,515	140.2	28,402	28,857	138.9	28,661	29,227	138.1
35–39	49,572	49,901	239.5	45,668	46,064	226.4	42,917	43,397	218.5	41,315	41,881	212.1
40–44	83,602	83,972	394.5	79,380	79,831	377.0	74,569	75,096	352.5	70,161	70,739	332.2
45–49	105,662	105,943	458.1	107,429	107,765	470.3	106,738	107,139	477.5	103,599	103,979	473.5
50–54	83,229	83,337	378.2	89,688	89,826	397.1	95,328	95,479	418.2	100,925	100,976	442.1
55–59	53,868	53,878	280.2	59,189	59,183	295.3	65,398	65,362	318.7	71,829	71,662	340.9
60–64	27,404	27,400	170.7	31,910	31,880	185.1	36,310	36,225	200.7	40,936	40,707	225.6
≥65	20,971	20,926	52.1	24,082	23,999	58.5	27,759	27,614	65.8	32,441	32,138	73.4
Race/ethnicity												
American Indian/Alaska Native	1,352	1,356	—	1,412	1,417	—	1,477	1,483	—	1,539	1,544	—
Asian[b]	4,883	4,927	—	5,191	5,249	—	5,486	5,557	—	5,788	5,878	—
Black/African American	193,674	194,277	—	200,417	201,203	—	206,409	207,362	—	212,686	213,559	—
Hispanic/Latino[c]	109,361	109,872	—	112,762	113,380	—	115,839	116,570	—	119,029	119,846	—
Native Hawaiian/other Pacific Islander	381	384	—	415	419	—	439	444	—	468	474	—
White	152,027	152,391	—	154,964	155,376	—	157,505	157,956	—	159,883	160,187	—
Multiple races	16,928	17,024	—	17,301	17,406	—	17,632	17,743	—	17,918	18,010	—
Transmission category												
Male adult or adolescent												
Male-to-male sexual contact	203,865	227,712	—	211,110	236,842	—	217,903	245,335	—	224,666	253,865	—
Injection drug use	50,858	59,621	—	50,208	59,199	—	49,535	58,663	—	48,931	58,127	—
Male-to-male sexual contact and injection drug use	30,416	33,113	—	30,512	33,330	—	30,492	33,418	—	30,457	33,436	—
Heterosexual contact[d]	33,768	41,109	—	34,973	42,843	—	36,097	44,398	—	37,085	45,849	—
Perinatal	2,144	2,151	—	2,230	2,238	—	2,300	2,310	—	2,346	2,355	—
Other[e]	43,780	2,283	—	46,246	2,262	—	48,355	2,246	—	50,777	2,238	—
Subtotal	364,831	365,989	291.2	375,279	376,714	297.4	384,682	386,369	302.2	394,262	395,870	306.7
Female adult or adolescent												
Injection drug use	26,477	33,265	—	26,329	33,355	—	26,050	33,275	—	25,851	33,197	—
Heterosexual contact[d]	60,090	77,018	—	62,090	80,370	—	63,860	83,429	—	65,495	86,367	—
Perinatal	2,227	2,236	—	2,348	2,360	—	2,445	2,459	—	2,512	2,526	—
Other[e]	24,442	1,180	—	25,968	1,199	—	27,384	1,212	—	28,886	1,230	—
Subtotal	113,236	113,699	86.7	116,735	117,283	88.1	119,739	120,375	89.7	122,744	123,320	91.1
Child (<13 yrs at end of year)												
Perinatal	518	521	—	428	432	—	344	348	—	288	292	—
Other[e]	21	21	—	20	20	—	22	22	—	17	17	—
Subtotal	539	543	1.0	448	452	0.8	366	370	0.7	305	309	0.6
Region of residence												
Northeast	132,381	133,326	241.2	134,265	135,322	244.4	135,858	137,035	246.5	137,523	138,725	248.7
Midwest	50,643	50,793	76.0	52,479	52,664	78.6	54,268	54,486	81.1	56,098	56,295	83.6
South	189,674	189,829	167.5	196,909	197,202	171.7	203,565	203,980	175.8	210,291	210,539	179.6
West	95,226	95,875	134.0	98,015	98,784	137.0	100,207	101,083	138.8	102,357	103,285	140.5
U.S. dependent areas	10,682	10,408	236.9	10,794	10,477	254.5	10,889	10,531	258.1	11,042	10,655	263.5
Total[f]	478,606	480,231	154.2	492,462	494,449	157.7	504,787	507,115	160.7	517,311	519,500	163.4

[a]Estimated numbers resulted from statistical adjustment that accounted for reporting delays and missing transmission category, but not for incomplete reporting. Rates are per 100,000 population. Rates by race/ethnicity are not provided because U.S. census information for U.S. dependent areas is limited. Rates are not calculated by transmission category because of the lack of denominator data.
[b]Includes Asian/Pacific Islander legacy cases
[c]Hispanics/Latinos can be of any race.
[d]Heterosexual contact with a person known to have, or to be at high risk for, HIV infection.
[e]Includes hemophilia, blood transfusion, and risk factor not reported or not identified.
[f]Because column totals for estimated numbers were calculated independently of the values for the subpopulations, the values in each column may not sum to the column total.

SOURCE: "Table 15b. Persons Living with Diagnosed HIV Infection Ever Classified As Stage 3 (AIDS), by Year and Selected Characteristics, 2009–2012—United States and 6 Dependent Areas," in *HIV Surveillance Report: Diagnoses of HIV Infection in the United States and Dependent Areas*, vol. 25, Centers for Disease Control and Prevention, National Center for HIV/AIDS, Viral Hepatitis, STD, and TB Prevention, Division of HIV/AIDS Prevention, February 2015, http://www.cdc.gov/hiv/pdf/g-l/hiv_surveillance_report_vol_25.pdf (accessed July 27, 2015)

urethra in males and the urethra and cervix in females. In addition, this bacterium can spread easily through the female reproductive tract causing pelvic inflammatory disease (PID). PID is an infection of the uterine (fallopian) tubes or other female reproductive organs and is a serious, painful condition that can result in sterility.

Figure 6.7 shows male and female chlamydia rates, by age, in 2013. As the graph clearly points out, young women are most affected by this STI, and at a much higher rate than young men. In 2013, 3,043.3 out of every 100,000 women aged 15 to 19 years and 3,621.1 out of every 100,000 women aged 20 to 24 years were infected with this STI. The CDC also reports in *Sexually Transmitted Disease Surveillance 2013* that African American females are disproportionately affected by this STI. In 2013 they were eight times more likely to become infected with chlamydia than white females. Native American or Alaskan Native females had the second-highest infection rate, followed closely by Native Hawaiian and Pacific Islander females.

Suicide

Kann et al. note that suicide is one of the four primary ways in which death occurs in people aged 20 to 24 years, just as it is with adolescents and teens aged 10 to 19 years. The researchers note that in 2013, 17% of high school students had seriously considered attempting suicide during the preceding 12 months. More females (22.4%) than males (11.6%) considered attempting suicide. The prevalence was higher among Hispanic students (18.9%) than among white (16.2%) and African American students (14.5%). Nationwide, 8% of high school students had attempted suicide, and 2.7% required medical attention as a result of the suicide attempt.

Violence in School

Violence in schools puts students at risk of injury or death, makes some students reluctant to attend school, and disrupts the educational process. In *Indicators of School Crime and Safety: 2014* (July 2015, http://nces.ed.gov/pubs2015/2015072.pdf), Simone Robers et al. note that children who are victims of school violence are more likely to perform poorly, drop out of school, and develop violent behaviors themselves. In addition, school violence drives some teachers out of the profession.

Many measures of school violence have decreased since the 1990s. According to the CDC, in "Trends in the Prevalence of Behaviors That Contribute to Violence, National YRBS: 1991–2013" (May 2015, http://www.cdc.gov/healthyyouth/data/yrbs/pdf/trends/us_violenceschool_trend_yrbs.pdf), the percentage of high school students involved in physical fights in school during the past year fell from 16.2% in 1993 to 8.1% in 2013. African American male high school students (14.5%) were the most

FIGURE 6.7

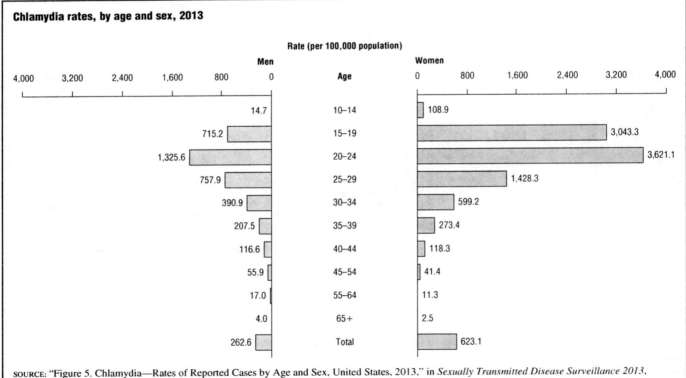

Chlamydia rates, by age and sex, 2013

Rate (per 100,000 population)

Men	Age	Women
14.7	10–14	108.9
715.2	15–19	3,043.3
1,325.6	20–24	3,621.1
757.9	25–29	1,428.3
390.9	30–34	599.2
207.5	35–39	273.4
116.6	40–44	118.3
55.9	45–54	41.4
17.0	55–64	11.3
4.0	65+	2.5
262.6	Total	623.1

SOURCE: "Figure 5. Chlamydia—Rates of Reported Cases by Age and Sex, United States, 2013," in *Sexually Transmitted Disease Surveillance 2013*, Centers for Disease Control and Prevention, National Center for HIV/AIDS, Viral Hepatitis, STD, and TB Prevention, Division of STD Prevention, December 2014, http://www.cdc.gov/std/stats13/surv2013-print.pdf (accessed July 27, 2015)

likely to have been involved in a physical fight on school grounds in 2013, followed by Hispanic males (12.1%) and white males (8.9%). (See Table 6.10.) Among female high school students, African Americans (11.2%) were considerably more likely than Hispanics (6.7%) or whites (3.8%) to have been involved in a physical fight on school property in 2013. (See Table 6.10.) Hispanic (8.5%) and African American (8.4%) high school students were substantially more likely than white high school students (5.8%)

to have been threatened or injured with a weapon on school grounds in 2013. (See Table 6.11.)

Crime that takes place at school can lead to a threatening, unsafe, and disorderly environment and to physical injury and stress among students. Although many measures of violence in school have decreased since the 1990s, students are feeling unsafe. As Table 6.10 shows, 7.1% of all high school students skipped school out of concern for their safety at some point in 2013.

TABLE 6.10

Percentage of high school students who were involved in a physical fight on school property and who stayed home from school out of fear for personal safety, by sex, race/ethnicity, and grade, 2013

Category	In a physical fight on school property			Did not go to school because of safety concerns		
	Female	Male	Total	Female	Male	Total
	%	%	%	%	%	%
Race/ethnicity						
White*	3.8	8.9	**6.4**	7.4	3.8	**5.6**
Black*	11.2	14.5	**12.8**	8.0	7.8	**7.9**
Hispanic	6.7	12.1	**9.4**	12.6	6.9	**9.8**
Grade						
9	8.6	13.0	**10.9**	9.9	5.5	**7.7**
10	6.3	10.2	**8.3**	10.7	5.3	**8.0**
11	4.1	10.9	**7.5**	8.1	5.8	**7.0**
12	2.6	7.3	**4.9**	5.9	5.0	**5.5**
Total	**11.5**	**10.7**	**8.1**	**8.7**	**5.4**	**7.1**

Note: Pertains to students were were in a physical fight on school property one or more times during the 12 months before the survey and who did not go to school because they felt unsafe at school or on their way to or from school on at least 1 day during the 30 days before the survey.
*Non-Hispanic.

SOURCE: Laura Kann et al., "Table 15. Percentage of High School Students Who Were in a Physical Fight on School Property and Who Did Not Go to School Because They Felt Unsafe at School or on Their Way to or from School, by Sex, Race/Ethnicity, and Grade—United States, Youth Risk Behavior Survey, 2013," in "Youth Risk Behavior Surveillance—United States, 2013," *MMWR*, vol. 63, no. 4, June 13, 2014, http://www.cdc.gov/mmwr/pdf/ss/ss6304.pdf?utm_source=rss&utm_ medium=rss&utm_campaign=youth-risk-behavior-surveillance-united-states-2013-pdf (accessed July 27, 2015)

TABLE 6.11

Percentage of high school students who carried a weapon on school property or who were threatened or injured with a weapon on school property, by sex, race/ethnicity, and grade, 2013

Category	Carried a weapon on school property			Threatened or injured with a weapon on school property		
	Female	Male	Total	Female	Male	Total
	%	%	%	%	%	%
Race/ethnicity						
White*	3.1	8.3	**5.7**	5.4	6.2	**5.8**
Black*	2.7	5.3	**3.9**	6.8	10.1	**8.4**
Hispanic	2.5	7.0	**4.7**	7.5	9.5	**8.5**
Grade						
9	3.3	6.4	**4.8**	7.7	9.3	**8.5**
10	2.9	6.7	**4.8**	7.4	6.6	**7.0**
11	3.3	8.7	**5.9**	5.6	8.1	**6.8**
12	2.1	8.7	**5.3**	3.1	6.8	**4.9**
Total	**3.0**	**7.6**	**5.2**	**6.1**	**7.7**	**6.9**

*Non-Hispanic.
Note: Pertains to students who carried a weapon such as a gun, knife, or a club on school property on at least 1 day during the 30 days before the survey and who were threatened or injured with a weapon on school property one or more times during the 12 months before the survey.

SOURCE: Laura Kann et al., "Table 11. Percentage of High School Students Who Carried a Weapon on School Property and Who Were Threatened or Injured with a Weapon on School Property, by Sex, Race/Ethnicity, and Grade—United States, Youth Risk Behavior Survey, 2013," in "Youth Risk Behavior Surveillance—United States, 2013," *MMWR*, vol. 63, no. 4, June 13, 2014, http://www.cdc.gov/mmwr/pdf/ss/ss6304.pdf?utm_source=rss&utm_medium=rss&utm_campaign=youth-risk-behavior-surveillance-united-states-2013-pdf (accessed July 27, 2015)

Perhaps many students are feeling unsafe in school because they are being bullied. Figure 6.8 shows the percentage of students aged 12 to 18 years who reported being bullied in various ways at school in 2013. More than one-fifth (21.5%) of students in this age group were bullied in some way at school. Female students (23.7%) were more likely than male students (19.5%) to report having been bullied at school in 2013. In addition, female students (8.6%) were considerably more likely than male students (5.2%) to have been cyber-bullied that year. (See Figure 6.9.) As Figure 6.10 shows, female students (6.7%) were slightly more likely than male students (6.6%) to report having been the target of hate speech in 2013.

FIGURE 6.8

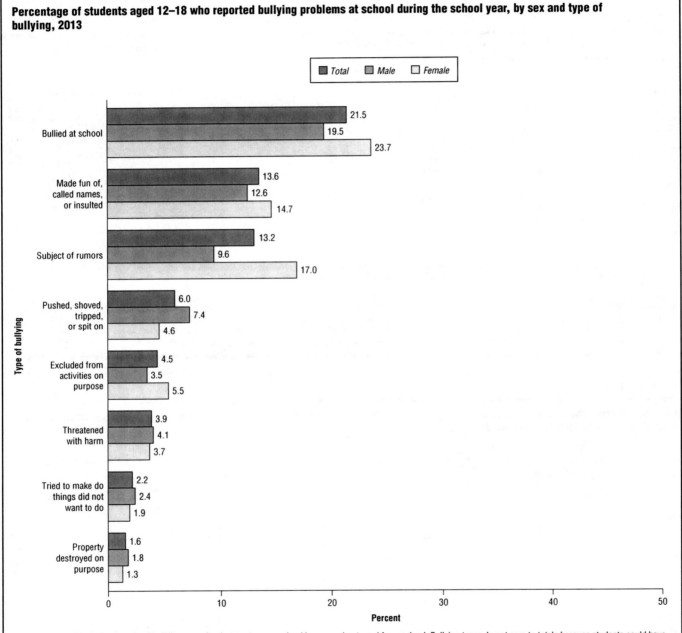

Percentage of students aged 12–18 who reported bullying problems at school during the school year, by sex and type of bullying, 2013

Note: "At school" includes the school building, on school property, on a school bus, or going to and from school. Bullying types do not sum to totals because students could have experienced more than one type of bullying. Students who reported experiencing more than one type of bullying at school were counted only once in the total for students bullied at school.

SOURCE: Simone Robers et al., "Figure 11.1. Percentage of Students Ages 12–18 Who Reported Being Bullied at School during the School Year, by Type of Bullying and Sex: 2013," in *Indicators of School Crime and Safety: 2014*, U.S. Department of Education, National Center for Education Statistics, and U.S. Department of Justice, Office of Justice Programs, Bureau of Justice Statistics, July 2015, http://nces.ed.gov/pubs2015/2015072.pdf (accessed July 27, 2015)

FIGURE 6.9

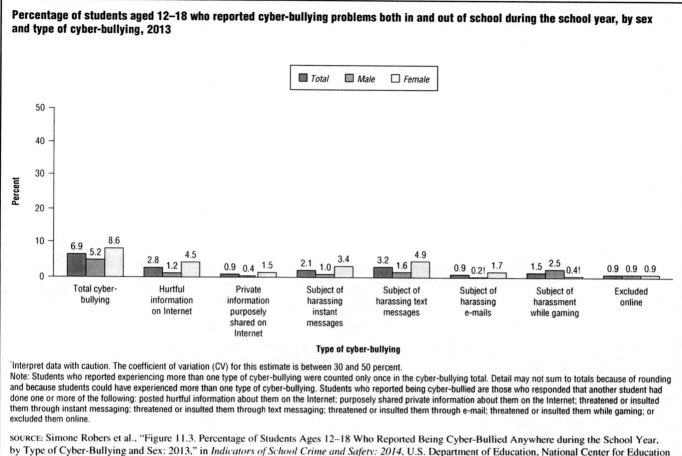

Percentage of students aged 12–18 who reported cyber-bullying problems both in and out of school during the school year, by sex and type of cyber-bullying, 2013

Legend: ■ Total ▨ Male □ Female

Type of cyber-bullying	Total	Male	Female
Total cyber-bullying	6.9	5.2	8.6
Hurtful information on Internet	2.8	1.2	4.5
Private information purposely shared on Internet	0.9	0.4	1.5
Subject of harassing instant messages	2.1	1.0	3.4
Subject of harassing text messages	3.2	1.6	4.9
Subject of harassing e-mails	0.9	0.2!	1.7
Subject of harassment while gaming	1.5	2.5	0.4!
Excluded online	0.9	0.9	0.9

!Interpret data with caution. The coefficient of variation (CV) for this estimate is between 30 and 50 percent.
Note: Students who reported experiencing more than one type of cyber-bullying were counted only once in the cyber-bullying total. Detail may not sum to totals because of rounding and because students could have experienced more than one type of cyber-bullying. Students who reported being cyber-bullied are those who responded that another student had done one or more of the following: posted hurtful information about them on the Internet; purposely shared private information about them on the Internet; threatened or insulted them through instant messaging; threatened or insulted them through text messaging; threatened or insulted them through e-mail; threatened or insulted them while gaming; or excluded them online.

SOURCE: Simone Robers et al., "Figure 11.3. Percentage of Students Ages 12–18 Who Reported Being Cyber-Bullied Anywhere during the School Year, by Type of Cyber-Bullying and Sex: 2013," in *Indicators of School Crime and Safety: 2014*, U.S. Department of Education, National Center for Education Statistics, and U.S. Department of Justice, Office of Justice Programs, Bureau of Justice Statistics, July 2015, http://nces.ed.gov/pubs2015/2015072.pdf (accessed July 27, 2015)

ALTERNATIVE SCHOOLS AND PROGRAMS

At-risk students who exhibit consistently disruptive behavior, have consistently failing grades, are pregnant, or are often absent from school are usually sent to alternative schools or programs to help meet their educational needs. In *Alternative Schools and Programs for Public School Students at Risk of Educational Failure: 2007–08* (March 2010, http://nces.ed.gov/pubs2010/2010026.pdf), the most recent report on alternative education as of September 2015, Priscilla Rouse Carver, Laurie Lewis, and Peter Tice report on the availability, enrollment, and locations of alternative schools and programs in the United States, and at which grades instruction was offered. The results show that, nationally, 64% of public school districts had at least one alternative school or program for at-risk students during the 2007–08 school year. Most (63%) of these schools and programs were housed in facilities separate from regular school facilities. Alternative schools were provided for grades nine to 12 in 88% to 96% of districts offering alternative schools, for grades six to eight in 41% to 63% of districts offering alternative schools, and for lower grades in 8% to 18% of districts offering

alternative schools. The districts most likely to offer alternative schools and programs were districts that had one or more of the following characteristics: urban, large (10,000 or more students), located in the Southeast, high minority student population, and high poverty.

Carver, Lewis, and Tice note that sometimes the goal is to return at-risk students to the regular school setting as soon as their risks have been minimized. Other times, students remain in alternative settings for the duration of their education, either by their own choice or by the choice of the school district. The factors of alternative schools and programs that appear to help at-risk students include a dedicated and well-trained staff, an effective curriculum, and support services that are offered in collaboration with other agencies, such as the juvenile justice system, community mental health agencies, the police or sheriff's department, child protective services, and parks and recreation departments.

In many cases, providing a quality learning experience to at-risk students requires educators to confront psychological or emotional issues that may present barriers to a young person's academic success. Typically, addressing

FIGURE 6.10

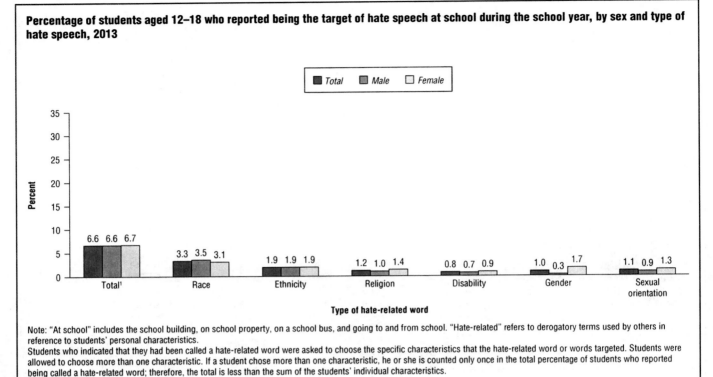

Percentage of students aged 12–18 who reported being the target of hate speech at school during the school year, by sex and type of hate speech, 2013

Note: "At school" includes the school building, on school property, on a school bus, and going to and from school. "Hate-related" refers to derogatory terms used by others in reference to students' personal characteristics.

Students who indicated that they had been called a hate-related word were asked to choose the specific characteristics that the hate-related word or words targeted. Students were allowed to choose more than one characteristic. If a student chose more than one characteristic, he or she is counted only once in the total percentage of students who reported being called a hate-related word; therefore, the total is less than the sum of the students' individual characteristics.

SOURCE: Simone Robers et al., "Figure 10.2. Percentage of Students Ages 12–18 Who Reported Being the Target of Hate-Related Words at School during the School Year, by Type of Hate-Related Word and Sex: 2013," in *Indicators of School Crime and Safety: 2014*, U.S. Department of Education, National Center for Education Statistics, and U.S. Department of Justice, Office of Justice Programs, Bureau of Justice Statistics, July 2015, http://nces.ed.gov/pubs2015/2015072.pdf (accessed July 27, 2015)

the mental health needs of at-risk students requires a strong commitment from the community, both to coordinate efforts between various schools and to ensure that initiatives are adequately funded. One school district that achieved some success with this approach during the early 21st century was in Sabine Parish, Louisiana. Working under the guidance of psychologists Howard Adelman and Linda Taylor, Sabine Parish implemented a new psychological support model, the "enabling component," designed to streamline intervention efforts while minimizing disruptions to a student's learning experience. Key elements in the enabling component model included having psychological support staff become directly involved with at-risk students in the classroom, offering parenting classes aimed at increasing family involvement in the schools, and boosting community investment through fundraising and other outreach programs. As Tori DeAngelis reports in "Helping At-Risk Students Succeed" (*Monitor on Psychology*, February 2012, vol. 43, no. 2), Sabine Parish schools quickly achieved positive results using the new model. Between 2007 and 2010, the district's high school graduation rate rose from 73% to 81.2%. By 2010 Sabine Parish schools were ranked 14th out of the state's 60 school districts in terms of academic performance, up from 37th in 2007.

In addition, educators have increasingly turned to technology as a way of helping at-risk students improve academically. According to Linda Darling-Hammond, Molly B. Zielezinski, and Shelley Goldman of Stanford University, in *Using Technology to Support At-Risk Students' Learning* (September 2014, https://edpolicy.stanford.edu/sites/default/files/scope-pub-using-technology-report.pdf), interactive learning tools, such as computer simulations and online games, can help foster increased creativity and engagement in students struggling to learn, in part by helping a student consider a particular academic problem or assignment from numerous points of view. At the same time, interactive technology has the capacity to adapt to a student's unique learning needs, diagnosing areas of weakness and developing study plans aimed at addressing specific problems. As Darling-Hammond, Zielezinski, and Goldman note, classroom technology is most effective when combined with individual interaction between an at-risk student and a teacher or peer.

DROPPING OUT

Patrick Stark, Amber M. Noel, and Joel McFarland note in *Trends in High School Dropout and Completion Rates in the United States: 1972–2012* (June 2015, http://

nces.ed.gov/pubs2015/2015015.pdf) that students who do not complete high school are at risk of experiencing many negative outcomes. For example, in 2012 the income of high school dropouts was only 54% of the income of those who had a high school credential, which includes a diploma or a General Educational Development (GED) certificate ($25,000 for dropouts versus $46,000 for those with a high school credential). High school dropouts are also more likely than others to be out of a job if they are in the workforce or to be out of the workforce altogether. In addition, dropouts aged 25 years and older tend to be in poorer health than those who have a high school credential, and dropouts make up a higher percentage of the U.S. prison and death row population. Clearly, an important educational goal is needed to help young people stay in school and graduate from high school.

Trends in Dropout Rates

In *Condition of Education 2015*, Kena et al. define the term *status dropout rate* as "the percentage of 16- through 24-year-olds who are not enrolled in school and have not earned a high school credential." Figure 6.11

shows the trend in status dropout rates of 16- to 24-year-olds by race and ethnicity between 1990 and 2013. During this period dropout rates fell most sharply for Hispanic students, from a high of 35% in 1991 to 12% in 2013. Dropout rates also declined for African American and white students between 1990 and 2013, although these changes were not as dramatic.

The Costs of Dropping Out

Young people who drop out before finishing high school usually pay a high price. Dropouts have a much harder time making the transition from school to work and economic independence. The unemployment rates of high school graduates and GED certificate holders have consistently been lower than those of dropouts, which is shown for the three-year period from 2012 to 2014 in Table 6.12.

In 2014 those aged 20 to 24 years with less than a high school education experienced a 25.3% unemployment rate, compared with 18.9% for those who completed high school, 12.2% for those who attended college but never completed a bachelor's degree, and 6.7% for those with a

FIGURE 6.11

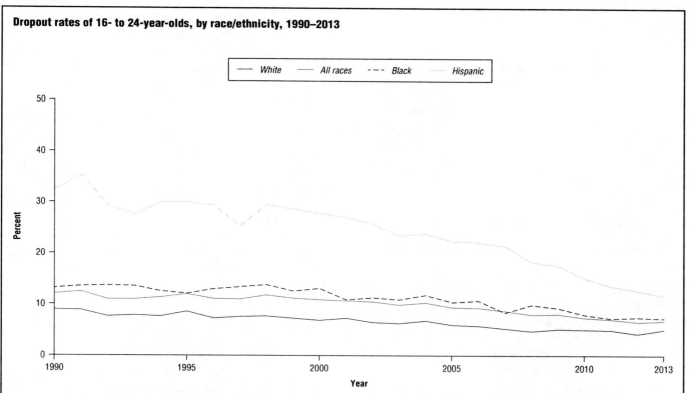

Dropout rates of 16- to 24-year-olds, by race/ethnicity, 1990–2013

Note: The "status dropout rate" represents the percentage of 16- through 24-year-olds who are not enrolled in school and have not earned a high school credential (either a diploma or an equivalency credential such as a General Educational Development [GED] certificate). Data are based on sample surveys of the civilian noninstitutionalized population, which excludes persons in prisons, persons in the military, and other persons not living in households. Data for all races include other racial/ethnic categories not separately shown. Race categories exclude persons of Hispanic ethnicity.

SOURCE: Grace Kena et al., "Figure 2. Status Dropout Rates of 16- through 24-year-olds, by Race/Ethnicity: 1990 through 2013," in *The Condition of Education 2015*, U.S. Department of Education, Institute of Education Sciences, National Center for Education Statistics, May 2015, http://nces.ed.gov/pubs2015/2015144.pdf (accessed July 27, 2015)

TABLE 6.12

Unemployment rates of persons aged 16 and older, by age and education level, 2012–14

Age group and highest level of educational attainment	2012	2013	2014
16 to 19 years old, all education levels[a]	30.6	29.4	22.9
Less than high school completion	41.1	36.3	22.9
High school completion[b]	28.7	29.2	25.0
At least some college	19.6	16.2	15.1
20 to 24 years old, all education levels[a]	15.5	15.2	14.9
Less than high school completion	27.6	29.2	25.3
High school completion[b]	18.3	17.5	18.9
Some college, no bachelor's degree[c]	12.7	12.2	12.2
Bachelor's or higher degree	6.0	7.0	6.7
25 to 34 years old, all education levels	9.2	8.0	7.4
Less than high school completion	16.8	15.1	13.7
High school completion[b]	12.8	12.1	10.5
Some college, no bachelor's degree[c]	10.1	8.0	7.8
Bachelor's or higher degree	4.1	3.6	3.7
35 to 44 years old, all education levels	7.1	6.4	5.7
Less than high school completion	14.1	11.5	11.5
High school completion[b]	9.1	8.5	7.4
Some college, no bachelor's degree[c]	7.4	6.7	6.1
Bachelor's or higher degree	3.6	3.6	2.8
45 to 54 years old, all education levels	6.8	6.0	4.9
Less than high school completion	13.5	12.3	8.0
High school completion[b]	7.8	7.8	6.1
Some college, no bachelor's degree[c]	6.9	5.2	4.8
Bachelor's or higher degree	3.9	3.8	3.2
55 to 64 years old, all education levels	6.6	5.7	5.2
Less than high school completion	11.5	11.2	8.2
High school completion[b]	7.1	6.4	5.6
Some college, no bachelor's degree[c]	7.1	5.8	5.5
Bachelor's or higher degree	4.8	4.2	4.0

[a]Data for 16- to 19-year-olds and 20- to 24-year-olds exclude persons enrolled in school.
[b]Includes equivalency credentials, such as the General Educational Development (GED) credential.
[c]Includes persons with no college degree as well as those with an associate's degree.
Note: The unemployment rate is the percentage of persons in the civilian labor force who are not working and who made specific efforts to find employment sometime during the prior 4 weeks. The civilian labor force consists of all civilians who are employed or seeking employment.

SOURCE: Adapted from "Table 501.80. Unemployment Rates of Persons 16 to 64 Years Old, by Age Group and Highest Level of Educational Attainment: Selected Years, 1975 through 2014," in "Most Current Digest Tables," *Digest of Education Statistics*, U.S. Department of Education, Institute of Education Sciences, National Center for Education Statistics, November 2014, https://nces.ed.gov/programs/digest/d14/tables/xls/tabn501.80.xls (accessed July 27, 2015)

bachelor's degree or higher. (See Table 6.12.) Among adults aged 25 to 64 years, the unemployment rate in 2014 was highest for those who never completed high school (10.6%), followed by high school graduates (7.4%), high school graduates who had taken some college courses (6.1%), and college graduates (3.4%).

People without high school diplomas or GED certificates tend to earn considerably less than those with more education. As the education level rises, so does income. According to Kena et al., the median incomes among adults between the ages of 25 and 34 years varied widely based on educational attainment. In 2013 the median yearly income for all adults between the ages of 25 and 34 years was $40,000. Among adults in that age group who never completed high school, the annual income was only $23,900. By comparison, 25- to 34-year-olds with a master's degree or higher earned a median annual income of $59,600 in 2013.

Many significant consequences of dropping out of school cannot be measured statistically. Some of those who drop out may likely experience lifelong poverty. Some who are poorly prepared to compete in society may turn to crime or substance abuse. Some become teenage parents without the ability to offer their children more than they had, possibly contributing to a cycle of dependence. Furthermore, the U.S. economy is deprived of the literate, technically trained, and dedicated workers it needs to compete internationally. In general, those without a high school diploma do not have the same opportunities that are available to the more highly educated.

DETACHED YOUTH

Some young people drop out not only from school but also from work. In *America's Children: Key National Indicators of Well-Being, 2015*, the Federal Interagency Forum on Child and Family Statistics applies the term *detached youth* to people aged 16 to 19 years "who are neither enrolled in school nor working." The forum notes that "such detachment, particularly if it lasts for several years, hinders a youth's opportunity to build a work history that contributes to future higher wages and employability. The percentage of youth who are not enrolled in school and not working is one measure of the proportion of young people who are at risk of limiting their future prospects."

Table 6.13 shows that the total percentage of detached youth fell from 11% in 1985 to 9% in 2014. Although a much higher percentage of females aged 16 to 19 years (13%) than males of the same age range (9%) was neither in school nor working in 1985, the gap disappeared by about 2007. In 2014, 8% of females and 9% of males were considered detached youth. A gap still exists, however, between non-Hispanic whites and other ethnic and racial groups. In 2014, 8% of non-Hispanic whites aged 16 to 19 years were not in school or working, whereas 11% of non-Hispanic African Americans and 10% of Hispanics of the same age group were not in school or working.

According to the Federal Interagency Forum on Child and Family Statistics, older youth aged 18 to 19 years were significantly more likely to be detached from school and work than were youth aged 16 to 17 years. Among youth aged 18 to 19 years, 14% were neither enrolled in school nor working in 2014, compared with 4% of youth aged 16 to 17 years.

TABLE 6.13

Percentage of youth aged 16–19 neither enrolled in school[a] nor working, by sex, age, and race/ethnicity, selected years 1985–2014

Characteristic	1985[b]	1990[b]	1995	2000[c]	2005	2008	2009	2010	2011	2012[d]	2013	2014
Ages 16–19												
Total	11	10	9	8	8	8	9	9	8	8	9	9
Gender												
Male	9	8	8	7	7	8	10	9	9	8	9	9
Female	13	12	11	9	8	8	9	9	8	8	9	8
Race and Hispanic origin[e]												
White, non-Hispanic	9	8	7	6	6	7	7	8	7	7	8	8
Black, non-Hispanic	18	15	14	13	12	11	12	12	11	11	11	11
Hispanic	17	17	16	13	12	11	13	11	11	11	11	10
Ages 16–17												
Total	5	5	4	4	3	4	4	3	3	3	5	4
Gender												
Male	5	4	4	3	3	4	4	4	3	3	4	5
Female	6	5	5	4	3	4	4	3	3	3	5	5
Race and Hispanic origin[e]												
White, non-Hispanic	5	4	3	3	3	3	3	3	3	3	4	4
Black, non-Hispanic	6	6	6	5	4	5	5	5	4	4	5	5
Hispanic	10	10	9	7	5	5	5	5	4	4	5	5
Ages 18–19												
Total	17	15	15	12	13	14	15	15	14	14	15	14
Gender												
Male	13	12	12	11	13	13	16	16	15	15	15	14
Female	20	18	17	13	13	14	14	15	14	13	15	13
Race and Hispanic origin[e]												
White, non-Hispanic	14	12	11	9	10	11	12	13	12	12	13	12
Black, non-Hispanic	30	23	24	21	20	20	20	21	19	19	18	19
Hispanic	24	24	23	18	19	19	21	19	18	18	18	16

[a]School refers to both high school and college.

[b]Data for 1985–1993 are not strictly comparable with data from 1994 onward because of revisions to the questionnaire and data collection methodology for the Current Population Survey (CPS).

[c]From 2000 to 2011, data incorporate population controls from Census 2000.

[d]Beginning in 2012, data incorporate population controls from Census 2010.

[e]For data before 2003, the 1977 Office of Management and Budget (OMB) Standards for Data on Race and Ethnicity were used to classify persons into on of the following four racial groups: white, black, American Indian or Alaskan Native, or Asian or Pacific Islander. The revised 1997 OMB standards were used for data for 2003 and later years. Persons could select one or more of five racial groups: white, black, or African American, American Indian or Alaska Native, Asian, or Native Hawaiian or other Pacific Islander. Included in the total but not shown separately are American Indian or Alaska Native, Asian, Native Hawaiian or other Pacific Islander, and "two or more races." Beginning in 2003, those in each racial category represent those reporting only one race. Data from 2003 onward are not directly comparable with data from earlier years. Data on race and Hispanic origin are collected separately. Persons of Hispanic origin may be of any race.

Note: Data relate to the labor force and enrollment status of persons ages 16–19 in the civilian noninstitutionalized population during an "average" week of the school year. The percentages represent an average based on responses to the survey questions for the months that youth are usually in school (January through May and September through December). Results are based on 9 months of data.

SOURCE: "Table ED5.A. Youth Neither Enrolled in School nor Working: Percentage of Youth Ages 16–19 Who Are Neither Enrolled in School nor Working by Age, Gender, and Race and Hispanic Origin, Selected Years 1985–2014," in *America's Children: Key National Indicators of Well-Being, 2015*, Federal Interagency Forum on Child and Family Statistics, July 2015, http://www.childstats.gov/pdf/ac2015/ac_15.pdf (accessed July 27, 2015)

CHAPTER 7
ISSUES IN EDUCATION

An issue is a matter on which various people or groups have opinions or take sides. In education there are many issues currently being debated. One major issue is school choice, which includes varied options such as voucher programs, tax credit and deduction programs, charter schools, homeschooling, open enrollment, and magnet schools. Other issues in education include privatization of public schools, religion, and bilingual education.

SCHOOL CHOICE

History of School Choice

One of the first school choice legal battles, which was settled in 1925, concerned parents' rights to send their children to private schools. The case involved an Oregon state law that required parents to send their children to public schools. In *Pierce v. Society of the Sisters of the Holy Names of Jesus* (268 U.S. 510 [1925]), the U.S. Supreme Court deemed it constitutional for parents to select a church-affiliated or private school for their children's education.

The opinion of the high court in *Pierce* asserted that "no question is raised concerning the power of the state reasonably to regulate all schools, to inspect, supervise and examine them, their teachers and pupils; to require that all children of proper age attend some school, that teachers shall be of good moral character and patriotic disposition, that certain studies plainly essential to good citizenship must be taught, and that nothing be taught which is manifestly inimical to the public welfare." However, because the law "unreasonably interferes with the liberty of parents and guardians to direct the upbringing and education of children ... under their control ... the fundamental theory of liberty upon which all governments in this Union repose excludes any general power of the state to standardize its children by forcing them to accept instruction from public teachers only." Therefore, parents cannot be forced to send their children to public schools. A family is free to choose private education or to leave one school district for another where it believes the public schools are better.

In 1954 the Supreme Court ruled in the landmark *Brown v. Board of Education* (347 U.S. 483) that having separate public schools for African American and white students was illegal. One year later the Nobel Prize–winning economist Milton Friedman (1912–2006) developed a plan that he believed would enhance and diversify American education in kindergarten to 12th grade. Friedman was a strong advocate of a free competitive market economy and the dissolution of monopolies. His plan for a school voucher system was designed to allow private schools to compete with what he saw as a monopoly of public schools.

Friedman suggested that government financing of education be separated from government administration of schools. The money for the education of a child would follow the child in the form of a voucher, explained Friedman, giving parents of all income levels and ethnicities freedom to choose the school they believed was most appropriate for their child. Without school vouchers, only parents of financial means could exercise school choice by buying homes and moving into neighborhoods with schools they wanted their children to attend. Parents of means could also afford to send their children to private schools if they preferred. Low-income families, however, were not able to exercise this manner of school choice.

Percentages of Those Taking Advantage of School Choice Options

A voucher system and school choice for every child as Friedman proposed has never been instituted nationally. However, there are school choice options available to families in many states. In *A Blueprint for Reform: The Reauthorization of the Elementary and Secondary Education Act* (March 2010, http://www2.ed.gov/policy/

elsec/leg/blueprint/blueprint.pdf), President Barack Obama (1961–) supports public school choice, such as the expansion of charter schools and magnet schools, as public education alternatives. The Obama administration does not, however, support voucher programs.

Between 2002 and 2012 the ethnic and racial makeup of U.S. public schools changed dramatically. In 2002 white students accounted for 59% of all public school enrollment. (See Figure 7.1.) That same year Hispanics accounted for 18% of overall enrollment in public schools, followed by African Americans (17%), Asians or Pacific Islanders (4%), and Native Americans or Alaskan Natives (1%). Within a decade these proportions had altered significantly. White students accounted for only 51% of public school enrollment in 2012, whereas Hispanic students represented nearly a quarter (24%) of total enrollment in public schools. Grace Kena et al. report in *The Condition of Education 2015* (May 2015, http://nces .ed.gov/pubs2015/2015144.pdf) that the number of white students attending public schools fell from 28.6 million in 2002 to 25.4 million in 2012, a decline of more than 11%. Over this same span Hispanic enrollment in public schools grew nearly 41%, from 8.6 million in 2002 to 12.1 million in 2012.

Voucher Programs

Voucher programs are one means of providing school choice. School vouchers are public funds in the form of tuition certificates that students may redeem to pay for all or part of their tuition at a private school of their choice. Typically, the money comes out of public school funds. In *School Choice Yearbook 2014–2015: Breaking Down Barriers to Choice* (2015, http://afcgrowthfund.org/wp-content/uploads/2015/04/AFC_2014-15_Yearbook.pdf), Matt Frendewey et al. reveal that as of 2015, 10 states, the District of Columbia, and Douglas County, Colorado, had implemented school voucher programs. According to the researchers, states were projected to dedicate roughly $1.5 billion to private education through voucher programs, tax credits, and other funding initiatives that year.

PROS AND CONS OF VOUCHER PROGRAMS. Those favoring voucher programs consider them an equitable means of helping low-income families provide their children with what they believe is a better education than in

FIGURE 7.1

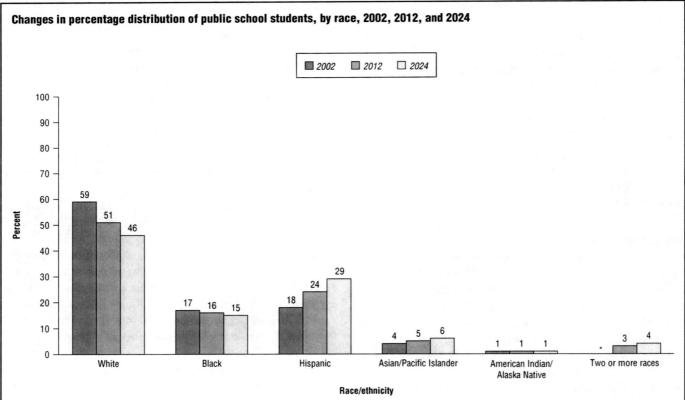

Changes in percentage distribution of public school students, by race, 2002, 2012, and 2024

*Not applicable.
Note: Race categories exclude persons of Hispanic ethnicity. Prior to 2008, separate data on students of two or more races were not collected. Detail may not sum to totals because of rounding. Data for 2024 are projected.

SOURCE: Grace Kena et al., "Figure 1. Percentage Distribution of Students Enrolled in Public Elementary and Secondary Schools, by Race/Ethnicity: Fall 2002, Fall 2012, and Fall 2024," in *The Condition of Education 2015*, U.S. Department of Education, Institute of Education Sciences, National Center for Education Statistics, May 2015, http://nces.ed.gov/pubs2015/2015144.pdf (accessed July 28, 2015)

their designated school. Voucher supporters like the idea that vouchers emphasize educational choices rather than requirements. In addition, many believe increased competition will force public schools to improve or face closure.

Those opposing vouchers believe the programs would help only a few students, leaving most low-income students in schools with reduced attendance and therefore reduced community commitment. Critics maintain that vouchers weaken public schools by diverting some tax money from public schools to voucher programs and, in effect, helping fund private schools. The debate becomes even more heated when voucher supporters advocate allowing students to attend religious schools with public voucher funds. A major dimension of that debate concerns whether the use of vouchers at religiously affiliated private schools violates the First Amendment (which specifies the separation of church and state) by directly supporting religious institutions, or whether vouchers avoid such violations by supporting only the children.

In 2015 opposition for voucher programs was stronger than support. According to "Testing Doesn't Measure Up for Americans: The 47th Annual PDK/Gallup Poll of the Public's Attitudes toward the Public Schools" (*Phi Delta Kappan*, vol. 97, no. 1, September 2015), 57% of Americans opposed the use of government funds to enable parents to send their children to private schools in 2015, compared with 31% of Americans who supported the use of public funds for private education. Both of these percentages represented a decline from 2014. William J. Bushaw and Valerie J. Calderon report in "Try It Again, Uncle Sam: The 46th Annual PDK/Gallup Poll of the Public's Attitudes toward the Public Schools" (*Phi Delta Kappan*, vol. 96, no. 1, September 2014) that 63% of Americans opposed the use of public funds to send students to private schools in 2014, compared with 37% who supported the use of government funds for private education. Opinion on the use of public funds for private education also varied according to how the funds were used. For example, in 2014 a majority of Americans supported the use of public funds to send students to charter schools (54%) or to provide vouchers to students from public schools that were failing (51%), whereas more than one-third (37%) supported the use of public funds to provide vouchers to low-income families. (See Figure 7.2.)

COURT RULINGS ON VOUCHER PROGRAMS. A Florida circuit court ruled in 2000 that Florida's voucher program, which was operated under the Opportunity Scholarships Program, was unconstitutional. The program provided funds for students attending a "failing" Florida school to attend a public or eligible private school of their choice. The state appealed the case to the Florida Supreme Court. In "Florida Supreme Court Blocks School Vouchers" (NYTimes.com, January 6, 2006),

FIGURE 7.2

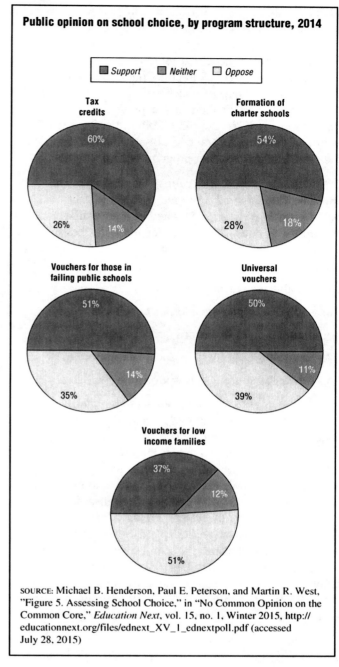

Public opinion on school choice, by program structure, 2014

■ *Support* ■ *Neither* □ *Oppose*

Tax credits
60% 26% 14%

Formation of charter schools
54% 28% 18%

Vouchers for those in failing public schools
51% 35% 14%

Universal vouchers
50% 39% 11%

Vouchers for low income families
37% 12% 51%

SOURCE: Michael B. Henderson, Paul E. Peterson, and Martin R. West, "Figure 5. Assessing School Choice," in "No Common Opinion on the Common Core," *Education Next*, vol. 15, no. 1, Winter 2015, http://educationnext.org/files/ednext_XV_1_ednextpoll.pdf (accessed July 28, 2015)

Sam Dillon reports that in January 2006 the Florida high court asserted that the voucher program violated Florida's constitution, which states that "adequate provision shall be made by law for a uniform, efficient, safe, secure and high quality system of free public schools." With this ruling the Florida Supreme Court was expressing the view that under Florida's constitution, public money was to be used for funding public schools and that the use of private schools did not constitute a "uniform" system allowable for public funding.

An Ohio federal court of appeals concluded in 2000 that the Cleveland voucher program, which gives low-income students scholarships to attend private secular or religious schools, violated the U.S. Constitution's stance on separation of church and state. The court rejected arguments that the Cleveland vouchers were a neutral form of aid to parents that only indirectly benefited religious schools. The ruling was appealed to the U.S. Supreme Court by the state of Ohio as well as by a group of voucher parents and several religious schools participating in the program. In *Zelman v. Simmons-Harris* (536 U.S. 639 [2002]), the Supreme Court overruled the Ohio federal court of appeals and determined that the Cleveland voucher program was constitutional.

With its landmark ruling in *Zelman*, the U.S. Supreme Court issued a private choice test that could be used by states to determine whether a particular voucher program was constitutional under the U.S. Constitution. To pass this test, five conditions of the voucher program would have to be met:

1. A valid secular purpose exists

2. Aid goes to parents and not to schools

3. A broad class of beneficiaries is covered

4. Neutrality exists with respect to religion

5. Adequate nonreligious options are available

In March 2009 the Arizona Supreme Court ruled in *Cain v. Horne* (No. 08-0819) that the state's school voucher program was unconstitutional. The Arizona constitution indicates that taxpayer money cannot be used to subsidize private schooling, whether it be a religious or nonreligious school, yet Arizona had instituted a school voucher program in 2006 that benefited disabled students and those living with foster parents. The voucher program was immediately challenged by groups that were opposed to school vouchers. The program was found (in 2009) to violate the Arizona state constitution because school vouchers use money drawn from the state treasury (taxpayer money) rather than use an individual's money as in the constitutional tuition tax credit program.

In 2011 the issue of providing vouchers that can be used at religious schools arose in Indiana. In May 2011 Indiana's voucher program was signed into law, but it was immediately challenged. Ken Kusmer explains in "Indiana Voucher Program Likely to Be Upheld, Judge Denies Block" (Associated Press, August 15, 2011) that those suing the state claimed the voucher program violated the state constitution because it provided public money to religious institutions. In August 2011 Judge Michael D. Keele of the Marion Superior Court denied a request for a temporary injunction to block the new voucher program until the case could be heard. The judge declared the program to be "religion-neutral," in that it was enacted "'for the benefit' of students, not religious institutions or activities." Proponents of the voucher program also contend the program does not violate the state

constitution because it gives vouchers to parents, not to the schools directly. Thus, they suggest, the state is not funding parochial (religious) schools. In March 2013 the Indiana Supreme Court voted unanimously that the state's school voucher program was constitutional, which enabled the system to remain intact.

Tax Credit and Deduction Programs

Tax credit programs or tax deduction programs are state school choice programs that advance parental choice via tax credits or deductions. Frendewey et al. indicate that 12 states had tax credit scholarship programs in 2015: Alabama, Arizona, Florida, Indiana, Iowa, Kansas, Louisiana, New Hampshire, Oklahoma, Pennsylvania, Rhode Island, and Virginia. According to Frendewey et al., the total funding for these programs topped $661 million during the 2014–15 school year, and served 209,808 students.

In some tax credit programs, state tax credits are given to families for public or private school expenses, possibly including tuition. (A tax credit lowers a tax bill by the amount of the credit. For example, if the credit is for $100, a person gets $100 off the taxes he or she owes.) Tax credits may also be given to individuals for contributions to public schools. In addition, tax credit programs may give individuals or corporations state tax credits for contributions to nonprofit scholarship funding organizations or school tuition organizations. The organizations then distribute the scholarships/tuitions to eligible children, often to those with limited financial resources.

Tax deduction programs operate in a similar way to tax credit programs, except that state tax deductions are given. (A tax deduction reduces taxable income by the amount of the deduction, so the value of the deduction depends on the individual's tax bracket. For example, a $100 deduction lowers the taxable income by $100. If the person is in the 30% tax bracket, the tax deduction is worth 30% of the $100, or $30.)

PROS AND CONS OF TAX CREDIT AND DEDUCTION PROGRAMS. As Figure 7.2 shows, more Americans support tax credit programs (60%) than any other use of public funds for private education. The proponents of tax credit and deduction programs argue that this mechanism can provide all families with financial access to school choice. In addition, tax credit and deduction proponents believe, as do school voucher proponents, that giving financial aid to families for school choice will encourage competition between private and public schools, which will enhance the quality of education. Moreover, some tax credit and deduction proponents believe that tax credit and deduction programs minimize associations between the government and religious schools more than do voucher programs. Many private schools prefer tax credits and deductions to vouchers because this mechanism of school choice subjects private schools to less governmental regulation than do voucher programs.

The opponents of tax credit and deduction programs argue that tax programs typically benefit families that have higher tax bills and that may already be sending their children to private schools. They contend that these programs do little to help economically disadvantaged families with school choice and that they provide tax relief only to families already financially able to send their children to the schools they choose. For example, families that are too poor to have a tax liability cannot take advantage of a tax credit. Many tax credit and deduction opponents favor vouchers that, instead, target low-income families with children attending schools in need of improvement.

Charter Schools

Charter schools are another element of the school choice movement. In charter schools teachers, parents, administrators, community groups, or private corporations design and operate a local school under charter (written contract) from a school district, state education agency, or other public institution. In some cases charter schools are nearly autonomous (self-directing) and are exempt from many state and district education rules. In other cases the schools function much like traditional public schools and must apply for the exemptions (exceptions to usual school operating rules) they want. In exchange for their autonomy, charter schools must keep careful track of student achievement. It should be noted that charter schools must meet all state and federal academic requirements. For example, charter schools cannot hold religious services and cannot charge tuition. They are required to accept all students—there is no admission test that must be passed—and students must be admitted by lottery if there are more student applicants than available places. In general, charters receive less government funding per pupil than traditional public schools.

The idea of charter schools was first suggested during the 1970s. Albert Shanker (1928–1997), the former president of the American Federation of Teachers, helped promote the idea. During the 1980s Philadelphia, Pennsylvania, piloted several model schools, calling them "charters." During the 1990s Minnesota developed charter schools based on three values: choice, opportunity, and accountability for results.

The Charter Schools Program (CSP) was authorized as part of the Improving America's Schools Act of 1994, an effort by the administration of Bill Clinton (1946–) to improve public schools. The CSP was intended as a school choice program with the goal of higher student achievement. To encourage the growth and quality of public charter schools, the CSP provided financial assistance for their planning, start-up, and implementation.

The CSP was amended in 1998 with the Charter School Expansion Act to increase the number of high-quality charter schools.

Figure 7.3 shows the steady rise in charter school enrollment between 1999–2000 and 2012–13. In 1999–2000 approximately 300,000 students were attending public charter schools. By 2012–13 this figure had risen to 2.3 million students, an increase of 667%. As Figure 7.4 shows, 4.6% of all public school students in the United States attended charter schools in 2012–13. Charter school enrollment ranged between 5% and 9.9% in 11 states and exceeded 10% in Arizona, Colorado, and District of Columbia. According to Bushaw and Calderon, 70% of Americans were in favor of charter schools in 2014.

Homeschooling

Practiced by parents who, among other reasons, wish to provide religious or moral instruction to their children, homeschooling is another part of the school choice movement. In *Digest of Education Statistics 2013* (May 2015, http://nces.ed.gov/pubs2015/2015011.pdf), Thomas D. Snyder and Sally A. Dillow report that nearly 1.8 million children between the ages of five and 17 years, or 3.4% of all students in that age group, were homeschooled in 2012. According to the U.S. Department of Education, in "Statistics about Nonpublic Education in the United States" (June 9, 2015, http://www2.ed.gov/about/offices/list/oii/nonpublic/statistics.html), more than nine out of 10 (91%) parents cited concern about the environment of other schools as one of their reasons for homeschooling in 2011–12. Roughly three-quarters of parents cited a desire to provide moral instruction (77%) or dissatisfaction with educational standards at other schools (74%) as reasons for homeschooling in 2011–12, while nearly two-thirds (64%) cited a desire to provide religious instruction to their children.

STATE HOMESCHOOLING REQUIREMENTS. Homeschooling is legal in all 50 states, but states vary widely in the way they govern homeschooling. Because all states' laws require school attendance, the states have jurisdiction over homeschools. Some states have set up elaborate requirements for homeschools, whereas others have taken a hands-off approach. No state will issue a high school diploma for homeschooled students. Parents have the option of providing a homeschool diploma to their children themselves (but usually transcripts are also needed for the parent-issued diploma to be accepted, as is the case with the armed forces); engaging an online or correspondence school that issues diplomas for homeschooled students; or having the student take the General Educational Development (GED) examination to obtain a GED certificate.

In "State Laws" (2015, http://www.hslda.org/laws/default.asp), the Home School Legal Defense Association

FIGURE 7.3

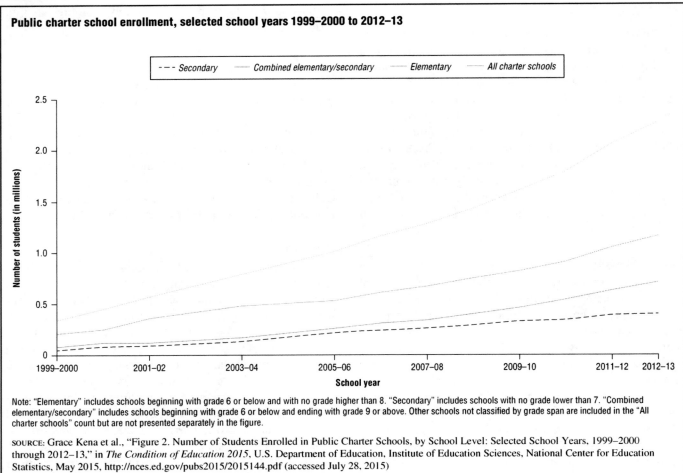

Public charter school enrollment, selected school years 1999–2000 to 2012–13

- - - Secondary   .... Combined elementary/secondary   .... Elementary   .... All charter schools

Note: "Elementary" includes schools beginning with grade 6 or below and with no grade higher than 8. "Secondary" includes schools with no grade lower than 7. "Combined elementary/secondary" includes schools beginning with grade 6 or below and ending with grade 9 or above. Other schools not classified by grade span are included in the "All charter schools" count but are not presented separately in the figure.

SOURCE: Grace Kena et al., "Figure 2. Number of Students Enrolled in Public Charter Schools, by School Level: Selected School Years, 1999–2000 through 2012–13," in *The Condition of Education 2015*, U.S. Department of Education, Institute of Education Sciences, National Center for Education Statistics, May 2015, http://nces.ed.gov/pubs2015/2015144.pdf (accessed July 28, 2015)

provides access to current homeschool laws for all 50 states. Three states—New York, Ohio, and Texas—illustrate the wide variance in homeschool requirements. New York has established extensive requirements for homeschools and is considered a state with high regulation. Elementary-age students must spend 900 hours per year in class, and those in grades seven to 12 must be in class 990 hours per year. Other requirements include providing annual notice of intent to homeschool to the superintendent of local schools, as well as records of attendance and assessment. Ohio, a state with moderate regulation, requires students to spend 900 hours per year in class, and the homeschool teacher must have a high school diploma or equivalent. Each year, advance notice of intent to homeschool and assessment of student performance must be filed with the superintendent of schools. Although the state specifies which subjects must be taught, it does not require homeschooling to include any concept, topic, or practice that is in conflict with the sincerely held religious beliefs of the parent. Texas is considered a state with "no notice" and has very few requirements for homeschools, because it regards them to be private schools (which are not regulated by the state).

The state requires no teacher certification, no advance notice, and no testing or attendance records. The only specified subjects are reading, spelling, grammar, mathematics, and good citizenship.

Open Enrollment

Open enrollment means that a student can transfer to a public school of his or her choosing. There are two types of open enrollment policies, and not all states have such policies. One type of open enrollment policy is intradistrict (meaning "within district"), which allows students to transfer to other schools within the district in which they live. The other type of open enrollment policy is interdistrict (meaning "between district"), which allows students to transfer to schools outside the district in which they live. Interdistrict open enrollment policies often require that both the sending and receiving districts agree to the transfer. Some states have voluntary open enrollment policies, whereas others have mandatory policies. Both types usually require that space be available to accommodate students, or transfers cannot be made. In "Open Enrollment: 50-State Report" (June 2013, http://ecs.force.com/mbdata/mbtab8OE?sid=a0i70000006fu14&rep=OE132T),

FIGURE 7.4

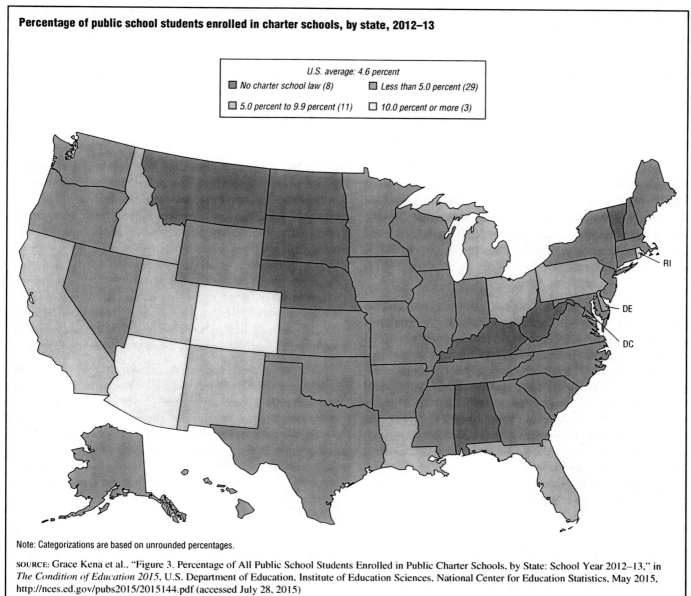

Percentage of public school students enrolled in charter schools, by state, 2012–13

U.S. average: 4.6 percent

- No charter school law (8)
- 5.0 percent to 9.9 percent (11)
- Less than 5.0 percent (29)
- 10.0 percent or more (3)

Note: Categorizations are based on unrounded percentages.

SOURCE: Grace Kena et al., "Figure 3. Percentage of All Public School Students Enrolled in Public Charter Schools, by State: School Year 2012–13," in *The Condition of Education 2015*, U.S. Department of Education, Institute of Education Sciences, National Center for Education Statistics, May 2015, http://nces.ed.gov/pubs2015/2015144.pdf (accessed July 28, 2015)

the Education Commission of the States provides information on the open enrollment policies for all 50 states. The report includes information on various practical considerations relating to open enrollment, including transportation costs and desegregation policies. For example, the California Department of Education indicates in "Open Enrollment" (July 17, 2015, http://www.cde.ca.gov/sp/eo/op) that the California Open Enrollment Act of 2010 granted students at 1,000 designated schools the right to transfer to institutions with stronger records of academic performance. In "Enrollment Choices" (2015, http://education.state.mn.us/MDE/StuSuc/EnrollChoice), the Minnesota Department of Education estimates that roughly 30% of the state's public school students took advantage of open enrollment and other forms of "school choice" in 2015.

Magnet Schools

Magnet schools were created as a desegregation measure, but they also provide school choice. Magnet schools offer specialized curricula, such as a focus on the arts, science and mathematics, or languages, to attract students from a variety of neighborhoods in a particular area. Parents, teachers, and community leaders often design the magnet school programs based on the needs of their communities so that interest is high and needs are met. Enrollment is generally regulated to ensure racial balance, and there are usually entrance requirements. Many people criticize magnet schools because of their entrance requirements, citing that students such as those with special needs, those not proficient in English, or those with behavioral problems are often not allowed to attend. Magnet schools are funded by federal grants, state grants, local school board contributions, corporate contributions, and, in some cases, tuition paid by parents. According to the Magnet Schools of America, in "About Magnet Schools of America" (http://www.magnet.edu/about), there were roughly 4,000 magnet schools in the United States in 2015.

PRIVATIZATION OF PUBLIC SCHOOLS

In some cases, school boards and state education offices have turned to privatizing their schools by contracting with private corporations called education management organizations (EMOs) to administer one or more local charter schools. Contracts for privatizing services are usually awarded based on bids submitted by the education companies. Most charter schools, which were discussed previously in this chapter, are not run by EMOs but are run independently by entities other than EMOs. The proportion varies by state.

In general, teachers' unions oppose privatizing schools. The National Education Association explains in "Privatization" (2015, http://www.nea.org/home/16355.htm) that privatization results in "a cut in services for the school, a cut in benefits and wages for employees, and a risk to safety for students and families." In "School Privatization Is a Hoax, 'Reformers' Aim to Destroy Public Schools" (Salon.com, September 15, 2013), the education reformer Diane Ravitch (1938–) levels a searing critique at the school privatization movement. Describing privatization as a "corporate idea of reform," she asserts that privatized schools "divert" public tax revenues away from educational initiatives to "pay profits to investors."

RELIGION IN PUBLIC SCHOOLS

The separation of church and state as outlined in the U.S. Constitution is one of the most widely debated educational issues. During the past two decades controversy has swirled around school prayer, prayers during graduation ceremonies, and other exercises of religious belief within public schools. The issue of bringing religion into the science classroom has been widely discussed since the Scopes "monkey" trial of the 1920s. In this trial a Tennessee high school teacher faced criminal charges for teaching evolution because, according to the Tennessee Evolution Statute (1925, http://www.law.umkc.edu/faculty/projects/ftrials/scopes/tennstat.htm), it was illegal in Tennessee "to teach any theory that denies the story of the Divine Creation of man as taught in the Bible, and to teach instead that man has descended from a lower order of animals."

The church and state separation clause in the First Amendment was intended to prohibit the establishment of a state religion or the coercion of citizens to belong to a particular group, either religious or antireligious.

Contrary to popular belief, the U.S. Supreme Court's interpretations of First Amendment rights do not prohibit the private expression of religion in the public school. They do not prevent students from praying at school or in the classroom, provided these activities do not disrupt the school's normal order or instruction. A student may pray either silently or quietly aloud whenever he or she is not actively participating in school activities. However, a student may not attempt to turn a class or meeting into a captive audience for a religious service.

Public school officials may not require prayers during the school day, make prayers a part of graduation exercises, or organize baccalaureate services (graduation services of hymns, worship, and sermons). Teachers and school administrators may not participate in, encourage, or insist on student religious or antireligious activities while they are acting in their capacities as representatives of the state. Doing so could be interpreted as coercion or as the establishment of a particular group as a state-sanctioned religion, which violates the First Amendment. Teachers and other school personnel may, however, exercise private religious activity in faculty lounges or private offices.

Public schools may teach about religion, but they cannot give religious instruction. The study of the Bible and other religious scriptures is permissible as part of literature, history, and social studies classes so that students can understand the contribution of religious ideas and groups to the nation's culture. Students may express their personal religious beliefs in reports, homework, and artwork on the condition that these expressions meet the goals of the assignments and are appropriate to the topics assigned.

The separation of church and state is very clear in some areas, but it can be ambiguous in others. For example, one of the biggest issues surrounding school vouchers is whether state funds, which are generated from taxes, can be used to pay tuition at parochial schools. In 1973 the Supreme Court ruled in *Committee for Public Education v. Nyquist* (413 U.S. 756) that doing so would be an unconstitutional mingling of church and state.

Nevertheless, a subsequent ruling by the Supreme Court indicates that the court has changed its stance on the necessity for a rigid barrier between public and parochial schools. Five justices criticized a 1985 finding in *Aguilar v. Felton* (473 U.S. 402), which ruled that sending public school teachers to parochial schools to conduct remedial classes was unconstitutional. In 1997 the court reheard the case, a most unusual procedure. Divided five to four, the Supreme Court ruled in *Agostini v. Felton* (521 U.S. 203) that *Aguilar* is "no longer good law." In reversing *Aguilar*, the court declared, "A federally funded program providing supplemental, remedial instruction to disadvantaged children on a neutral basis is not invalid under the Establishment Clause when such instruction is given on the premises of sectarian schools by government employees pursuant to a program containing safeguards.... This carefully constrained program also cannot reasonably be viewed as an endorsement of religion.... 'The mere circumstance that [an aid recipient] has chosen to use neutrally available state aid to help pay for [a] religious education [does not] confer any message of state endorsement of religion.'"

The Controversy over the Pledge of Allegiance

In 2001 Michael A. Newdow filed a lawsuit against his daughter's school district arguing that requiring his daughter to say the words "under God" in a public school while reciting the Pledge of Allegiance was unconstitutional. In *Elk Grove Unified School District v. Michael A. Newdow* (2002), a panel of the U.S. Court of Appeals for the Ninth Circuit agreed, issuing a two-to-one decision that requiring schoolchildren to say the phrase "under God" violates the First Amendment's prohibition of government sponsorship of religion. In 2003, however, the full U.S. Court of Appeals for the Ninth Circuit issued a 90-day stay, which allowed students in nine western states to continue saying the Pledge of Allegiance without the words removed, pending a decision by the U.S. Supreme Court on whether it would review the case.

The Supreme Court did agree to hear the case. In *Elk Grove Unified School District v. Newdow* (542 U.S. 1 [2004]), the court overturned the U.S. Court of Appeals for the Ninth Circuit's original decision, but it did so without actually ruling on the constitutionality of the pledge. The court determined that because Newdow did not have legal custody over his daughter (the child's mother had sole custody), he did not have legal standing to sue the school district on her behalf. This decision effectively kept the words "under God" in the Pledge of Allegiance but left the door open to future challenges on First Amendment grounds.

Teaching Evolution versus Teaching Creationism in the Science Classroom

The scientific theory of evolution explains that life changed from simple to complex forms over billions of years. Some people believe evolution contradicts their religious conviction that life was created directly by God in six days, a view known as special creation or, more generally, creationism. This view is contrary to evolution. Creationists have sought to ban the teaching of evolution and have creationism taught instead in public school science classrooms, or they want creationism taught alongside evolution. Some believe that various aspects of evolution and creationism can be compatible, but adding a supernatural component to evolution is not compatible with scientific thinking—it is not science.

In 1968 the Supreme Court ruled in *Epperson v. Arkansas* (393 U.S. 97) that banning the teaching of evolution in schools violated the Establishment Clause of the U.S. Constitution because the primary purpose of the ban was religious. In 1987 the court used the same reasoning in *Edwards v. Aguillard* (482 U.S. 578) to strike down a Louisiana law that required those who taught evolution to also discuss creation "science." Despite these historic rulings, the controversy over teaching evolution and creationism in schools continued. In 1999 the Kansas Board of Education voted to remove the subject of evolution from state standardized tests, but the old science standards were restored in 2001 after the election of a new board.

In 2004 the school board of Dover, Pennsylvania, mandated the teaching of intelligent design (ID), a theory proposing that the universe is so complex that it must have been created by a higher power. In the 2005 case *Kitzmiller v. Dover Area School District* (400 F.Supp.2d 707 [M.D.Pa.]), a group of parents and the American Civil Liberties Union sued the school board for adopting the policy. The lawsuit claimed that the Dover policy violated the Establishment Clause of the First Amendment by promoting a religious doctrine. The school board members who put ID into the curriculum were voted out of office in November 2005. The next month Judge John E. Jones (1955–) of the U.S. district court ruled that ID is a form of creationism and not science. He also ruled that members of Dover's school board lied under oath to hide their religious motivations. The judge barred the Dover Area School District from teaching ID in biology class. As of September 2015, the *Kitzmiller* case was the most significant legal ruling on teaching creationism in the science classroom.

Faith-Based Organizations Providing Services

As part of his education agenda, President George W. Bush (1946–) proposed using tax dollars to support after-school programs that were designed to improve academic performance. These programs would be provided by faith-based and religious organizations. Through Title I, Part A, of the 2002 No Child Left Behind (NCLB) Act, faith-based organizations were eligible to apply for approval to provide supplemental educational services to low-income students attending chronically underachieving schools. Federal funds were not to be used to support religious practices, such as religious instruction, worship, or prayer. Supported activities included extra help in reading, language arts, and mathematics before school, after school, on weekends, or during the summer.

Shortly after taking office in January 2009, President Obama renamed the Bush administration's Office of Faith-Based and Community Initiatives as the Office of Faith-Based and Neighborhood Partnerships. The White

House notes in the press release "Obama Announces White House Office of Faith-Based and Neighborhood Partnerships" (February 5, 2009, http://www.whitehouse.gov/the_press_office/ObamaAnnouncesWhiteHouseOffice ofFaith-basedandNeighborhoodPartnerships) that the newly renamed office "will work on behalf of Americans committed to improving their communities, no matter their religious or political beliefs." The White House also states that the "Office [of] Faith-Based and Neighborhood Partnerships will be a resource for nonprofits and community organizations, both secular and faith based, looking for ways to make a bigger impact in their communities, learn their obligations under the law, cut through red tape, and make the most of what the federal government has to offer."

BILINGUAL EDUCATION

In the United States, bilingual education refers to programs for public school students who have limited or no ability to speak English. In 1968 Congress passed the Bilingual Education Act to provide a linguistically appropriate education for students who, because of their limited English proficiency (LEP), were not getting an education equal to that of students fluent in English. The Bilingual Education Act provided funds for bilingual education and encouraged (but did not require) programs that were designed to teach students English. The goal was to teach English to students quickly so that within a year they could move into English-only classes. English instruction, however, was neglected in many schools, putting LEP students at a serious disadvantage.

In 1974 the Equal Educational Opportunity Act was passed, which required schools to take steps to help LEP students overcome their language barriers. Bilingual education moved from taking one year of transition to many years of transition before students could be instructed in English-only classes. In many schools, English instruction was limited to 30 minutes per day, and LEP students were still at a disadvantage.

One major issue with bilingual education is how to best teach LEP students English while instructing them in grade-level subjects. The Bilingual Education Act was amended in 1988 and defined a bilingual education program as one that provides instruction in English and in a native language to allow students to make progress in the educational system. This definition was still vague and did not prescribe a method of bilingual education.

Some students do not participate in bilingual education, even when it is offered, and many school districts have a shortage of bilingual teachers. Although it is difficult to measure the effectiveness of bilingual education, many observers believe children in bilingual programs acquire English at least as well as, and usually better than, children in all-English programs. However, others suggest that students in bilingual classes do not learn English more quickly and do not achieve better test scores.

The NCLB consolidated the U.S. Department of Education's bilingual and immigrant education programs. The new federal program focuses on helping LEP students learn English. States and school districts are held accountable for making annual increases in English proficiency from the previous year. States set performance objectives to ensure that LEP children achieve English fluency after they have attended school in the United States for three consecutive years. States that do not meet their performance objectives for LEP students can lose up to 10% of the administrative portion of their funding for all Elementary and Secondary Education Act programs.

The Obama administration supports transitional bilingual education. With this approach, students who do not speak English take their subject-matter classes taught in their native language while concurrently taking English-language classes. After a transition period of approximately three years, students move to English-only classes. The expectation is that these students have acquired sufficient content knowledge via their native-language instruction and sufficient English-language skills to do well in English-only classes after their transition period concludes.

Figure 7.5 shows the percentage of public school students who were English language learners during the 2012–13 school year. In six states (Alaska, California, Colorado, Nevada, New Mexico, and Texas) and the District of Columbia the proportion of public school students who were learning English as a second language exceeded 10%. In 18 other states this percentage ranged between 6% and 9.9%. By contrast, there were 14 states in 2012–13 where the proportion of English language learners in the public school system was less than 3%.

RACE, ETHNICITY, AND INCOME EQUALITY

The relationship between income levels and educational opportunities is one of the most troubling issues facing school reformers in the 21st century. In "Social Inequality and Educational Disadvantage" (2015, http://www.russell sage.org/research/social-inequality/social-inequality-and-educational-disadvantage), the Russell Sage Foundation, a social research organization based in New York City, outlines several key factors that can negatively impact the academic performance of disadvantaged students, including unstable social backgrounds, low educational attainment of parents, and poorly managed schools. Nowhere is the link between wealth and academic achievement more pronounced than in the area of early education. Sean F. Reardon of Stanford University asserts in the editorial "No Rich Child Left Behind" (NYTimes.com, April 27, 2013) that the rise of income inequality in the United States has resulted in a widening discrepancy in educational opportunities for high-income and low-income students. Reardon notes that between 1980 and 2010 the performance gap between affluent and underprivileged students on

FIGURE 7.5

Percentage of public school students who are English-language learners, by state, 2012–13

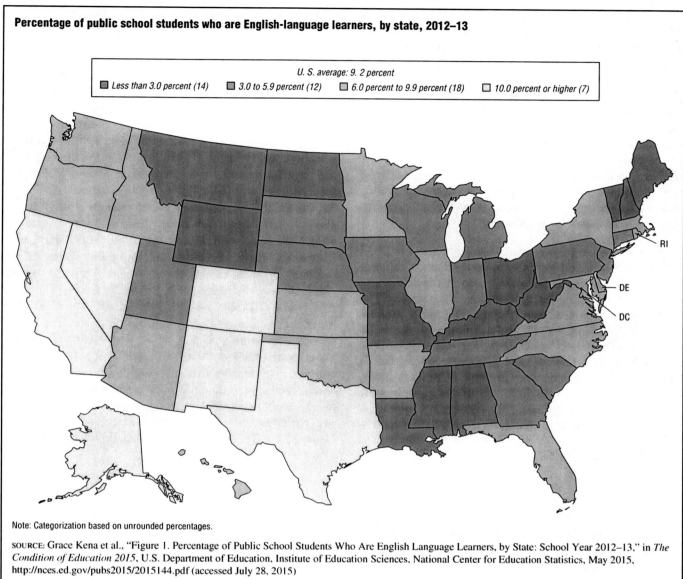

U. S. average: 9. 2 percent

Less than 3.0 percent (14)   3.0 to 5.9 percent (12)   6.0 percent to 9.9 percent (18)   10.0 percent or higher (7)

Note: Categorization based on unrounded percentages.

SOURCE: Grace Kena et al., "Figure 1. Percentage of Public School Students Who Are English Language Learners, by State: School Year 2012–13," in *The Condition of Education 2015*, U.S. Department of Education, Institute of Education Sciences, National Center for Education Statistics, May 2015, http://nces.ed.gov/pubs2015/2015144.pdf (accessed July 28, 2015)

standardized testing increased by 40%. According to Reardon, the key factor behind this growing divide was access to early education opportunities. "The academic gap is widening," he writes, "because rich students are increasingly entering kindergarten much better prepared to succeed in school than middle-class students."

In general, a majority of Americans support reforms that are aimed at providing early education opportunities to underprivileged children. William J. Bushaw and Shane J. Lopez reveal in "Which Way Do We Go? The 45th Annual PDK/Gallup Poll of the Public's Attitudes toward Public Schools" (*Phi Delta Kappan*, vol. 95, no. 1, September 2013) that in 2013, 73% of Americans (45% said "a great deal" and 28% said "quite a lot") believed that preschool education programs for low-income children had the potential to help those children become better students during their teenage years. This figure actually

represented a decline from 2006, when 81% of Americans (49% said "a great deal" and 32% said "quite a lot") felt that preschool programs for low-income children helped improve later academic performance. On the whole, public support for providing broader access to early education programs has grown since the 1990s. Bushaw and Lopez indicate that nearly two-thirds (63%) of Americans supported the idea of spending tax dollars on preschool programs in 2013, compared with 55% who supported such spending in 1991.

On other educational issues, Americans have proven to be more divided along racial and political lines. For example, Bushaw and Lopez reveal that in 2013 a slim majority of Americans opposed closing neighborhood schools for budgetary purposes, by a margin of 50% against to 47% in favor. Approximately 49% of whites favored closing neighborhood schools to save money, whereas 47% opposed this practice. In contrast, only 33% of nonwhite respondents favored shutting down neighborhood schools for budgetary reasons, compared with 64% who opposed such closings. This discrepancy in opinion most likely arises from the fact that these school closings frequently affect low-income and minority neighborhoods. Valerie Strauss reports in "How Closing Schools Hurts Neighborhoods" (WashingtonPost.com, March 6, 2013) that by 2013 this trend was affecting urban centers throughout the United States and threatened to devastate the social fabric that ties communities together. Strauss suggests that "when a neighborhood loses its schools, it also loses an institution that builds relationships among local residents and binds generations, while it serves local children."

Another divisive issue confronting educators in 2015 involved providing educational opportunities to children of illegal immigrants. Public opinion on this question was sharply divided along party lines. In "Americans Put Teacher Quality on Center Stage: The 46th Annual PDK/Gallup Poll of the Public's Attitudes toward the Public Schools, Part II" (*Phi Delta Kappan*, vol. 96, no. 2, October 2014), Bushaw and Calderon report that in 2014, 53% of Americans were in favor of providing free public education to children of illegal immigrants, whereas 43% were opposed. This discrepancy was even more pronounced among Democrats, with 85% supporting free public education to children of illegal immigrants and 14% opposing it. In contrast, 73% of Republicans opposed free educational benefits for children of illegal immigrants, while only 27% supported this policy.

SCHOOL SAFETY

The mass shooting at Sandy Hook Elementary School in Newtown, Connecticut, on December 14, 2012, in which 20-year-old Adam Lanza (1992–2012) murdered 20 children and six staff members before committing suicide, sparked furious debate over the question of school safety in the United States. In the aftermath of the tragedy, parents began expressing greater fear about their children's physical safety while at school. As Figure 7.6 shows, the proportion of parents who were concerned about school safety for their oldest child rose sharply after Newtown, from 25% to 33%. Still, this figure was far from a historical high point. Fear about school safety reached its peak in the wake of the April 20, 1999, massacre at Columbine High School in Colorado, when Eric Harris (1981–1999) and Dylan Klebold (1982–1999) murdered 12 students and a teacher before killing themselves. That same year 55% of all parents expressed fear about their oldest child's safety while at school. Meanwhile, the proportion of children who expressed concern about feeling unsafe at school peaked in 2001, when nearly a quarter (22%) of parents reported their school-age children felt afraid for their safety at school. (See Figure 7.7.) By 2014, however, this figure had dropped to 8%.

FIGURE 7.6

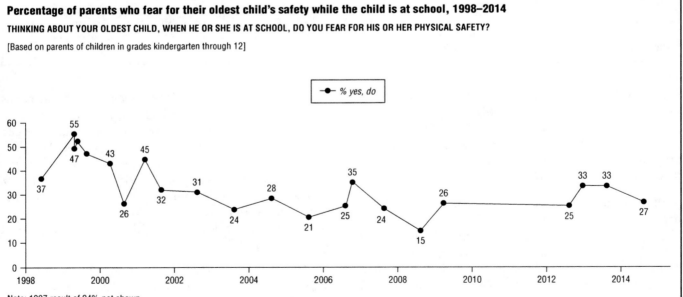

Percentage of parents who fear for their oldest child's safety while the child is at school, 1998–2014

THINKING ABOUT YOUR OLDEST CHILD, WHEN HE OR SHE IS AT SCHOOL, DO YOU FEAR FOR HIS OR HER PHYSICAL SAFETY?

[Based on parents of children in grades kindergarten through 12]

Note: 1997 result of 24% not shown.

SOURCE: Justin McCarthy, "Thinking about your oldest child, when he or she is at school, do you fear for his or her physical safety?" in *Fear for Child's Safety Nearly Back to Pre-Sandy Hook Levels*, The Gallup Organization, August 13, 2014, http://www.gallup.com/poll/174827/fear-child-safety-nearly-back-pre-sandy-hook-levels.aspx?utm_source=school%20safety&utm_medium=search&utm_campaign=tiles (accessed July 28, 2015). Copyright © 2015 Gallup, Inc. All rights reserved. The content is used with permission; however, Gallup retains all rights of republication.

FIGURE 7.7

Percentage of parents of K-12 students reporting that their children expressed fear about feeling unsafe at school, 2000–14

HAVE ANY OF YOUR SCHOOL-AGED CHILDREN EXPRESSED ANY WORRY OR CONCERN ABOUT FEELING UNSAFE AT THEIR SCHOOL WHEN THEY GO BACK TO SCHOOL THIS FALL?

[Based on parents of children in grades kindergarten through 12]

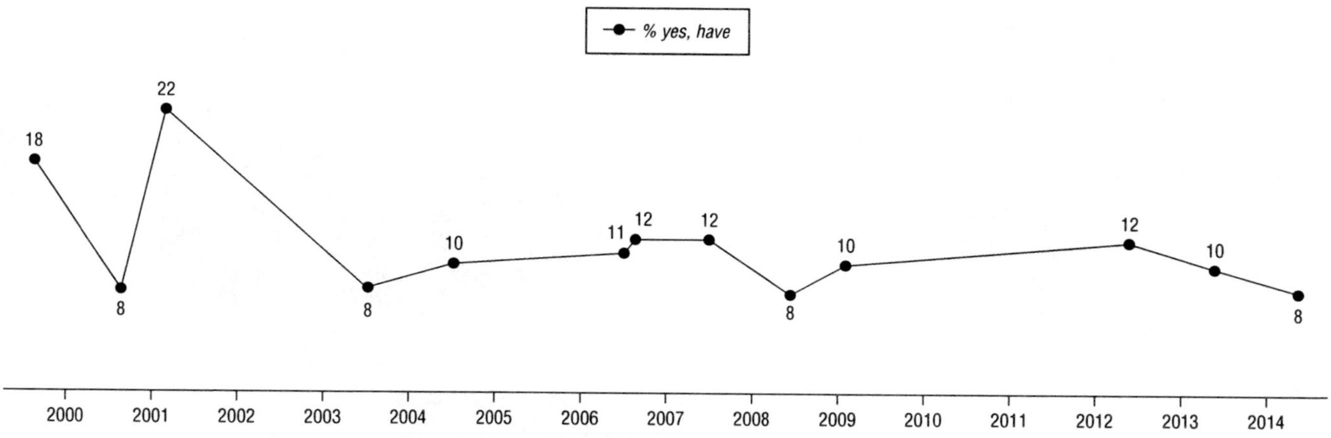

SOURCE: Justin McCarthy, "Have any of your school-aged children expressed any worry or concern about feeling unsafe at their school when they go back to school this fall?" in *Fear for Child's Safety Nearly Back to Pre-Sandy Hook Levels*, The Gallup Organization, August 13, 2014, http://www.gallup.com/poll/174827/fear-child-safety-nearly-back-pre-sandy-hook-levels.aspx?utm_source=school%20safety&utm_medium=search&utm_campaign=tiles (accessed July 28, 2015). Copyright © 2015 Gallup, Inc. All rights reserved. The content is used with permission; however, Gallup retains all rights of republication.

CHAPTER 8
TEACHERS

Teachers are the foundation of the education process. A well-designed, challenging curriculum, a first-class facility, and state-of-the-art equipment need motivated and well-trained teachers to complete the equation.

Since 1952 the Council of Chief State School Officers has sponsored the National Teacher of the Year Program as a way of recognizing excellence in the teaching profession. In 2015 the National Teacher of the Year award was given to Shanna Peeples, a high school English teacher from Amarillo, Texas. In addition, various organizations present Teacher of the Year awards at the state level. In "State Teachers of the Year" (http://www.ccsso .org/ntoy/State_Teachers.html), the council lists the recipients for 2015.

A growing number of teachers face situations that would have been inconceivable a generation ago, ranging from student apathy and disrespect to outright physical attacks. Teachers in inner-city schools particularly bear the brunt of many problems that are often a reflection of society's problems. Adding to the list of challenges that teachers face are large class sizes, inadequate funding, low salaries, and frequent testing mandates. Despite having to manage a host of difficult situations, teachers can derive a wonderful feeling of accomplishment from educating today's youth. This chapter will characterize the teacher workforce.

THE TEACHER WORKFORCE

Every four years the U.S. Census Bureau, working with the National Center for Education Statistics (NCES), administers the Schools and Staffing Survey (SASS) to school personnel in both public and private schools. As of September 2015, the most recent SASS report was *Characteristics of Public and Private Elementary and Secondary School Teachers in the United States: Results from the 2011–12 Schools and Staffing Survey* (August 2013, http://nces.ed.gov/pubs2013/2013314.pdf) by Rebecca Goldring, Lucinda Gray, and Amy Bitterman. The SASS

website overview page (http://nces.ed.gov/surveys/sass) lists topics that are researched in the SASS. These topics include teacher demand and shortage, teacher and administrator characteristics, school programs, general conditions in schools, school climate and problems, teacher compensation, district hiring practices, and basic characteristics of the student population.

In 2012 there were more than 3.5 million elementary and secondary school teachers in the United States. (See Table 8.1.) Of those teachers, 3.1 million taught in public schools and 414,000 taught in private schools. The total number of teachers peaked in 2008, when there were nearly 3.7 million elementary and secondary school teachers working in public and private schools. As Table 8.1 shows, the total number of elementary and secondary school teachers in the United States was not projected to match this number again until 2020.

Teacher Shortages

The U.S. Department of Education's Office of Postsecondary Education lists in *Teacher Shortage Areas Nationwide Listing, 1990–91 through 2015–2016* (March 2015, https://www2.ed.gov/about/offices/list/ope/pol/tsa .doc) the shortages of teachers in content areas for each state as well as schools within each state that have teacher shortages. A great number of factors affect teacher supply and demand, including student enrollments, particular subject area needs, the reserve pool of trained teachers, the pool of new teachers entering the profession, teacher retirement, and other reasons for teachers leaving the profession.

TEACHER MOBILITY. The Teacher Follow-Up Survey is conducted one year after the SASS and is administered to teachers who took the SASS the previous year, whether or not they are still teaching. In *Teacher Attrition and Mobility: Results from the 2012–13 Teacher Follow-Up Survey* (September 2014, http://nces.ed.gov/pubs

TABLE 8.1

Actual and projected numbers of elementary and secondary school teachers, and faculty at degree-granting postsecondary institutions, by control of institution, selected years 1970–2024

[In thousands]

Year	All levels			Elementary and secondary teachers[a]			Degree-granting institutions instructional staff[b]		
	Total	Public	Private	Total	Public	Private	Total	Public	Private
1970	2,766	2,373	393	2,292	2,059	233	474	314	160
1975	3,081	2,641	440	2,453	2,198	255[c]	628	443	185
1980	3,171	2,679	492	2,485	2,184	301	686[c,d]	495[c,d]	191[c,d]
1981	3,145	2,636	509	2,440	2,127	313[c]	705	509	196
1982	3,168	2,639	529	2,458	2,133	325[c]	710[c,d]	506[c,d]	204[c,d]
1983	3,200	2,651	549	2,476	2,139	337	724	512	212
1984	3,225	2,673	552	2,508	2,168	340[c]	717[c,d]	505[c,d]	212[c,d]
1985	3,264	2,709	555	2,549	2,206	343	715[c,d]	503[c,d]	212[c,d]
1986	3,314	2,754	560	2,592	2,244	348[c]	722[c,d]	510[c,d]	212[c,d]
1987	3,424	2,832	592	2,631	2,279	352	793	553	240
1988	3,472	2,882	590	2,668	2,323	345	804[c]	559[c]	245[c]
1989	3,537	2,934	603	2,713	2,357	356	824	577	247
1990	3,577	2,972	604	2,759	2,398	361[c]	817[c]	574[c]	244[c]
1991	3,623	3,013	610	2,797	2,432	365	826	581	245
1992	3,700	3,080	621	2,823	2,459	364[c]	877[c]	621[c]	257[c]
1993	3,784	3,154	629	2,868	2,504	364	915	650	265
1994	3,846	3,205	640	2,922	2,552	370[c]	923[c]	653[c]	270[c]
1995	3,906	3,255	651	2,974	2,598	376	932	657	275
1996	4,006	3,339	666	3,051	2,667	384[c]	954[c]	672[c]	282[c]
1997	4,127	3,441	687	3,138	2,746	391	990	695	295
1998	4,230	3,527	703	3,230	2,830	400[c]	999[c]	697[c]	303[c]
1999	4,347	3,624	723	3,319	2,911	408	1,028	713	315
2000	4,432	3,683	750	3,366	2,941	424	1,067[c]	741[c]	325[c]
2001	4,554	3,771	783	3,440	3,000	441	1,113	771	342
2002	4,631	3,829	802	3,476	3,034	442[c]	1,155[c]	794[c]	361[c]
2003	4,663	3,840	823	3,490	3,049	441	1,174	792	382
2004	4,774	3,909	865	3,538	3,091	447[c]	1,237[c]	818[c]	418[c]
2005	4,883	3,984	899	3,593	3,143	450	1,290	841	449
2006	4,944	4,021	924	3,622	3,166	456[c]	1,322[c]	854[c]	468[c]
2007	5,028	4,077	951	3,656	3,200	456	1,371	877	494
2008	5,065	4,107	958	3,670	3,222	448[c]	1,395[c]	885[c]	510[c]
2009	5,086	4,123	963	3,647	3,210	437	1,439	914	525
2010	5,038	4,044	994	3,529	3,099	429[c]	1,510[c]	945[c]	565[c]
2011	5,049	4,057	991	3,524	3,103	421	1,524	954	570
2012	5,054	4,067	987	3,523	3,109	414[e]	1,531[c]	958[c]	573[c]
2013[f]	5,071	4,087	983	3,527	3,120	407	1,544	968	576
2014[e]	—	—	—	3,520	3,122	398	—	—	—
2015[e]	—	—	—	3,521	3,129	391	—	—	—
2016[e]	—	—	—	3,525	3,138	387	—	—	—
2017[e]	—	—	—	3,577	3,185	392	—	—	—
2018[e]	—	—	—	3,617	3,224	393	—	—	—
2019[e]	—	—	—	3,660	3,264	395	—	—	—
2020[e]	—	—	—	3,700	3,302	398	—	—	—
2021[e]	—	—	—	3,743	3,342	401	—	—	—
2022[e]	—	—	—	3,788	3,383	405	—	—	—
2023[e]	—	—	—	3,840	3,429	410	—	—	—
2024[e]	—	—	—	3,881	3,466	415	—	—	—

—Not available.

[a]Includes teachers in local public school systems and in most private schools (religiously affiliated and nonsectarian). Teachers are reported in terms of full-time equivalents.

[b]Data through 1995 are for institutions of higher education, while later data are for degree-granting institutions. Degree-granting institutions grant associate's or higher degrees and participate in Title IV federal financial aid programs. The degree-granting classification is very similar to the earlier higher education classification, but it includes more 2-year colleges and excludes a few higher education institutions that did not grant degrees. Includes full-time and part-time faculty with the rank of instructor or above in colleges, universities, professional schools, and 2-year colleges. Excludes teaching assistants.

[c]Estimated.

[d]Inclusion of institutions is not consistent with surveys for 1987 and later years.

[e]Projected.

[f]Data for elementary and secondary teachers are projected and data for degree-granting institutions faculty are actual.

Note: Detail may not sum to totals because of rounding. Some data have been revised from previously published figures. Headcounts are used to report data for degree-granting institutions faculty.

SOURCE: "Table 105.40. Number of Teachers in Elementary and Secondary Schools, and Faculty in Degree-Granting Postsecondary Institutions, by Control of Institution: Selected Years, Fall 1970 through Fall 2024," in "Most Current Digest Tables," *Digest of Education Statistics*, U.S. Department of Education, Institute of Education Sciences, National Center for Education Statistics, March 2015, https://nces.ed.gov/programs/digest/d14/tables/xls/tabn105.40.xls (accessed July 31, 2015)

2014/2014077.pdf), Rebecca Goldring, Soheyla Tate, and Minsun Riddles provide some selected findings from the 2012–13 Teacher Follow-Up Survey. The percentage of teachers who left teaching each year increased between the 1988–89 and 2004–05 academic years. In 1988–89, 5.6% of public school teachers left the profession, and in 2004–05, 8.4% left. (See Table 8.2.) This percentage dropped slightly during the 2008–09 academic year, with 8% of public school teachers leaving the profession. By 2012–13 the percentage of public school teachers who left the profession fell to 7.7%. Of the 8.1% of public school teachers who moved to a different school during the 2012–13 academic year, 58.8% moved to a different public school in the same district, 38.2% moved to a public school in a different district, and 2.9% left public school to teach in a private school.

TABLE 8.2

Percentage of public elementary and secondary school teachers who remained at the same school, moved to a different school, or left teaching, by selected teacher and school characteristics, selected years 1987–88 to 2012–13

	Percent of public school teachers										
							2011–12 to 2012–13				
								Moved to another school			
			Left teaching						Teachers who moved, by destination		
Selected teacher or school characteristic	1987–88 to 1988–89	1993–94 to 1994–95	1999–2000 to 2000–01	2003–04 to 2004–05	2007–08 to 2008–09	Remained in same school	Total moving to another school	Public school in same school district	Public school in different district	Private school	Left teaching
Total	5.6	6.6	7.4	8.4	8.0	84.3	8.1	58.8	38.2	2.9	7.7
Sex											
Male	5.1	5.2	7.4	7.7	7.9	85.7	7.9	46.4	51.2	2.3!	6.4
Female	5.8	7.1	7.4	8.6	8.0	83.8	8.1	62.6	34.3	3.1	8.1
Race/ethnicity											
White	5.7	6.5	7.5	8.2	8.0	85.0	7.5	58.7	37.7	3.6	7.5
Black	5.1!	6.6	7.4	11.0	9.0	78.2	11.7!	64.2	35.2!	‡	10.1!
Hispanic	2.9	9.1	7.5	9.3	5.6!	79.4	12.6	57.9	41.4	‡	8.0!
Asian/Pacific Islander	‡	2.4	2.1!	‡	8.0!	95.5	‡	‡	‡	‡	‡
Asian	—	—	—	‡	9.6!	95.8	‡	‡	‡	‡	‡
Pacific Islander	—	—	—	‡	‡	‡	‡	‡	‡	‡	‡
American Indian/Alaska Native	‡	3.5!	7.6!	1.9!	‡	‡	‡	‡	‡	‡	‡
Two or more races	—	—	—	‡	‡	88.8	‡	‡	‡	‡	‡
Age											
Less than 25	4.3	3.8	9.3	4.8	8.7!	73.8	17.1	35.1	60.0	‡	‡
25 to 29	9.0	10.0	9.7	10.6	9.4	80.0	12.9	50.9	43.9	5.2!	7.1
30 to 39	5.8	6.7	6.5	6.8	8.4	86.3	8.5	59.0	39.7	1.3!	5.3
40 to 49	2.4	3.9	4.6	5.3	3.9	90.1	5.9	65.9	33.3	‡	4.0
50 to 59	5.7	6.3	8.1	9.8	8.4	83.0	6.6	67.5	29.0	‡	10.5
60 to 64	23.4	30.5	25.7	28.0	17.5	73.3	7.0!	52.9!	‡	‡	19.7
65 and over	‡	34.1	16.6!	21.2	10.4!	70.0	‡	‡	‡	‡	24.8!
Full- and part-time teaching experience											
1 year or less	7.9	5.7	10.5	9.6	11.4!	79.0	13.4!	43.2	52.6	‡	7.6!
2 years	7.3	9.1	8.5	6.4	8.8!	78.0	14.5	26.0	68.1	5.9!	7.5!
3 years	9.3	9.8	7.5	7.7	9.0!	84.0	9.8	46.1	48.0	‡	6.2
4 to 10 years	6.4	6.8	7.3	8.1	8.1	81.3	11.3	62.0	36.3	1.8!	7.4
11 to 20 years	3.5	4.9	5.2	5.5	4.3	89.5	5.3	63.1	35.6	‡	5.2
21 to 25 years	3.5	4.0	4.2	6.6	5.8!	87.5	6.6!	63.1	35.1!	‡	5.9
More than 25 years	11.3	12.0	11.4	14.3	12.6	79.4	4.5	73.5	‡	‡	16.1
Grade level taught											
Elementary (preK–grade 8)	5.5	6.4	6.8	8.4	7.9	84.1	8.9	66.5	30.5	3.0!	7.1
Secondary (grades 9–12)	5.6	6.7	8.6	8.4	8.0	84.5	7.2	48.8	48.4	2.8	8.3
School size											
Less than 150	7.3	6.4	9.5	12.1	‡	85.4	7.6!	36.5	59.0	‡	7.0
150 to 349	4.8	7.8	6.7	10.3	7.3	84.2	8.1	49.1	47.1	3.7!	7.7
350 to 499	6.1	5.8	7.4	8.6	9.4	84.2	8.0	66.0	30.8	‡	7.8
500 to 749	5.6	7.6	7.1	7.0	5.3	82.9	9.2	68.6	28.2	‡	7.8
750 or more	5.0	5.7	7.7	8.2	8.9	85.1	7.3	51.9	45.9	2.2!	7.5
Percent of students who are Black, Hispanic, Asian, Pacific Islander, American Indian/Alaska Native, or two or more races*											
Less than 5 percent	5.1	8.0	6.8	7.6	8.6	85.9	7.6!	79.2	‡	‡	6.5
5 to 19 percent	5.8	6.0	6.8	7.5	7.8	87.6	5.4	46.8	50.6	2.6!	7.0
20 to 49 percent	5.2	6.2	9.4	6.5	8.1	86.4	7.3	62.0	34.2	3.8!	6.3
50 percent or more	5.3	6.8	6.8	10.3	7.9	80.5	10.4	62.7	34.1	3.2!	9.1

TABLE 8.2

Percentage of public elementary and secondary school teachers who remained at the same school, moved to a different school, or left teaching, by selected teacher and school characteristics, selected years 1987–88 to 2012–13 [CONTINUED]

	Percent of public school teachers										
						2011–12 to 2012–13					
								Moved to another school			
		Left teaching						Teachers who moved, by destination			
Selected teacher or school characteristic	1987–88 to 1988–89	1993–94 to 1994–95	1999–2000 to 2000–01	2003–04 to 2004–05	2007–08 to 2008–09	Remained in same school	Total moving to another school	Public school in same school district	Public school in different district	Private school	Left teaching
Percent of students approved for free or reduced-price lunch											
0 to 25.0 percent	—	—	—	7.3	9.8	87.8	6.2	61.4	36.3	‡	6.0
25.1 to 50.0 percent	—	—	—	9.0	8.8	85.8	6.2	58.4	39.1	‡	7.9
50.1 to 75.0 percent	—	—	—	10.4	5.5	84.1	8.7	55.9	40.5	‡	7.1
More than 75.0 percent	—	—	—	14.3	14.3	77.9	12.3	60.8	36.7	2.5!	9.9
School did not respond or did not participate in program	—	—	—	8.1	8.4	85.8	‡	40.0!	36.7!	‡	10.7!
Locale											
City	—	—	—	10.1	7.5	82.3	9.7	66.2	30.9	2.9!	7.9
Suburban	—	—	—	8.3	8.3	84.9	7.8	60.0	36.9	3.1!	7.3
Town	—	—	—	6.5	7.5!	86.3	7.3	55.0	39.9	‡	6.4
Rural	—	—	—	7.9	8.4	84.6	7.0	48.9	49.3	‡	8.4

—Not available.

!Interpret data with caution. The coefficient of variation (CV) for this estimate is between 30 and 50 percent.

‡Reporting standards not met. Either there are too few cases for a reliable estimate or the coefficient of variation (CV) is 50 percent or greater..

*Data were not available for approximately 4 percent of teachers for 2011–12 to 2012–13.

Note: Race categories exclude persons of Hispanic ethnicity. Detail may not sum to totals because of rounding.

SOURCE: Adapted from "Table 210.30. Mobility of Public Elementary and Secondary Teachers, by Selected Teacher and School Characteristics: Selected Years, 1987–88 through 2012–13," in "Most Current Digest Tables," *Digest of Education Statistics*, U.S. Department of Education, Institute of Education Sciences, National Center for Education Statistics, October 2014, https://nces.ed.gov/programs/digest/d14/tables/xls/tabn210.30.xls (accessed July 31, 2015)

Teacher Education

Goldring, Gray, and Bitterman examine the percentage distribution of school teachers by the highest degree earned for the 2011–12 academic year. Most teachers (96.3% of all public school teachers and 91.6% of all private school teachers) had earned at least a bachelor's degree. A high percentage of teachers held graduate degrees; 47.7% of public school teachers and 35.8% of private school teachers had earned a master's degree. In addition, 8.7% of public school teachers and 7.3% of private school teachers had earned degrees higher than a master's degree, such as an educational specialist or professional diploma, a certificate of advance graduate studies, or a doctorate or first professional degree.

Goldring, Gray, and Bitterman also reveal that public school teachers on the secondary level were slightly more likely than public school teachers on the elementary level to have a master's degree (49.6% versus 47.3%, respectively). In addition, public school teachers on the middle school level (9.2%) were slightly more likely than public school teachers on the secondary level (8.8%) or the elementary (8.4%) level to hold a degree higher than a master's. This difference was much more pronounced within the population of private school teachers. Secondary private school teachers were much more likely than elementary private

school teachers to hold master's degrees (45% versus 32.7%, respectively) or to have a higher degree (8.7% versus 6.1%, respectively). With respect to charter schools, their teachers were much less likely to have a master's degree than teachers in traditional public schools (37.3% versus 48%, respectively) or to have a degree higher than a master's (6.3% versus 8.8%, respectively).

Besides holding postsecondary degrees, U.S. teachers typically earn some level of certification to teach in public schools. As Table 8.3 shows, certification requirements vary by state. In many instances public school teachers must pass a basic skills exam, a subject matter exam, and a knowledge of teaching exam to receive certification. In addition, most states require that teachers receive a satisfactory assessment of their performance in the classroom to be certified. In 2013 and 2014 Iowa was the only state with no certification exam or in-class assessment for public school teachers; six other states (Maine, Mississippi, New Jersey, North Carolina, Oklahoma, and Wyoming) did not provide certification data for either year.

Student-Teacher Ratio and Teacher Supply

The student-teacher ratio is the number of students per teacher. Educators prefer a low number of students

TABLE 8.3

Teacher certification requirements, by assessment type and state, 2013 and 2014

State	Assessment for certification, 2013				Assessment for certification, 2014			
	Basic skills exam	Subject-matter exam	Knowledge of teaching exam	Assessment of teaching performance	Basic skills exam	Subject-matter exam	Knowledge of teaching exam	Assessment of teaching performance
Alabama	X	X	X	X	X	X	X	X
Alaska	X				X			
Arizona		X	X			X	X	
Arkansas	X	X	X		X	X	X	X
California	X	—		X	X	—		X
Colorado		X				X		
Connecticut	X	X	—	—	X	X	—	—
Delaware	X	X			X	X		
District of Columbia	X	X	X		X	X	X	
Florida	X			X	X			X
Georgia	X	X			X	X		
Hawaii	X	X		—	X	X		—
Idaho		X		X		X		X
Illinois	X	X	X		X	X	X	
Indiana	X	X		X	X	X		X
Iowa								
Kansas		X	X			X	X	
Kentucky	X	X	X	X	X	X	X	X
Louisiana	X	X	X	X	X	X	X	X
Maine	—	—	—	—	—	—	—	—
Maryland	X	X	X	X	X	X	X	X
Massachusetts	X	X		X	X	X		X
Michigan	X	X		X	X	X		X
Minnesota	X	X	X			X	X	
Mississippi	—	—	—	—	—	—	—	—
Missouri	X	X		X	X	X		X
Montana								
Nebraska	X				X			
Nevada	—	X	—	—	—	X	—	—
New Hampshire	X	X			X	X		
New Jersey	—	—	—	—	—	—	—	—
New Mexico	X	X	X	X	X	X	X	X
New York		X	X			X	X	
North Carolina	—	—	—	—	—	—	—	—
North Dakota	—	X	—	—		X	—	—
Ohio		X	X	X		X	X	X
Oklahoma	—	—	—	—	—	—	—	—
Oregon	X	X		X	X	X		X
Pennsylvania	X	X	X	X	X	X	X	X
Rhode Island			X	X			X	X
South Carolina		X	X			X	X	
South Dakota	X	X	X	X	X	X	X	X
Tennessee	X	X	X		X	X	X	
Texas	X	X	X	X	X	X	X	X
Utah		X		X		X		X
Vermont	X	X			X	X		
Virginia	X	X	X		X	X	X	
Washington	X	X		X	X	X		X
West Virginia	X	X	X	X	X	X	X	X
Wisconsin	X	X			X	X		
Wyoming	—		—	—	—		—	—

—Not available.

X = Denotes that the state requires testing. A blank denotes that the state does not require testing.

SOURCE: "Table 234.50. Required Testing for Initial Certification of Elementary and Secondary School Teachers, by Type of Assessment and State: 2013 and 2014," in "Most Current Digest Tables," *Digest of Education Statistics*, U.S. Department of Education, Institute of Education Sciences, National Center for Education Statistics, November 2014, https://nces.ed.gov/programs/digest/d14/tables/xls/tabn234.50.xls (accessed July 31, 2015)

per teacher, which allows teachers to spend more time with each student. Table 8.4 provides data on student-teacher ratios between 1955 and 2012. Overall, the average number of students in public elementary and secondary classrooms fell steadily during this period, from 26.9 in 1955 to 16 in 2012. Private school class sizes experienced an even more dramatic decrease over this span, falling from 31.7 in 1955 to 12.5 in 2012.

According to the NCES (March 2015, https://nces .ed.gov/programs/digest/d14/tables/dt14_208.10.asp?current =yes), schools with smaller total enrollments typically have smaller class sizes. For example, in schools with a total enrollment of under 300 students in 2012, the average class size was 12.7. By contrast, schools with an overall student body of 1,500 or more had an average class size of 18.8. On average, combined elementary and

TABLE 8.4

Actual and projected numbers of elementary and secondary school teachers, with total enrollment, student-teacher ratios, and new teacher hires, by type of institution, selected years 1955–2024

Year	Teachers (in thousands)			Enrollment (in thousands)			Pupil/teacher ratio			Number of new teacher hires (in thousands)[a]		
	Total	Public	Private	Total	Public	Private	Total	Public	Private	Total	Public	Private
1955	1,286	1,141	145[b]	35,280	30,680	4,600[b]	27.4	26.9	31.7[b]	—	—	—
1960	1,600	1,408	192[b]	42,181	36,281	5,900[b]	26.4	25.8	30.7[b]	—	—	—
1965	1,933	1,710	223	48,473	42,173	6,300	25.1	24.7	28.3	—	—	—
1970	2,292	2,059	233	51,257	45,894	5,363	22.4	22.3	23.0	—	—	—
1971	2,293	2,063	230[b]	51,271	46,071	5,200[b]	22.4	22.3	22.6[b]	—	—	—
1972	2,337	2,106	231[b]	50,726	45,726	5,000[b]	21.7	21.7	21.6[b]	—	—	—
1973	2,372	2,136	236[b]	50,445	45,445	5,000[b]	21.3	21.3	21.2[b]	—	—	—
1974	2,410	2,165	245[b]	50,073	45,073	5,000[b]	20.8	20.8	20.4[b]	—	—	—
1975	2,453	2,198	255[b]	49,819	44,819	5,000[b]	20.3	20.4	19.6[b]	—	—	—
1976	2,457	2,189	268	49,478	44,311	5,167	20.1	20.2	19.3	—	—	—
1977	2,488	2,209	279	48,717	43,577	5,140	19.6	19.7	18.4	—	—	—
1978	2,479	2,207	272	47,637	42,551	5,086	19.2	19.3	18.7	—	—	—
1979	2,461	2,185	276[b]	46,651	41,651	5,000[b]	19.0	19.1	18.1[b]	—	—	—
1980	2,485	2,184	301	46,208	40,877	5,331	18.6	18.7	17.7	—	—	—
1981	2,440	2,127	313[b]	45,544	40,044	5,500[b]	18.7	18.8	17.6[b]	—	—	—
1982	2,458	2,133	325[b]	45,166	39,566	5,600[b]	18.4	18.6	17.2[b]	—	—	—
1983	2,476	2,139	337	44,967	39,252	5,715	18.2	18.4	17.0	—	—	—
1984	2,508	2,168	340[b]	44,908	39,208	5,700[b]	17.9	18.1	16.8[b]	—	—	—
1985	2,549	2,206	343	44,979	39,422	5,557	17.6	17.9	16.2	—	—	—
1986	2,592	2,244	348[b]	45,205	39,753	5,452[b]	17.4	17.7	15.7[b]	—	—	—
1987	2,631	2,279	352	45,488	40,008	5,479	17.3	17.6	15.6	—	—	—
1988	2,668	2,323	345[b]	45,430	40,189	5,242[b]	17.0	17.3	15.2[b]	—	—	—
1989	2,713	2,357	356	46,141	40,543	5,599	17.0	17.2	15.7	—	—	—
1990	2,759	2,398	361[b]	46,864	41,217	5,648[b]	17.0	17.2	15.6[b]	—	—	—
1991	2,797	2,432	365	47,728	42,047	5,681	17.1	17.3	15.6	—	—	—
1992	2,823	2,459	364[b]	48,694	42,823	5,870[b]	17.2	17.4	16.1[b]	—	—	—
1993	2,868	2,504	364	49,532	43,465	6,067	17.3	17.4	16.7	—	—	—
1994	2,922	2,552	370[b]	50,106	44,111	5,994[b]	17.1	17.3	16.2[b]	—	—	—
1995	2,974	2,598	376	50,759	44,840	5,918	17.1	17.3	15.7	—	—	—
1996	3,051	2,667	384[b]	51,544	45,611	5,933[b]	16.9	17.1	15.5[b]	—	—	—
1997	3,138	2,746	391	52,071	46,127	5,944	16.6	16.8	15.2	—	—	—
1998	3,230	2,830	400[b]	52,526	46,539	5,988[b]	16.3	16.4	15.0[b]	—	—	—
1999	3,319	2,911	408	52,875	46,857	6,018	15.9	16.1	14.7	305	222	83
2000	3,366	2,941	424[b]	53,373	47,204	6,169[b]	15.9	16.0	14.5[b]	—	—	—
2001	3,440	3,000	441	53,992	47,672	6,320	15.7	15.9	14.3	—	—	—
2002	3,476	3,034	442[b]	54,403	48,183	6,220[b]	15.7	15.9	14.1[b]	—	—	—
2003	3,490	3,049	441	54,639	48,540	6,099	15.7	15.9	13.8	311	236	74
2004	3,536	3,091	445[b]	54,882	48,795	6,087[b]	15.5	15.8	13.7[b]	—	—	—
2005	3,593	3,143	450	55,187	49,113	6,073	15.4	15.6	13.5	—	—	—
2006	3,622	3,166	456[b]	55,307	49,316	5,991[b]	15.3	15.6	13.2[b]	—	—	—
2007	3,656	3,200	456	55,201	49,291	5,910	15.1	15.4	13.0	241	173	68
2008	3,670	3,222	448[b]	54,973	49,266	5,707[b]	15.0	15.3	12.8[b]	—	—	—
2009	3,647	3,210	437	54,849	49,361	5,488	15.0	15.4	12.5	—	—	—
2010	3,529	3,099	429[b]	54,867	49,484	5,382[b]	15.5	16.0	12.5[b]	—	—	—
2011	3,524	3,103	421	54,790	49,522	5,268	15.5	16.0	12.5	241	173	68
2012	3,523	3,109	414[b]	54,952	49,771	5,181[c]	15.6	16.0	12.5[c]	321	247	74
2013[c]	3,527	3,120	407	55,036	49,942	5,094	15.6	16.0	12.5	319	250	69
2014[c]	3,520	3,122	398	54,965	49,986	4,979	15.6	16.0	12.5	310	244	66
2015[c]	3,521	3,129	391	54,994	50,094	4,899	15.6	16.0	12.5	316	249	67
2016[c]	3,525	3,138	387	55,077	50,229	4,848	15.6	16.0	12.5	318	250	68
2017[c]	3,577	3,185	392	55,447	50,584	4,863	15.5	15.9	12.4	364	288	76
2018[c]	3,617	3,224	393	55,719	50,871	4,848	15.4	15.8	12.3	358	283	74
2019[c]	3,660	3,264	395	56,031	51,183	4,848	15.3	15.7	12.3	361	286	76
2020[c]	3,700	3,302	398	56,404	51,547	4,856	15.2	15.6	12.2	362	285	76
2021[c]	3,743	3,342	401	56,779	51,910	4,869	15.2	15.5	12.1	367	289	77
2022[c]	3,788	3,383	405	57,151	52,260	4,891	15.1	15.4	12.1	371	292	79
2023[c]	3,840	3,429	410	57,524	52,601	4,922	15.0	15.3	12.0	381	300	81
2024[c]	3,881	3,466	415	57,872	52,920	4,952	14.9	15.3	11.9	375	293	81

secondary schools (14.3) had smaller class sizes than elementary schools (16.3) or secondary schools (16.5) in 2012.

CAREER OUTLOOK FOR TEACHERS

In August 2012 the Executive Office of the President issued the report *Investing in Our Future: Returning Teachers to the Classroom* (http://www.whitehouse.gov/sites/default/files/Investing_in_Our_Future_Report.pdf). The report notes that 312,700 educator jobs were lost between June 2009 and August 2012. Unlike the seven previous recessions dating to 1958, the 2009–12 downturn was the only instance when the education sector suffered a net employment loss 37 months after the end of a recession. For example, in the three years following

TABLE 8.4

Actual and projected numbers of elementary and secondary school teachers, with total enrollment, student-teacher ratios, and new teacher hires, by type of institution, selected years 1955–2024 [CONTINUED]

—Not available.

[a]A teacher is considered to be a new hire for a public or private school if the teacher had not taught in that control of school in the previous year. A teacher who moves from a public to private or a private to public school is considered a new teacher hire, but a teacher who moves from one public school to another public school or one private school to another private school is not considered a new teacher hire.

[b]Estimated.

[c]Projected.

Note: Data for teachers are expressed in full-time equivalents (FTE). Counts of private school teachers and enrollment include prekindergarten through grade 12 in schools offering kindergarten or higher grades. Counts of public school teachers and enrollment include prekindergarten through grade 12. The pupil/teacher ratio includes teachers for students with disabilities and other special teachers, while these teachers are generally excluded from class size calculations. Ratios for public schools reflect totals reported by states and differ from totals reported for schools or school districts. Some data have been revised from previously published figures. Detail may not sum to totals because of rounding.

SOURCE: "Table 208.20. Public and Private Elementary and Secondary Teachers, Enrollment, Pupil/Teacher Ratios, and New Teacher Hires: Selected Years, Fall 1955 through Fall 2024," in "Most Current Digest Tables," *Digest of Education Statistics*, U.S. Department of Education, Institute of Education Sciences, National Center for Education Statistics, March 2015, https://nces.ed.gov/programs/digest/d14/tables/xls/tabn208.20.xls (accessed July 31, 2015)

the recession of 2001, education employment rose 3.2%. In contrast, between June 2009 and July 2012 education employment fell 3.9%.

The administration of Barack Obama (1961–) notes in *Investing in Our Future* that cuts in education resulting from state and local governmental budget shortfalls, including the loss of teacher jobs, were having a devastating effect on the U.S. education system. The report states that, as part of his 2013 budget, President Obama proposed designating $25 billion to help state and local governments "retain, rehire, and hire early childhood, elementary, and secondary educators."

In spite of high teacher job loss from 2009 through 2012, the U.S. Bureau of Labor Statistics (BLS) still foresees average job growth for most teaching sectors in the period between 2012 and 2022. The BLS predicts in "Kindergarten and Elementary School Teachers" (January 8, 2014, http://www.bls.gov/ooh/education-training-and-library/kindergarten-and-elementary-school-teachers.htm) the addition of 188,400 kindergarten and elementary teachers to the education workforce between 2012 and 2022, an increase of 12%. The BLS predicts similar percentage growth at the middle school level in "Middle School Teachers" (January 8, 2014, http://www.bls.gov/ooh/education-training-and-library/middle-school-teachers.htm), forecasting the addition of 76,000 positions to the middle school workforce by 2022. The only teachers expected to see lower-than-average job growth were on the high school level. In "High School Teachers" (January 8, 2014, http://www.bls.gov/ooh/education-training-and-library/high-school-teachers.htm), the BLS predicts that the number of high school teachers is expected to grow by only 6% between 2012 and 2022, with the addition of 52,900 new positions.

Teacher Tenure

In most states teachers are unionized and have relatively good job security through state tenure laws. In states with "time-served" teacher tenure, teachers are eligible

TABLE 8.5

Public opinion on the practice of granting tenure to teachers, by parent/teacher status and race/ethnicity, 2014

	Public	Parents	Teachers	African Americans	Hispanics
Strongly favor	5%	5%	23%	8%	7%
Somewhat favor	21	20	28	29	23
Somewhat oppose	32	25	30	26	29
Strongly oppose	25	29	8	11	23
Neither favor nor oppose	18	22	11	26	19

SOURCE: Michael B. Henderson, Paul E. Peterson, and Martin R. West, "Table 24b. Teachers with tenure cannot be dismissed unless a school district follows detailed procedures. Some say that tenure provides teachers with the necessary independence for their work. Others say that it makes it too difficult to replace ineffective teachers. We want to know what you think of tenure. Do you favor or oppose giving tenure to teachers?" in "*Education Next*—Program on Education Policy and Governance—Survey 2014," *Education Next*, Harvard Program on Education Policy and Governance, 2015, http://educationnext.org/files/2014ednextpoll.pdf (accessed July 31, 2015)

for tenure when they satisfactorily complete a probationary period, which protects them from being fired without a full investigation and due process procedures. Those who favor teacher tenure say it helps protect teachers from being fired for political or arbitrary reasons. Those who oppose teacher tenure say the policy makes it difficult to fire ineffective teachers. Many states are eliminating or reforming teacher tenure laws as they grapple with heavy deficits so that they can more easily fire underperforming teachers. The American Federation of Teachers (AFT) and the National Education Association (NEA) favor reform of teacher tenure rather than its elimination.

In general, the American public is opposed to the practice of granting public school teachers tenure. In 2014 over half (57%) of Americans either strongly opposed (25%) or somewhat opposed (32%) giving tenure to public school teachers; a little over a quarter (26%) of Americans either strongly favored (5%) or somewhat favored (21%) the practice of granting tenure, while 18% expressed no opinion either way. (See Table 8.5.) African Americans and

Hispanics were decidedly mixed on the issue of giving public school teachers tenure. Thirty-seven percent of African Americans either strongly favored (8%) or somewhat favored (29%) granting tenure to public school teachers, compared with 37% who either strongly opposed (11%) or somewhat opposed (26%) the practice; 26% expressed no opinion about teacher tenure in 2014. Hispanics viewed teacher tenure less favorably. That year, 30% of Hispanics either strongly favored (7%) or somewhat favored (23%) tenure for public school teachers, while 52% either strongly opposed (23%) or somewhat opposed (29%) teacher tenure, and 19% neither opposed nor supported the idea.

TEACHER EXPERIENCE

Goldring, Gray, and Bitterman note that most of the U.S. teacher workforce is experienced, with 88.1% of public school teachers during the 2011–12 school year having four or more years of full-time teaching experience. Percentages were lower for charter schools (73.7%) and schools with enrollments of less than 100 students (83.9%).

For private school teachers, Goldring, Gray, and Bitterman note that 83.9% had four or more years of full-time teaching experience during the 2011–12 school year. Percentages were higher in some types of schools. Catholic schools (86.2%) and large schools with enrollments of between 500 and 749 students (88%) had the highest percentages of private school teachers with four or more years of teaching experience. Private school teachers in cities (85.6%) were more likely to have four or more years of experience than private school teachers in towns (81.9%) in 2011–12.

SALARIES

Table 8.6 shows teachers' salaries for selected school years between 1959–60 and 2013–14. Using constant 2013–14 dollars is a way to examine the salaries over the years to see if they have comparatively increased or decreased. Salaries rose from an equivalent of $39,943 in 1959–60 to $53,655 in 1969–70. Salaries continued to rise through the 1972–73 school year, to $55,843. During these years student enrollments increased as the majority of the baby boomers (people born between 1946 and 1964) made their way through elementary and high school. Teachers were recruited to instruct burgeoning school populations.

According to Grace Kena et al., in *The Condition of Education 2015* (May 2015, http://nces.ed.gov/pubs2013/2013037.pdf), school enrollments began falling during the early 1970s and declined through 1985. As school enrollments fell, the average teacher salary fell as well. Table 8.6 shows that the average teacher salary for the 1980–81 school year was $47,858 in constant 2013–14 dollars, which was nearly $8,000 less than the 1972–73

school year. However, by the 1986–87 school year the average teacher salary had risen again as enrollments rose when children of the baby boomers entered and made their way through school. The average teacher salary has leveled off since then. The average teacher salaries of the 2012–13 ($56,979) and 2013–14 ($56,689) school years were not much different from that of the 1986–87 ($56,124) school year in constant 2013–14 dollars.

Table 8.7 provides a breakdown of public school teacher salaries by state for selected school years between 1969–70 and 2013–14. Massachusetts had the highest teacher salaries in 2013–14, paying an average of $73,736 to public elementary and secondary school teachers that year; the District of Columbia had the second-highest annual teacher salaries, paying public school teachers $73,162 on average. By contrast, South Dakota ($40,023), Mississippi ($42,187), and Oklahoma ($44,277) paid the lowest annual public school teacher salaries in the nation in 2013–14.

Comparisons of Teacher Salaries

According to the BLS, in the press release *Occupational Employment and Wages—May 2014* (March 25, 2015, http://www.bls.gov/news.release/pdf/ocwage.pdf), the mean (average) annual salary of full-time elementary and middle school teachers was $57,080 in 2014, which was slightly lower than full-time secondary school teachers ($59,180). On average, kindergarten teachers earned $53,480. Average preschool teacher salaries were considerably lower, at $32,040. By contrast, special education preschool teachers earned considerably more in 2014, with an average annual salary of $57,860. Overall, special education teachers at all levels earned an average salary of $58,850 in 2014.

According to the BLS, the mean annual earnings of full-time college and university teachers was $75,780 in 2014, which was significantly higher than earnings for elementary and secondary teachers. With an average annual salary of $126,270, law professors earned more than teachers in any other field at the postsecondary level in 2014; other postsecondary disciplines commanding high average salaries in 2014 included health specialties ($112,950), health ($102,260), economics ($102,120), and engineering ($102,000). By contrast, postsecondary vocational education instructors earned average salaries of $53,130 in 2014, while graduate assistants at the postsecondary level earned $32,970.

Merit Pay: Payment for Student Performance?

One debate in the public forum is whether teachers' salaries should be based on their students' academic progress on state tests. John Rosales of the NEA notes in "Pay Based on Test Scores?" (2015, http://www.nea.org/home/36780.htm) that the Obama administration favors using

TABLE 8.6

Estimated annual salary of teachers in public elementary and secondary schools, selected years 1959–60 to 2013–14

| School year | Current dollars | | | | | Average public school teachers' salary in constant 2013–14 dollars[a] | | |
| | Average public school teachers' salary | | | Wage and salary accruals per full-time-equivalent (FTE) employee[b] | Ratio of average teachers' salary to accruals per FTE employee | | | |
	All teachers	Elementary teachers	Secondary teachers			All teachers	Elementary teachers	Secondary teachers
1959–60	$4,995	$4,815	$5,276	$4,749	1.05	$39,943	$38,504	$42,190
1961–62	5,515	5,340	5,775	5,063	1.09	43,111	41,743	45,144
1963–64	5,995	5,805	6,266	5,478	1.09	45,672	44,225	47,737
1965–66	6,485	6,279	6,761	5,934	1.09	47,755	46,238	49,787
1967–68	7,423	7,208	7,692	6,533	1.14	51,287	49,801	53,145
1969–70	8,626	8,412	8,891	7,486	1.15	53,655	52,324	55,303
1970–71	9,268	9,021	9,568	7,998	1.16	54,818	53,358	56,593
1971–72	9,705	9,424	10,031	8,521	1.14	55,415	53,811	57,277
1972–73	10,174	9,893	10,507	9,056	1.12	55,843	54,301	57,671
1973–74	10,770	10,507	11,077	9,667	1.11	54,275	52,950	55,822
1974–75	11,641	11,334	12,000	10,411	1.12	52,812	51,419	54,441
1975–76	12,600	12,280	12,937	11,194	1.13	53,384	52,028	54,812
1976–77	13,354	12,989	13,776	11,971	1.12	53,461	52,000	55,150
1977–78	14,198	13,845	14,602	12,811	1.11	53,263	51,939	54,779
1978–79	15,032	14,681	15,450	13,807	1.09	51,562	50,358	52,996
1979–80	15,970	15,569	16,459	15,050	1.06	48,335	47,122	49,815
1980–81	17,644	17,230	18,142	16,461	1.07	47,858	46,736	49,209
1981–82	19,274	18,853	19,805	17,795	1.08	48,123	47,072	49,449
1982–83	20,695	20,227	21,291	18,873	1.10	49,543	48,422	50,970
1983–84	21,935	21,487	22,554	19,781	1.11	50,637	49,603	52,066
1984–85	23,600	23,200	24,187	20,694	1.14	52,428	51,540	53,732
1985–86	25,199	24,718	25,846	21,685	1.16	54,412	53,373	55,809
1986–87	26,569	26,057	27,244	22,700	1.17	56,124	55,042	57,550
1987–88	28,034	27,519	28,798	23,777	1.18	56,862	55,818	58,412
1988–89	29,564	29,022	30,218	24,752	1.19	57,318	56,268	58,586
1989–90	31,367	30,832	32,049	25,762	1.22	58,044	57,054	59,306
1990–91	33,084	32,490	33,896	26,935	1.23	58,048	57,006	59,473
1991–92	34,063	33,479	34,827	28,169	1.21	57,910	56,917	59,209
1992–93	35,029	34,350	35,880	29,245	1.20	57,749	56,629	59,152
1993–94	35,737	35,233	36,566	30,030	1.19	57,428	56,618	58,760
1994–95	36,675	36,088	37,523	30,857	1.19	57,293	56,376	58,618
1995–96	37,642	37,138	38,397	31,822	1.18	57,247	56,480	58,395
1996–97	38,443	38,039	39,184	33,058	1.16	56,843	56,246	57,939
1997–98	39,350	39,002	39,944	34,635	1.14	57,165	56,659	58,027
1998–99	40,544	40,165	41,203	36,277	1.12	57,897	57,356	58,838
1999–2000	41,807	41,306	42,546	38,144	1.10	58,025	57,330	59,051
2000–01	43,378	42,910	44,053	39,727	1.09	58,211	57,583	59,117
2001–02	44,655	44,177	45,310	40,589	1.10	58,883	58,252	59,746
2002–03	45,686	45,408	46,106	41,629	1.10	58,947	58,588	59,489
2003–04	46,542	46,187	46,976	43,259	1.08	58,765	58,317	59,313
2004–05	47,516	47,122	47,688	44,908	1.06	58,243	57,760	58,453
2005–06	49,086	48,573	49,496	46,626	1.05	57,960	57,354	58,444
2006–07	51,052	50,740	51,529	48,713	1.05	58,762	58,403	59,311
2007–08	52,800	52,385	53,262	50,504	1.05	58,602	58,142	59,115
2008–09	54,319	53,998	54,552	51,409	1.06	59,458	59,107	59,713
2009–10	55,202	54,918	55,595	52,413	1.05	59,845	59,537	60,271
2010–11	55,623	55,217	56,225	53,975	1.03	59,115	58,683	59,755
2011–12	55,418	54,704	56,226	55,435	1.00	57,220	56,483	58,055
2012–13	56,103	55,344	57,077	56,361	1.00	56,979	56,208	57,969
2013–14	56,689	56,015	57,593	—	—	56,689	56,015	57,593

—Not available.

[a]Constant dollars based on the Consumer Price Index, prepared by the Bureau of Labor Statistics, U.S. Department of Labor, adjusted to a school-year basis.

[b]The average monetary remuneration earned by FTE employees across all industries in a given year, including wages, salaries, commissions, tips, bonuses, voluntary employee contributions to certain deferred compensation plans, and receipts in kind that represent income. Calendar-year data from the U.S. Department of Commerce, Bureau of Economic Analysis, have been converted to a school-year basis by averaging the two appropriate calendar years in each case.

Note: Some data have been revised from previously published figures.

SOURCE: Table 211.50. Estimated Average Annual Salary of Teachers in Public Elementary and Secondary Schools: Selected Years, 1959–60 through 2013–14," in "Most Current Digest Tables," *Digest of Education Statistics*, U.S. Department of Education, Institute of Education Sciences, National Center for Education Statistics, August 2014, https://nces.ed.gov/programs/digest/d14/tables/xls/tabn211.50.xls (accessed July 28, 2015)

student achievement data in the evaluation of teachers. The administration's Race to the Top program appears to give grant funding preference to states that do just that. Rosales notes, however, that there are pitfalls with granting merit pay for increases in student achievement scores: only a narrow portion of the teacher's work is measured, the plan can pit teacher against teacher if a quota system exists, and some teachers do not teach the tested subjects. Opponents also suggest that payment for student performance is not a fair way to compensate teachers due to

TABLE 8.7

Estimated annual salaries of public elementary and secondary school teachers, by state, selected years 1969–70 to 2013–14

State	Current dollars							Constant 2013–14 dollars*							Percent change, 1999–2000 to 2013–14
	1969–70	1979–80	1989–90	1999–2000	2009–10	2012–13	2013–14	1969–70	1979–80	1989–90	1999–2000	2009–10	2012–13	2013–14	
United States	$8,626	$15,970	$31,367	$41,807	$55,202	$56,103	$56,689	$53,655	$48,335	$58,044	$58,025	$59,845	$56,979	$56,689	-2.3
Alabama	6,818	13,060	24,828	36,689	47,571	47,949	48,413	42,409	39,528	45,944	50,922	51,572	48,698	48,413	-4.9
Alaska	10,560	27,210	43,153	46,462	59,672	65,468	66,739	65,685	82,354	79,854	64,486	64,691	66,491	66,739	3.5
Arizona	8,711	15,054	29,402	36,902	46,952	49,885	51,109	54,184	45,563	54,408	51,218	50,901	50,664	51,109	-0.2
Arkansas	6,307	12,299	22,352	33,386	46,700	46,631	46,950	39,230	37,224	41,362	46,338	50,628	47,359	46,950	1.3
California	10,315	18,020	37,998	47,680	68,203	69,324	70,126	64,161	54,540	70,315	66,177	73,940	70,407	70,126	6.0
Colorado	7,761	16,205	30,758	38,163	49,202	49,844	50,651	48,275	49,046	56,917	52,968	53,341	50,623	50,651	-4.4
Connecticut	9,262	16,229	40,461	51,780	64,350	69,397	70,584	57,611	49,119	74,873	71,867	69,763	70,481	70,584	-1.8
Delaware	9,015	16,148	33,377	44,435	57,080	59,679	60,571	56,075	48,874	61,764	61,673	61,881	60,611	60,571	-1.8
District of Columbia	10,285	22,190	38,402	47,076	64,548	70,906	73,162	63,974	67,161	71,063	65,338	69,978	72,014	73,162	12.0
Florida	8,412	14,149	28,803	36,722	46,708	46,598	46,691	52,324	42,824	53,300	50,968	50,637	47,326	46,691	-8.4
Georgia	7,276	13,853	28,006	41,023	53,112	52,880	52,924	45,258	41,928	51,825	56,937	57,580	51,742	52,924	-7.0
Hawaii	9,453	19,920	32,047	40,578	55,063	54,300	56,291	58,799	60,290	59,303	56,320	59,695	55,148	56,291	-0.1
Idaho	6,890	13,611	23,861	35,547	46,283	49,734	50,945	42,857	41,195	44,155	49,337	50,176	50,511	50,945	3.3
Illinois	9,569	17,601	32,794	46,486	62,077	59,113	60,124	59,521	53,271	60,685	64,520	67,299	60,036	60,124	-6.8
Indiana	8,833	15,599	30,902	41,850	49,986	50,065	50,644	54,943	47,212	57,184	58,085	54,191	50,847	50,644	-12.8
Iowa	8,355	15,203	26,747	35,678	49,626	50,946	51,662	51,969	46,014	49,495	49,519	53,800	51,742	51,662	4.3
Kansas	7,612	13,690	28,744	34,981	46,657	47,464	48,221	47,348	41,434	53,190	48,551	50,582	48,205	48,221	-0.7
Kentucky	6,953	14,520	26,292	36,380	49,543	50,203	50,705	43,249	43,946	48,653	50,493	53,710	50,987	50,705	0.4
Louisiana	7,028	13,760	24,300	33,109	48,903	51,381	52,259	43,715	41,646	44,967	45,953	53,017	52,184	52,259	13.7
Maine	7,572	13,071	26,881	35,561	46,106	48,430	49,232	47,099	39,561	49,743	49,356	49,984	49,186	49,232	-0.3
Maryland	9,383	17,558	36,319	44,048	63,971	64,248	64,868	58,364	53,141	67,208	61,136	69,352	65,252	64,868	6.1
Massachusetts	8,764	17,253	34,712	46,580	69,273	72,334	73,736	54,513	52,218	64,234	64,650	75,100	73,464	73,736	14.1
Michigan	9,826	19,663	37,072	49,044	57,958	61,560	61,866	61,119	59,512	68,601	68,070	62,833	62,522	61,866	-9.1
Minnesota	8,658	15,912	32,190	39,802	52,431	56,268	57,230	53,854	48,159	59,567	55,243	56,841	57,147	57,230	3.6
Mississippi	5,798	11,850	24,292	31,857	45,644	41,814	42,187	36,064	35,865	44,952	44,215	49,483	42,467	42,187	-4.6
Missouri	7,799	13,682	27,094	35,656	45,317	47,517	48,329	48,511	41,410	50,137	49,488	49,129	48,259	48,329	-2.3
Montana	7,606	14,537	25,081	32,121	45,759	48,855	49,893	47,310	43,998	46,412	44,582	49,608	49,618	49,893	11.9
Nebraska	7,375	13,516	25,522	33,237	46,227	48,997	49,545	45,874	40,908	47,228	46,131	50,115	49,762	49,545	7.4
Nevada	9,215	16,295	30,590	39,390	51,524	55,957	57,391	57,319	49,319	56,606	54,671	55,858	56,831	57,391	5.0
New Hampshire	7,771	13,017	28,986	37,734	51,443	55,599	57,057	48,337	39,397	53,638	52,372	55,770	56,467	57,057	8.9
New Jersey	9,130	17,161	35,676	52,015	65,130	68,797	70,060	56,790	51,940	66,018	72,193	70,608	69,872	70,060	-3.0
New Mexico	7,796	14,887	24,756	32,554	46,258	45,453	45,727	48,492	45,057	45,811	45,183	50,149	46,163	45,727	1.2
New York	10,336	19,812	38,925	51,020	71,633	75,279	76,566	64,291	59,963	72,030	70,812	77,658	76,455	76,566	8.1
North Carolina	7,494	14,117	27,883	39,404	46,850	45,737	45,355	46,614	42,727	51,597	54,690	50,791	46,451	45,355	-17.1
North Dakota	6,696	13,263	23,016	29,863	42,964	47,344	48,666	41,650	40,142	42,591	41,448	46,578	48,083	48,666	17.4
Ohio	8,300	15,269	31,218	41,436	55,958	56,307	57,270	51,627	46,213	57,769	57,510	60,665	57,186	57,270	-0.4
Oklahoma	6,882	13,107	23,070	31,298	47,691	44,373	44,277	42,807	39,670	42,691	43,440	51,703	45,066	44,277	1.9
Oregon	8,818	16,266	30,840	42,336	55,224	57,612	58,597	54,849	49,231	57,069	58,760	59,869	58,512	58,597	-0.3
Pennsylvania	8,858	16,515	33,338	48,321	59,156	62,994	64,072	55,098	49,984	61,692	67,066	64,132	63,978	64,072	-4.5
Rhode Island	8,776	18,002	36,057	47,041	59,686	63,474	64,696	54,588	54,485	66,723	65,290	64,707	64,465	64,696	-0.9
South Carolina	6,927	13,063	27,217	36,081	47,508	48,375	48,425	43,087	39,537	50,365	50,078	51,504	49,131	48,425	-3.3
South Dakota	6,403	12,348	21,300	29,071	38,837	39,018	40,023	39,828	37,373	39,415	40,349	42,104	39,627	40,023	-0.8
Tennessee	7,050	13,972	27,052	36,328	46,290	47,563	48,049	43,852	42,288	50,059	50,421	50,184	48,306	48,049	-4.7
Texas	7,255	14,132	27,496	37,567	48,261	48,819	49,270	45,127	42,772	50,881	52,141	52,321	49,582	49,270	-5.5
Utah	7,644	14,909	23,686	34,946	45,885	49,393	50,659	47,547	45,124	43,831	48,503	49,745	50,164	50,659	4.4
Vermont	7,968	12,484	29,012	37,758	49,084	52,526	53,656	49,562	37,784	53,686	52,406	53,213	53,346	53,656	2.4
Virginia	8,070	14,060	30,938	38,744	50,015	48,670	49,233	50,197	42,554	57,250	53,774	54,222	49,430	49,233	-8.4
Washington	9,225	18,820	30,457	41,043	53,003	52,234	52,236	57,381	56,961	56,360	56,965	57,461	53,050	52,236	-8.3
West Virginia	7,650	13,710	22,842	35,009	45,959	45,453	45,583	47,584	41,495	42,269	48,590	49,825	46,163	45,583	-6.2
Wisconsin	8,963	16,006	31,921	41,153	51,264	53,797	54,717	55,751	48,444	59,069	57,118	55,576	54,637	54,717	-4.2
Wyoming	8,232	16,012	28,141	34,127	55,861	56,775	57,910	51,204	48,462	52,075	47,366	60,560	57,662	57,910	22.3

TABLE 8.7

Estimated annual salaries of public elementary and secondary school teachers, by state, selected years 1969–70 to 2013–14 [CONTINUED]

*Constant dollars based on the Consumer Price Index (CPI), prepared by the Bureau of Labor Statistics, U.S. Department of Labor, adjusted to a school-year basis. The CPI does not account for differences in inflation rates from state to state.
Note: Some data have been revised from previously published figures.

SOURCE: "Table 211.60. Estimated Average Annual Salary of Teachers in Public Elementary and Secondary Schools, by State: Selected Years, 1969–70 through 2013–14," in "Most Current Digest Tables," *Digest of Education Statistics*, U.S. Department of Education, Institute of Education Sciences, National Center for Education Statistics, August 2014, https://nces.ed.gov/programs/digest/d14/tables/xls/tabn211.60.xls (accessed July 31, 2015)

the complexities of the classroom and the differences among children.

According to "Testing Doesn't Measure Up for Americans: The 47th Annual PDK/Gallup Poll of the Public's Attitudes toward the Public Schools" (*Phi Delta Kappan*, vol. 97, no. 1, September 2015), a majority of Americans oppose including information about student results on standardized testing in teacher evaluations. In 2015, 55% of Americans were against the practice, while 43% favored it. Democrats (60%) were somewhat more opposed to including standardized test scores in teacher evaluations than Republicans (56%) or Independents (53%).

In "*Education Next*—Program on Education Policy and Governance—Survey 2014" (2015, http://educationnext .org/files/2014ednextpoll.pdf), Michael B. Henderson, Paul E. Peterson, and Martin R. West of the Harvard Program on Education Policy and Governance survey parents, teachers, and the general public on a range of issues relating to public education in the United States. Table 8.8 looks at public opinion on whether teacher compensation should be linked to how much students learn in the classroom. A majority (59%) of parents either completely favored (21%) or somewhat favored (38%) the idea of basing teacher pay on how much their students learned. Conversely, just over two out of 10 (21%) of all teachers either completely favored (4%) or somewhat favored (17%) basing their salary on how much their students learned in the classroom. Meanwhile, in 2014 a majority of Americans supported paying more to teachers who work with disadvantaged students, with nearly two-thirds (63%) of respondents either completely favoring (14%) or somewhat favoring (49%) the idea. (See Table 8.9.)

In 2014 a majority of the population supported the idea of paying their state's public school teachers more money. Among the general public, 62% believed teacher salaries should be increased (51%) or greatly increased (11%). (See Table 8.10.) These figures were even higher for African Americans and Hispanics. Overall, nearly three-quarters (73%) of African Americans supported either some form of increase (54%) or a significant increase (19%) in teacher salaries. Slightly more than two-thirds (68%) of Hispanics supported the idea of raising teacher salaries, with 54% in favor of increasing and 14% in favor of greatly increasing the salaries of their state's teachers. Nearly two-thirds (62%) of all parents supported the idea of raising teacher salaries, with 49% supporting some form of increase and 13% believing their compensation should be greatly increased. In contrast, roughly one-third (32%) of all parents felt teacher salaries should remain about the same. Among teachers, 35% favored a significant increase in their compensation; another 50% supported some form of increase, while 14% felt their salary should remain about the same.

TABLE 8.8

Public opinion on whether to base teacher salaries, in part, on how much their students learn, by race/ethnicity and parent/teacher status, 2014

	Public	Parents	Teachers	African Americans	Hispanics
Completely favor	18%	21%	4%	18%	21%
Somewhat favor	39	38	17	37	35
Somewhat oppose	21	21	28	22	18
Completely oppose	11	10	45	11	11
Neither favor nor oppose	11	10	6	12	14

SOURCE: Michael B. Henderson, Paul E. Peterson, and Martin R. West, "Table 22. Do you favor or oppose basing part of the salaries of teachers on how much their students learn?" in "*Education Next*—Program on Education Policy and Governance—Survey 2014," *Education Next*, Harvard Program on Education Policy and Governance, 2015, http://educationnext.org/files/2014ednextpoll.pdf (accessed July 30, 2015)

TABLE 8.9

Public opinion on whether to base teacher salaries, in part, on whether they work with disadvantaged students, by parent/teacher status and race/ethnicity, 2014

	Public	Parents	Teachers	African Americans	Hispanics
Completely favor	14%	15%	13%	13%	23%
Somewhat favor	49	47	44	39	40
Somewhat oppose	14	17	20	22	15
Completely oppose	5	4	8	8	5
Neither favor nor oppose	18	17	14	18	17

SOURCE: Michael B. Henderson, Paul E. Peterson, and Martin R. West, "Table 23b. Schools with disadvantaged students face substantial problems finding good teachers. Do you favor or oppose basing part of the salaries of teachers on whether or not they teach in those schools?" in "*Education Next*—Program on Education Policy and Governance—Survey 2014," *Education Next*, Harvard Program on Education Policy and Governance, 2015, http://educationnext.org/files/2014ednextpoll.pdf (accessed July 31, 2015)

TABLE 8.10

Public opinion on whether teacher pay should increase, decrease, or remain the same, by race/ethnicity and parent/teacher status, 2014

	Public	Parents	Teachers	African Americans	Hispanics
Greatly increase	11%	13%	35%	19%	14%
Increase	51	49	50	54	54
Stay about the same	32	32	14	21	27
Decrease	5	5	1	3	1
Greatly decrease	1	1	0	2	4

SOURCE: Michael B. Henderson, Paul E. Peterson, and Martin R. West, "Table 21a. Do you think that public school teacher salaries should increase, decrease, or stay about the same?" in "*Education Next*—Program on Education Policy and Governance—Survey 2014," *Education Next*, Harvard Program on Education Policy and Governance, 2015, http://educationnext.org/files/2014ednextpoll.pdf (accessed July 30, 2015)

Teacher Unions

The two largest national teachers' unions for public school teachers are the AFT and the NEA. State and local affiliates of these national unions exist as well. For example, the California Federation of Teachers is affiliated with the AFT, and the California State Teachers Association is affiliated with the NEA. United Teachers Los Angeles (UTLA) is affiliated with all four organizations.

In 2015 Henderson, Peterson, and West asked Americans whether unionization has helped, hurt, or made no difference in the quality of public school education in the United States. As Table 8.11 shows, public opinion is sharply divided on the issue of teacher unionization. In general, 40% of Americans felt teacher unions had a somewhat negative effect (24%) or a strongly negative effect (16%) on the quality of public schools. By contrast, only 33% of the general population felt such unionization was a somewhat positive (26%) or a strongly positive (7%) development. A little over a quarter (26%) believed teacher unionization had neither a positive nor a negative impact on schools. Among parents, 33% believed unionization had a somewhat positive effect (26%) or a strongly positive effect (7%) on schools, versus 37% of parents who believed it had a somewhat negative effect (22%) or a strongly negative effect (15%) on schools; 29% of all parents surveyed felt teacher unions were neither positive nor negative. A majority (59%) of teachers believed their unions exerted a somewhat positive effect (39%) or a strongly positive effect (20%) on schools. In contrast, 23% of teachers believed their unions had a somewhat negative impact (17%) or a strongly negative impact (6%) on schools; 18% of all teachers surveyed believed their unions were neither positive nor negative.

African Americans and Hispanics had a somewhat more positive view of teacher unions than the general population. As Table 8.11 reveals, 43% of African Americans believed teacher unions had either a somewhat positive effect (32%) or a strongly positive effect (11%) on the quality of public schools. Opinions among Hispanics were comparable, with 43% feeling that teacher unions had either a somewhat positive effect (34%) or a strongly positive effect (9%) on schools. Among African Americans, 19% felt teacher unions had a somewhat negative effect (15%) or a strongly negative effect (4%) on school quality, while 29% of Hispanics viewed teacher unions as having a somewhat negative impact (20%) or a strongly negative impact (9%) on schools. More than one-third (37%) of African Americans believed teachers unions were neither positive nor negative, compared with over a quarter (28%) of Hispanics who expressed the same view.

CRIMES AGAINST TEACHERS

For teaching and learning to take place, one basic necessity is that the environment be safe. Theft and violence at school produces a threatening environment and can lead to physical injury, emotional stress, and academic underperformance.

Chapter 6 looks at school violence from the student perspective. Although Chapter 6 notes that some measures of violence in school were down since the 1990s, it also indicates that a greater percentage of students were nonetheless feeling threatened than during the 1990s and that many students were bullied and therefore felt unsafe. Regardless, Kena et al. report that the percentage of students who experienced at least one serious violent incident decreased between 1992 and 2013. In 1992, 68 out of every 1,000 students aged 12 to 18 years were the victim of an act of violence while at school; by 2013 this proportion had fallen to 37 out of every 1,000 students. The rate of violent incidents was notably higher among students aged 12 to 14 years, 52 out of every 1,000 of whom suffered an act of violence at school in 2013, than students aged 15 to 18 years, for whom the rate of school violence was only 24 out of every 1,000.

Crimes against teachers have declined as well. In *Indicators of School Crime and Safety: 2014* (July 2015, http://nces.ed.gov/pubs2015/2015072.pdf), Simone Robers et al. note that the percentage of public school teachers who reported that they were threatened with injury had declined from 11.7% during the 1993–94 academic year to 9.2% during the 2011–12 academic year. In 2011–12 public school teachers (10%) were three times more likely than private school teachers (3.1%) to be threatened with violence. African American teachers (13.8%) were considerably more likely than Hispanic (9.4%) or white (8.8%) teachers to be threatened with injury during the 2011–12 school year.

Although the rate of teachers who were threatened with violence declined between 1993–94 and 2011–12,

TABLE 8.11

Public opinion on whether teacher unions have a positive or negative impact on schools, by race/ethnicity and parent/teacher status, 2014

	Public	Parents	Teachers	African Americans	Hispanics
Strongly positive effect	7%	7%	20%	11%	9%
Somewhat positive effect	26	26	39	32	34
Somewhat negative effect	24	22	17	15	20
Strongly negative effect	16	15	6	4	9
Neither positive nor negative effect	26	29	18	37	28

SOURCE: Michael B. Henderson, Paul E. Peterson, and Martin R. West, "Table 26. Some people say that teacher unions are a stumbling block to school reform. Others say that unions fight for better schools and better teachers. What do you think? Do you think teacher unions have a generally positive effect on schools, or do you think they have a generally negative effect?" in *"Education Next—Program on Education Policy and Governance—Survey 2014," Education Next,* Harvard Program on Education Policy and Governance, 2015, http://educationnext.org/files/2014ednextpoll.pdf (accessed July 30, 2015)

the percentage of teachers who were physically attacked by a student rose during that span. In 1993–94, 4.1% of all teachers suffered physical attacks by students; in 2011–12, 5.4% of all teachers reported having been attacked by a student during the previous year. Female teachers (6%) were nearly twice as likely as male teachers (3.5%) to have been attacked by a student in 2011–12. That year, elementary school teachers (8.2%) were over three times more likely to have suffered an attack than high school teachers (2.6%).

CHAPTER 9
COLLEGES AND UNIVERSITIES

As noted in Chapter 1, the United States has many of the best colleges and universities in the world. In "World University Rankings, 2014–15" (2015, https://www.timeshighereducation.co.uk/world-university-rankings/2015/world-ranking#), Times Higher Education, a leading higher education news publication located in the United Kingdom, notes that 29 U.S. universities were listed among the top 50 in the world in 2014–15. (See Table 1.2 in Chapter 1.) Three of the top-five spots were held by U.S. universities—California Institute of Technology (number 1 overall), Harvard University (2), and Stanford University (4). In addition, 11 of the top-15 universities were in the United States.

THE LEVEL OF POSTSECONDARY EDUCATION OF THE POPULACE

Students are taking advantage of the excellent postsecondary education (often called higher education) that is available in the United States. In 2014, 37% of all female adults aged 25 to 29 years and 31% of all male adults in that age group had completed bachelor's degrees. (See Figure 9.1.) In addition, among adults aged 25 to 29 years, 9% of women and 6% of men had earned master's degrees in 2014.

ENROLLMENT IN COLLEGE

Table 9.1 shows actual enrollment numbers for selected years between the fall of 1997 and the fall of 2011 and projected numbers through the fall of 2022 for students attending postsecondary institutions full time. Between 1997 and 2011 the total number of full-time postsecondary students rose 50%, from 10.6 million to 15.9 million. Roughly 70% of all full-time postsecondary students, or over 11.3 million, were attending four-year colleges in 2011; of these, 6.7 million attended public institutions and 4.5 million attended private colleges or universities. By 2022 the total number of full-time postsecondary students is expected to be nearly 18 million.

Enrollment by Gender

According to Grace Kena et al., in *The Condition of Education 2015* (May 2015, http://nces.ed.gov/pubs2015/2015144.pdf), undergraduate enrollment increased steadily between 1990 and 2013. College enrollment increased 46% over this span, from 12 million undergraduate students in 1990 to 17.5 million undergraduate students in 2013. Of all undergraduates enrolled in postsecondary institutions in 2013, 9.8 million (56%) were women and 7.7 million (44%) were men. (See Figure 9.2.) Kena et al. indicate that between 2013 and 2024 the total number of female undergraduates is projected to grow 15%, from 9.8 million to 11.3 million, while the total number of male undergraduates is projected to grow 9%, from 7.7 million to 8.3 million. According to Kena et al., total enrollment in all degree-granting postsecondary institutions, including undergraduate and graduate students, reached 20.4 million during the fall of 2013.

Minority Enrollment

The enrollment of minority students (African Americans, Hispanics, Asians or Pacific Islanders, and Native Americans or Alaskan Natives) in higher education has been rising steadily. Table 9.2 shows enrollment figures at degree-granting postsecondary institutions for select years between 1976 and 2013, by race, ethnicity, and gender. In 1976 the total undergraduate population of the United States was 9.4 million; of these, 7.7 million (83.4%) were white students. That same year African American students accounted for 943,400 (10.2%) of the overall undergraduate population, Hispanics accounted for 352,900 (3.8%), Asians or Pacific Islanders accounted for 169,300 (1.8%), and Native Americans or Alaskan Natives accounted for 69,700 (0.8%) of the total undergraduate population.

By 2013 the U.S. undergraduate population had increased 86%, to 17.5 million. (See Table 9.2.) That

FIGURE 9.1

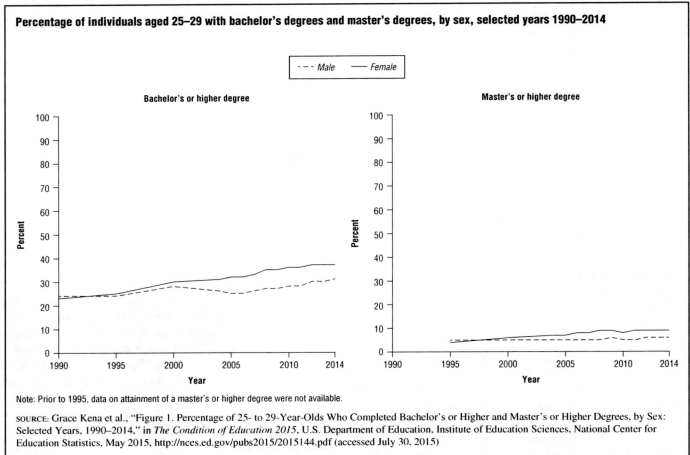

Percentage of individuals aged 25–29 with bachelor's degrees and master's degrees, by sex, selected years 1990–2014

- - - Male   —— Female

Bachelor's or higher degree

Master's or higher degree

Note: Prior to 1995, data on attainment of a master's or higher degree were not available.

SOURCE: Grace Kena et al., "Figure 1. Percentage of 25- to 29-Year-Olds Who Completed Bachelor's or Higher and Master's or Higher Degrees, by Sex: Selected Years, 1990–2014," in *The Condition of Education 2015*, U.S. Department of Education, Institute of Education Sciences, National Center for Education Statistics, May 2015, http://nces.ed.gov/pubs2015/2015144.pdf (accessed July 30, 2015)

same year there were 9.9 million white undergraduates attending degree-granting institutions; these students accounted for 58.3% of the overall undergraduate population in 2013. There were 2.5 million African Americans attending degree-granting undergraduate institutions, accounting for 14.7% of the total undergraduate population. Hispanics accounted for 16.9% of the total undergraduate enrollment, with nearly 2.9 million Hispanic students attending degree-granting undergraduate institutions. Other races also saw increases in college enrollment between 1976 and 2013. In 2013 Asians or Pacific Islanders (1.1 million) accounted for 6.3% of the nation's undergraduate enrollment, and Native Americans or Alaskan Natives (147,800) accounted for 0.9% of the total undergraduate enrollment.

International Students

According to the Institute of International Education (IIE), in "Open Doors 2014 Fast Facts: International Students in the U.S." (November 2014, http://www.iie.org/~/media/Files/Corporate/Open-Doors/Fast-Facts/Fast-Facts-2014.ashx?la=en), 886,052 international students were enrolled at institutions of higher learning in the United States during the 2013–14 school year. This

figure was an increase of 8.1% from the previous year's figure of 819,614. The IIE notes that during the 2013–14 school year 31% (274,439) of international students in U.S. institutions of higher learning were from China, 11.6% (102,673) were from India, 7.7% (68,047) were from South Korea, 6.1% (53,919) were from Saudi Arabia, and 3.2% (28,304) were from Canada. Another 2.4% (21,266) were from Taiwan and 2.2% (19,334) were from Japan.

The IIE reports that California hosted the largest number of international students (121,647) during the 2013–14 school year. New York University, with 11,164 foreign students, had the largest international student population of any college or university in the United States. Business and management (21.2% of students) and engineering (19.2%) were the leading areas of study for international students.

Studying Abroad

Many college students from the United States also participate in study abroad programs. According to the IIE, in "Open Doors 2014 Fast Facts," the number of U.S. students studying abroad more than tripled between the 1994–95 and 2012–13 academic years. The IIE

TABLE 9.1

Actual and projected enrollment in degree-granting institutions, by type of institution, 1997–2022

[In thousands]

| Year | Total | Public | | Private | |
		4-year	2-year	4-year	2-year
Actual					
1997	10,615	4,814	3,056	2,525	220
1998	10,699	4,869	3,011	2,599	220
1999	10,975	4,950	3,109	2,684	231
2000	11,267	5,026	3,241	2,770	231
2001	11,766	5,194	3,445	2,894	233
2002	12,331	5,406	3,655	3,033	237
2003	12,689	5,558	3,684	3,186	260
2004	13,001	5,641	3,707	3,377	276
2005	13,201	5,728	3,662	3,533	277
2006	13,403	5,825	3,679	3,631	268
2007	13,783	5,994	3,745	3,775	268
2008	14,394	6,140	3,922	4,030	302
2009	15,496	6,452	4,298	4,357	389
2010	15,943	6,636	4,385	4,490	433
2011	15,886	6,733	4,216	4,532	405
Projected					
2012	15,886	6,736	4,201	4,545	404
2013	16,036	6,794	4,243	4,591	407
2014	16,287	6,896	4,310	4,668	413
2015	16,436	6,953	4,352	4,713	417
2016	16,619	7,025	4,404	4,768	422
2017	16,827	7,108	4,464	4,828	428
2018	17,058	7,199	4,531	4,893	434
2019	17,305	7,300	4,603	4,961	442
2020	17,521	7,389	4,666	5,019	448
2021	17,767	7,494	4,730	5,089	455
2022	17,966	7,579	4,782	5,145	460

Note: Detail may not sum to totals because of rounding. Some data have been revised from previously published figures.

SOURCE: William J. Hussar and Tabitha M. Bailey, "Table 31. Actual and Projected Numbers for Full-Time-Equivalent Enrollment in All Postsecondary Degree-Granting Institutions, by Control and Level of Institution: Fall 1997 through Fall 2022," in *Projections of Education Statistics to 2022*, 41st ed., U.S. Department of Education, Institute of Education Sciences, National Center for Education Statistics, February 2014, http://nces.ed.gov/pubs2014/2014051.pdf (accessed July 30, 2015)

estimates that during the 2012–13 school year there were 289,408 U.S. students studying abroad, an increase of 2.1% over the previous year.

The IIE indicates that the countries with the largest numbers of Americans enrolled in institutions of higher learning during the 2012–13 school year included the United Kingdom (36,210), Italy (29,848), Spain (26,281), France (17,210), China (14,413), Germany (9,544), Costa Rica (8,497), Australia (8,320), and Ireland (8,084). The largest number of U.S. students abroad studied science, technology, engineering, and mathematics (65,223, or 22.5% of U.S. students abroad), followed by social sciences (63,914, or 22.1%), business (59,147, or 20.4%), and the humanities (30,167, or 10.4%).

SIZE OF DEGREE-GRANTING INSTITUTIONS

The National Center for Education Statistics (NCES; May 2015, http://nces.ed.gov/programs/digest/d14/tables/dt14_317.40.asp?current=yes) reveals that most students go to large colleges and universities. During the fall of 2013 only 584 (12.4%) out of the nation's 4,716 degree-granting colleges and universities had enrollments

of 10,000 students or more. However, 12.2 million (59.7%) of the nation's 20.4 million postsecondary students attended these schools. Conversely, 2,069 (43.9%) of the nation's 4,716 degree-granting postsecondary institutions had enrollment levels of under 1,000 students, but accounted for only 802,553 (3.9%) of the nation's 20.4 million postsecondary students. According to the NCES (April 2015, http://nces.ed.gov/programs/digest/d14/tables/dt14_312.10.asp?current=yes), during the fall of 2013 the postsecondary institutions with the largest enrollments were the University of Phoenix Online Campus (212,044 students), Ivy Tech Community College (98,778 students), Liberty University (77,338 students), and Miami Dade College (66,298 students). By contrast, as Samantha Lindsay reports in "Complete List: The Smallest Colleges in the United States" (August 23, 2015, http://blog.prepscholar.com/the-smallest-colleges-in-the-united-states), among postsecondary institutions with a total enrollment of at least 50 students, the Shasta Bible College and Graduate School (59 students), Knoxville College (73 students), Kentucky Mountain Bible College (74 students), the Webb Institute (79 students), and Shimer College (81 students) were the

FIGURE 9.2

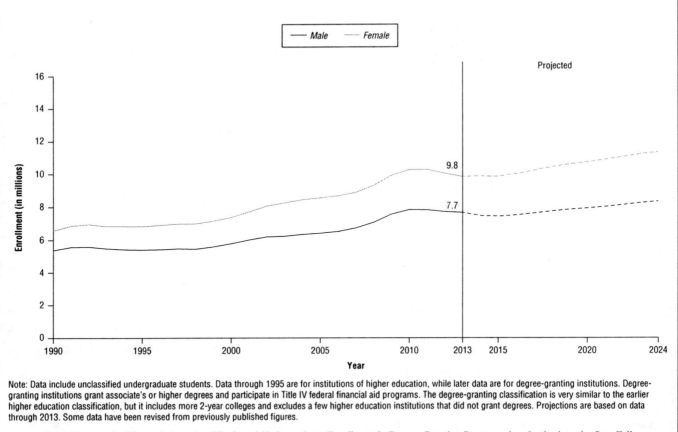

Actual and projected undergraduate enrollment, by sex, 1990–2024

Note: Data include unclassified undergraduate students. Data through 1995 are for institutions of higher education, while later data are for degree-granting institutions. Degree-granting institutions grant associate's or higher degrees and participate in Title IV federal financial aid programs. The degree-granting classification is very similar to the earlier higher education classification, but it includes more 2-year colleges and excludes a few higher education institutions that did not grant degrees. Projections are based on data through 2013. Some data have been revised from previously published figures.

SOURCE: Grace Kena et al., "Figure 1. Actual and Projected Undergraduate Enrollment in Degree-Granting Postsecondary Institutions, by Sex: Fall 1990–2024," in *The Condition of Education 2015*, U.S. Department of Education, Institute of Education Sciences, National Center for Education Statistics, May 2015, http://nces.ed.gov/pubs2015/2015144.pdf (accessed July 30, 2015)

nation's smallest degree-granting postsecondary institutions in 2015.

ADULT EDUCATION

The NCES (November 2014, http://nces.ed.gov/programs/digest/d14/tables/dt14_507.20.asp?current=yes) examines nationwide trends in adult education enrollment between 2000 and 2012. According to NCES data, enrollment in adult education programs peaked in 2000, when 2.6 million adults were taking state-administered basic, secondary, or English as a second language education courses nationwide. This figure dropped steadily over the course of the next decade. In 2005 adult education enrollment fell to 2.5 million, and by 2010 enrollment had fallen below 2 million. In 2012 nationwide enrollment in adult education classes dipped to 1.7 million. Of this total, 819,465 adults were enrolled in basic education courses, 193,979 were taking classes at the secondary level, and 676,767 were studying English as a second language.

Not surprisingly, a number of individual states saw adult education enrollment fall between 2000 and 2012. In terms of total numbers, Florida experienced the single largest decline in adult education enrollment during this period. In 2000 the number of students participating in adult education programs in Florida was 404,912; by 2012 this figure had dropped to 147,474, a decrease of 64%. Between 2000 and 2005 California experienced a sizable increase in adult education enrollment, with the number of students participating in adult education programs rising from 473,050 to 591,893. However, California's adult education enrollment figures declined significantly over the next seven years, falling to 302,169 by 2012. In contrast, some states experienced growth in adult education enrollments between 2000 and 2012. From a percentage standpoint, Vermont experienced the largest gain during this span, as adult education enrollment rose from 1,146 in 2000 to 2,097 in 2012, an increase of 83%. In Maryland adult education enrollment rose from 22,702 in 2000 to 31,029 in 2012, an increase of 37%, while Kentucky saw participation in adult

TABLE 9.2

Fall enrollment in degree-granting institutions, by demographic characteristics, selected years 1976–2013

Level of enrollment, sex, attendance status, and race/ethnicity of student	Fall enrollment (in thousands)											Percentage distribution of U.S. residents										
	1976	1980	1990	2000	2005	2008	2009	2010	2011	2012	2013	1976	1980	1990	2000	2005	2008	2009	2010	2011	2012	2013
All students, total	10,985.6	12,086.8	13,818.6	15,312.3	17,487.5	19,102.8	20,313.6	21,019.4	21,010.6	20,642.8	20,375.8	100.0	100.0	100.0	100.0	100.0	100.0	100.0	100.0	100.0	100.0	100.0
White	9,076.1	9,833.0	10,722.5	10,462.1	11,495.4	12,088.8	12,668.9	12,720.8	12,401.9	11,981.1	11,590.7	84.3	83.5	79.9	70.8	68.0	65.5	64.5	62.6	61.2	60.3	59.3
Total, selected races/ethnicities	1,690.8	1,948.8	2,704.7	4,321.5	5,407.2	6,353.5	6,962.5	7,591.0	7,868.2	7,878.8	7,944.8	15.7	16.5	20.1	29.2	32.0	34.5	35.5	37.4	38.8	39.7	40.7
Black	1,033.0	1,106.8	1,247.0	1,730.3	2,214.6	2,584.5	2,883.9	3,039.0	3,079.2	2,962.1	2,872.1	9.6	9.4	9.3	11.7	13.1	14.0	14.7	15.0	15.2	14.9	14.7
Hispanic	383.8	471.7	782.4	1,461.8	1,882.0	2,272.9	2,537.4	2,748.8	2,893.0	2,979.4	3,091.1	3.6	4.0	5.8	9.9	11.1	12.3	12.9	13.5	14.3	15.0	15.8
Asian/Pacific Islander	197.9	286.4	572.4	978.2	1,134.4	1,302.8	1,335.3	1,281.6	1,277.0	1,259.2	1,259.6	1.8	2.4	4.3	6.6	6.7	7.1	6.8	6.3	6.3	6.3	6.4
Asian	—	—	—	—	—	—	—	1,217.6	1,211.0	1,195.6	1,198.5	—	—	—	—	—	—	—	6.0	6.0	6.0	6.1
Pacific Islander	—	—	—	—	—	—	—	64.0	66.0	63.6	61.1	—	—	—	—	—	—	—	0.3	0.3	0.3	0.3
American Indian/Alaska Native	76.1	83.9	102.8	151.2	176.3	193.3	205.9	196.2	186.2	172.9	162.6	0.7	0.7	0.8	1.0	1.0	1.0	1.0	1.0	0.9	0.9	0.8
Two or more races	—	—	—	—	—	—	—	325.4	432.7	505.1	559.4	†	†	†	†	†	†	†	1.6	2.1	2.5	2.9
Nonresident alien	218.7	305.0	391.5	528.7	584.8	660.6	682.2	707.7	740.5	782.9	840.3											
Male	5,794.4	5,868.1	6,283.9	6,721.8	7,455.9	8,188.9	8,733.0	9,045.8	9,034.3	8,919.1	8,860.8	100.0	100.0	100.0	100.0	100.0	100.0	100.0	100.0	100.0	100.0	100.0
White	4,813.7	4,772.9	4,861.0	4,634.6	5,007.2	5,302.9	5,572.8	5,605.8	5,457.2	5,285.0	5,133.1	85.3	84.4	80.5	72.1	70.1	67.7	66.6	64.7	63.2	62.2	61.1
Total, selected races/ethnicities	826.6	884.4	1,176.6	1,789.8	2,139.2	2,532.8	2,794.6	3,060.3	3,177.9	3,209.4	3,267.6	14.7	15.6	19.5	27.9	29.9	32.3	33.4	35.3	36.8	37.8	38.9
Black	469.9	463.7	484.7	635.3	774.1	911.8	1,028.1	1,089.0	1,107.8	1,079.4	1,065.0	8.3	8.2	8.0	9.9	10.8	11.6	12.3	12.6	12.8	12.7	12.7
Hispanic	209.7	231.6	353.9	627.1	774.6	946.7	1,063.0	1,157.6	1,215.8	1,254.3	1,306.5	3.7	4.1	5.9	9.8	10.8	12.1	12.7	13.4	14.1	14.8	15.6
Asian/Pacific Islander	108.4	151.3	294.9	465.9	522.0	597.4	620.7	600.6	600.7	593.7	594.3	1.9	2.7	4.9	7.3	7.3	7.6	7.4	6.9	7.0	7.0	7.1
Asian	—	—	—	—	—	—	—	572.1	571.6	565.3	567.0	—	—	—	—	—	—	—	6.6	6.6	6.7	6.7
Pacific Islander	—	—	—	—	—	—	—	28.5	29.1	28.5	27.3	—	—	—	—	—	—	—	0.3	0.3	0.3	0.3
American Indian/Alaska Native	38.5	37.8	43.1	61.4	68.4	76.9	82.8	78.7	73.8	68.6	64.8	0.7	0.7	0.7	1.0	1.0	1.0	1.0	0.9	0.9	0.8	0.8
Two or more races	—	—	—	—	—	—	—	134.4	179.8	213.3	236.9	†	†	†	†	†	†	†	1.6	2.1	2.5	2.8
Nonresident alien	154.1	210.8	246.3	297.3	309.5	353.3	365.6	379.6	399.1	424.7	460.1											
Female	5,191.2	6,218.7	7,534.7	8,590.5	10,031.6	10,913.9	11,580.6	11,973.7	11,976.3	11,723.7	11,515.0	100.0	100.0	100.0	100.0	100.0	100.0	100.0	100.0	100.0	100.0	100.0
White	4,262.4	5,060.1	5,861.5	5,827.5	6,488.2	6,785.9	7,096.1	7,115.0	6,944.6	6,696.1	6,457.6	83.1	82.6	79.3	69.7	66.5	64.0	63.0	61.1	59.7	58.9	58.0
Total, selected races/ethnicities	864.2	1,064.4	1,528.1	2,531.7	3,268.0	3,820.7	4,167.9	4,530.7	4,690.4	4,669.4	4,677.2	16.9	17.4	20.7	30.3	33.5	36.0	37.0	38.9	40.3	41.1	42.0
Black	563.1	643.0	762.3	1,095.0	1,440.4	1,672.7	1,855.8	1,949.9	1,971.4	1,882.7	1,807.1	11.0	10.5	10.3	13.1	14.8	15.8	16.5	16.7	16.9	16.6	16.2
Hispanic	174.1	240.1	428.5	834.7	1,107.3	1,326.1	1,474.4	1,591.2	1,677.2	1,725.1	1,784.6	3.4	3.9	5.8	10.0	11.4	12.5	13.1	13.7	14.4	15.2	16.0
Asian/Pacific Islander	89.4	135.2	277.5	512.3	612.4	705.4	714.6	681.0	676.4	665.5	665.3	1.7	2.2	3.8	6.1	6.3	6.7	6.3	5.8	5.8	5.9	6.0
Asian	—	—	—	—	—	—	—	645.5	639.4	630.3	631.5	—	—	—	—	—	—	—	5.5	5.5	5.5	5.7
Pacific Islander	—	—	—	—	—	—	—	35.5	36.9	35.2	33.8	—	—	—	—	—	—	—	0.3	0.3	0.3	0.3
American Indian/Alaska Native	37.6	46.1	59.7	89.7	107.9	116.4	123.2	117.5	112.5	104.3	97.7	0.7	0.8	0.8	1.1	1.1	1.1	1.1	1.0	1.0	0.9	0.9
Two or more races	—	—	—	—	—	—	—	191.0	253.0	291.8	322.5	†	†	†	†	†	†	†	1.6	2.2	2.6	2.9
Nonresident alien	64.6	94.2	145.2	231.4	275.3	307.3	316.6	328.0	341.4	358.2	380.2											
Full-time	6,703.6	7,088.9	7,821.0	9,009.6	10,797.0	11,747.7	12,605.4	13,087.2	13,002.5	12,737.0	12,597.1	100.0	100.0	100.0	100.0	100.0	100.0	100.0	100.0	100.0	100.0	100.0
White	5,512.6	5,717.0	6,016.5	6,231.1	7,220.5	7,593.5	8,016.2	8,053.5	7,781.2	7,485.6	7,239.2	84.2	83.4	79.9	72.5	69.8	67.6	66.4	64.3	62.7	61.9	60.8
Total, selected races/ethnicities	1,030.9	1,137.5	1,514.9	2,368.5	3,117.1	3,631.9	4,049.6	4,468.5	4,623.1	4,610.0	4,662.5	15.8	16.6	20.1	27.5	30.2	32.4	33.6	35.7	37.3	38.1	39.2
Black	659.2	685.6	718.3	982.6	1,321.7	1,530.7	1,727.6	1,811.3	1,807.3	1,720.1	1,669.3	10.1	10.0	9.5	11.4	12.8	13.6	14.3	14.5	14.6	14.2	14.0
Hispanic	211.1	247.0	394.7	710.3	979.7	1,177.2	1,350.9	1,501.0	1,593.3	1,632.4	1,700.3	3.2	3.6	5.2	8.3	9.5	10.5	11.2	12.0	12.8	13.5	14.3
Asian/Pacific Islander	117.7	162.0	347.4	591.2	710.1	808.9	845.9	820.8	822.1	815.4	821.3	1.8	2.4	4.6	6.9	6.9	7.2	7.0	6.6	6.6	6.7	6.9
Asian	—	—	—	—	—	—	—	783.0	782.9	778.5	785.5	—	—	—	—	—	—	—	6.3	6.3	6.4	6.6
Pacific Islander	—	—	—	—	—	—	—	37.8	39.2	36.9	35.7	—	—	—	—	—	—	—	0.3	0.3	0.3	0.3

TABLE 9.2

Fall enrollment in degree-granting institutions, by demographic characteristics, selected years 1976–2013 [CONTINUED]

Level of enrollment, sex, attendance status, and race/ethnicity of student	Fall enrollment (in thousands)											Percentage distribution of U.S. residents										
	1976	1980	1990	2000	2005	2008	2009	2010	2011	2012	2013	1976	1980	1990	2000	2005	2008	2009	2010	2011	2012	2013
American Indian/Alaska Native	43.0	43.0	54.4	84.4	105.6	115.1	125.2	118.3	110.8	102.1	94.5	0.7	0.6	0.7	1.0	1.0	1.0	1.0	0.9	0.9	0.8	0.8
Two or more races	—	—	—	—	—	—	—	217.2	289.6	340.0	377.2	—	—	—	—	—	—	—	1.7	2.3	2.8	3.2
Nonresident alien	160.0	234.4	289.6	410.0	459.4	522.3	539.6	565.2	598.2	641.4	695.3	†	†	†	†	†	†	†	†	†	†	†
Part-time	**4,282.1**	**4,997.9**	**5,997.7**	**6,302.7**	**6,690.5**	**7,355.1**	**7,708.2**	**7,932.3**	**8,008.1**	**7,905.8**	**7,778.7**	**100.0**	**100.0**	**100.0**	**100.0**	**100.0**	**100.0**	**100.0**	**100.0**	**100.0**	**100.0**	**100.0**
White	3,563.5	4,116.0	4,706.0	4,231.0	4,274.9	4,495.3	4,652.7	4,667.3	4,620.6	4,495.5	4,351.5	84.4	83.5	79.8	68.4	65.1	62.3	61.5	59.9	58.7	57.9	57.0
Total, selected races/ethnicities	659.9	811.3	1,189.8	1,953.0	2,290.1	2,721.5	2,912.9	3,122.5	3,245.2	3,268.8	3,282.2	15.6	16.5	20.2	31.6	34.9	37.7	38.5	40.1	41.3	42.1	43.0
Black	373.8	421.2	528.7	747.7	892.9	1,053.7	1,156.3	1,227.7	1,272.0	1,242.1	1,202.9	8.9	8.5	9.0	12.1	13.6	14.6	15.3	15.8	16.2	16.0	15.8
Hispanic	172.7	224.8	387.7	751.5	902.2	1,095.7	1,186.5	1,247.9	1,299.7	1,347.0	1,390.8	4.1	4.6	6.6	12.2	13.7	15.2	15.7	16.0	16.5	17.3	18.2
Asian/Pacific Islander	80.2	124.4	225.1	387.1	424.3	493.9	489.4	460.8	454.9	443.8	438.3	1.9	2.5	3.8	6.3	6.5	6.8	6.5	5.9	5.8	5.4	5.7
Asian	—	—	—	—	—	—	—	434.6	428.1	417.1	413.0	—	—	—	—	—	—	—	5.6	5.4	5.4	5.4
Pacific Islander	—	—	—	—	—	—	—	26.2	26.8	26.7	25.3	—	—	—	—	—	—	—	0.3	0.3	0.3	0.3
American Indian/Alaska Native	33.1	40.9	48.4	66.8	70.7	78.2	80.7	78.0	75.4	70.8	68.1	0.8	0.8	0.8	1.1	1.1	1.1	1.1	1.0	1.0	0.9	0.9
Two or more races	—	—	—	—	—	—	—	108.2	143.2	165.0	182.1	—	—	—	—	—	—	—	1.4	1.8	2.1	2.4
Nonresident alien	58.7	70.6	101.8	118.7	125.5	138.3	142.6	142.5	142.3	141.5	145.0	†	†	†	†	†	†	†	†	†	†	†
Undergraduate, total	**9,419.0**	**10,469.1**	**11,959.1**	**13,155.4**	**14,964.0**	**16,365.7**	**17,464.2**	**18,082.4**	**18,077.3**	**17,732.4**	**17,474.8**	**100.0**	**100.0**	**100.0**	**100.0**	**100.0**	**100.0**	**100.0**	**100.0**	**100.0**	**100.0**	**100.0**
White	7,740.5	8,480.7	9,272.6	8,983.5	9,828.6	10,339.2	10,859.4	10,895.9	10,618.6	10,247.4	9,899.2	83.4	82.7	79.0	69.8	67.1	64.6	63.6	61.6	60.1	59.3	58.3
Total, selected races/ethnicities	1,535.3	1,778.5	2,467.7	3,884.0	4,820.7	5,666.2	6,228.3	6,788.1	7,036.1	7,034.6	7,092.3	16.6	17.3	21.0	30.2	32.9	35.4	36.4	38.4	39.9	40.7	41.7
Black	943.4	1,018.8	1,147.2	1,548.9	1,955.4	2,269.3	2,545.9	2,677.1	2,708.3	2,592.8	2,504.8	10.2	9.9	9.8	12.0	13.3	14.2	14.9	15.1	15.3	15.0	14.7
Hispanic	352.9	433.1	724.6	1,351.0	1,733.6	2,103.5	2,354.4	2,551.0	2,687.9	2,766.1	2,870.2	3.8	4.2	6.2	10.5	11.8	13.1	13.8	14.4	15.2	16.0	16.9
Asian/Pacific Islander	169.3	248.7	500.5	845.5	971.4	1,117.9	1,140.3	1,087.3	1,079.6	1,063.2	1,064.4	1.8	2.4	4.3	6.6	6.7	7.0	6.7	6.1	6.1	6.2	6.3
Asian	—	—	—	—	—	—	—	1,029.8	1,020.2	1,006.5	1,010.1	—	—	—	—	—	—	—	5.8	5.8	5.8	5.9
Pacific Islander	—	—	—	—	—	—	—	57.5	59.4	56.7	54.2	—	—	—	—	—	—	—	0.3	0.3	0.3	0.3
American Indian/Alaska Native	69.7	77.9	95.5	138.5	160.4	175.6	187.6	179.1	170.2	157.5	147.8	0.8	0.8	0.8	1.1	1.1	1.1	1.1	1.0	1.0	0.9	0.9
Two or more races	—	—	—	—	—	—	—	293.7	390.2	455.0	505.2	—	—	—	—	—	—	—	1.7	2.2	2.6	3.0
Nonresident alien	143.2	209.9	218.7	288.0	314.7	360.3	376.5	398.4	422.6	450.5	483.4	†	†	†	†	†	†	†	†	†	†	†
Male	**4,896.8**	**4,997.4**	**5,379.8**	**5,778.2**	**6,408.9**	**7,066.6**	**7,563.2**	**7,836.3**	**7,823.0**	**7,713.9**	**7,659.6**	**100.0**	**100.0**	**100.0**	**100.0**	**100.0**	**100.0**	**100.0**	**100.0**	**100.0**	**100.0**	**100.0**
White	4,052.2	4,054.9	4,184.4	4,010.1	4,330.4	4,598.6	4,840.7	4,861.0	4,725.5	4,571.9	4,439.6	84.4	83.5	79.6	71.3	69.2	66.8	65.6	63.7	62.1	61.1	60.0
Total, selected races/ethnicities	748.2	802.7	1,069.3	1,618.0	1,926.6	2,290.3	2,534.2	2,773.8	2,879.8	2,904.9	2,961.6	15.6	16.5	20.4	28.7	30.8	33.2	34.4	36.3	37.9	38.9	40.0
Black	430.7	428.2	448.0	577.0	697.5	821.3	930.4	982.9	998.6	969.7	955.4	9.0	8.8	8.5	10.3	11.1	11.9	12.6	12.9	13.1	13.0	12.9
Hispanic	191.7	211.2	326.9	582.6	718.5	884.0	994.5	1,082.9	1,137.8	1,173.0	1,222.9	4.0	4.3	6.2	10.4	11.5	12.8	13.5	14.2	15.0	15.7	16.5
Asian/Pacific Islander	91.1	128.5	254.5	401.9	448.1	514.6	533.4	513.4	512.0	505.5	507.4	1.9	2.6	4.8	7.1	7.2	7.5	7.2	6.7	6.7	6.8	6.9
Asian	—	—	—	—	—	—	—	487.4	485.5	479.9	482.9	—	—	—	—	—	—	—	6.4	6.4	6.4	6.5
Pacific Islander	—	—	—	—	—	—	—	26.0	26.5	25.6	24.5	—	—	—	—	—	—	—	0.3	0.3	0.3	0.3
American Indian/Alaska Native	34.8	34.8	39.9	56.4	62.5	70.3	75.9	72.3	67.9	62.9	59.5	0.7	0.7	0.8	1.0	1.0	1.0	1.1	0.9	0.9	0.8	0.8
Two or more races	—	—	—	—	—	—	—	122.3	163.6	193.8	216.3	—	—	—	—	—	—	—	1.6	2.2	2.6	2.9
Nonresident alien	96.4	139.8	126.1	150.2	151.8	177.7	188.3	201.5	217.7	237.1	258.4	†	†	†	†	†	†	†	†	†	†	†
Female	**4,522.1**	**5,471.7**	**6,579.3**	**7,377.1**	**8,555.1**	**9,299.1**	**9,901.0**	**10,246.1**	**10,254.3**	**10,018.5**	**9,815.2**	**100.0**	**100.0**	**100.0**	**100.0**	**100.0**	**100.0**	**100.0**	**100.0**	**100.0**	**100.0**	**100.0**
White	3,688.3	4,425.8	5,088.2	4,973.3	5,498.2	5,740.6	6,018.6	6,035.0	5,893.1	5,675.5	5,459.6	82.4	81.9	78.4	68.7	65.5	63.0	62.0	60.1	58.6	57.9	56.9
Total, selected races/ethnicities	787.0	975.8	1,398.5	2,266.0	2,894.0	3,375.9	3,694.1	4,014.3	4,156.4	4,129.1	4,130.6	17.6	18.1	21.6	31.3	34.5	37.0	38.0	39.9	41.4	42.1	43.1
Black	512.7	590.6	699.2	971.9	1,257.8	1,448.0	1,615.5	1,694.2	1,709.7	1,623.1	1,549.4	11.5	10.9	10.8	13.4	15.0	15.9	16.6	16.9	17.0	16.6	16.2
Hispanic	161.2	221.8	397.6	768.4	1,015.0	1,219.5	1,359.9	1,468.1	1,550.1	1,593.0	1,647.2	3.6	4.1	6.1	10.6	12.1	13.4	14.0	14.6	15.4	16.2	17.2

TABLE 9.2

Fall enrollment in degree-granting institutions, by demographic characteristics, selected years 1976–2013 [CONTINUED]

Level of enrollment, sex, attendance status, and race/ethnicity of student	Fall enrollment (in thousands)											Percentage distribution of U.S. residents										
	1976	1980	1990	2000	2005	2008	2009	2010	2011	2012	2013	1976	1980	1990	2000	2005	2008	2009	2010	2011	2012	2013
Asian/Pacific Islander	78.2	120.2	246.0	443.6	523.2	603.2	607.0	573.9	567.6	557.7	556.9	1.7	2.2	3.8	6.1	6.2	6.6	6.2	5.7	5.6	5.7	5.8
Asian	—	—	—	—	—	—	—	542.4	534.7	526.6	527.3	—	—	—	—	—	—	—	5.4	5.3	5.4	5.5
Pacific Islander	—	—	—	—	—	—	—	31.5	32.9	31.1	29.7	—	—	—	—	—	—	—	0.3	0.3	0.3	0.3
American Indian/Alaska Native	34.9	43.1	55.5	82.1	98.0	105.2	111.7	106.8	102.3	94.6	88.2	0.8	0.8	0.9	1.1	1.2	1.2	1.2	1.1	1.0	1.0	0.9
Two or more races	—	—	—	—	—	—	—	171.3	226.7	261.3	288.8	†	†	†	†	†	†	†	1.7	2.3	2.7	3.0
Nonresident alien	46.8	70.1	92.6	137.8	162.9	182.6	188.2	196.9	204.9	213.3	225.0	†	†	†	†	†	†	†	†	†	†	†
Postbaccalaureate, total	1,566.6	1,617.7	1,859.5	2,156.9	2,523.5	2,737.1	2,849.4	2,937.0	2,933.3	2,910.4	2,901.0	100.0	100.0	100.0	100.0	100.0	100.0	100.0	100.0	100.0	100.0	100.0
White	1,335.6	1,352.4	1,449.8	1,478.6	1,666.8	1,749.6	1,809.5	1,824.9	1,783.3	1,733.8	1,691.5	89.6	88.8	86.0	77.2	74.0	71.8	71.1	69.4	68.2	67.3	66.5
Total, selected races/ethnicities	155.5	170.3	237.0	437.5	586.6	687.2	734.2	802.8	832.1	844.2	852.5	10.4	11.2	14.0	22.8	26.0	28.2	28.9	30.6	31.8	32.7	33.5
Black	89.7	87.9	99.8	181.4	259.2	315.2	338.0	361.9	370.9	369.3	367.3	6.0	5.8	5.9	9.5	11.5	12.9	13.3	13.8	14.2	14.3	14.4
Hispanic	30.9	38.6	57.9	110.8	148.4	169.4	183.0	197.8	205.1	213.4	221.0	2.1	2.5	3.4	5.8	6.6	7.0	7.2	7.5	7.8	8.3	8.7
Asian/Pacific Islander	28.6	37.7	72.0	132.7	163.0	184.9	194.9	194.3	197.4	196.0	195.2	1.9	2.5	4.3	6.9	7.2	7.6	7.7	7.4	7.5	7.6	7.7
Asian	—	—	—	—	—	—	—	187.8	190.8	189.1	188.4	—	—	—	—	—	—	—	7.1	7.3	7.3	7.4
Pacific Islander	—	—	—	—	—	—	—	6.5	6.7	6.9	6.8	—	—	—	—	—	—	—	0.2	0.3	0.3	0.3
American Indian/Alaska Native	6.4	6.0	7.3	12.6	15.9	17.7	18.3	17.1	16.1	15.4	14.8	0.4	0.4	0.4	0.7	0.7	0.7	0.7	0.7	0.6	0.6	0.6
Two or more races	—	—	—	—	—	—	—	31.7	42.5	50.1	54.2	†	†	†	†	†	†	†	1.2	1.6	1.9	2.1
Nonresident alien	75.5	95.1	172.7	240.7	270.1	300.3	305.7	309.3	317.9	332.4	356.9	†	†	†	†	†	†	†	†	†	†	†
Male	897.6	870.7	904.2	943.5	1,047.1	1,122.3	1,169.8	1,209.5	1,211.3	1,205.2	1,201.2	100.0	100.0	100.0	100.0	100.0	100.0	100.0	100.0	100.0	100.0	100.0
White	761.6	718.1	676.6	624.5	676.8	704.3	732.0	744.9	731.8	713.1	693.1	90.7	89.8	86.3	78.4	76.1	74.4	73.8	72.2	71.1	70.1	69.4
Total, selected races/ethnicities	78.4	81.7	107.4	171.9	212.5	242.5	260.4	286.5	298.1	304.5	306.0	9.3	10.2	13.7	21.6	23.9	25.6	26.2	27.8	28.9	29.9	30.6
Black	39.2	35.5	36.7	58.3	76.6	90.5	97.7	106.1	109.3	109.7	109.6	4.7	4.4	4.7	7.3	8.6	9.6	9.8	10.3	10.6	10.8	11.0
Hispanic	18.1	20.4	27.0	44.5	56.1	62.7	68.6	74.7	78.0	81.3	83.6	2.2	2.5	3.4	5.6	6.3	6.6	6.9	7.2	7.6	8.0	8.4
Asian/Pacific Islander	17.4	22.8	40.4	64.0	73.9	82.7	87.3	87.2	88.7	88.3	86.9	2.1	2.8	5.2	8.0	8.3	8.7	8.8	8.5	8.6	8.7	8.7
Asian	—	—	—	—	—	—	—	84.7	86.1	85.4	84.2	—	—	—	—	—	—	—	8.2	8.4	8.4	8.4
Pacific Islander	—	—	—	—	—	—	—	2.5	2.6	2.8	2.7	—	—	—	—	—	—	—	0.2	0.3	0.3	0.3
American Indian/Alaska Native	3.7	3.0	3.2	5.0	5.9	6.5	6.8	6.4	5.9	5.7	5.3	0.4	0.4	0.4	0.6	0.7	0.7	0.7	0.6	0.6	0.6	0.5
Two or more races	—	—	—	—	—	—	—	12.0	16.2	19.6	20.6	†	†	†	†	†	†	†	1.2	1.6	1.9	2.1
Nonresident alien	57.7	71.0	120.2	147.1	157.7	175.5	177.4	178.2	181.4	187.5	201.7	†	†	†	†	†	†	†	†	†	†	†
Female	669.1	747.0	955.4	1,213.4	1,476.5	1,614.8	1,679.6	1,727.5	1,722.0	1,705.2	1,699.8	100.0	100.0	100.0	100.0	100.0	100.0	100.0	100.0	100.0	100.0	100.0
White	574.1	634.3	773.2	854.1	990.0	1,045.3	1,077.5	1,080.0	1,051.5	1,020.6	998.0	88.1	87.7	85.6	76.3	72.6	70.2	69.5	67.7	66.3	65.4	64.6
Total, selected races/ethnicities	77.2	88.6	129.6	265.7	374.0	444.8	473.8	516.4	534.0	539.7	546.5	11.9	12.3	14.4	23.7	27.4	29.8	30.5	32.3	33.7	34.6	35.4
Black	50.5	52.4	63.1	123.1	182.6	224.7	240.3	255.8	261.7	259.6	257.7	7.7	7.2	7.0	11.0	13.4	15.1	15.5	16.0	16.5	16.6	16.7
Hispanic	12.8	18.3	30.9	66.3	92.3	106.7	114.5	123.1	127.1	132.1	137.4	2.0	2.5	3.4	5.9	6.8	7.2	7.4	7.7	8.0	8.5	8.9
Asian/Pacific Islander	11.2	15.0	31.5	68.7	89.1	102.2	107.6	107.0	108.7	107.8	108.4	1.7	2.1	3.5	6.1	6.5	6.9	6.9	6.7	6.9	6.9	7.0
Asian	—	—	—	—	—	—	—	103.1	104.7	103.7	104.2	—	—	—	—	—	—	—	6.5	6.6	6.6	6.7
Pacific Islander	—	—	—	—	—	—	—	3.9	4.0	4.1	4.1	—	—	—	—	—	—	—	0.2	0.3	0.3	0.3
American Indian/Alaska Native	2.7	3.0	4.1	7.6	10.0	11.2	11.5	10.7	10.2	9.8	9.5	0.4	0.4	0.5	0.7	0.7	0.8	0.7	0.6	0.6	0.6	0.6
Two or more races	—	—	—	—	—	—	—	19.7	26.3	30.5	33.6	†	†	†	†	†	†	†	1.2	1.7	2.0	2.2
Nonresident alien	17.8	24.1	52.5	93.6	112.4	124.8	128.3	131.1	136.5	144.9	155.2	†	†	†	†	†	†	†	†	†	†	†

—Not available.

†Not applicable.

Note: Race categories exclude persons of Hispanic ethnicity. Because of underreporting and nonreporting of racial/ethnic data, some figures are slightly lower than corresponding data in other tables. Data through 1990 are for institutions of higher education, while later data are for degree-granting institutions. Degree-granting institutions grant associate's or higher degrees and participate in Title IV federal financial aid programs. The degree-granting classification is very similar to the earlier higher education classification, but it includes more 2-year colleges and excludes a few higher education institutions that did not grant degrees. Some data have been revised from previously published figures. Detail may not sum to totals because of rounding.

SOURCE: "Table 306.10. Total Fall Enrollment in Degree-Granting Postsecondary Institutions, by Level of Enrollment, Sex, Attendance Status, and Race/Ethnicity of Student: Selected Years, 1976 through 2013," in "Most Current Digest Tables," Digest of Education Statistics, U.S. Department of Education, Institute of Education Sciences, National Center for Education Statistics, November 2014, https://nces.ed.gov/programs/digest/d14/tables/xls/tabn306.10.xls (accessed July 30, 2015)

FIGURE 9.3

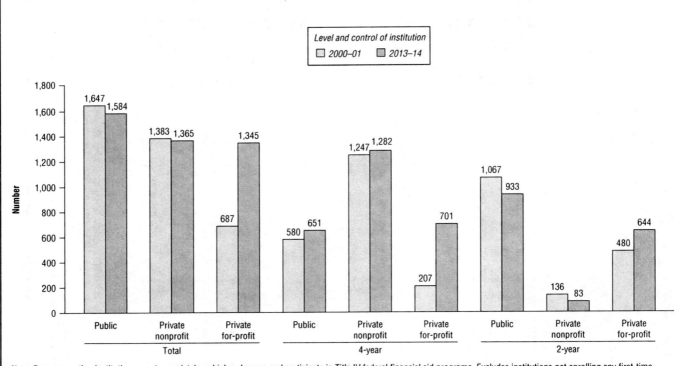

Number of degree-granting institutions, by school type, 2000–01 and 2013–14

Note: Degree-granting institutions grant associate's or higher degrees and participate in Title IV federal financial aid programs. Excludes institutions not enrolling any first-time degree/certificate-seeking undergraduates.

SOURCE: Grace Kena et al., "Figure 1. Number of Degree-Granting Institutions with First-Year Undergraduates, by Level and Control of Institution: Academic Years 2000–01 and 2013–14," in *The Condition of Education 2015*, U.S. Department of Education, Institute of Education Sciences, National Center for Education Statistics, May 2015, http://nces.ed.gov/pubs2015/2015144.pdf (accessed July 30, 2015)

education programs expand from 31,050 in 2000 to 37,909 in 2012, an increase of 22%. Other states that experienced modest growth in adult education enrollment during this period included Alabama, Delaware, Minnesota, North Carolina, and Rhode Island.

DEGREE-GRANTING INSTITUTIONS

Types

Figure 9.3 shows the total numbers of degree-granting institutions with first-year undergraduates by control (public, private nonprofit, and private for-profit) and by type of institution (two year and four year) for the 2000–01 and 2013–14 academic years. Public degree-granting institutions are those that are funded predominantly by public means. In the United States, most public universities are funded and run by the state. They are generally recognizable by having the name of the state as part of the name of the university, such as the University of Missouri or Arizona State University. (However, the University of Pennsylvania, which was founded by Benjamin Franklin [1706–1790], is a private institution.) Private universities are not run by the government. Nonprofit private universities are run as educational and research organizations with primarily private funding. Examples are

Columbia University, Cornell University, Dartmouth College, Harvard University, Princeton University, and Yale University. Some nonprofit private universities are affiliated with religious institutions (such as the University of Notre Dame) or run by religious institutions (such as Brigham Young University).

For-profit institutions are also commonly called career colleges, trade schools, or proprietary schools. The word *proprietary* in this context means privately owned and managed and run as a profit-making business. For-profits focus on training students for specific careers and providing job-specific skills. Examples of the varied programs offered by career colleges are accounting, information systems, dental hygiene, criminal justice, and construction management. Large career colleges offer a wide variety of programs, but some career colleges focus on just one or a few areas, such as plumbing technology. A person wanting to major in classical languages or to pursue a liberal arts education for personal growth, for example, would not attend a career college. Examples of for-profit postsecondary schools are the University of Phoenix, Argosy University, Kaplan University, Capella University, DeVry University, and ITT Technical Institute.

Numbers

During the 2013–14 school year there were 4,294 degree-granting institutions in the United States—1,584 public and 2,710 private. (See Figure 9.3.) Approximately 61.3% (2,634) of all degree-granting institutions were four-year schools and 38.7% (1,660) were two-year schools. Although most four-year schools were private (1,983 private versus 651 public institutions), most two-year schools were public (933 public versus 727 private schools). The total number of degree-granting institutions in the United States increased 15.5% between the 2000–01 and 2011–12 school years, from 3,717 to 4,294.

THE RISE IN NUMBER OF FOR-PROFIT DEGREE-GRANTING INSTITUTIONS. The number of for-profit degree-granting institutions has increased dramatically since the 2000–01 academic year. In that year there were 687 for-profit degree-granting postsecondary institutions in the United States. (See Figure 9.3.) By 2013–14 there were 1,345 for-profit degree-granting institutions in the United States, nearly twice the number that were operating only 13 years earlier. In addition, the number of four-year for-profits in 2013–14 (701) was comparable to the number of two-year for-profits (644), whereas in 2000–01 there were more than twice as many for-profit two-year institutions (480) than for-profit four-year institutions (207).

COLLEGES THAT SERVE SPECIFIC POPULATIONS

Women's Colleges

Women's colleges are those that identify themselves as having an institutional mission that is primarily related to promoting and expanding educational opportunities for women. Women's colleges were founded during the late 19th century in response to a need for advanced education for women at a time when most institutions of higher education admitted only men.

Most of the independent nonprofit women's colleges that developed at that time were located in the Northeast. Educational opportunities in the South during the 19th century were limited to whites, but some higher education institutions for African Americans were formed there after the Civil War (1861–1865). These institutions included a few colleges that were founded especially to serve African American women, two of which still survive: Bennett College in Greensboro, North Carolina, and Spelman College in Atlanta, Georgia. These were the only African American women's colleges in the United States in 2015.

In "Women's Colleges in the United States" (http://www.college-scholarships.com/women_colleges.htm), the American Educational Guidance Center indicates that in 2015 there were 60 women's colleges in 24 states and the District of Columbia. The majority of women's colleges were private four-year institutions, were independent nonprofit institutions or affiliated with the Roman Catholic Church, and were located in the Northeast. Eight were in Massachusetts and seven in Pennsylvania. In 2015 graduates of women's colleges accounted for 2% of the total number of women in the United States who held undergraduate degrees.

Historically Black Colleges and Universities

Historically black colleges and universities (HBCUs) are accredited institutions of higher learning established before 1964, whose principal mission was to educate African Americans. The first HBCU was Cheyney University in Pennsylvania, established in 1837, well before the Civil War. At that time, most African Americans in the nation were still slaves, and the prevailing practice was to limit or prohibit their education.

Richard Humphreys (1750–1832) founded Cheyney University, which began as a high school and then became a college (Cheyney State College), awarding its first baccalaureate degree during the 1930s, almost 100 years after its founding. Two HBCUs were established during the 1850s: Lincoln University in Pennsylvania (1854) and Wilberforce College in Ohio (1856). Both of these colleges were founded by African Americans to promote education among other African Americans.

Another institution whose beginnings go back to the 1850s is now known as the University of the District of Columbia. First known as Miner Normal School, this institution was started in 1851 by Myrtilla Miner (1815–1864) as a teachers school for African American women. In 1955 it united with Wilson Normal School to become the District of Columbia Teachers College. In 1976 the District of Columbia Teachers College, the Federal City College, and Washington Technical Institute merged to form the University of the District of Columbia.

Following the Civil War, educating freed slaves became a top priority of the federal government, the African American community, and private philanthropic groups. Public support in the various states generally came in the form of land grants for school buildings. Many of the HBCUs founded during this period were religious schools, such as Edward Waters College in Florida (1866), Fisk University in Tennessee (1867), and Talladega College in Alabama (1867). Howard University in the District of Columbia was founded in 1867 by an act of Congress. The university was established as a coeducational and multiracial private school.

Table 9.3 shows that during the fall of 2012 there were 101 HBCUs in the United States; 51 were public

TABLE 9.3

Selected statistics on degree-granting historically black colleges and universities, selected years 1990–2013

Selected statistics	Total	Public			Private		
		Total	4-year	2-year	Total	4-year	2-year
Number of institutions, fall 2012	101	51	40	11	50	48	2
Fall enrollment							
Total enrollment, fall 1990	257,152	187,046	171,969	15,077	70,106	68,528	1,578
Males	105,157	76,541	70,220	6,321	28,616	28,054	562
Males, black	82,897	57,255	54,041	3,214	25,642	25,198	444
Females	151,995	110,505	101,749	8,756	41,490	40,474	1,016
Females, black	125,785	86,949	80,883	6,066	38,836	38,115	721
Total enrollment, fall 2000	275,680	199,725	175,404	24,321	75,955	75,306	649
Males	108,164	78,186	68,322	9,864	29,978	29,771	207
Males, black	87,319	60,029	56,017	4,012	27,290	27,085	205
Females	167,516	121,539	107,082	14,457	45,977	45,535	442
Females, black	139,920	96,677	89,260	7,417	43,243	42,810	433
Total enrollment, fall 2010	326,614	249,146	205,774	43,372	77,468	77,325	143
Males	127,437	95,883	78,528	17,355	31,554	31,482	72
Males, black	101,644	72,668	65,552	7,116	28,976	28,904	72
Females	199,177	153,263	127,246	26,017	45,914	45,843	71
Females, black	164,267	121,175	107,686	13,489	43,092	43,021	71
Total enrollment, fall 2012	312,438	237,782	198,568	39,214	74,656	74,465	191
Males	121,722	90,928	75,191	15,737	30,794	30,690	104
Males, black	96,084	68,207	61,571	6,636	27,877	27,773	104
Females	190,716	146,854	123,377	23,477	43,862	43,775	87
Females, black	155,446	114,812	103,008	11,804	40,634	40,548	86
Full-time enrollment, fall 2012	245,872	176,792	157,476	19,316	69,080	68,894	186
Males	98,626	70,192	62,075	8,117	28,434	28,333	101
Females	148,837	106,600	95,401	11,199	42,237	40,561	85
Part-time enrollment, fall 2012	66,566	60,990	41,092	19,898	5,576	5,571	5
Males	23,096	20,736	13,116	7,620	2,360	2,357	3
Females	43,470	40,254	27,976	12,278	3,216	3,214	2
Earned degrees conferred, 2011–12							
Associate's	4,631	4,393	840	3,553	238	183	55
Males	1,579	1,460	190	1,270	119	95	24
Males, black	625	526	99	427	99	75	24
Females	3,052	2,933	650	2,283	119	88	31
Females, black	1,651	1,538	334	1,204	113	82	31
Bachelor's	34,013	24,045	24,045	†	9,968	9,968	†
Males	11,780	8,406	8,406	†	3,374	3,374	†
Males, black	9,833	6,759	6,759	†	3,074	3,074	†
Females	22,233	15,639	15,639	†	6,594	6,594	†
Females, black	19,123	12,914	12,914	†	6,209	6,209	†
Master's	7,654	6,518	6,518	†	1,136	1,136	†
Males	2,332	1,976	1,976	†	356	356	†
Males, black	1,576	1,285	1,285	†	291	291	†
Females	5,322	4,542	4,542	†	780	780	†
Females, black	3,948	3,278	3,278	†	670	670	†
Doctor's[a]	2,285	1,214	1,214	†	1,071	1,071	†
Males	913	499	499	†	414	414	†
Males, black	524	226	226	†	298	298	†
Females	1,372	715	715	†	657	657	†
Females, black	944	442	442	†	502	502	†
Financial statistics, 2011–12[b]			In thousands of current dollars				
Total revenue	$7,885,680	$5,208,919	$4,802,727	$406,193	$2,676,760	$2,672,510	$4,250
Student tuition and fees	1,798,213	943,209	895,296	47,913	855,004	854,508	496
Federal government[c]	2,282,322	1,415,372	1,231,672	183,701	866,949	865,503	1,446
State governments	1,894,960	1,825,546	1,697,442	128,103	69,415	69,415	0
Local governments	110,642	91,996	62,872	29,124	18,646	18,646	0
Private gifts and grants[d]	351,507	105,272	104,897	375	246,235	244,841	1,394
Investment return (gain or loss)	−83,271	31,446	30,893	553	−114,717	−114,729	12
Auxiliary (essentially self-supporting) enterprises	860,291	525,576	518,338	7,238	334,714	333,812	902
Hospitals and other sources	671,017	270,503	261,317	9,185	400,514	400,514	0
Total expenditures	7,734,318	4,963,760	4,589,134	374,626	2,770,558	2,766,473	4,086

institutions and 50 were private institutions. During the fall of 2012, 312,438 students were enrolled. Full-time students (245,872) outnumbered part-time students (66,566) by nearly four to one. Women (190,716, or 61%) made up a majority of all students at these institutions. Most HBCU students were African American— 81.5% (155,446 out of 190,716) of the women and 78.9% (96,084 out of 121,722) of the men.

TABLE 9.3

Selected statistics on degree-granting historically black colleges and universities, selected years 1990–2013 [CONTINUED]

Selected statistics	Total	Public			Private		
		Total	4-year	2-year	Total	4-year	2-year
Instruction	1,958,551	1,347,622	1,224,585	123,037	610,929	609,700	1,229
Research	463,800	309,023	308,522	502	154,777	154,708	68
Academic support	522,044	372,900	346,405	26,495	149,145	149,145	0
Institutional support	1,132,392	628,204	578,169	50,036	504,188	503,287	901
Auxiliary (essentially self-supporting) enterprises	746,153	546,358	536,091	10,267	199,795	199,715	80
Other expenditures	2,911,377	1,759,652	1,595,363	164,289	1,151,725	1,149,918	1,807

†Not applicable.

ᵃIncludes Ph.D., Ed.D., and comparable degrees at the doctoral level, as well as such degrees as M.D., D.D.S., and law degrees that were formerly classified as first-professional degrees.

ᵇTotals (column 2) of public and private institutions together are approximate because public and private not-for-profit institutions fill out different survey forms with different accounting concepts.

ᶜIncludes independent operations.

ᵈIncludes contributions from affiliated entities.

Note: Degree-granting institutions grant associate's or higher degrees and participate in Title IV federal financial aid programs. Historically black colleges and universities are degree-granting institutions established prior to 1964 with the principal mission of educating black Americans. Federal regulations, 20 U.S. Code, Section 1061 (2), allow for certain exceptions to the founding date. Federal, state, and local governments revenue includes appropriations, grants, and contracts. Totals include persons of other racial/ethnic groups not separately identified. Detail may not sum to totals because of rounding.

SOURCE: "Table 313.30. Selected Statistics on Degree-Granting Historically Black Colleges and Universities, by Control and Level of Institution: Selected Years, 1990 through 2013," in "Most Current Digest Tables," *Digest of Education Statistics*, U.S. Department of Education, Institute of Education Sciences, National Center for Education Statistics, May 2014, https://nces.ed.gov/programs/digest/d14/tables/xls/tabn313.30.xls (accessed July 30, 2015)

Hispanic-Serving Institutions

Hispanic-serving institutions (HSIs) are colleges and universities that have a minimum of 25% Hispanic student enrollment. The Hispanic Association of Colleges and Universities reports in *2013 Annual Report* (http://www.hacu.net/images/hacu/about/HACU2013_AnnualReport.pdf) that during the fall of 2014 it had 480 member institutions, affiliates, partners, associated school districts, and faculty and staff caucus members in 35 states, the District of Columbia, Puerto Rico, and 10 countries in South America and Europe. The states that had the most HSIs were California (97), Texas (63), New York (30), Florida (19), and New Mexico (19). Puerto Rico had 32 HSIs.

Native American Colleges

Although Native American (tribally controlled) colleges and universities differ widely in their stages of development, they share some similarities. The governing boards of most are made up primarily of Native Americans or Alaskan Natives, as are their student bodies. According to the NCES (May 2015, http://nces.ed.gov/programs/digest/d14/tables/dt14_312.50.asp?current=yes), during the fall of 2013 there were 34 tribally controlled colleges located in 13 states, most in rural or isolated areas. Eight were private nonprofit institutions, and the rest were public institutions.

Overall, tribal colleges served 18,274 full- and part-time students during the fall of 2013. The college with the smallest enrollment during the fall of 2013 was the White Earth Tribal and Community College in Minnesota, with an enrollment of 60 students. The college with the largest enrollment during the fall of 2013 was Fond du Lac Tribal and Community College in Minnesota, with an enrollment of 2,272 students.

One of the major thrusts of Native American schools is to reinforce traditional cultures and pass them on to coming generations. Their curricula are primarily practical and geared to local needs. Many of them are strongly oriented toward community service.

Most funding for tribally controlled colleges comes from the federal government under the Tribally Controlled College or University Assistance Act. Tribal colleges typically do not receive state support because they have been established as sovereign nations and are usually located on federal trust land.

TRENDS IN DEGREES GRANTED

Trends in Enrollment

Table 9.4 shows that undergraduate enrollment grew from 12.5 million during the fall of 1997 to 18.1 million during the fall of 2011, a 45% increase. During the fall of 2011 women outnumbered men—10.2 million (57%) of those enrolled were women. Total undergraduate enrollment is projected to reach 20.4 million by the fall of 2022. William J. Hussar and Tabitha M. Bailey report in *Projections of Education Statistics to 2022* (February 2014, http://nces.ed.gov/pubs2014/2014051.pdf) that the total number of students enrolled in all postsecondary degree-granting institutions rose from 14.5 million in 1997 to 21 million in 2011, an increase of 45%. Women (12 million) outnumbered men (9 million) in all postsecondary institutions in 2011. According to Hussar and Bailey, total enrollment in all postsecondary

TABLE 9.4

Actual and projected undergraduate enrollment in degree-granting institutions, by sex, attendance status, and type of institution, 1997–2022

[In thousands]

Year	Total	Sex		Attendance status		Control	
		Men	Women	Full-time	Part-time	Public	Private
Actual							
1997	12,451	5,469	6,982	7,419	5,032	10,007	2,443
1998	12,437	5,446	6,991	7,539	4,898	9,950	2,487
1999	12,739	5,584	7,155	7,754	4,986	10,174	2,565
2000	13,155	5,778	7,377	7,923	5,232	10,539	2,616
2001	13,716	6,004	7,711	8,328	5,388	10,986	2,730
2002	14,257	6,192	8,065	8,734	5,523	11,433	2,824
2003	14,480	6,227	8,253	9,045	5,435	11,523	2,957
2004	14,781	6,340	8,441	9,284	5,496	11,651	3,130
2005	14,964	6,409	8,555	9,446	5,518	11,698	3,266
2006	15,184	6,514	8,671	9,571	5,613	11,847	3,337
2007	15,604	6,728	8,876	9,841	5,763	12,138	3,466
2008	16,366	7,067	9,299	10,255	6,111	12,591	3,775
2009	17,565	7,595	9,970	11,144	6,422	13,387	4,179
2010	18,079	7,835	10,244	11,452	6,627	13,704	4,374
2011	18,063	7,817	10,246	11,359	6,704	13,689	4,374
Projected							
2012	18,006	7,771	10,235	11,334	6,672	13,642	4,364
2013	18,187	7,820	10,368	11,390	6,797	13,788	4,400
2014	18,467	7,872	10,595	11,536	6,931	14,002	4,465
2015	18,639	7,881	10,758	11,609	7,030	14,136	4,503
2016	18,848	7,918	10,930	11,711	7,138	14,299	4,550
2017	19,086	7,980	11,106	11,836	7,250	14,482	4,603
2018	19,349	8,055	11,295	11,986	7,363	14,685	4,664
2019	19,634	8,146	11,487	12,169	7,465	14,900	4,733
2020	19,887	8,234	11,653	12,336	7,551	15,092	4,795
2021	20,169	8,335	11,834	12,521	7,648	15,303	4,865
2022	20,399	8,423	11,976	12,673	7,726	15,476	4,923

Note: Detail may not sum to totals because of rounding. Some data have been revised from previously published figures.

SOURCE: William J. Hussar and Tabitha M. Bailey, "Table 27. Actual and Projected Numbers for Undergraduate Enrollment in All Postsecondary Degree-Granting Institutions, by Sex, Attendance Status, and Control of Institution: Fall 1997 through Fall 2022," in *Projections of Education Statistics to 2022*, 41st ed., U.S. Department of Education, Institute of Education Sciences, National Center for Education Statistics, February 2014, http://nces.ed.gov/pubs2014/2014051.pdf (accessed July 30, 2015)

degree-granting institutions is expected to reach 23.9 million by 2022.

Trends in Degrees Conferred

The number of degrees conferred by degree-granting institutions increased tremendously during the past four decades, and the numbers are projected to continue to increase at all levels through the 2023–24 academic year. (See Table 9.5.) The number of associate's degrees conferred increased nearly five times between the 1969–70 and 2011–12 academic years, rising from 206,023 to just over 1 million. During this same period the number of bachelor's degrees conferred more than doubled, from 792,316 to 1.8 million; master's degrees increased 253%, from 213,589 to 754,229; and doctoral degrees conferred nearly tripled, from 59,486 to 170,062.

As Table 9.5 shows, during the 2011–12 school year more women than men earned associate's degrees, bachelor's degrees, master's degrees, and doctoral degrees as had been the case since 1979–80 for associate's degrees,

1989–90 for bachelor's degrees, 1989–90 for master's degrees, and 2009–10 for doctoral degrees.

In *America's Children: Key National Indicators of Well-Being, 2015* (July 2015, http://www.childstats.gov/pdf/ac2015/ac_15.pdf), the Federal Interagency Forum on Child and Family Statistics reports that between 1980 and 2013 the percentage of those aged 16 to 24 years who completed high school and immediately enrolled in college increased from 49% to 66%. In 2013 the immediate enrollment rate for non-Hispanic whites (67%) was comparable to the enrollment rate for Hispanics (66%), while the enrollment rate for non-Hispanic African Americans was 57%. (See Figure 9.4.)

Associate's Degrees

During the 2011–12 school year just over 1 million students earned associate's degrees. (See Table 9.6.) Nearly three-quarters (756,084, or 74%) of those degrees were earned at public institutions. Liberal arts and sciences/general studies/humanities, health professions and related programs, and business were the most popular

TABLE 9.5

Actual and projected degrees conferred, by level of degree and sex of student, selected years 1869–70 to 2023–24

Year	Associate's degrees				Bachelor's degrees				Master's degrees				Doctor's degrees[a]			
	Total	Males	Females	Percent	Total	Males	Females	Percent	Total	Males	Females	Percent	Total	Males	Females	Percent
1869–70	—	—	—	—	9,371[b]	7,993[b]	1,378[b]	14.7	0	0	0	—	1	1	0	0.0
1879–80	—	—	—	—	12,896[b]	10,411[b]	2,485[b]	19.3	879	868	11	1.3	54	51	3	5.6
1889–90	—	—	—	—	15,539[b]	12,857[b]	2,682[b]	17.3	1,015	821	194	19.1	149	147	2	1.3
1899–1900	—	—	—	—	27,410[b]	22,173[b]	5,237[b]	19.1	1,583	1,280	303	19.1	382	359	23	6.0
1909–10	—	—	—	—	37,199[b]	28,762[b]	8,437[b]	22.7	2,113	1,555	558	26.4	443	399	44	9.9
1919–20	—	—	—	—	48,622[b]	31,980[b]	16,642[b]	34.2	4,279	2,985	1,294	30.2	615	522	93	15.1
1929–30	—	—	—	—	122,484[b]	73,615[b]	48,869[b]	39.9	14,969	8,925	6,044	40.4	2,299	1,946	353	15.4
1939–40	—	—	—	—	186,500[b]	109,546[b]	76,954[b]	41.3	26,731	16,508	10,223	38.2	3,290	2,861	429	13.0
1949–50	—	—	—	—	432,058[b]	328,841[b]	103,217[b]	23.9	58,183	41,220	16,963	29.2	6,420	5,804	616	9.6
1959–60	—	—	—	—	392,440[b]	254,063[b]	138,377[b]	35.3	74,435	50,898	23,537	31.6	9,829	8,801	1,028	10.5
1969–70	206,023	117,432	88,591	43.0	792,316	451,097	341,219	43.1	213,589	130,799	82,790	38.8	59,486	53,792	5,694	9.6
1979–80	400,910	183,737	217,173	54.2	929,417	473,611	455,806	49.0	305,196	156,882	148,314	48.6	95,631	69,526	26,105	27.3
1989–90	455,102	191,195	263,907	58.0	1,051,344	491,696	559,648	53.2	330,152	158,052	172,100	52.1	103,508	63,963	39,545	38.2
1994–95	539,691	218,352	321,339	59.5	1,160,134	526,131	634,003	54.6	403,609	183,043	220,566	54.6	114,266	67,324	46,942	41.1
1999–2000	564,933	224,721	340,212	60.2	1,237,875	530,367	707,508	57.2	463,185	196,129	267,056	57.7	118,736	64,930	53,806	45.3
2004–05	696,660	267,536	429,124	61.6	1,439,264	613,000	826,264	57.4	580,151	237,155	342,996	59.1	134,387	67,257	67,130	50.0
2009–10	849,452	322,916	526,536	62.0	1,650,014	706,633	943,381	57.2	693,025	275,197	417,828	60.3	158,558	76,605	81,953	51.7
2010–11	942,327	361,309	581,018	61.7	1,715,913	734,133	981,780	57.2	730,635	291,551	439,084	60.1	163,765	79,654	84,111	51.4
2011–12	1,017,538	391,990	625,548	61.5	1,791,046	765,317	1,025,729	57.3	754,229	302,191	452,038	59.9	170,062	82,611	87,451	51.4
2014–15	1,046,000	418,000	628,000	60.0	1,835,000	778,000	1,057,000	57.6	821,000	327,000	495,000	60.3	177,500	88,000	89,600	50.5
2019–20	1,239,000	492,000	746,000	60.2	1,953,000	808,000	1,145,000	58.6	935,000	361,000	575,000	61.5	197,600	96,500	101,100	51.2
2023–24	1,410,000	556,000	854,000	60.6	2,061,000	842,000	1,219,000	59.1	1,032,000	385,000	647,000	62.7	208,500	100,300	108,100	51.8

—Not available.

[a]Includes Ph.D., Ed.D., and comparable degrees at the doctoral level. Includes most degrees formerly classified as first-professional, such as M.D., D.D.S., and law degrees.

[b]Includes some degrees classified as master's or doctor's degrees in later years.

[c]Projected.

Notes: Data through 1994–95 are for institutions of higher education, while later data are for degree-granting institutions. Degree-granting institutions grant associate's or higher degrees and participate in Title IV federal financial aid programs. Some data have been revised from previously published figures. Detail may not sum to totals because of rounding.

SOURCE: Adapted from "Table 318.10. Degrees Conferred by Degree-Granting Postsecondary Institutions, by Level of Degree and Sex of Student: Selected Years, 1869–70 through 2023–24," in "Most Current Digest Tables," *Digest of Education Statistics*, U.S. Department of Education, Institute of Education Sciences, National Center for Education Statistics, March 2014, https://nces.ed.gov/programs/digest/d13/tables/xls/tabn318.10.xls (accessed July 30, 2015)

FIGURE 9.4

Percentage of high school completers who enrolled in college immediately after high school, by race/ethnicity, 1980–2013

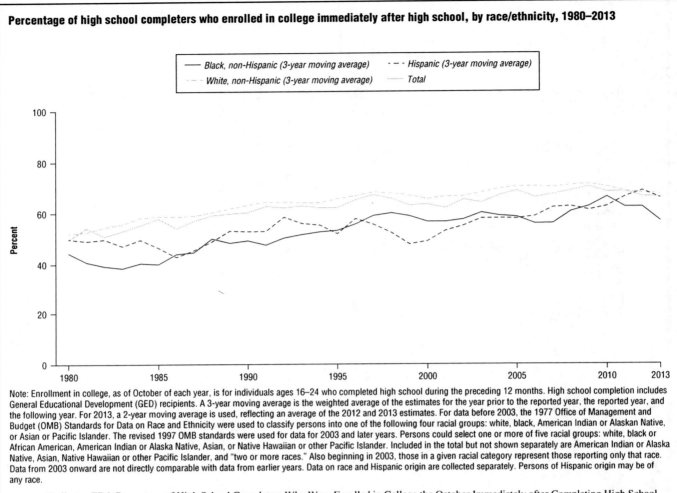

Note: Enrollment in college, as of October of each year, is for individuals ages 16–24 who completed high school during the preceding 12 months. High school completion includes General Educational Development (GED) recipients. A 3-year moving average is the weighted average of the estimates for the year prior to the reported year, the reported year, and the following year. For 2013, a 2-year moving average is used, reflecting an average of the 2012 and 2013 estimates. For data before 2003, the 1977 Office of Management and Budget (OMB) Standards for Data on Race and Ethnicity were used to classify persons into one of the following four racial groups: white, black, American Indian or Alaskan Native, or Asian or Pacific Islander. The revised 1997 OMB standards were used for data for 2003 and later years. Persons could select one or more of five racial groups: white, black or African American, American Indian or Alaska Native, Asian, or Native Hawaiian or other Pacific Islander. Included in the total but not shown separately are American Indian or Alaska Native, Asian, Native Hawaiian or other Pacific Islander, and "two or more races." Also beginning in 2003, those in a given racial category represent those reporting only that race. Data from 2003 onward are not directly comparable with data from earlier years. Data on race and Hispanic origin are collected separately. Persons of Hispanic origin may be of any race.

SOURCE: "Indicator ED6. Percentage of High School Completers Who Were Enrolled in College the October Immediately after Completing High School by Race and Hispanic Origin, 1980–2013," in *America's Children: Key National Indicators of Well-Being, 2015*, Federal Interagency Forum on Child and Family Statistics, July 2015, http://www.childstats.gov/pdf/ac2015/ac_15.pdf (accessed July 30, 2015)

areas of study at public institutions conferring associate's degrees. At both private nonprofit institutions and private for-profit institutions conferring associate's degrees, health professions and related programs were the top area of study.

Bachelor's Degrees

During the 2011–12 academic year, students earned nearly 1.8 million bachelor's degrees. (See Table 9.6.) More than 1.1 million undergraduates earned their bachelor's degrees at public colleges or universities, 526,506 earned their bachelor's degrees at private nonprofit institutions, and 132,654 earned their bachelor's degrees at private for-profit institutions. Among all institutions, the largest number of bachelor's degrees granted were in the area of business (366,815), which accounted for 20.5% of all bachelor's degrees conferred in 2011–12; other areas of study conferring large numbers of degrees included social sciences and history (178,543), health professions and related programs (163,440), and psychology (108,986).

Master's Degrees

As Table 9.5 shows, the number of master's degrees awarded annually increased between 1969–70 and 2011–12, from 213,589 to 754,229. The proportion earned by women has steadily increased as well. During the 1969–70 school year women earned 38.8% (82,790) of all master's degrees; during the 2011–12 academic year the proportion rose to 59.9% (452,038) and was projected to rise to 62.7% (647,000) by the 2023–24 school year. The fields with the greatest numbers of master's degrees awarded in 2011–12 were business (191,571) and education (178,062). (See Table 9.6.)

Doctor's Degrees

According to the NCES, a doctor's degree refers both to a degree earned at the doctoral level, such as a doctor of philosophy or a doctor of education, and to a number of professional degrees (formerly known as first-professional degrees), such as a doctor of medicine, a doctor of law, or

TABLE 9.6

Degrees conferred, by level of degree, type of institution, and field of study, 2011–12

Field of study	All institutions				Public institutions				Private nonprofit institutions				Private for-profit institutions			
	Associate's degrees	Bachelor's degrees	Master's degrees	Doctor's degrees[a]	Associate's degrees	Bachelor's degrees	Master's degrees	Doctor's degrees[a]	Associate's degrees	Bachelor's degrees	Master's degrees	Doctor's degrees[a]	Associate's degrees	Bachelor's degrees	Master's degrees	Doctor's degrees[a]
All fields, total	**1,017,538**	**1,791,046**	**754,229**	**170,062**	**756,084**	**1,131,886**	**349,311**	**84,727**	**54,346**	**526,506**	**325,427**	**79,483**	**207,108**	**132,654**	**79,491**	**5,852**
Agriculture and natural resources	7,066	30,929	6,390	1,333	6,785	25,963	4,985	1,255	281	4,644	1,315	78	0	322	90	0
Architecture and related services	593	9,728	8,448	255	562	7,055	5,207	190	31	2,620	3,140	65	0	53	101	0
Area, ethnic, cultural, gender, and group studies	194	9,232	1,947	302	181	6,012	1,156	180	13	3,219	791	122	0	1	0	0
Biological and biomedical sciences	3,834	95,849	12,415	7,935	3,694	65,732	7,525	5,300	138	29,979	4,890	2,635	2	138	0	0
Business	142,338	366,815	191,571	2,531	83,893	202,276	66,464	961	11,585	111,974	88,410	689	46,860	52,565	36,697	881
Communication, journalism, and related programs	3,495	83,770	9,005	563	3,243	58,473	4,032	465	102	23,876	4,756	98	150	1,421	217	0
Communications technologies	5,000	4,982	491	4	3,198	1,285	85	0	162	1,415	239	4	1,640	2,282	167	0
Computer and information sciences	41,161	47,384	20,917	1,698	20,422	23,176	10,510	1,170	1,879	11,132	8,269	498	18,860	13,076	2,138	30
Construction trades	5,752	377	5	0	4,563	359	5	0	212	17	0	0	977	1	0	0
Education	20,531	105,785	178,062	9,990	16,499	73,277	85,247	5,676	738	29,283	76,115	3,009	3,294	3,225	16,700	1,305
Engineering	3,382	81,382	40,323	8,722	3,310	62,850	26,883	6,404	29	18,218	13,191	2,318	43	314	249	0
Engineering technologies and engineering-related fields[b]	36,510	16,531	4,769	134	24,097	12,894	2,874	56	1,398	1,782	1,632	78	11,015	1,855	263	0
English language and literature/letters	2,137	53,767	9,939	1,427	1,518	37,640	6,282	1,084	21	15,859	3,468	343	598	268	189	0
Family and consumer sciences/human sciences	9,503	23,428	3,157	325	8,821	19,221	1,983	270	452	3,949	842	45	230	258	332	10
Foreign languages, literatures, and linguistics	1,980	21,764	3,827	1,231	1,689	15,559	2,778	786	291	6,198	1,049	445	0	7	0	0
Health professions and related programs	218,041	163,440	83,893	62,090	129,382	91,828	38,206	31,830	18,059	52,023	35,123	29,282	70,600	19,589	10,564	978
Homeland security, law enforcement, and firefighting	50,695	53,767	8,402	117	28,921	30,599	3,236	85	1,922	11,250	2,645	5	19,852	11,918	2,521	27
Legal professions and studies	12,182	4,592	6,614	46,836	6,350	2,299	1,694	15,554	680	1,272	4,728	29,686	5,152	1,021	192	1,596
Liberal arts and sciences, general studies, and humanities	336,554	46,925	3,791	93	3,22,318	32,304	1,396	43	10,641	14,394	2,343	22	3,595	227	52	28
Library science	159	95	7,441	60	159	95	6,146	59	0	0	1,295	1	0	0	0	0
Mathematics and statistics	1,529	18,842	6,245	1,669	1,514	12,776	4,496	1,248	15	6,065	1,749	421	0	1	0	0
Mechanic and repair technologies/technicians	20,714	250	0	0	12,566	178	0	0	1,726	72	0	0	6,422	0	0	0
Military technologies and applied sciences	986	86	29	0	959	57	27	0	13	7	2	0	14	22	0	0
Multi/interdisciplinary studies	27,267	45,716	7,745	727	21,692	31,063	4,249	490	270	9,763	2,845	237	5,305	4,890	651	0
Parks, recreation, leisure, and fitness studies	3,123	38,993	7,047	288	1,940	28,756	5,086	271	244	9,873	1,797	17	939	364	164	0
Philosophy and religious studies	308	12,651	2,003	778	135	5,735	664	351	173	6,735	1,220	426	0	181	119	1
Physical sciences and science technologies	5,824	26,663	6,910	5,370	5,742	18,643	5,237	3,827	81	8,016	1,673	1,543	1	4	0	0
Precision production	3,320	37	11	0	2,975	8	0	0	88	29	11	0	257	0	0	0

TABLE 9.6

Degrees conferred, by level of degree, type of institution, and field of study, 2011–12 [CONTINUED]

Field of study	All institutions				Public institutions				Private nonprofit institutions				Private for-profit institutions			
	Associate's degrees	Bachelor's degrees	Master's degrees	Doctor's degrees[a]	Associate's degrees	Bachelor's degrees	Master's degrees	Doctor's degrees[a]	Associate's degrees	Bachelor's degrees	Master's degrees	Doctor's degrees[a]	Associate's degrees	Bachelor's degrees	Master's degrees	Doctor's degrees[a]
Psychology	4,717	108,986	26,834	5,928	4,372	72,921	8,282	2,398	275	32,754	14,103	2,660	70	3,311	4,449	870
Public administration and social services	9,143	29,695	41,680	884	5,752	18,017	24,694	513	474	8,517	15,164	253	2,917	3,161	1,822	118
Social sciences and history	14,132	178,543	21,889	4,597	14,007	121,679	11,898	3,046	95	54,181	9,410	1,551	30	2,683	581	0
Social sciences	13,321	143,422	17,734	3,628	13,227	97,743	9,068	2,404	83	43,353	8,422	1,224	11	2,326	244	0
History	811	35,121	4,155	969	780	23,936	2,830	642	12	10,828	988	327	19	357	337	0
Theology and religious vocations	839	9,369	13,396	2,447	1	1	0	0	817	9,286	13,341	2,441	21	82	55	6
Transportation and materials moving	2,098	4,876	1,702	0	1,591	2,204	86	0	430	2,552	1,561	0	77	120	55	0
Visual and performing arts	22,431	95,797	17,331	1,728	13,233	50,951	7,898	1,215	1,011	35,552	8,310	511	8,187	9,294	1,123	2

[a]Includes Ph.D., Ed.D., and comparable degrees at the doctoral level, as well as such degrees as M.D., D.D.S., and law degrees that were formerly classified as first-professional degrees.

[b]Excludes "Construction trades" and "Mechanic and repair technologies/technicians," which are listed separately.

Note: Data are for postsecondary institutions participating in Title IV federal financial aid programs. To facilitate trend comparisons, certain aggregations have been made of the degree fields as reported in the Integrated Postsecondary Education Data System (IPEDS): "Agriculture and natural resources" includes agriculture, agriculture operations, and related sciences and natural resources and conservation; and "Business" includes business management, marketing, and related support services and personal and culinary services.

SOURCE: "Table 318.50. Degrees Conferred by Postsecondary Institutions, by Control of Institution, Level of Degree, and Field of Study: 2011–12," in "Most Current Digest Tables," *Digest of Education Statistics*, U.S. Department of Education, Institute of Education Sciences, National Center for Education Statistics, July 2013, https://nces.ed.gov/programs/digest/d13/tables/xls/tabn318.50.xls (accessed July 30, 2015)

a doctor of dental surgery. Table 9.5 indicates that the number of doctor's degrees conferred jumped dramatically between 1959–60 and 1969–70. In 1959–60, 9,829 students received doctor's degrees; in 1969–70 this figure jumped to 59,486, an increase of 505%. By 1989–90 there were 103,508 doctor's degrees conferred in the United States. This number continued to climb, reaching 170,062 by the 2011–12 academic year. The proportion of women earning doctor's degrees also rose dramatically during this span. In 1979–80, 27.3% of all doctor's degrees were earned by women; by 2011–12 the proportion of doctor's degrees earned by women (51.4%) exceeded the proportion earned by men (48.6%). As Table 9.6 shows, more doctor's degrees were conferred in the area of health professions and related programs (62,090) than in any other field of study in 2011–12.

Among the disciplines formerly granting first-professional degrees—dentistry, medicine, and law—a total of 68,481 doctor's degrees were conferred in 2011–12. (See Table 9.7.) The largest number of degrees were conferred in law (46,445), followed by medical degrees (16,927) and dentistry degrees (5,109). Table 9.7 also shows the dramatic increase in the number of legal professionals between the mid-1950s and 2011–12. In 1955–56, there were 8,262 law degrees conferred in the United States. By comparison, 6,810 students earned medical degrees that year, or roughly 82% of the total number of students who earned law degrees. By 1975–76 the number of medical degrees conferred had nearly doubled, to 13,426; meanwhile, the number of students receiving law degrees more than tripled, to 32,293. The number of law degrees conferred fluctuated over the next two decades. In 1984–85, 37,491 law degrees were conferred; this figure subsequently dipped to 35,397 in 1987–88, rose to 40,302 in 1992–93, then fell again to 37,904 in 2000–01, before rising steadily over the next decade.

INSTRUCTORS IN DEGREE-GRANTING INSTITUTIONS

During the fall of 2013 there were 791,391 full-time faculty members employed at degree-granting institutions. (See Table 9.8.). Of these, 181,530 were full professors, 155,095 were associate professors, and 166,045 were assistant professors. The remaining 288,701 full-time faculty members consisted of instructors, lecturers, and other faculty.

Gender

Table 9.8 shows that during the fall of 2013, 436,456 men accounted for 55.2% of all full-time faculty members at degree-granting institutions. More than a quarter of male full-time faculty (125,836, or 28.8%) were full professors in 2013. Of the 354,935 full-time female faculty members at degree-granting institutions during the fall of 2013, only 15.7% (55,694) were full professors.

Race and Ethnicity

During the fall of 2013, 575,491 whites made up 72.7% of all full-time faculty at degree-granting institutions. (See Table 9.8.) African Americans accounted for 5.5% (43,188) of full-time faculty, Hispanics made up 4.2% (33,217), Asians or Pacific Islanders made up 9.1% (72,246), and Native Americans or Alaskan Natives made up 0.4% (3,538). Nonresident aliens accounted for 4.9% (38,407) of full-time faculty during the fall of 2013. Nonresident aliens are people who are not U.S. citizens and do not meet certain government requirements for residency; employees who are nonresident aliens include visiting teachers and researchers.

Faculty Salaries

According to Kena et al., average salaries for full-time faculty at private nonprofit institutions were $86,800 during the 2013–14 academic year. These salaries were somewhat higher than the average salaries received by full-time faculty at public degree-granting institutions ($75,200), and considerably higher than those received by full-time faculty at private for-profit institutions ($50,700). Furthermore, Kena et al. note that the average faculty salaries at private for-profit schools actually rose the fastest between 1999–2000 and 2013–14, increasing 24% during that span. By comparison, the average faculty salaries at private nonprofit institutions increased only 7% between 1999–2000 and 2013–14, while faculty salaries at public institutions actually decreased 1% over the same period.

Figure 9.5 shows the average salaries for full-time faculty members at a range of degree-granting institutions during the 2013–14 academic year. Faculty at private nonprofit doctoral institutions received the highest compensation in 2013–14, with an average salary of $101,700 per year; by comparison, professors at public doctoral institutions earned an average of $85,900 per year. The lowest compensation for full-time faculty were found at private for-profit institutions, where instructors earned an average annual salary of $50,700.

THE COST OF HIGHER EDUCATION

According to the College Board, in *Trends in College Pricing, 2014* (2014, http://trends.collegeboard.org/sites/default/files/2014-trends-college-pricing-final-web.pdf), the average annual cost of tuition and fees at private nonprofit four-year postsecondary institutions (in constant 2014 dollars) nearly doubled between 1989–90 and 2014–15, from $16,591 to $31,231 per year. Public four-year colleges and universities saw an even higher proportional rise in annual tuition and fees, rising from $3,248 in 1989–90 to $9,139 in 2014–15, an increase of 181%.

TABLE 9.7

Doctor's degrees conferred in dentistry, medicine, and law, by sex of student, selected years 1949–50 to 2011–12

Year	Dentistry (D.D.S. or D.M.D.) Number of institutions conferring degrees	Number of degrees conferred Total	Males	Females	Medicine (M.D.) Number of institutions conferring degrees	Number of degrees conferred Total	Males	Females	Law (LL.B. or J.D.) Number of institutions conferring degrees	Number of degrees conferred Total	Males	Females
1949–50	40	2,579	2,561	18	72	5,612	5,028	584	—	—	—	—
1951–52	41	2,918	2,895	23	72	6,201	5,871	330	—	—	—	—
1953–54	42	3,102	3,063	39	73	6,712	6,377	335	—	—	—	—
1955–56	42	3,009	2,975	34	73	6,810	6,464	346	131	8,262	7,974	288
1957–58	43	3,065	3,031	34	75	6,816	6,469	347	131	9,394	9,122	272
1959–60	45	3,247	3,221	26	79	7,032	6,645	387	134	9,240	9,010	230
1961–62	46	3,183	3,166	17	81	7,138	6,749	389	134	9,364	9,091	273
1963–64	46	3,180	3,168	12	82	7,303	6,878	425	133	10,679	10,372	307
1964–65	46	3,108	3,086	22	81	7,304	6,832	472	137	11,583	11,216	367
1965–66	47	3,178	3,146	32	84	7,673	7,170	503	136	13,246	12,776	470
1967–68	48	3,422	3,375	47	85	7,944	7,318	626	138	16,454	15,805	649
1968–69	—	3,408	3,376	32	—	8,025	7,415	610	—	17,053	16,373	680
1969–70	48	3,718	3,684	34	86	8,314	7,615	699	145	14,916	14,115	801
1970–71	48	3,745	3,703	42	89	8,919	8,110	809	147	17,421	16,181	1,240
1971–72	48	3,862	3,819	43	92	9,253	8,423	830	147	21,764	20,266	1,498
1972–73	51	4,047	3,992	55	97	10,307	9,388	919	152	27,205	25,037	2,168
1973–74	52	4,440	4,355	85	99	11,356	10,093	1,263	151	29,326	25,986	3,340
1974–75	52	4,773	4,627	146	104	12,447	10,818	1,629	154	29,296	24,881	4,415
1975–76	56	5,425	5,187	238	107	13,426	11,252	2,174	166	32,293	26,085	6,208
1976–77	57	5,138	4,764	374	109	13,461	10,891	2,570	169	34,104	26,447	7,657
1977–78	57	5,189	4,623	566	109	14,279	11,210	3,069	169	34,402	25,457	8,945
1978–79	58	5,434	4,794	640	109	14,786	11,381	3,405	175	35,206	25,180	10,026
1979–80	58	5,258	4,558	700	112	14,902	11,416	3,486	179	35,647	24,893	10,754
1980–81	58	5,460	4,672	788	116	15,505	11,672	3,833	176	36,331	24,563	11,768
1981–82	59	5,282	4,467	815	119	15,814	11,867	3,947	180	35,991	23,965	12,026
1982–83	59	5,585	4,631	954	118	15,484	11,350	4,134	177	36,853	23,550	13,303
1983–84	60	5,353	4,302	1,051	119	15,813	11,359	4,454	179	37,012	23,382	13,630
1984–85	59	5,339	4,233	1,106	120	16,041	11,167	4,874	181	37,491	23,070	14,421
1985–86	59	5,046	3,907	1,139	120	15,938	11,022	4,916	181	35,844	21,874	13,970
1986–87	58	4,741	3,603	1,138	121	15,428	10,431	4,997	179	36,056	21,561	14,495
1987–88	57	4,477	3,300	1,177	122	15,358	10,278	5,080	180	35,397	21,067	14,330
1988–89	58	4,265	3,124	1,141	124	15,460	10,310	5,150	182	35,634	21,069	14,565
1989–90	57	4,100	2,834	1,266	124	15,075	9,923	5,152	182	36,485	21,079	15,406
1990–91	55	3,699	2,510	1,189	121	15,043	9,629	5,414	179	37,945	21,643	16,302
1991–92	52	3,593	2,431	1,162	120	15,243	9,796	5,447	177	38,848	22,260	16,588
1992–93	55	3,605	2,383	1,222	122	15,531	9,679	5,852	184	40,302	23,182	17,120
1993–94	53	3,787	2,330	1,457	121	15,368	9,544	5,824	185	40,044	22,826	17,218
1994–95	53	3,897	2,480	1,417	119	15,537	9,507	6,030	183	39,349	22,592	16,757
1995–96	53	3,697	2,374	1,323	119	15,341	9,061	6,280	183	39,828	22,508	17,320
1996–97	52	3,784	2,387	1,397	118	15,571	9,121	6,450	184	40,079	22,548	17,531
1997–98	53	4,032	2,490	1,542	117	15,424	9,006	6,418	185	39,331	21,876	17,455
1998–99	53	4,143	2,673	1,470	118	15,566	8,972	6,594	185	38,297	21,102	17,195
1999–2000	54	4,250	2,547	1,703	118	15,286	8,761	6,525	190	38,152	20,638	17,514
2000–01	54	4,391	2,696	1,695	118	15,403	8,728	6,675	192	37,904	19,981	17,923
2001–02	53	4,239	2,608	1,631	118	15,237	8,469	6,768	192	38,981	20,254	18,727
2002–03	53	4,345	2,654	1,691	118	15,034	8,221	6,813	194	39,067	19,916	19,151
2003–04	53	4,335	2,532	1,803	118	15,442	8,273	7,169	195	40,209	20,332	19,877
2004–05	53	4,454	2,505	1,949	120	15,461	8,151	7,310	198	43,423	22,297	21,126
2005–06	54	4,389	2,435	1,954	119	15,455	7,900	7,555	197	43,440	22,597	20,843
2006–07	55	4,596	2,548	2,048	120	15,730	7,987	7,743	200	43,486	22,777	20,709
2007–08	55	4,795	2,661	2,134	120	15,646	7,935	7,711	201	43,769	23,197	20,572
2008–09	55	4,918	2,637	2,281	120	15,987	8,164	7,823	203	44,045	23,860	20,185
2009–10	55	5,062	2,745	2,317	120	16,356	8,468	7,888	205	44,345	23,394	20,951
2010–11	55	5,071	2,764	2,307	120	16,863	8,701	8,162	206	44,445	23,493	20,952
2011–12	55	5,109	2,748	2,361	120	16,927	8,809	8,118	207	46,445	24,576	21,869

—Not available.

Note: Data are for postsecondary institutions participating in Title IV federal financial aid programs.

SOURCE: "Table 324.40. Number of Postsecondary Institutions Conferring Doctor's Degrees in Dentistry, Medicine, and Law, and Number of Such Degrees Conferred, by Sex of Student: Selected Years, 1949–50 through 2011–12," in "Most Current Digest Tables," *Digest of Education Statistics*, U.S. Department of Education, Institute of Education Sciences, National Center for Education Statistics, July 2013, https://nces.ed.gov/programs/digest/d13/tables/xls/tabn324.40.xls (accessed July 30, 2015)

Institutional Revenues

The primary sources of revenue for public institutions of higher education are state appropriations (funds received from acts of state legislature), local appropriations (funds received from legislatures lower than the state), student tuition and fees, gifts, and portions of faculty grants and contracts that are deemed useable for overhead expenses. Private postsecondary institutions do not include state and

TABLE 9.8

Full-time faculty members in degree-granting institutions, by sex, race/ethnicity, and academic rank, 2009, 2011, and 2013

Year, sex, and academic rank	Total	White	Black, Hispanic, Asian, Pacific Islander, American Indian/ Alaska Native, and two or more races				Asian/Pacific			American Indian/ Alaska Native	Two or more races	Race/ ethnicity unknown	Non- resident alien[b]
			Total	Percent[a]	Black	Hispanic	Total	Asian	Pacific Islander				
2009													
Total	729,152	551,230	130,903	19.2	39,706	28,022	59,480	—	—	3,458	—	16,059	31,197
Professors	177,566	149,553	24,633	14.1	6,086	4,683	13,281	—	—	580	—	1,923	1,460
Associate professors	148,959	117,241	26,779	18.6	8,162	5,382	12,626	—	—	601	—	2,387	2,560
Assistant professors	171,622	117,794	37,199	24.0	10,974	6,783	18,634	—	—	717	—	4,616	12,104
Instructors	104,554	78,346	20,951	21.1	7,807	6,575	5,546	—	—	1,002	—	3,399	1,879
Lecturers	33,372	24,925	5,851	19.0	1,813	1,583	2,319	—	—	139	—	882	1,711
Other faculty	93,079	63,371	15,490	19.7	4,864	3,016	7,074	—	—	419	—	2,852	11,483
2011													
Total	762,114	564,218	147,495	20.7	41,662	31,335	66,842	65,469	1,373	3,534	4,122	16,999	33,402
Professors	181,509	150,364	27,559	15.5	6,517	5,180	14,617	14,425	192	589	656	2,202	1,384
Associate professors	155,201	119,415	30,605	20.4	8,695	6,144	14,364	14,129	235	597	805	2,477	2,704
Assistant professors	174,052	118,022	39,986	25.3	10,994	7,428	19,820	19,445	375	701	1,043	4,926	11,118
Instructors	109,042	80,690	23,162	22.3	8,602	6,907	5,807	5,448	359	981	865	3,262	1,928
Lecturers	34,473	25,821	6,261	19.5	1,688	1,773	2,455	2,420	35	135	210	848	1,543
Other faculty	107,837	69,906	19,922	22.2	5,166	3,903	9,779	9,602	177	531	543	3,284	14,725
Males	427,214	316,133	79,707	20.1	18,63	16,341	40,989	40,368	621	1,752	1,989	9,600	21,774
Professors	128,649	106,069	19,812	15.7	3,984	3,499	11,550	11,420	130	362	417	1,643	1,125
Associate professors	89,742	68,493	17,820	20.6	4,373	3,437	9,260	9,142	118	313	437	1,574	1,855
Assistant professors	88,173	58,538	19,877	25.3	4,458	3,692	10,970	10,820	150	303	454	2,694	7,064
Instructors	48,124	35,864	9,750	21.4	3,138	3,133	2,668	2,525	143	463	348	1,486	1,024
Lecturers	15,690	11,721	2,740	18.9	751	753	1,110	1,090	20	47	79	410	819
Other faculty	56,836	35,448	9,708	21.5	1,932	1,827	5,431	5,371	60	264	254	1,793	9,887
Females	334,900	248,085	67,788	21.5	23,02	14,994	25,853	25,101	752	1,782	2,133	7,399	11,628
Professors	52,860	44,295	7,747	14.9	2,533	1,681	3,067	3,005	62	227	239	559	259
Associate professors	65,459	50,922	12,785	20.1	4,322	2,707	5,104	4,987	117	284	368	903	849
Assistant professors	85,879	59,484	20,109	25.3	6,536	3,736	8,850	8,625	225	398	589	2,232	4,054
Instructors	60,918	44,826	13,412	23.0	5,464	3,774	3,139	2,923	216	518	517	1,776	904
Lecturers	18,783	14,100	3,521	20.0	937	1,020	1,345	1,330	15	88	131	438	724
Other faculty	51,001	34,458	10,214	22.9	3,234	2,076	4,348	4,231	117	267	289	1,491	4,838
2013[c]													
Total	791,391	575,491	157,480	21.5	43,188	33,217	72,246	71,038	1,208	3,538	5,291	20,013	38,407
Professors	181,530	148,577	29,111	16.4	6,665	5,604	15,417	15,247	170	573	852	2,323	1,519
Associate professors	155,095	116,817	32,580	21.8	8,812	6,381	15,809	15,626	183	591	987	2,859	2,839
Assistant professors	166,045	112,262	38,011	25.3	10,542	7,130	18,402	18,070	332	683	1,254	5,695	10,077
Instructors	99,304	73,859	20,684	21.9	7,448	6,340	5,236	4,950	286	879	781	3,180	1,581
Lecturers	36,728	27,453	6,591	19.4	1,728	2,015	2,436	2,403	33	117	295	1,151	1,533
Other faculty	152,689	96,523	30,503	24.0	7,993	5,747	14,946	14,742	204	695	1,122	4,805	20,858
Males	436,456	316,912	83,905	20.9	18,90	17,198	43,519	42,928	591	1,736	2,547	10,813	24,826
Professors	125,836	102,520	20,450	16.6	4,018	3,669	11,882	11,772	110	350	531	1,664	1,202
Associate professors	87,420	65,320	18,552	22.1	4,321	3,533	9,897	9,810	87	287	514	1,727	1,821
Assistant professors	82,331	54,700	18,387	25.2	4,169	3,506	9,887	9,725	162	304	521	2,957	6,287
Instructors	42,877	32,014	8,665	21.3	2,714	2,888	2,304	2,179	125	430	329	1,349	849
Lecturers	16,588	12,464	2,756	18.1	760	834	992	983	9	39	131	580	788
Other faculty	81,404	49,894	15,095	23.2	2,923	2,768	8,557	8,459	98	326	521	2,536	13,879
Females	354,935	258,579	73,575	22.2	24,28	16,019	28,727	28,110	617	1,802	2,744	9,200	13,581
Professors	55,694	46,057	8,661	15.8	2,647	1,935	3,535	3,475	60	223	321	659	317
Associate professors	67,675	51,497	14,028	21.4	4,491	2,848	5,912	5,816	96	304	473	1,132	1,018
Assistant professors	83,714	57,562	19,624	25.4	6,373	3,624	8,515	8,345	170	379	733	2,738	3,790
Instructors	56,427	41,845	12,019	22.3	4,734	3,452	2,932	2,771	161	449	452	1,831	732
Lecturers	20,140	14,989	3,835	20.4	968	1,181	1,444	1,420	24	78	164	571	745
Other faculty	71,285	46,629	15,408	24.8	5,070	2,979	6,389	6,283	106	369	601	2,269	6,979

—Not available.

[a]Combined total of faculty who were black, Hispanic, Asian, Pacific Islander, American Indian/Alaska Native, and of two or more races as a percentage of total faculty, excluding race/ethnicity unknown and nonresident alien.

[b]Race/ethnicity not collected.

[c]Only instructional faculty were classified by academic rank. Primarily research and primarily public service faculty, as well as faculty without ranks, appear under "other faculty."

Note: Degree-granting institutions grant associate's or higher degrees and participate in Title IV federal financial aid programs. Includes institutions with fewer than 15 full-time employees; these institutions did not report staff data prior to 2007. Race categories exclude persons of Hispanic ethnicity. Some data have been revised from previously published figures.

SOURCE: "Table 315.20. Full-Time Faculty in Degree-Granting Postsecondary Institutions, by Race/Ethnicity, Sex, and Academic Rank: Fall 2009, Fall 2011, and Fall 2013," in "Most Current Digest Tables," *Digest of Education Statistics*, U.S. Department of Education, Institute of Education Sciences, National Center for Education Statistics, March 2015, https://nces.ed.gov/programs/digest/d14/tables/xls/tabn315.20.xls (accessed July 30, 2015)

FIGURE 9.5

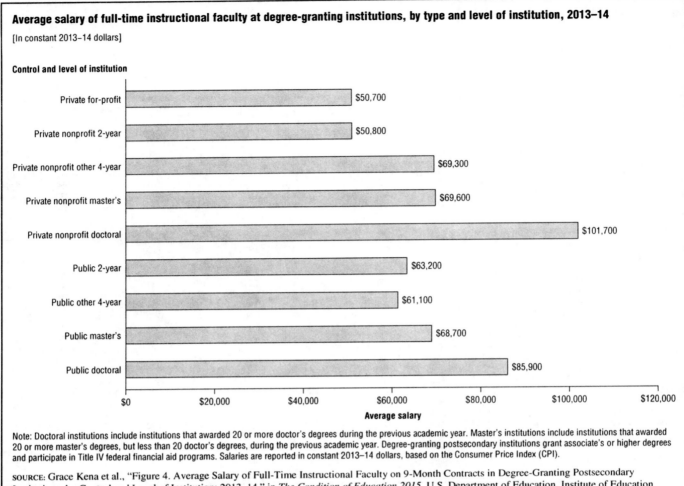

Average salary of full-time instructional faculty at degree-granting institutions, by type and level of institution, 2013–14

[In constant 2013–14 dollars]

Control and level of institution

Private for-profit	$50,700
Private nonprofit 2-year	$50,800
Private nonprofit other 4-year	$69,300
Private nonprofit master's	$69,600
Private nonprofit doctoral	$101,700
Public 2-year	$63,200
Public other 4-year	$61,100
Public master's	$68,700
Public doctoral	$85,900

Average salary

Note: Doctoral institutions include institutions that awarded 20 or more doctor's degrees during the previous academic year. Master's institutions include institutions that awarded 20 or more master's degrees, but less than 20 doctor's degrees, during the previous academic year. Degree-granting postsecondary institutions grant associate's or higher degrees and participate in Title IV federal financial aid programs. Salaries are reported in constant 2013–14 dollars, based on the Consumer Price Index (CPI).

SOURCE: Grace Kena et al., "Figure 4. Average Salary of Full-Time Instructional Faculty on 9-Month Contracts in Degree-Granting Postsecondary Institutions, by Control and Level of Institution: 2013–14," in *The Condition of Education 2015*, U.S. Department of Education, Institute of Education Sciences, National Center for Education Statistics, May 2015, http://nces.ed.gov/pubs2015/2015144.pdf (accessed July 30, 2015)

local appropriations in their sources of revenue. In addition, some postsecondary institutions have endowments, which are gifts of money or property given with the stipulation that the gift be invested and the proceeds be used for university purposes while the principal remains intact. Endowments are usually large gifts from wealthy donors and can provide funds in perpetuity. The College Board notes in *Trends in College Pricing, 2014* that only a relatively small number of public and private institutions have endowment wealth, and most are universities that award doctoral degrees. The National Association of College and University Business Officers finds in *U.S. and Canadian Institutions Listed by Fiscal Year (FY) 2014 Endowment Market Value and Change in Endowment Market Value from FY2013 to FY2014* (February 2015, http://www.nacubo.org/Documents/EndowmentFiles/2014_Endowment_Market_Values_Revised.pdf) that 92 universities in the United States and Canada—headed by Harvard University, the University of Texas system, and Yale University—each had over $1 billion in endowment wealth in 2014.

According to the College Board, total state appropriations for public postsecondary instruction decreased 16% between the 2007–08 and 2013–14 school years after adjusting for inflation. Enrollments, however, increased 9% over this six-year span. The College Board notes that appropriations per student at public institutions declined between 2005–06 and 2011–12, when they fell to $6,800 per student (in 2013 dollars), before rising to $7,161 per student in 2013–14.

What Students Pay

In *Trends in College Pricing, 2014*, the College Board states that during the 2014–15 school year the average residential student (living on campus) paid $23,410 in total costs if he or she attended an in-state, public four-year college, including $9,193 in tuition and fees, $9,804 in room and board, $1,225 in books and supplies, $1,146 in transportation, and $2,096 in other costs. At a private nonprofit four-year college, total costs were $46,272 per residential student, of which $31,231 was for tuition and fees, $11,188 was for room and board, $1,244 was for books and supplies, $1,002 was for transportation, and $1,607 was for other expenses.

The cost of a postsecondary education varies regionally. The College Board indicates that in 2014–15 the South had the lowest average tuition rate for private nonprofit four-year institutions, while the Southwest had the lowest average tuition rate for public four-year institutions. New England had the highest average rate for both public and private four-year institutions in that academic year.

In "America's 20 Most Expensive Colleges" (August 26, 2015, http://www.businessinsider.com/most-expensive-colleges-in-america-2015-8), Peter Jacobs charts the 20 most expensive colleges and universities in the United States in 2015–16. Harvey Mudd College in Claremont, California, topped the list, at a cost of $67,255 per year. This total included $50,749 in tuition and fees and $16,506 in room and board. The second-most expensive institution, Columbia University in New York City, had the highest tuition and fees of any college or university on the list, with tuition and fees accounting for $53,523 of the total costs of $66,383 in 2015–16. Other colleges and universities in the top five included New York University ($65,860), Sarah Lawrence College ($65,630) in Yonkers, New York, and the University of Chicago ($64,965).

Financial Assistance for Students

According to the College Board, in *Trends in Student Aid, 2014* (2014, http://trends.collegeboard.org/sites/default/files/2014-trends-student-aid-final-web.pdf), total undergraduate aid during the 2013–14 academic year consisted of federal loans (Stafford loans to students, Perkins loans to high-need students, and parent loans for undergraduate students [PLUS]; 34%), institutional grants (21%), federal Pell grants (18%), education tax benefits (8%), other federal programs (7%), private and employer grants (6%), state grants (5%), and federal work-study programs (0.9%).

Stafford loans (named after U.S. senator Robert T. Stafford [1913–2006; R-VT]) are student loans that have low interest rates and deferred payments until graduation. Students who are eligible for low-interest Perkins loans (named after U.S. representative Carl Dewey Perkins [1912–1984; D-KY]) can have their loan canceled if they participate in military, teaching, or public service employment. PLUS loans have a higher interest rate than student loans, and payments begin right away, but usually the parents have 10 years to pay off the loan. Pell grants (named after U.S. senator Claiborne Pell [1918–2009; D-RI]) are awarded based on need to low-income undergraduate and certain graduate students. Grants do not have to be paid back.

Richard Fry of the Pew Research Center reports in *The Changing Profile of Student Borrowers* (October 7, 2014, http://www.pewsocialtrends.org/files/2014/10/2014-10-07_Student-Debtors-FINAL.pdf) that total student borrowing for higher education has grown dramatically since the early 1990s. According to Fry, student debt topped $24 billion (in 2012 dollars) in 1990–91; by 2012–13, this figure had grown to $110 billion, an increase of 352%. (See Figure 9.6.) The median (half were higher and half were lower) debt amount owed at graduation by undergraduates who had taken out student loans also rose significantly during this period. In 1992–93 the average

FIGURE 9.6

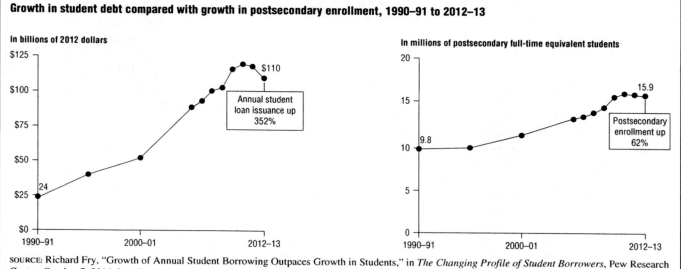

Growth in student debt compared with growth in postsecondary enrollment, 1990–91 to 2012–13

SOURCE: Richard Fry, "Growth of Annual Student Borrowing Outpaces Growth in Students," in *The Changing Profile of Student Borrowers*, Pew Research Center, October 7, 2014, http://www.pewsocialtrends.org/files/2014/10/2014-10-07_Student-Debtors-FINAL.pdf (accessed July 30, 2015)

FIGURE 9.7

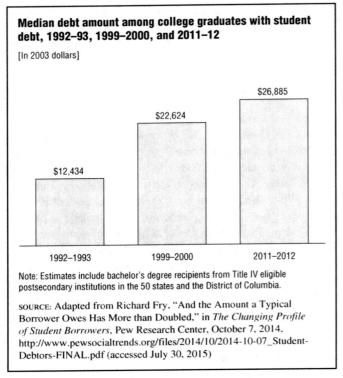

Median debt amount among college graduates with student debt, 1992–93, 1999–2000, and 2011–12

[In 2003 dollars]

$12,434 (1992–1993)
$22,624 (1999–2000)
$26,885 (2011–2012)

Note: Estimates include bachelor's degree recipients from Title IV eligible postsecondary institutions in the 50 states and the District of Columbia.

SOURCE: Adapted from Richard Fry, "And the Amount a Typical Borrower Owes Has More than Doubled," in *The Changing Profile of Student Borrowers*, Pew Research Center, October 7, 2014, http://www.pewsocialtrends.org/files/2014/10/2014-10-07_Student-Debtors-FINAL.pdf (accessed July 30, 2015)

FIGURE 9.8

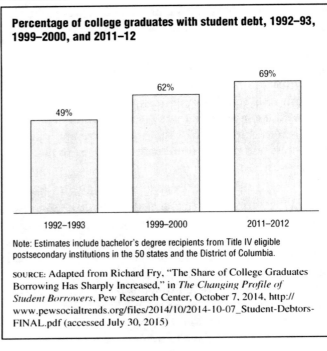

Percentage of college graduates with student debt, 1992–93, 1999–2000, and 2011–12

49% (1992–1993)
62% (1999–2000)
69% (2011–2012)

Note: Estimates include bachelor's degree recipients from Title IV eligible postsecondary institutions in the 50 states and the District of Columbia.

SOURCE: Adapted from Richard Fry, "The Share of College Graduates Borrowing Has Sharply Increased," in *The Changing Profile of Student Borrowers*, Pew Research Center, October 7, 2014, http://www.pewsocialtrends.org/files/2014/10/2014-10-07_Student-Debtors-FINAL.pdf (accessed July 30, 2015)

college student with student loan debt owed $12,434 at graduation. (See Figure 9.7.) By 2011–12 this figure had more than doubled, to $26,885.

The proportion of college students graduating with student loan debt also rose during this span. Although fewer than half (49%) of all undergraduates financed their education with student loans in 1992–93, by 2011–12 more than two-thirds (69%) of college graduates had student loan debt. (See Figure 9.8.) As Figure 9.9 shows, graduates from high-income families assumed a higher proportion of overall student debt between 1993 and 2012. During this span the share of student loans taken on by high-income families rose 105%. In contrast, the share of total student debt assumed by graduates from low-income families rose only 16%. African American students bore a disproportionate share of student debt during these years. Between 2000 and 2014, 39% of white students graduated from college without student loan debt, whereas only 22% of African American students left college without loan debt. (See Table 9.9.) Meanwhile, African American students with student loan debt owed more at graduation than white students. Between 2000 and 2014, 50% of all African American students borrowed $25,000 or more in student loans to help pay for their education, compared with 34% of white students.

ONLINE EDUCATION

In the face of rising costs that are associated with attending traditional colleges and universities, many students are seeking alternative ways to pursue a higher education. The early 21st century has seen the emergence of a broad range of online institutions and programs aimed at enabling students to earn college credit, certificates, and even advanced degrees over the Internet. Besides offering students the opportunity to take college courses at lower prices, online universities also provide students with a level of flexibility and convenience not typically available at conventional schools. Meanwhile, an increasing number of traditional institutions are beginning to include online classes in their course catalogs. According to Eric Brooks and Robert Morse, in "Methodology: Best Online Bachelor's Programs Rankings" (USNews.com, January 6, 2015), by 2014 nearly 300 schools nationwide, or 17% of all institutions surveyed in the *U.S. News and World Report*'s annual rankings of the country's colleges and universities, offered students the opportunity to earn a bachelor's degree over the Internet. Brooks and Morse note that most students pursuing a college education online in 2014 were older adults who had already earned some credit toward the completion of their degree.

As a result, online certification and degree programs are receiving growing acceptance as a viable alternative to traditional institutes of higher education. In "Experimenting with Aid" (InsideHigherEd.com, July 21, 2015), Paul Fain explains that in 2015 the U.S. Department of Education was exploring ways to expand federal financial aid to help students complete their degree online. As part of this process, the federal government created a process for evaluating qualified online programs, initially consisting of approved partnerships

FIGURE 9.9

Growth in student borrowing for postsecondary education, by sex of student, family income, and educational attainment of parents, 1993–2012

[% increase in share of college graduates borrowing, class of 1993 to class of 2012]

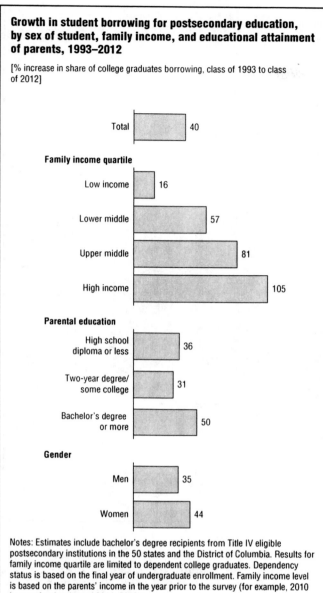

Notes: Estimates include bachelor's degree recipients from Title IV eligible postsecondary institutions in the 50 states and the District of Columbia. Results for family income quartile are limited to dependent college graduates. Dependency status is based on the final year of undergraduate enrollment. Family income level is based on the parents' income in the year prior to the survey (for example, 2010 income for the class of 2011–2012).

SOURCE: Richard Fry, "The Growth in Borrowing Has Been More Acute among Affluent and Among Women," in *The Changing Profile of Student Borrowers*, Pew Research Center, October 7, 2014, http://www.pewsocialtrends.org/files/2014/10/2014-10-07_Student-Debtors-FINAL.pdf (accessed July 30, 2015)

TABLE 9.9

Percentage of college graduates with student debt, by race and debt level, 2000–14

Undergraduate Student Loan Debt, by Race: 2000–2014 Graduates

APPROXIMATELY HOW MUCH MONEY DID YOU BORROW IN STUDENT LOANS TO OBTAIN YOUR UNDERGRADUATE DEGREE?

	2000–2004
	%
Blacks	
No loans	22
$1–$25,000	28
More than $25,000	50
Whites	
No loans	39
$1–$25,000	28
More than $25,000	34
Total	
No loans	37
$1–$25,000	28
More than $25,000	35

Feb. 4-March 7, 2014.
Figures adjusted for inflation in 2014 dollars.

SOURCE: Andrew Dugan and Scott Vanderbilt, "Undergraduate Student Loan Debt, by Race: 2000–2014 Graduates," in *Black College Grads More Likely to Graduate With Debt*, The Gallup Organization, September 18, 2014, http://www.gallup.com/poll/176051/black-college-graduates-likely-graduate-debt.aspx?utm_source=student%20loans&utm_medium=search&utm_campaign=tiles (accessed July 30, 2015). Copyright © 2015 Gallup, Inc. All rights reserved. The content is used with permission; however, Gallup retains all rights of republication.

offers impressive returns. According to Kena et al., in 2013 the median annual income for people aged 25 to 34 years with a master's degree or higher was $59,600, 22.9% higher than the median annual income of $48,500 earned by young adults with only a bachelor's degree. Among individuals aged 25 to 34 years with a high school diploma or equivalent, median annual earnings were $30,000 in 2013.

Figure 9.10 indicates a clear gender gap in the area of earnings. Whereas men aged 25 to 34 years with a master's degree or higher earned a median annual income of $66,800 in 2013, 25- to 34-year-old women with equivalent educational attainment earned a median annual income of only $53,900, 19.3% less than their male counterparts.

An inverse correlation is seen between the level of education and the unemployment rate. That is, as the level of education rises, the unemployment level falls. The percentage of unemployed people between the ages of 25 and 64 years with a bachelor's degree or higher in 2014 was 3.4%, compared with 10.6% for adults aged 25 to 64 years who did not graduate from high school. (See Figure 9.11.)

between universities and nontraditional institutions. According to Fain, these "experimental sites" will allow the partnerships to bypass established college accreditation requirements, provided their online programs meet predetermined quality benchmarks in their course offerings.

THE BENEFITS OF HIGHER EDUCATION

Regardless of the increases in costs of postsecondary school attendance, the investment in higher education

FIGURE 9.10

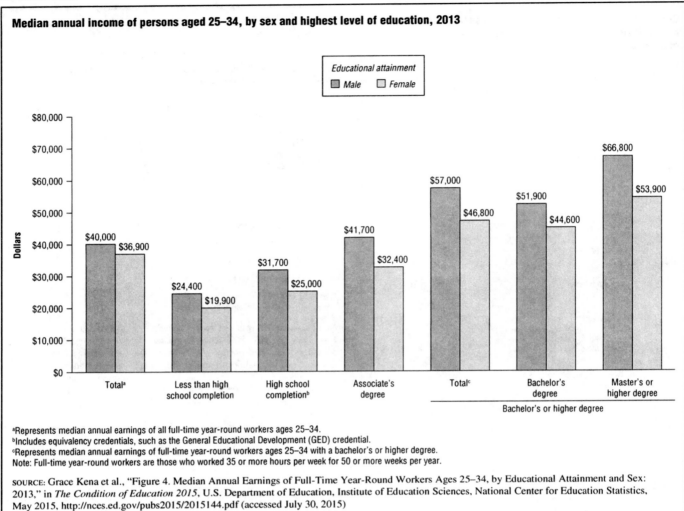

Median annual income of persons aged 25–34, by sex and highest level of education, 2013

aRepresents median annual earnings of all full-time year-round workers ages 25–34.
bIncludes equivalency credentials, such as the General Educational Development (GED) credential.
cRepresents median annual earnings of full-time year-round workers ages 25–34 with a bachelor's or higher degree.
Note: Full-time year-round workers are those who worked 35 or more hours per week for 50 or more weeks per year.

SOURCE: Grace Kena et al., "Figure 4. Median Annual Earnings of Full-Time Year-Round Workers Ages 25–34, by Educational Attainment and Sex: 2013," in *The Condition of Education 2015*, U.S. Department of Education, Institute of Education Sciences, National Center for Education Statistics, May 2015, http://nces.ed.gov/pubs2015/2015144.pdf (accessed July 30, 2015)

SUBSTANCE ABUSE AMONG COLLEGE STUDENTS

Illicit Drug Use

In *Monitoring the Future: National Survey Results on Drug Use, 1975–2014. Volume 1, Secondary School Students* (June 2015, http://www.monitoringthefuture.org/pubs/monographs/mtf-vol1_2014.pdf), Richard A. Miech et al. of the University of Michigan's Institute for Social Research examine information on drug use among college students and young adults aged 19 to 28 years as well as secondary school students. The college students surveyed were full-time students who were one to four years out of high school and were enrolled in two- or four-year institutions.

Miech et al. note that compared with their nonstudent peers, college students showed a slightly higher annual prevalence of illicit drug use in 2014 (38.6%, compared with 37.5% for nonstudent young adults aged 19 to 28 years). (See Table 9.10.) Annual prevalence means using a drug at any time within the year preceding the survey, and illicit drugs are both illegal drugs and controlled

substances that are used illegally. Drug use among college students has generally increased since 1991, when the annual prevalence of illicit drug use was 29.2%.

In 2014 slightly more than one-third (34.4%) of college students said they had used marijuana at some time during the previous year, compared with 31.6% of nonstudents. (See Table 9.10.) Fewer students used cocaine (4.4%) than did their nonstudent peers (5%). Use of cocaine within the previous year declined for both college students and young adults not in college from the 2005 statistics. Heroin use remained well under 1% among both students and nonstudents in 2014.

Alcohol Use

College students were slightly less likely to have used alcohol in the past year than their nonstudent peers (76.1%, compared with 82.3%). (See Table 9.10.) The high incidence of heavy or binge drinking (five or more drinks in a row in the past two weeks) among college students has been a topic of concern in recent years.

FIGURE 9.11

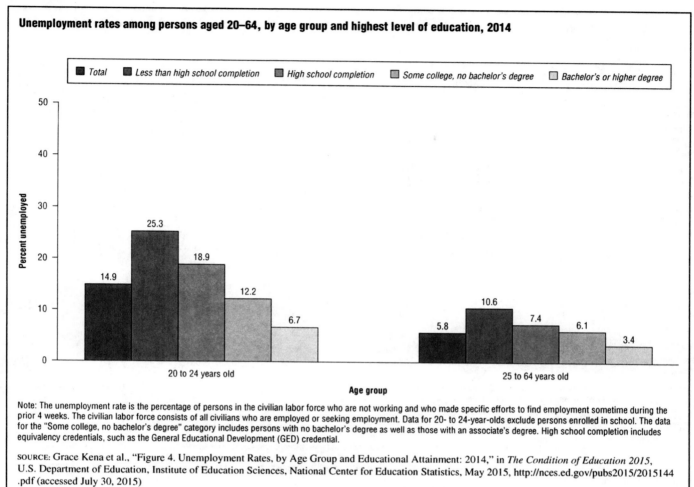

Unemployment rates among persons aged 20–64, by age group and highest level of education, 2014

☐ Total ☐ Less than high school completion ☐ High school completion ☐ Some college, no bachelor's degree ☐ Bachelor's or higher degree

Note: The unemployment rate is the percentage of persons in the civilian labor force who are not working and who made specific efforts to find employment sometime during the prior 4 weeks. The civilian labor force consists of all civilians who are employed or seeking employment. Data for 20- to 24-year-olds exclude persons enrolled in school. The data for the "Some college, no bachelor's degree" category includes persons with no bachelor's degree as well as those with an associate's degree. High school completion includes equivalency credentials, such as the General Educational Development (GED) credential.

SOURCE: Grace Kena et al., "Figure 4. Unemployment Rates, by Age Group and Educational Attainment: 2014," in *The Condition of Education 2015*, U.S. Department of Education, Institute of Education Sciences, National Center for Education Statistics, May 2015, http://nces.ed.gov/pubs2015/2015144 .pdf (accessed July 30, 2015)

Lloyd D. Johnston et al. of the University of Michigan's Institute for Social Research reveal in *Monitoring the Future: National Survey Results on Drug Use, 1975–2014. Volume 2, College Students and Adults Ages 19–55* (July 2015, http://www.monitoringthefuture.org/pubs/monographs/mtf-vol2_2014.pdf) that in 2014 approximately 35% of college students reported bouts of heavy drinking in the previous two weeks, compared with 31% of nonstudents. Binge drinking has decreased among both groups since 1980.

Tobacco Use

Table 9.10 shows that full-time college students in 2014 were less likely than other people in the same age group to have smoked cigarettes at any time within the year preceding the survey. In that year, 22.6% of college students reported smoking at some time during the past year, down from 41.3% in 2000. By comparison, 27% of nonstudents in the same age group reported smoking within the past year in 2014, down from 40.9% in 2000.

TABLE 9.10

Trends in annual prevalence of drug, alcohol, and tobacco use among college students and young adults, selected years 1991–2014

[Entries in percents]

	1991	1995	2000	2005	2010	2013	2014	2013–2014 change
Any illicit drug[a]								
College students	29.2	33.5	36.1	36.6	35.0	40.5	38.6	−1.9
Young adults	27.0	29.8	30.8	32.8	33.2	36.7	37.5	+0.9
Marijuana/hashish								
College students	26.5	31.2	34.0	33.3	32.7	35.5	34.4	−1.1
Young adults	23.8	26.5	27.9	28.2	28.7	32.2	31.6	−0.6
Cocaine								
College students	3.6	3.6	4.8	5.7	3.5	2.7	4.4	+1.7 s
Young adults	6.2	4.4	5.4	6.9	4.7	3.9	5.0	+1.1 ss
Heroin[b]								
College students	0.1	0.3	0.5	0.3	0.2	0.3	0.0	−0.2
Young adults	0.1	0.4	0.4	0.4	0.5	0.6	0.4	−0.2
Alcohol[c]								
Any use								
College students	88.3	83.2	83.2	83.0	78.6	75.6	76.1	+0.5
Young adults	86.9	84.7	84.0	83.8	82.7	82.5	82.3	−0.1
Cigarettes								
Any use								
College students	35.6	39.3	41.3	36.0	28.1	23.2	22.6	−0.5
Young adults	37.7	38.8	40.9	39.1	33.0	29.8	27.0	−2.8 ss

[a]Use of any illicit drug includes any use of marijuana, LSD, other hallucinogens, crack, other cocaine, or heroin; or any use of narcotics other than heroin, amphetamines, sedatives (barbiturates), or tranquilizers not under a doctor's orders. Due to changes in the amphetamines questions 2013 data for any illicit drug and any illicit drug other than marijuana are based on half the population indicated. For any illicit drug including inhalants, college students and young adults are based on one half the population indicated for 2013; 12th graders are based on one sixth of population indicated in 2013.
[b]In 1995, the heroin question was changed two of six forms for college students and young adults. Separate questions were asked for use with and without injection. Data presented here represent the combined data from all forms.
[c]The 1993 data are based on the changed forms only; population is one half of population indicated for these groups. In 1994 the remaining forms were changed to the new wording. The data are based on all forms beginning in 1994. In 2004, the question text was changed slightly in half of the forms. An examination of the data did not show any effect from the wording change. The remaining forms were changed in 2005. The revision of the question text resulted in rather little change in the reported prevalence of use. The data for all forms are used to provide the most reliable estimate of change.
Notes: Level of significance of difference between the two most recent classes: s = .05, ss = .01.
Any apparent inconsistency between the change estimate and the prevalence estimates for the two most recent years is due to rounding.

SOURCE: Adapted from Richard A. Miech et al., "Table 2-2. Trends in Annual Prevalence of Use of Various Drugs for 8th, 10th, and 12th Graders, College Students, and Young Adults (Ages 19–28)," in *Monitoring the Future: National Survey Results on Drug Use, 1975–2014. Volume I, Secondary School Students*, University of Michigan, Institute for Social Research, June 2015, http://www.monitoringthefuture.org/pubs/monographs/mtf-vol1_2014.pdf (accessed July 30, 2015)

CHAPTER 10
PUBLIC OPINION ABOUT EDUCATION

Every year Phi Delta Kappa, a professional education fraternity, publishes a survey of the American public on education issues. This annual questionnaire is considered to be one of the best measurements of current American attitudes toward education. Some of the information in this chapter comes from "Try It Again, Uncle Sam: The 46th Annual PDK/Gallup Poll of the Public's Attitudes toward the Public Schools" (*Phi Delta Kappan*, vol. 96, no. 1, September 2014) and "Americans Put Teacher Quality on Center Stage: The 46th Annual PDK/Gallup Poll of the Public's Attitudes toward the Public Schools, Part II" (*Phi Delta Kappan*, vol. 96, no. 2, October 2014) by William J. Bushaw and Valerie J. Calderon. In addition, some questions are from Gallup Organization polls.

It should be noted that these are surveys of people's opinions and feelings about public education, which may or may not coincide with facts about the nation's schools. Instead, the survey results illustrate trends in current American thought on educational subjects.

OVERALL SATISFACTION WITH KINDERGARTEN TO 12TH-GRADE EDUCATION

Rebecca Riffkin of the Gallup Organization reports in *Americans' Satisfaction with Education System Increases* (August 28, 2014, http://www.gallup.com/poll/175517 /americans-satisfaction-education-system-increases.aspx) that in August 2014 Gallup pollsters asked parents of school children if they were satisfied with their oldest child's education and asked members of the general public if they were satisfied with the state of schools nationwide. Gallup has asked these questions since 1999, and the results for the general public are shown in Figure 10.1.

According to Riffkin, three-quarters (75%) of parents were satisfied with their oldest child's education in 2014. This represented a notable rise from 2013, when 67% of parents expressed satisfaction with their oldest child's education. In contrast, parents' satisfaction with the nation's education system was considerably higher than that of the general public (48%) in 2014. (See Figure 10.1.) Likewise, parents were somewhat more likely to approve of the teachers' performance in their local schools than the general public in 2014. (See Table 10.1.)

THE BIGGEST PROBLEMS FACING LOCAL PUBLIC SCHOOLS

Since Phi Delta Kappa began surveying the public's opinions about education in 1969, lack of financial support, use of drugs, and lack of discipline have been among the top-three problems on respondents' list of concerns. In "Try It Again, Uncle Sam," Bushaw and Calderon examine the public's attitudes toward the biggest problems facing schools in 2014. In that year roughly one-third of both public school parents (36%) and the general public (32%) felt that a lack of financial support was the most serious challenge facing public education in the United States. Democrats (45%) were considerably more likely than Independents (33%) or Republicans (21%) to view funding as the most serious problem confronting public schools in 2014. Republicans (11%) were more likely than Independents (10%) or Democrats (6%) to say that a lack of educational standards was the most serious issue in education that year. By contrast, Democrats (16%) were the most likely to say that finding quality teachers was the most serious issue, followed by Republicans (8%) and Independents (3%).

GRADING THE SCHOOLS

Phi Delta Kappa/Gallup pollsters frequently ask respondents to grade the public schools on the same A, B, C, D, and Fail scale that is used to grade students. In general, the survey has found for many years that the respondents' relationships to schools influence the way they rank them. That is, people generally give their children's schools a higher grade than the schools in the community as a whole, and local community schools are

FIGURE 10.1

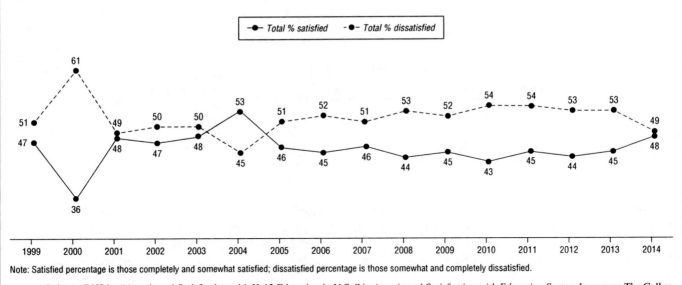

Public satisfaction with K-12 education, 1999–2014

OVERALL, HOW SATISFIED ARE YOU WITH THE QUALITY OF EDUCATION STUDENTS RECEIVE IN KINDERGARTEN THROUGH GRADE 12 IN THE U.S. TODAY—WOULD YOU SAY YOU ARE COMPLETELY SATISFIED, SOMEWHAT SATISFIED, SOMEWHAT DISSATISFIED OR COMPLETELY DISSATISFIED?

Note: Satisfied percentage is those completely and somewhat satisfied; dissatisfied percentage is those somewhat and completely dissatisfied.

SOURCE: Rebecca Riffkin, "Americans' Satisfaction with K-12 Education in U.S.," in *Americans' Satisfaction with Education System Increases*, The Gallup Organization, August 28, 2014, http://www.gallup.com/poll/175517/americans-satisfaction-education-system-increases.aspx?utm_source=how%20satisfied%20are%20you%20with%20the%20quality%20of%20educatio&utm_medium=search&utm_campaign=tiles (accessed July 30, 2015). Copyright © 2015 Gallup, Inc. All rights reserved. The content is used with permission; however, Gallup retains all rights of republication.

TABLE 10.1

Public opinion on the quality of teachers in their local schools, by parent/teacher status and race/ethnicity, 2014

	Public	Parents	Teachers	African Americans	Hispanics
A	25%	28%	41%	23%	25%
B	26	28	28	23	25
C	25	23	18	24	21
D	13	11	8	14	13
Fail	9	10	5	11	11

SOURCE: Michael B. Henderson, Paul E. Peterson, and Martin R. West, "Table 20a. Suppose you had to grade each teacher in your local school for the quality of their work using the grades A, B, C, D, and F. What percent of teachers in your local schools would you give each grade? Your answers should add to 100%," in *Education Next*—Program on Education Policy and Governance—Survey 2014," *Education Next*, Harvard Program on Education Policy and Governance, 2015, http://educationnext.org/files/2014ednextpoll.pdf (accessed July 31, 2015)

generally given higher grades than the nation's school system as a whole. For example, Bushaw and Calderon reveal in "Try It Again, Uncle Sam" that half (50%) of all people surveyed gave the public schools in their community a grade of A or B in 2014. By contrast, 70% of respondents gave the public schools nationwide a grade of C (51%) or D (19%).

Overall, parents tend to express stronger support for schools than the general public. Bushaw and Calderon report that just about two-thirds (67%) of public school parents awarded an A or B to the school attended by their oldest child in 2014. By comparison, 50% of the general public believed the schools in their community deserved an A or B grade in 2014; this percentage was slightly down from 53% in 2013. According to Bushaw and Calderon, respondents graded the U.S. public school system as a whole much more harshly. In 2014 only 17% thought the nation's public schools deserved an A or B grade, down from 19% in 2013.

EDUCATION AS PREPARATION FOR THE WORKFORCE

In 2014 Phi Delta Kappa/Gallup pollsters asked Americans whether high school dropouts, high school graduates, and college graduates are ready for the working world. Pollsters asked for responses using a five-point scale, with five meaning "strongly agree" and one meaning "strongly disagree." The three statements relating to work readiness were: "Today's high school dropout is ready for the world of work," "Today's high school graduate is ready for the world of work," and "Today's college graduate is ready for the world of work." In addition, pollsters asked those surveyed how important they felt a college education was in today's world.

Perhaps not surprisingly, the Phi Delta Kappa/Gallup poll found that an overwhelming majority of both public school parents and the general population felt that high school dropouts were not prepared to enter the workforce in 2014. In "Americans Put Teacher Quality on Center Stage," Bushaw and Calderon note that 62% of both groups strongly disagreed that high school dropouts were ready to work; another 25% of both groups responded with a ranking of two on the five-point scale. These figures suggest that, overall, 87% of the general population and public school parents felt high school dropouts were not ready for the world of work. By contrast, only 2% of public school parents and 1% of the general population believed high school dropouts were prepared to enter the workforce in 2014.

The general population and public school parents also tended to agree on how prepared high school graduates were for the world of work in 2014. Bushaw and Calderon report that nearly half (48%) of public school parents either strongly disagreed (17%) or disagreed (31%) that high school graduates were ready to enter the workforce in 2014. A comparable proportion of the general public (49%) also strongly disagreed (18%) or disagreed (31%) that high school graduates were ready to work. As these numbers show, although a large percentage of public school parents and the general population disagreed with the idea that high school graduates were ready for work, the feeling of disagreement was considerably less intense than that expressed when asked about the work readiness of high school dropouts. At the same time, a large proportion of both public school parents (40%) and the general public (38%) responded with a ranking of three on the five-point scale, suggesting that they neither agreed nor disagreed that high school graduates were ready to work in 2014.

According to Bushaw and Calderon, public school parents and the general population had mixed feelings about the value of a college degree in preparing young people to enter the workforce. More than two-thirds of both the general populace (36%) and public school parents (34%) responded with a ranking of three on the five-point scale when asked whether or not college graduates were ready to work in 2014. A slightly higher proportion of the general population (37%) either strongly agreed (5%) or agreed (32%) that college graduates were ready for work after leaving school; by comparison, one-third (33%) of public school parents either strongly agreed (5%) or agreed (28%) with the same conclusion. An identical proportion of public school parents (33%) either strongly disagreed (14%) or disagreed (19%) that college graduates were ready to work in 2014, compared with over a quarter (28%) of the general public who either strongly disagreed (9%) or disagreed (19%) that college graduates were ready to enter the workforce that year.

A COLLEGE EDUCATION AND ITS COSTS

Bushaw and Calderon note in "Americans Put Teacher Quality on Center Stage" that the public's attitude toward the importance of higher education changed substantially between the late 1970s and the first decade of the 21st century. In 1978 more than four out of five (82%) of the general population felt that a college education was either very important or fairly important. This figure rose steadily over the following years. In 1983 nearly nine out of 10 (89%) people surveyed believed a college education was either very important or somewhat important, while by 2010, 96% of the general public felt it was either very important or fairly important to graduate from college. Even more notable than the increase in support for higher education during this span was the gradual shift in intensity of people's views. For example, in 1978 just over one-third (36%) of the general population felt getting a college education was very important, while nearly half (46%) believed it was fairly important. Within five years these proportions were reversed. In 1983 well over half (58%) of people surveyed felt a college education was very important, while less than one-third (31%) felt it was fairly important. By 2010 three-quarters (75%) of the population viewed a college education as very important, compared with only 21% who regarded it as fairly important.

However, by 2014 the public's attitude toward the value of higher education had once again begun to shift. According to Bushaw and Calderon, 91% of the general population believed a college education was either very important or fairly important that year, down five percentage points from four years earlier. More significantly, well below half (43%) of the general population believed a college degree was very important in 2014, 32 percentage points lower than the proportion of respondents who felt that way in 2010. Public school parents were slightly less likely than the general population to believe in the value of a college education in 2014, with 89% of public school parents reporting that they felt a college degree was either very important (41%) or fairly important (48%) that year.

Despite the steadily rising costs of higher education, most parents remain reasonably confident that they will be able to afford to send their oldest child to college. Bushaw and Calderon note that in 1995 nearly seven out of 10 (69%) public school parents believed it was very likely (30%) or somewhat likely (39%) that they would be able to pay for their oldest child's college education. By 2010 the overall proportion of public school parents who felt prepared to pay for their oldest child's higher education rose to 77%, with 36% stating it was very likely and 41% stating it was somewhat likely. However, this number subsequently declined over the next four years. In 2014, 69% of public school parents believed it was very likely (28%) or somewhat likely (41%) that they would be able to cover the costs of their oldest child's higher education.

IMPORTANT NAMES
AND ADDRESSES

**American Association for
Employment in Education**
PO Box 173
Slippery Rock, PA 16057
(614) 485-1111
FAX: (360) 244-7802
E-mail: info@aaee.org
URL: http://www.aaee.org/

American College Testing
500 ACT Dr.
Iowa City, IA 52243
(319) 337-1000
URL: http://www.act.org/

American Federation for Children
1660 L St. NW, Ste. 1000
Washington, DC 20036
(202) 280-1990
FAX: (202) 280-1989
URL: http://www.federationforchildren.org/

**American Federation of Teachers
American Federation of Labor–Congress
of Industrial Organizations**
555 New Jersey Ave. NW
Washington, DC 20001
(202) 879-4400
URL: http://www.aft.org/

**Brown Center on Education Policy
Brookings Institution**
1775 Massachusetts Ave. NW
Washington, DC 20036
(202) 797-6000
URL: http://www.brookings.edu/about/
centers/brown

Child Trends
7315 Wisconsin Ave. NW, Ste. 1200W
Bethesda, MD 20814
(240) 223-9200
FAX: (240) 200-1238
URL: http://www.childtrends.org/

College Board
250 Vesey St.
New York, NY 10281
(212) 713-8000
URL: http://www.collegeboard.org/

Council of Chief State School Officers
One Massachusetts Ave. NW, Ste. 700
Washington, DC 20001-1431
(202) 336-7000
FAX: (202) 408-8072
URL: http://www.ccsso.org/

Council of the Great City Schools
1301 Pennsylvania Ave. NW, Ste. 702
Washington, DC 20004
(202) 393-2427
FAX: (202) 393-2400
URL: http://www.cgcs.org/

Education Commission of the States
700 Broadway, Ste. 810
Denver, CO 80203-3442
(303) 299-3600
FAX: (303) 296-8332
E-mail: ecs@ecs.org
URL: http://www.ecs.org/

**Education Next
Program on Education Policy
and Governance
Harvard Kennedy School**
79 JFK St.
Cambridge, MA 02138
(617) 496-5488
FAX: (617) 496-4428
URL: http://educationnext.org/

Educational Testing Service
660 Rosedale Rd.
Princeton, NJ 08541
(609) 921-9000
FAX: (609) 734-5410
URL: http://www.ets.org/

Institute of International Education
809 United Nations Plaza
New York, NY 10017
(212) 883-8200
FAX: (212) 984-5452
URL: http://www.iie.org/

**National Center for Education Statistics
Institute of Education Sciences**
1990 K St. NW, Eight and Ninth Floors
Washington, DC 20006
(202) 502-7300
FAX: (202) 502-7466
URL: http://nces.ed.gov/

National Education Association
1201 16th St. NW
Washington, DC 20036-3290
(202) 833-4000
FAX: (202) 822-7974
URL: http://www.nea.org/

**National Forum to Accelerate
Middle-Grades Reform**
PO Box 224
Savoy, IL 61874
(217) 351-2196
FAX: (217) 351-1068
E-mail: nationalforum@middlegradesforum
.org
URL: http://middlegradesforum.org/

Phi Delta Kappa International
1525 Wilson Blvd., Ste. 705
Arlington, VA 22209
(812) 339-11561-800-766-1156
FAX: (812) 339-0018
URL: http://www.pdkintl.org/

U.S. Department of Education
400 Maryland Ave. SW
Washington, DC 20202
1-800-872-5327
URL: http://www.ed.gov/

RESOURCES

The U.S. Department of Education's National Center for Education Statistics (NCES) is a valuable source of information about the state of education in the United States. Its two annual publications, *Digest of Education Statistics* and *The Condition of Education*, provide a detailed compilation of education statistics from prekindergarten to graduate school. In addition, its *Most Current Digest Tables* provides a number of tables used in this book.

Many other NCES publications were of major assistance in the preparation of this book, including *A First Look: 2013 Mathematics and Reading* (November 2013), *The Nation's Report Card 2013: Vocabulary* (2013), *The Nation's Report Card: 2014 U.S. History Assessment* (2014), and *Are the Nation's Twelfth Graders Making Progress in Math and Reading?* (2013).

The NCES also published *Timeline for National Assessment of Education Progress (NAEP) Assessments from 1969 to 2017* (July 2014), *Revenues and Expenditures for Public Elementary and Secondary Education: School Year 2011–12 (Fiscal Year 2012)* (Stephen Q. Cornman, January 2015), *Selected Statistics from the Public Elementary and Secondary Education Universe: School Year 2012–13* (Patrick Keaton, October 2014), *Projections of Education Statistics to 2022* (William J. Hussar and Tabitha M. Bailey, February 2014), *Performance of U.S. 15-Year-Old Students in Mathematics, Science, and Reading Literacy in an International Context: First Look at PISA 2012* (Dana Kelly et al., December 2013), and *Characteristics of Public and Private Elementary and Secondary School Teachers in the United States: Results from the 2011–12 Schools and Staffing Survey* (Rebecca Goldring, Lucinda Gray, and Amy Bitterman, August 2013).

The U.S. Department of Justice monitors the problem of crime and violence among the school-age population.

A publication produced by the Department of Justice in collaboration with the Department of Education was used in this book: *Indicators of School Crime and Safety: 2014* (Simone Robers et al., July 2015). U.S. Census Bureau publications were also consulted, including *Income and Poverty in the United States: 2013* (Carmen DeNavas-Walt and Bernadette D. Proctor, September 2014).

The Centers for Disease Control and Prevention (CDC) published *Sexually Transmitted Disease Surveillance 2013* (December 2014), "Youth Risk Behavior Surveillance—United States, 2013" (Laura Kann et al., June 2014), and *HIV Surveillance Report: Diagnoses of HIV Infection in the United States and Dependent Areas* (February 2015). Richard A. Miech et al. of the University of Michigan's Institute for Social Research, with support from the National Institute on Drug Abuse, annually perform the *Monitoring the Future* study, an in-depth survey of drug use among high school and college students. The U.S. Department of Health and Human Services' Administration for Children and Families produced the *Head Start Program Facts Fiscal Year 2014* (April 2015).

Other important sources of information include the International Association for the Evaluation of Educational Achievement, which publishes *Progress in International Reading Literacy Study (PIRLS) 2011 International Results in Reading* (Ina V. S. Mullis et al., 2012), *Trends in International Mathematics and Science Study (TIMSS) 2011 International Results in Mathematics* (Ina V.S. Mullis, et al., 2012), and *Trends in International Mathematics and Science Study (TIMSS) 2011 International Results in Science* (Michael O. Martin et al., 2012).

Also referenced was *America's Children: Key National Indicators of Well-Being, 2015* (July 2015), which is part of an annual series prepared by the Federal Interagency Forum on Child and Family Statistics. This report provided statistics on early childhood education and detached youth.

Phi Delta Kappa, a professional education fraternity, publishes numerous reports on the condition of education in the United States. It also conducts an annual poll, the Phi Delta Kappa/Gallup Poll of the Public's Attitudes toward the Public Schools.

The College Board produced *Trends in College Pricing, 2014* (2014) and *Trends in Student Aid, 2014* (2014), which were consulted for this book.

Lastly, the journal *Education Next* publishes the annual "*Education Next*—Program on Education Policy and Governance," which is conducted by the Harvard Program on Education Policy and Governance.

INDEX

M

Magnet schools, 129–130
Mainstreaming. *See* Inclusive education
Marijuana, 105–108, 109*t*
Marland, Sidney, 42
Marland definition, 42
Master's degrees, 151, 152*f*, 164
Master's degrees of teachers, 140
Mathematics
    achievement levels, 61–62
    A Blueprint for Reform (Obama
        administration), 93
    international comparisons of
        achievement in, 1–2, 3(*t*1.3), 67, 74,
        85*f*–86*f*
    mathematics proficiency levels, 12th
        grade, 76*f*
    NAEP achievement levels, 74(*f*4.10),
        75*f*, 77*t*–78*t*
    NAEP scores, 57, 60–62, 67*f*, 70*t*–71*t*,
        72*t*–73*t*
    NAEP scores and achievement levels,
        68*t*–69*t*
    No Child Left Behind Act, 91, 92
    student attitudes toward, 60–61, 74(*f*4.9)
    12th-grade proficiency levels, 76*f*
    See also STEM education
Medical degrees, 164, 167, 168*t*
Mental disorders, 46
MEP (Migrant Education Program), 44
Merit pay for teachers, 144–145, 148
Methamphetamines, 105
Migrant Education Program (MEP), 44
Migrant students, 43–44
Miner, Myrtilla, 159
Miner Normal School, 159
Minorities. *See* Race/ethnicity
Mobility, teacher, 137–139, 139*t*–140*t*
Monitoring the Future (Institute for Social
    Research), 104, 174
Mortality, 104
Multiple intelligences, 40–41

N

NAEHCY (National Association for the
    Education of Homeless Children and
    Youth), 44
NAEP. *See* National Assessment of
    Educational Progress
NASSP (National Association of Secondary
    School Principals), 95
*A Nation at Risk: The Imperative for
    Educational Reform* (National
    Commission on Excellence in
    Education), 89
National Aeronautics and Space
    Administration, 90
National Assessment Governing Board, 49
National Assessment of Educational
    Progress (NAEP)
    goals, 49

history achievement scores, 81*f*, 82*f*
history assessment, 66
mathematics achievement levels,
    74(*f*4.10), 77*t*–78*t*
mathematics achievement levels, by
    state, 75*f*
mathematics scores, 57, 60–62, 67*f*
mathematics scores, by attitudes toward
    mathematics, 70*t*–71*t*, 72*t*–73*t*
mathematics scores and achievement
    levels, 68*t*–69*t*
reading, 51–52, 51*t*, 57, 63*t*–64*t*
reading scores, 52*f*, 53*t*–54*t*, 55*t*–56*t*, 57
reading scores, by race/ethnicity, 58*t*–59*t*
results, reporting of, 50–51
schedule, 49, 50*t*
science, 62, 65–66
science scores, 79*t*–80*t*
vocabulary scores, 65*f*
vocabulary scores, by race/ethnicity, 66*f*
National Association for the Education of
    Homeless Children and Youth
    (NAEHCY), 44
National Association of Elementary School
    Principals, 95
National Association of Secondary School
    Principals (NASSP), 95
National Center for Children in Poverty, 103
National Center for Education Statistics
    (NCES), 49
National Commission on Excellence in
    Education, 89
National Education Association (NEA), 94,
    130, 148–149
National Education Goals, 89–90
National Governors Association, 39
National Science Foundation, 90
National Teacher of the Year Program, 137
Native Americans
    Head Start program, 48*t*
    tribal colleges, 161
NCES (National Center for Education
    Statistics), 49
NCLB. *See* No Child Left Behind Act
NEA (National Education Association), 94,
    130, 148–149
Neighborhood school closings, 133–134
*Newdow, Elk Grove Unified School District
    v.*, 131
No Child Left Behind (NCLB) Act
    A Blueprint for Reform (Obama
        administration), 93–94
    faith-based organizations, 131
    financial considerations, 20
    reauthorization, 92, 96–97
    requirements, 90–92
Norway, 24
Nursery school. *See* Preprimary education
Nyquist, Committee for Public Education v.,
    130

O

Obama, Barack
    bilingual education, 132
    A Blueprint for Reform (Obama
        administration), 93–94, 95–96
    career and technical education, 31
    federal funding for teacher retention and
        hiring, 143
    merit pay, 144–145
    No Child Left Behind Act, 20, 97
    Office of Faith-Based and Neighborhood
        Partnerships, 131–132
    public opinion of education policies of,
        92–93
    school choice, 124
    STEM education, 90
OECD (Organisation for Economic
    Co-operation and Development), 1, 23–24
Office of Faith-Based and Neighborhood
    Partnerships, 131–132
Office of Special Education Programs, U.S.
    Department of Education, 40
Ohio, 125–126
Open enrollment, 128–129
Opportunity Scholarships Program, 125
Oregon, 123
Organisation for Economic Co-operation
    and Development (OECD), 1, 23–24

P

Parental educational attainment
    illicit drug use, 108, 109*t*
    mathematics scores, by attitudes toward
        mathematics, 70*t*–71*t*, 72*t*–73*t*
    reading achievement levels, 62*f*
    science scores, 79*t*–80*t*
    student debt, 173(*f*9.9)
Peeples, Shanna, 137
Pell, Claiborne, 171
Pell grants, 171
Pelvic inflammatory disease (PID), 114
Perkins, Carl Dewey, 171
Perkins loans, 171
Per-pupil expenditures, 19–20
Philadelphia, PA, 127
*Pierce v. Society of the Sisters of the Holy
    Names of Jesus*, 123
PID (pelvic inflammatory disease), 114
PIRLS (Progress in International Reading
    Literary Study), 67
PISA (Program for International Student
    Assessment), 1–2
Pledge of Allegiance, 131
Political affiliation, 92–93, 92*t*, 97
Postsecondary degrees of teachers, 140
Poverty and low-income students
    at-risk students, 99–101, 102–103
    children in poverty, by race/ethnicity and
        family structure, 103*f*
    dropouts, high school, 120

APACK

9 781573 026673